1980

Educational
Research
and
Evaluation
Methods

J. WILLIAM ASHER
Purdue University

Little, Brown and Company
Boston • Toronto

I am grateful to the Literary Executor of the late Sir Ronald A. Fisher F.R.S., to Doctor Frank Yates, F.R.S., and to Longman Group Ltd., London, for permission to reprint Tables I, III, IV, V, VII and XXXIII from their book *Statistical Tables for Biological, Agricultural and Medical Research* (6th Edition 1974).

Definitions of "research," "perception," and "sensation" reprinted by permission:

From Webster's Third New International Dictionary ©1971 by G. & C. Merriam Co., Publishers of the Merriam-Webster Dictionaries.

From Webster's New Collegiate Dictionary ©1975 by G. & C. Merriam Co., Publishers of the Merriam-Webster Dictionaries.

From Webster's New Collegiate Dictionary ©1961 by G. & C. Merriam Co., Publishers of the Merriam-Webster Dictionaries.

Library of Congress Catalog Card No: 75-30262

First Printing

Published simultaneously in Canada by Little, Brown & Company (Canada) Limited

Printed in the United States of America

Teaching of others
Teacheth the teacher

Thomas Fuller
Gnomologia, 1732

Preface

PURPOSE AND SCOPE

This book shows how professional educators apply behavioral science methods to practical, educational problems. It presents the most up-to-date, useful, and accurate information available about behavioral science research procedures. Modern computers and small electronic calculators enable professional educators to apply new research techniques to their decisions. If we do so semester by semester, the result will be better education.

Research methods in behavioral science have evolved rapidly in the last 15 to 20 years. Often new concepts in science are difficult to understand at first, but the overarching explanations become much simpler as more knowledge emerges to clarify the concepts. This is happening now in educational research. Educators cannot become experts overnight in the methodology of the behavioral sciences, but they can gain an overview and learn basic techniques. With this background they can consult effectively with experts about the rest. I hope this book will also help its readers to be alert to technical errors and possible propaganda found in the professional and research literature in education.

The major emphasis of this book is on understanding and using experimental and quasi-experimental research designs in various research and evaluation studies in education. True experiments, quasi-experiments, descriptive studies, sampling methods, and prediction and classification procedures are presented in Chapters Two, Five, Six,

Seven, and Eight and illustrated with their use in educational problems. For instance, the Chapter Two discussion of the logic of comparisons in research and true experimental design includes a detailed actual example of a professional educator's research study.

Additional features of this book include an overview of the nature of science, research, evaluation, and professionalism (Chapter One) and brief introductions to statistical analysis and measurement methods (Chapters Three and Four). Further, there are chapters on educational evaluation (Chapter Nine), reading professional literature and writing reports of research and evaluations (Chapter Ten), common errors to avoid (Chapter Eleven), implementing change, sources of support, and ethics (Chapter Twelve). An appendix presents an overview of the rest of the most commonly used statistical methods for those who want to become more familiar with them. A glossary of research terms further enhances the usefulness of the book.

ACKNOWLEDGMENTS

My commitment as a researcher and teacher primarily interested in the problems of education can be traced to my childhood in Gary, Indiana. Both my parents were teachers actively involved in helping to improve the curriculum and organization of the public schools. They faced then many of the challenges we still face today: minority and non-English-speaking students and the development of ethnic pride, early childhood education, and the place of recreation and social education and education for citizenship and political participation. My parents and their friends enthusiastically discussed their problems and strategies, their achievements and failures. I thank them for introducing me to the excitement of attacking educational problems with ever-evolving new research methods.

When I have taught evening courses in research methods, teachers and administrators have taught me much by presenting me the problems they met during the day and challenging me to show how research methods could be used to help resolve them. Some of their results are found in these pages.

More specifically, a number of people have supported my efforts in preparing this book. My colleagues here at Purdue were most encouraging. Professors John Feldhusen, Ernest McDaniel, and Robert Kane deserve special mention for their numerous suggestions about topics to include and discussions about the dimensions of the effort. Professor Georgia Baker read the manuscript as it was being written, chapter by chapter. Her notes on the presentation, organization, and clarification of educational research concepts in light of her experiences as a classroom teacher and faculty member were exceedingly helpful and are most appreciated. Professors Curtis Stafford of San Jose State College; Ronald P. Curcio, University of New Hampshire; Richard McCowan, State University College at Buffalo; Helen I. Snyder, The Pennsylvania State University; and Roger A. Koehler, University of Nebraska–Lincoln also reviewed the manuscript and made many useful suggestions.

It is standard procedure to thank one's typist. My secretary, Mrs. Phyllis Willman, however, is also an excellent critic and an expert in the A.P.A. style manual. Best of all, she knows what I should be saying even when she can't read my handwriting. She has an admirable theory of followership to counteract administrative theories of leadership: Don't do what the boss tells you to do; do what he would tell you to do if he knew what he was talking about. Who could ask for better assistance?

Ms. Majorie Zumstein, in charge of the Purdue Psychology and Education Libraries, was most generous in giving her time in reading and making invaluable suggestions in the chapter dealing with the use of libraries.

My wife proofread and edited the entire manuscript under pressure of deadlines. She has been a teacher, struggled with a statistics course, collected data for me, and read and commented on many of my prior manuscripts. This cumulation of experience and her expertise in the use of language make this book better.

In 1973 and 1974 my Introduction to Educational Research classes at Purdue tested a prior version of this manuscript. The experience reinforced my conviction that the material is understandable and useful to teachers working on masters degrees and to education under-graduates. My students also offered many suggestions which I incorporated into this book.

While I owe a great deal of gratitude to these many people for their help and encouragement, I did consider each suggestion carefully before accepting it and shaping it to fit. If I inadvertently distorted concepts or "muddied" their presentation, the fault is mine.

I plan to continue teaching and working in the area of educational research. Therefore I welcome suggestions from readers on ways to do research and evaluation better, to add to the scope of the problems attacked, and to clarify the concepts presented.

Contents

Chapter 1

Research, Science, and Educational Research

Enhancing broad educational research skills of professional and preprofessional educators is the purpose of this book. However, just reading about research does not make an educational researcher, nor can one book or course accomplish that aim. The preparation to become an educational researcher requires courses in a combination of statistical and measurement methods, educational research design, and some practice under the supervision of an experienced researcher. In addition, a thorough knowledge is needed of a substantive field of education such as English, history, mathematics, reading, education of exceptional children, educational guidance, or educational administration. For some it is possible to make major contributions to education and become an educational researcher by applying knowledge and research methods from fields upon which many of educational methods are based, such as psychology, sociology, administration, etc.

Additional aims of this work are: (1) to make the readers more sophisticated in their study of the research and professional literature in education; (2) to help them recognize where educational research methods can be used readily to improve the educational procedures and systems in which they are involved as professional educators; and (3) to give them minimum skills in educational research. Readers will be able to develop initial research designs, identify predictors of criteria and possibilities fo classification and measurement, and, as a result, be able to talk with statistical analysts and measurement specialists and to consult effectively with educational researchers. If these skills are achieved, the result will be more effective educational decisions and procedures and thus the enhancement of the education of children, adolescents, and adults.

Toward this end then, this book will present some of the bases of skills needed for educational research. Primarily these skills are used to determine what is factual in reading the professional education literature and to derive knowledge from observations made of the educational world (or at least the social and behavioral aspects of it) and are called research methods. The most important part of research methods is research design. Knowledge of research design is the methodological base upon which the profession rests.

Research design opens many doors to knowledge. It is fundamental to the ability to understand and accept or reject evidence about the effectiveness of educational programs. Further, research design is less quantitatively oriented than statistics or measurement and thus is learned easier and remembered longer by many educators whose fields are nonmathematical and nonscientific. Some of the basic concepts of statistics and measurement will be presented, as well as the relationship of these concepts to prediction and classification problems in education. Many examples will be presented in the context of actual educational research studies which were done by education students in beginning and advanced educational research methods courses. These students aided in the improvement of education. So can you.

Research, especially educational research, encompasses many types of activities. Research connotes status and prestige in academic institutions so that many persons claim that their activities fall within the scope of the word. Modifiers are added to the word "research" to broaden its meaning and also to help accomplish the aim of gaining status. Others will perform activities and conduct investigations for which they decline to use the word research at all, perhaps to avoid the sometimes proclaimed lack of direct application of the results of basic research. "Evaluation," "dissemination," "adoption," "trial," "design," "demonstration," "test," "assessment," "analysis," "examination," "effectiveness," "efficiency," and even "common sense" are words and phrases chosen to describe their activities. These terms all fall well within the realm of the words used in the definitions of the word research: "investigation," "correct interpretation," "practical application," "knowledge," "acquaintance with ascertained principles" and "having information."

Research is defined in *Webster's Third New International Dictionary* as, "Studious inquiry or examination; esp. critical and exhaustive

investigation or experimentation having for its aim the discovery of
new facts and their correct interpretation, the revision of accepted
conclusions, theories, or laws in the light of newly discovered facts, or
the practical applications of such new or revised conclusions, theories,
or laws." The *Oxford English Dictionary* (1933) has a one word definition, "Knowledge," which is extended to, "having information acquired by study or research; acquaintance with ascertained truths,
facts, or principles." Bergen Evans and his sister Cornelia in their
Dictionary of Contemporary American Usage (1957) say, "Research . . .
means diligent and systematic inquiry or investigation into a subject in
order to discover facts or principles." However, they suggest that the
word is widely overused and extended beyond this meaning. "A
schoolboy looking up the meaning of a word in the dictionary is now
said to be doing research."

In this chapter science and the several varieties of research and
educational research will be discussed. What is science and what does it
encompass? What are its goals and methods? What is knowledge? What
is engineering and how does educational research relate to engineering? What attempts are made to build status into some types of
research? Particular concern will be given to answering the questions:
What is educational research? and How does educational research relate
to the professional educator?

Educational research has many aspects. Development, innovation,
trial, installation, and institutionalization of change all have research
aspects. In recent years the developments in educational evaluation
have been many, and educational research methods are used in
evaluation. Innovation and change are important with many new
administrative methods being implemented in education. Systems
analysis, accountability, cost-benefit, and cost-effectiveness procedures
are some of these, and research is needed to determine facts when these
methods are used. Measurement plays a part in educational research,
too. Educational research, such as action research and curriculum
research, has a special purpose. Results of curriculum innovation and
the dissemination process are also important in educational research.

SCIENCE

Science is a word with status connotations but also with connotations of inapplicability to certain aspects of man's affairs, particularly to
his humanistic aspects. The word "science" is derived from the Latin
scire which means "to know." Conant in his book *Science and Common
Sense* (1951), stated that science is a way of explaining the universe in
which we live. He suggested that "experimental science can be thought

of as an activity which increases the adequacy of the concepts and conceptual schemes . . . . It is one extension of common sense" (p. 24). It is accumulated knowledge which includes a vast amount of practical as well as theoretical knowledge. He further argued that the progress made in the art of government, the treatment of criminals, the spread of education, and social reform in general, while no part of social science, does bear the same relationship to the science of man as the improvements in manufacturing processes and transportation have to the physical sciences. He suggested that it might be profitable to the social sciences for man to study the way that the physical and biological sciences have evolved from the everyday activities of artisans and agriculturists. The social sciences, and the behavioral sciences as well, could benefit from examination of the everyday problems that professional educators face rather than the disregard for applied problems that is sometimes expressed. Garner (1972) indicates, "The term 'pure' is certainly intended to have a morally favorable connotation, while the term 'applied' may or may not have an unfavorable connotation" (p. 941).

Among the often-stated goals of science are those of description, prediction, and understanding. Applied research, done on an emergency basis on specific problems, leads to specific information of little use in understanding later problems. However, applied research can be both goal oriented *and* productive of general knowledge if it is done with a long-term perspective. A long-term view, however, requires excellent communication between the scientist and the profession with the problems. This communication is essential both to those who apply knowledge and those who develop it. The relationship is symbiotic.

One of the necessary conditions for scientific investigations is an exact and impartial analysis of the facts. This emphasis on exactness and impartiality, increased adequacy of concepts, and improvement, truth, knowledge, and so forth suggests that science embodies many of the major virtues of mankind. Antithetically it is noted that science is undemocratic and elitist. One scientist with facts derived from replicable observations can win scientific arguments over thousands who lack these data. For the scientist in his area of competence, his jury is a body of well-informed peers to whom he presents accurate reports with a minimum of emotion. Science is a self-correcting, adapting field composed of an interrelated set of principles, theories, and a vast amount of organized information, facts, and knowledge. Since scientific knowledge is public knowledge, the process of "publication," whether in print, in papers presented at conventions, or lectures in classrooms, is a necessary part of the self-correcting and adaption process.

SCIENCE AND CERTAINTY

Thus science's knowledge is subjected to replication and confirmation or rejection. New ideas, concepts, and discoveries, spread rapidly via the publication process, which breeds new ideas and discoveries. Errors in observations or interpretations of data are checked and corrected as a result of the public nature of the process. Science is *not* a quest for certainty. It is a search for a reasonable approximation and greater conceptual power in understanding the world and the universe. Scientific theories and explanations are provisional. The best that can be done in the scientific world is that other scientists attempt to verify observations under similar conditions over a period of time. Nothing can be proved scientifically. All that can be done is to bring evidence to bear that a proposition is true. Proof is a matter of deduction, and in the interpretations of analyses of data, the word "proof" cannot be used in a logical sense. Interpretations of data analyses must be concerned with the evidence for or against the validity of hypotheses and theories. Thus an attitude of healthy skepticism without disdain and a lack of dogma about scientific findings is important for scientists and the consumers of science.

SCIENCE AND COMMON SENSE

Science perhaps can be comprehended more readily if it is considered as a human activity which increases the adequacy of man's ideas and conceptual systems as they relate to his perception of the natural world. Conant stated (1951), "[science] may be thought of as a series of concepts and conceptual schemes which have proved highly satisfactory for the practical uses of mankind" (pp. 32-33). He argued for further support for the scientific study of man as a social animal. He hoped that his ideas would be influential for investigators who seek a better understanding of man and the society he creates.

Huxley is said to have defined science as organized common sense. Unfortunately in many instances common sense is rather uncommon or poorly defined. But with common sense, as in science, what was commonly sensible in George Washington's time may be no longer common or sensible. Science is concerned with the objective study of the world of nature, including not only the physical and biological aspects of nature, but man's cognitive, social, and emotional domains, as well as the dynamic interrelationships of his groups.

SCIENCE AND OBJECTIVITY

The emotional and social aspects of man are definitely included in objective scientific study even though they are subjective phenomena. To define "objective," the word "subjective" needs definition. Scriven noted (1972) two distinct meanings to the word subjective. In the first definition "'subjective' refers to what concerns or occurs to the individual subject and his experiences, qualities, and dispositions" (p. 95). In the second, nonscientific aspects of the definition, "'subjective' means unreliable, biased or probably biased, a matter of opinion" (p. 95). What is objective about science is "what a *number* of subjects or judges experience—in short, . . . phenomena in the public domain" (p. 95). Scriven also stated that "A man's tastes, attitudes and values as well as his thoughts and feelings are quite properly thought of as characteristics of him or of his state at a particular time and are no less objective facts about him than his weight . . . or his strength or his ability to multiply seven by seven" (p. 96). Thus man's attitudes, values, thoughts, and feelings as a part of the objective world, are amenable to study by scientific methods.

PHILOSOPHY OF EDUCATION AND SCIENCE

These descriptions of scientific areas must be distinguished from other scholarly areas, particularly in education. The function of education in part is to declare the worth or value of certain goals. Science cannot determine the worth of morals or ethics or values except for the ethics of man as a scientist. The basic ethic of science is that it is better to know than not to know and that this knowledge is public. Thus moral, ethical, and value judgments in education are left to the philosophers of education.

The two scholarly areas of educational philosophy and educational research meet (and sometimes inadvertently clash) in education when the scientist chooses criteria on which to assess the educational effectiveness of treatments. Because selection of criteria always implies some value system, scientists thus declare their value judgments about what they feel the educational system is supposed to accomplish.

Alternately, when philosophers or judges of education declare that a given curriculum or method of instruction should be used *because*, from their point of view, logically it produces certain benefits to the students involved, they wander into the territory of the educational researcher. Such cause-and-effect statements can only be made on the basis of data and facts.

The goals and objectives of education are many and are sometimes as conflicting as they are in men's value systems generally. Educational researchers should be aware that they are selecting only a few of the criteria for a study from the many that are available. The determination of cause-and-effect relationships between program variables and these criteria are within the realm of the scientist and are subject to the rules of scientific evidence, not simply rhetoric or oratory.

OTHER KNOWLEDGE

Knowledge of the natural world can be gained by methods other than the formal ones of science. Experience, observation of events as they occur in the world, trial and error where one discards what does not work, tradition, and custom are other sources of knowledge about the natural world. In fact, it has been said that if man waits long enough, much of the observation and experimentation in science may occur naturally and knowledge would accrue. Research is merely a more accurate method, accelerating the process in a systematic manner.

ENGINEERING AND EDUCATIONAL RESEARCH

Education is both a profession and an applied field. Education's purposes are comparable, particularly in research functions, to other applied fields such as engineering. According to Smith, "Engineering is the professional art of applying science to the efficient conversion of natural resources to the benefit of man" (1956, p. 9). Educational research is the professional art of applying science to the efficient use of man's inner resources as well as for his educational benefit. Smith elaborated that an art is based on a set on a set of principles and rules for doing a certain work well and includes the systematic application of knowledge. The scientist attempts to explain and predict while engineering is a decision-making process in which the engineer attempts to maximize the benefits of the use of resources while minimizing costs. The major part of engineering work consists of solving problems. This involves making clear statements of the problems, marshalling facts, analyzing these facts, checking the results, and drawing conclusions. Major engineering functions are research, development, design, application, and management. These are similar to the functions of educational research. Smith differentiated between the research engineer and the research scientist by a sole characteristic. The aim of the research scientist is to know, to discover truth for truth's sake. The research engineer has a definite use in mind for the new information, new principles, or new methods he is seeking.

Often the educational researcher also has a definite use in mind for his research in the educational processes. His or her purpose is to improve the functioning of an educational system by finding out how it works and developing a more adequate causal-theoretical understanding of it. The educational researcher's aim is to establish facts about cause-and-effect relationships in education and to assist in either doing the equivalent educational job at a lower cost or getting more educational output for the same cost. They may develop new thrusts and approaches to the educational task. Their purpose is not simply developing behavioral and social science knowledge for its own sake.

BASIC AND APPLIED RESEARCH

Sometimes a distinction is made in research by calling one type of research pure, or basic, and the other type, applied research. Basic research is sometimes said to be generalizable knowledge while applied research, or evaluation, particularly as used in education, is said to be information for specific program decisions. Stetten in an editorial in *Science* (1972) said, "Research is the invasion of the unknown . . . . One cannot know where one will be a day hence, one cannot be certain of either distance to be covered or direction taken. In short, one cannot plan . . . . Once the trail has been blazed, to pave it into a road can be a planned operation, but . . . this is no longer research . . . research proper remains an unplanned exercise." Stetten has a very narrow definition of the word research, and his definition applies only to basic or pure research.

Conant (1951, p. 61) suggested an interchanging of functions—that those trained as engineers become applied scientists by reducing the degree of empiricism in problem solving; and conversely, that men trained as scientists often operate as engineers. In prior centuries even the giants of basic science moved back and forth between basic and applied work: Davy, in chemistry and agriculture, Kelvin, in physics and in telegraphy, and Pasteur, in chemistry and in wine and silk-worm problems.

A certain snobbery, however, has developed, with a restrained disdain by basic researchers for applied researchers and engineers. This attitude may be in part due to a need for status among those who would label themselves basic researchers. Conspicuous consumption may play a role here also. This concept, described by the sociologist Veblen, suggests that man achieves status by the use of resources in a deliberate, nonproductive way. An example from Veblen's time was the conversion of pasture land used for grazing cattle to lawns, and vegetable plots used for food production to decorative gardens. Similarly, some basic researchers to attain status declare that their research has no applied purpose; their work is being supported by society, it is implied, solely because of their genius. Too often, however, the lack of application of these proclaimers' research occurs because the basic researchers' "results" simply do not hold up in the transfer from their laboratories to the real world when the attempt is made to apply them.

This snobbery is not new. James Clark-Maxwell, a famous nineteenth-century English physicist, in referring to Alexander Graham Bell's telephone suggested that, while the telephone was an example of a constructive skill that went beyond the common bell-pull, it was capable of being put together by an amateur. Maxwell indicated his disappointment was only partially relieved on finding that the instrument really was able to talk. He declared that Bell was not an electrician who made a tinplate speak, but a speaker who, to gain his private ends, had become an electrician.

There is a persistent tendency to believe that ideas flow from majestic founts of knowledge which are recharged only by the genius and exhaustive efforts of basic researchers. In fact, perhaps a great portion of the ideas for work in new scientific theory comes from the engineering and applied science solutions of society's problems. Even Nobel prizes and other major scientific honors are now granted to researchers in industry and medicine.

EDUCATORS, PROFESSIONS, KNOWLEDGE, AND DECISIONS

How does an educator fit into this schema? Educators are professionals. They have codes of ethics, are generally licensed by the state, and have accepted standards of practice. But perhaps one of the most definitive criteria of a profession is that it is based on abstract and theoretical knowledge. Leggatt (1970), in a chapter titled "Teaching as a Profession," said that the characteristic of professionals appearing with the greatest regularity is that their practice is founded upon a base of theoretical, esoteric knowledge. Turner and Hodge (1970) stated, "An ubiquitous assumption in writing on professions appears to be that a profession has an essential underpinning of abstract principles which have been organized into a theory, set of theories, or at least a complex web of theoretical orientations" (p. 26). Many sociologists agree that the core characteristic of professions is their foundation upon systematic, technical knowledge. The theme of theoretical knowledge runs throughout these descriptions of a profession. Theoretical knowledge is the major common ground on which research, science, engineering, and professional education meet; all else is dependent on it. It is assumed professional educators have some rational knowledge basis for their actions. Further, it is assumed that this knowledge is sufficiently unique that others are not likely to have major aspects of it at their command. This system of knowledge continues to grow and develop to meet new educational situations and to resolve old problems more effectively. As in medicine, where a great deal of the knowledge arises from basic biological research, much research covers problems generated from within medical practice. Educators also should do research on problems arising from their professional work while drawing on basic research from psychology, sociology, and so forth.

TEACHERS AND ADMINISTRATORS AND RESEARCH

Evaluating, appraising, measuring, or controlling (in the sense of measuring output or results of the organization), comparing end products with some standard, or adjusting inputs to outputs of the system are among the several functions of educational administrators according to Knezevich (1969). He added that knowledge is "necessary for objective assessment of operations" (p. 32). Any educational decision involves making a choice among alternative methods through which educational objectives can be achieved. Teaching and the organization of learning experiences; or the structuring of the physical environment of the buildings, playground, classrooms and shop, band, and cafeterias; or the development of rules for teachers and students— all involve instructional, curricular, or administrative decisions. All of these and other administrative decisions in education are based on the fundamental rationale that there is a cause-and-effect relationship between the educational objectives and the alternative methods of achieving them. It is assumed that some educational objectives can be achieved faster, or better, more completely, or less expensively through the use of certain procedures and choices rather than through others. These cause-and-effect relationships may not be made explicit when the decisions are being made, but they are at the basis of every administrative decision in education. The teachers and educational administrators consider all the alternatives and select one or two which are felt to be "best" in the sense that they are most likely to achieve the educational objective with the most effective balance of costs, effort, unwanted side effects, and numerous additional factors.

Decision-making is the central process in administration (Griffiths, 1959), and knowledge is a basic ingredient in decision-making. In the past, administrative decision-makers in education were concerned primarily with summary data collected for central and accounting purposes, social bookkeeping, enforcement of regulations and laws, and the distribution of reimbursement funds. It is suggested that these were after-the-fact pieces of information for before-the-fact decisions. If professional educators are to be actively engaged in administering and guiding education with decision-making processes, it must be assumed they have a choice of alternatives from which they can choose and also, that they have the knowledge to select which alternative is best for a given educational situation. Research design knowledge is implicit in educational administration and decision-making, and research must be done formally if knowledge is to accumulate and better decisions are to be made.

EDUCATIONAL RESEARCH

Certainly educational research is a field of science since it deals at least with cognitive, emotional, and physical learning, and social interrelationships of children, adolescents, and adults. It is an applied scientific field because of the direction implied by the word "educational." However, not all research done in schools is educational research. There is a great deal of behavioral and social science research that takes place in schools because schools happen to be a marvelous source of captive audiences, ranging from children and adolescents to college sophomores. Boring, the great historian of psychology, inadvertently expressed the attitude of too many of his colleagues when, in speaking about the greater availability of subjects for experimental psychology (other than the professors and the experimenters themselves in earlier times), he noted (1954), "Such studies . . . are supplemented nowadays by researchers which utilize large numbers of rats and school-children, subjects which, besides being inexpensive and plentiful, make the sample examined more representative." (p. 588).

Scriven (1972) wrote that "the aims of educational research need some proletarianizing, and some serious concern with teaching manual skills in a more effective and respectful way" (p. 140). He hoped to see researchers working on improving shorthand, speed reading, memory skills, "speed-speak," "fast-think," and much of the work in the learning area providing the chance for practical payoff as well as theoretical gain. "In every dimension one is faced with the list of things that have long needed doing and that have been kept out by status considerations of the crudest and least rational kind" (p. 141). Among these things suggested were proof of the effectiveness on education of school buildings and curriculum materials, ways to get evaluations into the planning of schools of the future, and ways to specify the designs for them.

The purposes of educational research are: (1) to generate knowledge to advance the effectiveness and quality of educational systems, (2) to be used by professional educators for this end, and (3) to reduce the costs of the educational system if effectiveness can be maintained or improved while doing so. Educational research is oriented toward the problems of education. It includes a broad variety of activities which involve the generation and use of scientific knowledge by professionals and others in education. However, investigators working on practical educational problems may aid basic researchers in gaining insight into understanding broader facets of human behavior; thus educational research contributes to basic research knowledge. Many of the questions which arise from attempts to solve educational problems are productive areas into which basic researchers can delve. Educational research is distinctive when criteria for both education and research can be used. Science, research, and education are inextricably intertwined and each needs the others if all are to prosper.

PROBLEMS

On what kinds of problems do teachers and administrators work? Where do these problems come from? How are everyday problems developed into formal research problems?

Basic research activities often are aimed at being able to ask better questions than currently are being asked. In fields related to education, basic research is done by scientists in psychology, sociology, anthropology, and political science. While basic research is done involving educational systems and procedures of significance to education, few educational professionals may be interested in doing basic research themselves.

On the other hand, professionals are more likely to be interested in applied research and an engineering approach to education, involving the development of solutions to day-to-day and year-in and year-out problems that are recognized only too well. These are the problems to which professionals can make major contributions. In fact, it might be said that anyone who has been in the field of education for a few years and is unable to recognize the many major and minor problems in the area, is either not too aware of his surroundings or is in a very sheltered corner of the profession.

In the view of educational research taken in this book, there is little need for a list of top-quality scientific problems needing solutions; rather, it is a knowledge of methods of attack for existing problems and protection against pseudo-solutions for problems which are recognized readily. Problems in education are abundant. Educators are almost overrun by the problems they and their colleagues face everyday. The problems of educating the disadvantaged and minority culture groups, of financing public education, of obtaining appropriate materials, problems in organizing education, of retaining able personnel, of developing vocational programs, special education programs and programs for alienated youth are just a few of the areas in recent years where more problems than solutions exist. The position is taken here that all of these areas and many other areas as well are worthy ones in which professionals can work toward solutions via scientific methods, or in other words, do research as defined in this book. The big issue probably will not be in finding a problem area but in being able to reduce the problem to a size manageable with the resources available to attack it.

There are some methods by which important problems can be brought into manageable range. In some areas there are lists of succinct problems that seem to be next in line for solutions based on the knowledge just becoming available. The *Encyclopedia of Educational Research* (Ebel, 1969) often includes these problem areas at the end of its articles. Sometimes good areas for continued probing appear in articles found when the literature review is made of the problem area. The lack of congruence between solutions appearing in the literature in the problem area and programs working in the schools is a good place to document, to do research, and to publish results. Documenting the effectiveness of a particular program through a research project is a good educational research approach. A series of articles or books in a field of education that has presented findings based on methodological errors is also a good area in which to further research. The next study can improve the design, analysis, and methodology and correct the information previously obtained. Often statements which have little basis in research data will be made about educational practice.

Overgeneralizations and conclusions which do not follow from data also are often found in the literature. These, too, are good areas for research.

However, there are four words in educational questions which cannot be used in the statement of scientific problems. These are "ought," "should," "good," and "bad." The answers to questions such as what *should* education be doing about this or that problem, or what *ought* the goals of this educational program be, are value-oriented questions and fall within the realm of philosophy, not science. Given an educational objective, though, the methods by which the objective can be accomplished are subject to systematic investigation, or in other words, research. The words "good" and "bad" imply moral or ethical values and need to be translated into what happens to students or a system when something is done. After the scientific data and results are available, then the moral and ethical evaluations can be considered.

Once the general area of a problem has been selected, there are several steps that need to be taken. A first step is to frame worthwhile research questions. Just any sentence ending with a question mark is not adequate. In order for a research question to be meaningful, it must be answerable with statements that refer to sources of information and to procedures for collecting data about the question. Both these sources and procedures must refer to the observations that are needed to answer the questions. Who are the subjects, what are the data, what is to be done, what is to be described, what criterion or evidence is acceptable, and what are the conditions, are some of the questions that are asked in order to develop a good statement of a problem. These types of questions will lead to *operational definitions* of variables and to subject groups and measuring instruments. Questions of these types will lead to operations, conditions, and subjects that will produce evidence which, in turn, will lead toward answers to problems and to futher questions.

The scientific method involves continuous questioning. As older ideas are changed as a result of data and questions, more questions will develop and answers to these questions will be sought. Then further questions are asked, more observations made, new answers recognized, and then the process of questioning starts again.

The fundamental aspect of a good question is that it will specify the procedures to be used in making the needed observations to answer the question. These skills can be sharpened by developing research questions and asking whether the questions specify methods and observations that can be used to answer them. If it is felt that they do, a colleague might then be asked to indicate what these procedures would be, based on the questions. Then the search is renewed with more detailed questions.

Of course, for some of the questions asked, some answers may already exist. To locate these answers is the purpose of a literature review. Other questions may be rather narrow in scope or of value to only a small segment of the educational world. These questions need to be stated so that if they are answered, the results apply more generally to education. This is the purpose of theory development. Good theories attempt to answer general questions. The theories will generate the questions that attempt to answer the query "How?" and later, "Why?"

RESEARCH, DEVELOPMENT, DIFFUSION, AND ADOPTION

The several processes of educational research have been classified by several authorities. Clark and Guba (1965) use the following: implementation, design, application, use, and introduction of research results. The Development, Diffusion, and Adoption (DD & A) aspects of the model are concerned primarily with implementation and use of the research knowledge. The Clark-Guba model suggested that knowledge develops from an inquiry process and proceeds through the Development, Diffusion, and Adoption processes in order. Gideonse (1968) developed a more complex model further dividing the classifications of the process: Development into invention and design; Diffusion into dissemination and demonstration; and Adoption into trial, installation, and institutionalization. For the Diffusion process Gideonse uses words such as "examine and assess" and "evidential assessment" to describe the demonstration components of Development. At the far end of the DD & A continuum, Adoption, where changes are being incorporated into the schools' operations, one of the three components listed is "trial." Here part of the objective is, "To . . . provide a basis for assessing the quality, value, fit, and utility of the invention . . . i.e., *to test.*"

Even in the other two components of adoption, installation and institutionalization, words used to indicate the criteria of these are "effectiveness," "efficiency," and "valuation." Certainly these words and functions typically fit under the general term "educational research." Definitions of educational research found in journals and books cover almost the entire range of the Gideonse Research, Development, Diffusion, and Adoption (RDD & A) model of educational research.

RESEARCH DESIGN AND EDUCATIONAL RESEARCH

What methodological skills and knowledge areas then are common to the various educational research sequences? Again, the words that are used to describe the components of educational research can be examined: "relative contribution," "generalizability," "extent which it affects," "examination and assessment of operating qualities," "evidential assessment," "assessing quality," "to test," "effectiveness," "efficiency," and "valuation." These terms are drawn from all seven components of the Gideonse educational research processes which are related to and necessary for change in education. They can be encompassed by the concepts found in the general terms "research," "the theory of measurement," and, to some extent, "statistics." While it might be argued that effectiveness, efficiency, assessment, etc., can be defined by common sense, authoritative "eyeball analysis," or administrative judgment, the range of problems to which these processes can be applied is limited. It is now rather well established that all types of data—from the most subjective to the most objective—should be used in the assessment and evaluation of human activities (Scriven, 1972).

Perhaps the fundamental difference between basic research and the evaluation, effectiveness, and assessment functions of educational research is that of external research validity versus internal research validity. External validity refers to the generalizability of any knowledge gained. Internal validity answers the more fundamental question: Are the interpretations of the results of the research true even in the research situation from which they were developed? The indicated evaluation, effectiveness, relative contribution, evidential assessment, and testing functions in all of these aspects of educational research then are continual checks of the internal validity of the effectiveness of the educational innovation. For example, does it still work in this particular school, class, or learning situation? Basic research's primary goal is to develop broad principles and theory about behavior which hold true in most of the situations to which they are applied. The concept of broad truth is necessary to a definition of theory. This is the aspect of theory that makes it so valuable and useful. In the adage ascribed to Kurt Lewin, nothing is more useful than a good theory.

EVALUATION AND EDUCATIONAL RESEARCH

"Educational evaluation is the process of delineating, obtaining, and providing useful information for judging decision alternatives"

(1971, p. 40) is the definition of evaluation written by the Phi Delta Kappa National Study Committee. Chaired by Daniel Stufflebeam, a prominent evaluation theorist, the Committee declared that the basic rationale for acceptable evaluations is that the results be "in data or findings which might be thought of as information" (p. 26). Two kinds of information are described. The first kind refers to the standard *scientific* criteria such as reliability and validity. Informing or being informed is the second kind. Stufflebeam, *et al.* present four scientific criteria for information: internal validity, external validity, reliability, and objectivity; and six practical criteria: relevance, importance, scope, credibility, timeliness, and pervasiveness. It is clear the committee included almost all of educational research within their definition of evaluation.

However, there are differences between research and evaluation. Evaluation goes well beyond educational research, Provus (1969) describes evaluation as agreeing upon program standards, determining discrepancies between aspects of the program and the program standards, and using discrepancy information to identify the weaknesses of the program. *Evaluation then implies judgments based on facts which research methods supply.*

Hemphill (1969) and Stake and Denny (1969) described similar comparisons. However, Stake and Denny suggest that the distinction between research and evaluation can be overstated as well as understated. They feel the principal difference between the two is the degree to which the findings are generalizable beyond their application to a given product, program, or locale. Researchers and evaluators use the same inquiry paradigms. Hemphill (1969) indicates that in many instances there are no distinctions between evaluation and research.

Evaluation, then, is more than research and at the same time completely encompasses research methods. If these methodological components are weak, the evaluation which builds upon them can be no stronger. Evaluation decisions can be no better than the validity of the information upon which they rest. For educational dissemination and adoption purposes, the concern can be the quality of the generalizations and information presented to others through the communication channels.

CHANGE AND EDUCATIONAL RESEARCH

In the book *Innovation in Education* (Miles, 1964), several authors make a number of statements about evaluation and change as a part of the educational research process. A theme of the book was that educational organization could be conceived of as an open system with inputs and outputs, but it is quite apparent that changes typically occur not because of noted changes in *output*. There are few meaningful output data getting into existing feedback loops from which change for demonstrated improvement could result. Kendall in her chapter in the book suggests that the creators of experimental programs feel little need for systematic evaluation. Their assumption is that the courses were developed under the best possible conditions. However, without good evaluatory evidence, the results of a curricular change are said to be self-evident. Frequently, the opinions of users and clients are invoked, and informal student reactions and teachers responses are assessed. Seldom are data found which could be interpreted reasonably in a cause-and-effect relationship and decisions to terminate or continue innovations are often based on little evidence. Adequate evaluation of an innovation is expensive. Serious evaluation of a new curriculum may cost nearly three times the amount needed for its original production. This inability, or lack of resources, to determine whether an innovation has achieved results often goes unnoticed.

SYSTEMS EVALUATION AND EDUCATIONAL RESEARCH

Systems evaluation along with accountability, cost-benefit, and cost effectiveness have recently been hailed as among the new saviors of education. And well they might be since systems evaluation, according to Gagné (1962) is "the set of procedures used to determine what the system can do and how well it performs the operations implied by its purposes" (p. 8). He indicates that systems evaluation implies the necessity for observation and measurement relative to the systems' total functioning. In discussing systems research, Davis and Behan (1962) indicate that it is necessary to arrive at some clearcut understanding of the system to be investigated. Then the methodologies must be developed for experimentally investigating proposed hypotheses, and finally, experiments and studies must be designed and conducted to test hypotheses. They feel that evaluation of a complex system involves combining these three elements into a total evaluation strategy.

Oettinger's (1968) expert view perhaps sums up thinking on systems analysis as applied to education. "The myth of systems analysis holds that educational salvation lies in applying to education the planning and control techniques commonly believed to have been successful in the defense and aerospace industries" (p. 77). Systems analysis cannot be dismissed, however, out of hand. He feels the best formulations of systems analysis are indistinguishable from descriptions of the scientific method.

Accountability definitions vary but a reasonable accepted core of meaning is ascribed to the concept. Lieberman (1970) implies cause-and-effect relationships as well as close ties to educational research in his broad definition. Grayson defines a cost-benefit analysis in many ways as identical to the purposes of the more formal types of research; it thus uses many of the same methods. These methods, of course, would be subject to the same types of research design criticisms as educational research.

MEASUREMENT AND EDUCATIONAL RESEARCH

The terms evaluation, assessment, effectiveness, etc., used in educational research imply that measured variables are used by which the evaluations are made. It is assumed that these measures exist in a real world and have some lasting substance over time.

This existence in a real world is the basic concept of reliability as defined by internal consistency, test-retest, and alternate form methods. It is also assumed that the measures reflect relevant current and future behaviors, or that they possess concurrent and predictive validity. The "effective procedures, including provision for appropriate objective measurements" called for in Title I of the Elementary and Secondary Education Act can be considered as a need for reliable, replicable conclusions inferred from a research design.

Kerlinger defines an objective procedure as "one in which agreement among observers is at a maximum" (1964, p. 479). Objectivity then, is another word for reliability. For objective agreement about cause-and-effect relationships among variables, the principles of internal validity must be accepted, or experienced observers will not agree on the causal relationships.

ACTION RESEARCH, CURRICULUM RESEARCH, AND EDUCATIONAL RESEARCH

Some investigators rationalize that their investigations are action research and therefore should not be held to the more formal research design standards. However, Corey (1953, pp. 100, 142–144) declared that action research is a responsible and fruitful curricular experimentation which results in dependable evidence obtained by the scientific method. He claims that differences in methodology between action research and traditional research are minor. The major difference is that the motivation of action researchers is improvement of their own practices.

Smith, Stanley, and Shores, in an early edition of their book *Fundamentals of Curriculum Development* (1950), state that to appraise experimental studies of curriculum patterns, the following conditions must be understood and satisfied: the theory of the curriculum patterns must be stated unequivocally, the conditions under which the curriculum pattern is to be tried must be described in detail, hypotheses derived from the curriculum theory must be stated, and data collected to ascertain whether or not the hypotheses derived from the curriculum theory were borne out by observed facts. If two curricular theories are being compared, then there must be experiments to determine which is superior. This language and the required activities for curriculum research fall well within the definitions of scientific educational research which have been presented.

EDUCATIONAL INNOVATIONS: POOR EXAMPLES

Driver education has a well-developed and defined curriculum. It has been actively diffused and promoted throughout the United States by safety councils, industry, business, and professional organizations, some devoted almost entirely to its welfare. Considerable pressure has been exerted by the public which demands that state and local school systems adopt driver education. Financial aid has been made available to encourage the process further. State certification in driver education has helped focus attention on driver education instructors and has helped in setting professional standards in the field. Much applied research has been done over a period of thirty years or more, the predominance of which clearly demonstrates that students who take driver education courses in high school do indeed have fewer accidents. These studies have been collated, summarized, reviewed, and the preceding conclusion certified in a study sponsored and widely disseminated by the National Education Association (1961). Thus, conviction has been built of the value of the system.

Three nationwide conferences were held over a period of years. Subcommittees met and passed resolutions making strong recommendations to the education profession and to state educational agencies about the content and methods used in driver education, including the famed thirty and six recommendation—thirty hours of classroom work and six hours of behind-the-wheel instruction. The industrial giants of our society, the automobile manufacturers, have strongly supported driver education from time to time both by corporate policy and fiscal support. Many insurance companies promote driver education in their advertising campaigns.

Computers were used on very large populations exceeding 500,000 people to further certify to the results. Finally, in a move hardly contemplated by either the Guba-Clark or the Gideonse educational change process models, the U.S. Congress passed a law which made driver education *mandatory* throughout a state with the penalty being a fine of 10 percent of the state's federal highway construction subsidy. (This is a sum on the order of many million dollars each year; institutionalization in the Gideonse model with a vengeance!) Here then is an educational process in which careful attention and large expenditures of energy were devoted to the change process in education. Many aspects of the DD & A model can be examined in relationships to data and gaps filled, concepts shaped, and new interrelationships established.

In fact there is only one small problem in this model. To anyone who had managed to recognize clearly that a relationship is *not* necessarily a *cause-and-effect relationship*, it is apparent that driver education may very well *not* cause a reduction in accidents. Driver education, with its high equipment cost needs and its small student-teacher ratio, is one of the more expensive courses in the standard educational system. Implementation of such a program on the basis of correlational information with little if any testing of alternative hypotheses is a poor decision-making process.

When alternative hypotheses were tested (Conger, *et al.*, 1966, Asher, 1968a, Shively, 1968), it became very apparent that a general relationship between socioeconomic status and fewer accidents could account for the correlation between driver education and reduction in accidents. McGuire's research in Mississippi (McGuire & Kersh, 1968), which won a National Safety Council prize, demonstrated no relationship at all between accident reduction and driver education when careful measurement procedures and research controls were instituted. Asher (1968a) also has shown, for a nationwide sample of high school seniors, that there is no relationship.

Even some of the top-level systems analysts evidently naively accepted the correlation between taking driver education and reduced accidents as a cause-and-effect relationship (Moynihan, 1968). Systems analysts and cost effectiveness specialists evaluated driver education against other accident-reducing systems. They correctly concluded that such components as seat-belt installations, drunken-driver control, and emergency medical services would have a greater "pay off" than further implementation of driver education programs. So far, so good. How-

ever, the report further states that the economic return on driver
education is estimated to be 5 percent above costs! Again the systems
analysts blithely accepted the correlational relationships as cause-and-
effect. From the work of McGuire and Kersh, and Asher, it is obvious
that the cost of driver education for the specific benefit of accident
reduction is perhaps a 100 percent *loss*, not a 5 percent gain. It is clear
that at least some systems analysts need to know more about research
methodology and the interpretation of educational research data.

Other examples of negative information in the development,
dissemination, and adoption change in education can be given.
Language laboratories have long been subsidized by the United States
Office of Education support programs. The result has been widespread
installation and institutionalization in the adoption process; that is, a
language lab in many schools. Yet the eminent authority on foreign
language learning, Carroll (1963), writing in the *Handbook of Research on
Teaching*, indicates that there have been few experimental studies on
the question of how much and in what ways a tape recorder or language
laboratories may be expected to take over the duties of an instructor. In
one of his own studies he found no significant differences between
methods of instruction except that the class that used the language
laboratory did poorer on tests of reading, vocabulary, and grammar.
Auditory comprehension skills were the same in both groups tested.
Frymier (1968) more recently supports this view. He indicated that the
use of language laboratories represented a very extensive kind of
change which had little basis in empirical data to support it, even
though most of the "experts" in the field are convinced of its
advantages. Yet Miles (1954, p. 4) states that Titles III and VII of the
National Defense Education Act supported the appearance of approximately 5,000 language laboratories.

The Initial Teaching Alphabet (i/t/a) is another educational innovation widely disseminated in education. The research underpinnings for
it have been sparse. The USOE supported one study which was further
monitored by the professional organization in the area, the International Reading Association. However, the research design was clearly
faulty in the project and the statistical analysis was also in error (Asher,
1968b). The follow-up study was equally in error (Asher, 1968c).

In the last decade or so, major curricular innovations have been
supported by various arms of the federal government and their
"results" widely proclaimed as saving the schools from many dire fates.
As time cools the passions and developers are less identified with their
products, diminishing federal money is no longer used to keep
educational administrators and practitioners seduced (or discreetly
bribed). Thus, more objective evaluations of the results of the cur-

riculum changes can be made. Frymier (1968) makes a telling statement for those more concerned with really improving education rather than just being innovative.

> The purpose here is not to argue that the "new curriculum ventures are not sound, theoretically, or desirable, operationally. They may very well be. The basic point here is that to date very few of the innovations have withstood careful experimental scrutiny and prove, in practice, their superiority to the 'traditional' programs or plans. However, changes have been made and have not been made, *regardless of the data avalable,* simply because education as a social system has no systematic way to utilize feedback data effectively and creatively to improve clarification." (p. 2) (Emphasis added.)

EDUCATIONAL INNOVATIONS: GOOD EXAMPLES

It may be said that the systematic examination, assessment, evaluation, efficiency, valuation, and testing components of educational research are often lacking, at least to a reasonable or acceptable degree. This lack of research, editing, critiques, and comments in the literature in the educational DD & A process hurts in another way as well. It is often stated that everybody knows the quality of the literature in education and this is particularly true of doctoral dissertations. But numerous well-done studies exist in the literature which could be of value to education but are not widely used. Early entrance into school (see the study by Birch, Tisdale, Barney & Marks, 1965) is one example.

Another example is a study done on the use of a heel bar instead of the standard heel cleats on football shoes. Nedwidek, for a doctoral thesis at the University of Pittsburgh (1965), did a study for which the basic theory seemed well developed. He was concerned about ankle and knee injuries of his players and also the diffusion of this theoretical information and its adoption by his fellow coaches. This information was clearly beyond the invention and design stage aspects of the Development stage of educational research. Since ankle and knee injuries constitute about 70 percent of football injuries, and football is so widely played in educational institutions, the problem is obviously significant, especially for the public which supports education in the United States. A true experiment was designed and measurement procedures developed. An interested othopedic surgeon assisted in the medical aspects of the problem. Nedwidek, a respected high school football coach himself, obtained the cooperation of a number of high school coaches in the area, and replaced heel cleats with heel bars on the shoes of randomly selected players. The results were clear cut. A 74 percent reduction in the number of ankle and knee injuries in the experimental group was observed!

Some have stated that educational research only yields trivial or minimal results. Here is a clear refutation of the statement. Yet heel bars are not widely used in this part of the educational system in which the results are of such considerable interest to those concerned with athletics in schools and colleges.

The preceding study is an example of educational research in its broader, more general meaning. It is clearly not basic research nor, under the Gideonse definition, even applied research. It is not Development either; the invention has been made and the design work done (and it was commercially available). It is clearly educational research at the Diffusion and Adoption stage because it was meant to inform and build conviction about the invention. It presented evidential assessment of the operating qualities of the invention. This adoption was an open, in-service test of the invention which would indicate its effectiveness, help operationalize its installation, and establish its value to the institution. Thus it becomes clearer that much educational research done by professionals in education would be called DD & A in the Clark-Guba and Gideonse terminology. But it is also clear that research design methods, measurement, and statistics—the technical methods for obtaining knowledge in the behavioral sciences—are obviously required in the educational DD & A process because of the testing and evaluation being done.

Research and development in the physical sciences is also of value to education. Findings in these areas are generally more accepted as fact, but even here education has not implemented the Dissemination and Adoption components for change. Perhaps it is because the RDD & A literature in education is so loaded with "data" that is towards the fantasy end of the information continuum, that much of that which is near the factual end, is lost in the overall noise of the system.

An example comes from acoustics. The acoustical qualities of various types, sizes, and contents of rooms are reasonably well known. However, the Massachusetts Institute of Technology (Newman, 1949) did applied research on the acoustical properties of school classrooms. Their conclusions were firm and well documented. Acoustical tile, when used, should be placed around the *tops* of the *walls*. Acoustical tile should *not* be placed on the ceilings of classrooms because that hard surface is used to transmit the instructional voice and classroom discussion to all listeners in the class. This knowledge was also included in a Diffusion journal article directed at educational administrators (Ryden & Asher, 1955) and later in a book of readings in educational psychology (Remmers, Rivlin, Ryans & Ryden, 1957). Later the article was also brought to the personal attention of one of the members of a leading national firm of school architects. Yet, as important as speaking and listening are in elementary and secondary classrooms, it is still relatively unusual to see this concept applied. In fact, the exact opposite of the recommendation is in widespread use.

Again, the total volume of the educational research literature is so large and generally of such indifferent quality that often the educator's strategy in using the literature is to implement those research "findings" presented most recently, that is, most popular at the moment. This practice hardly builds enduring quality in educational systems. Meanwhile, communications and information of high quality tend to become obliterated in the mass of the literature.

SUMMARY

This chapter has introduced the reader to the field of educational research. Definitions and concepts from research, science, education, engineering, professionalism, knowledge, and administration were presented.

An overview has also been presented of the broadly defined field of educational research, including the Development, Dissemination, and Adoption Processes. The relationship of educational research to research design, evaluation, change, systems evaluation, measurement, action and curriculum research, and the quality of educational research literature were discussed. Examples of good and poor research were presented, and the need to study educational research by professionals was implied throughout the chapter.

STUDY AND DISCUSSION PROBLEMS

1. Indicate areas of education where the methods of science cannot be used to resolve problems.
2. Suggest several types of problems in your area of education where scientific methods can be used to advantage.
3. In your own words briefly tell what research is.
4. Indicate areas and problems of education which fall in the domain of educational research and in the domain of educational philosophy.
5. Find new terms or phrases in the chapter and describe the concepts in your own words.
6. Does educational research involve more basic research or applied research? Give examples of each.

7. What is the purpose of educational research?
8. Can the word "proof" be used in educational research?
9. How are engineering and educational research alike?
10. What are the purposes of this book?
11. What are the areas of skills needed for educational research?
12. Do the methods of science lead to certainty?
13. Define "objectivity" and "subjectivity" and relate them to one another.
14. What is "engineering" and how might the concept apply to education?
15. What is a profession? When does a teacher or an administrator become a professional?
16. Why, as a professional educator, is it important to you to have an understanding of educational research methods?
17. Check several classrooms to see if the recommendations for their acoustic treatment have been used.
18. What are some of the differences and similarities between educational research and educational evaluation?
19. Indicate a teaching method, device, or technique which has been recommended to you. Justify its use from the research literature.
20. Describe "internal validity."
21. Describe "external validity" and distinguish it from internal validity.
22. How does educational evaluation use the concepts of internal and external validity?
23. Indicate briefly the views of several authorities with respect to what evaluation is.
24. How do the concepts of systems analysis, accountability, and cost-benefit analysis relate to education and educational research?
25. Indicate where measurement concepts are important in education.
26. What are some principles of measurement that are useful in understanding educational research?
27. Define a problem in the area of education. Is it researchable? What are the populations involved? What are the variables? How could they be measured? What are the relationships among the variables of interest? What comparisons among the groups are to be made?

REFERENCES

Asher, J. W. Do driver training courses produce better drivers? An alternative hypothesis. *Traffic Safety Research Review,* 1968a, *12*(1), 2–6.

Asher, J. W. Comment on "A comparison of i/t/a and T. O. reading achievement when methodology is controlled." *Elementary English,* 1968b, *XLV*(4), 452–457, 484.

Asher, J. W. Comment on "Spelling achievement following i.t.a. instruction." *The Reading Teacher,* November, 1968c, *22*(2), 153–156, & 169.

Birch, J. W., Tisdale, W. J., Barney, W. D., and Marks, C. H. A field demonstration of the effectiveness and feasibility of early admission to school for mentally advanced children. Pittsburgh, Pa.: University of Pittsburgh School of Education, December 1965, ERIC Ed 0001336.

Boring, E.G. The Nature and the history of experimental control. *American Journal of Psychology*, 1954, *67*, 573–589.

Campbell, D.T., and Stanley, J.C. Experimental and quasi-experimental designs for research on teaching. In N.L. Gate (Ed.) *Handbook of research on teaching*. Chicago: Rand McNally, 1963, 171-246.

Carroll, J.B. Research on teaching foreign languages. In N.L. Gage (Ed.) *Handbook of research on teaching*. Chicago: Rand McNally, 1963, 1060–1100.

Clark, D.L., and Guba, E.G. An explanation of potential change roles in education. October 1965, 33 pp. (mimeo).

Conant, J.B. *Science and common sense*. New Haven, Conn.: Yale University Press, 1951.

Conger, J.J., Miller, W.C., and Rainey, R.V. Effects of driver education: The role of motivation, intelligence, social class, and exposure. *Traffic Safety Research Review*, 1966, *10*, 67-71.

Corey, S.M. *Action research to improve school practices*. New York: Teachers College, Columbia, 1953.

Davis, R.H., and Behan, R.A. Evaluating performance in simulated environments. In R.M. Gagné (Ed.) *Psychological principles in system development*. New York: Holt, Rinehart and Winston, 1962, 477–515.

Ebel, R. (Ed.) *Encylcopedia of educational research*. New York: Macmillan, 1969.

Evans, B., and Evans, C. *Dictionary of contemporary American usage*. New York: Random House, 1957.

Frymier, J.R. Teachers: Not will but can they change? Strategies for educational change. *Newsletter*, 1968, *2*(6), 1–4.

Gagné, R.M. *Psychological principles in systems development*. New York: Holt, Rinehart and Winston, 1962.

Garner, W.R. The acquisition and application of knowledge: A symbiotic relation. *American Psychologist*, 1972, *27*(10), 941–946.

Gideonse, H.D. An output-oriented model of research and development and its relationship to educational improvement. *Journal of Experimental Education*, 1968, *37*(1), 157–163.

Griffiths, D.E. *Administrative theory*. New York: Appleton-Century-Crofts, 1959.

Hemphill, J.M. The relationship between research and evaluation studies. In R. Tyler (Ed.) *Educational evaluation: New roles, new means*. Chicago: NSSE, 1969, 189–220.

Kerlinger, F.M. *Foundations of behavioral research*. New York: Holt, Rinehart and Winston, 1964.

Knezevich, S.J. *Administration of public education*. New York: Harper and Row, 1969.

Leggatt, T. Teaching as a profession. In J.A. Jackson (Ed.) *Professions and professionalization*. London: Cambridge University Press, 1970, 153–178.

Lieberman, M. An overview of accountability. *Phi Delta Kappan*, 1970, *LII*(4), 194 and 195.

McGuire, F.L., and Kersh, R.C. *A summary of an experimental evaluation of driver education in the United States*, 1968.

Miles, M.B. Innovations in education: Some generalizations. In M.B. Miles (Ed.). *Innovation in education.* New York: Teachers College, Columbia, 1964, 631–662.

Moynihan, P. What the Moynihan report really said about driver education. *Traffic Safety Research Review,* 1968, *12,* 25.

National Education Association. Summary of results of studies evaluating driver education. Washington, D.C., 1961.

Nedwidek, R.A. Football cleats and knee and ankle injuries in high school football. University of Pittsburgh, Ed. D. Thesis, 1965.

Newman, R.B. Notes on how to improve sound insulation in the school and hearing conditions in the classroom. *Architectural Forum,* 1949, *91*(4), 152–153.

Oettinger, A. The myths of educational technology. *Saturday Review,* 1968, *LI*(20), 77.

The Oxford English Dictionary. Oxford: Clarendon Press, 1933.

Provus, M. Evaluation of ongoing programs in the public school system. In R. Tyler (Ed.) *Educational evaluation: New roles, new means.* Chicago, NSSE, 1969, 242–283.

Remmers, H.H., Rivlin, H.N., Ryans, D.G., and Ryden, E.R. *Growth, teaching, and learning.* New York: Harper, 1957.

Ryden, E.R., and Asher, J.W. Intelligibility and the classroom. *Educational Administration and Supervision.* 1955, *41*(8), 475–484.

Shively, J.E. Characteristics of high school students unable to take driver training. Masters Thesis, Purdue University, 1968.

Smith, B.O., Stanley, W.O., and Shores, J.H. *Fundamentals of curriculum development* (rev. ed). New York: Harcourt, Brace, & World, 1950, 583, 1957, 390.

Smith, R.J. *Engineering as a career.* New York: McGraw-Hill, 1956.

Stake, R.E., and Denny, T. Needed concepts and techniques for utilizing more fully the potential of evaluation. In R. Tyler, (Ed.) *Educational evaluation: New roles, new means.* Chicago: NSSE, 1969, 370–390.

Stetten, D., Jr. Editorial. *Science,* August 1972, *177* (4049).

Stufflebeam, D.L., *et al. Educational evaluation and decision making.* Itasca, Ill.: Peacock, 1971.

Turner, C., and Hodge, M.N. Occupations and professions. In Jackson, J.A. (Ed.) *Professions and professionalization,* London: Cambridge University Press, 1970, pp. 17-50.

Vockell, E., and Asher, W. Perceptions of Document Quality and Use by Educational Decision Makers and Researchers. *American Educational Research Journal,* 1974, *11*(3), 249–259.

Webster's Third New International Dictionary. Springfield, Mass.: Merriam, 1971.

Chapter 2

Research Design and Educational Knowledge

The logic of comparisons in educational research and their value for experimental inferences will be the concern of this chapter. The role of randomization in developing comparison groups and the components of an experiment in education also will be presented. The chapter also will include definitions and explanations of concepts used in research, such as internal and external validity, theory, hypothesis, generalization, and interaction. An actual educational research experiment done by a doctoral student and its implications for scientific statements and educational decisions are used as a method of explaining these several concepts.

COMPARISONS AND KNOWLEDGE

Comparisons are the key to all knowledge about the natural world. The better the quality of the comparisons, the better is the quality of knowledge gained from the comparisons. The more strained the comparisons, the more tenuous will be the knowledge gained. People have a limited number of senses through which they can detect the natural world, make comparisons of it, and gain knowledge. Hearing, vision, touch, taste, smell, detecting warmth, and determining the location of one's limbs and the position of the body commonly describe these sensory channels.

Sensation differs from perception. The latter connotes understanding, or again, knowledge, of what it is that is sensed. Even at this basic level, it is through comparisons that perception, or knowledge, is gained. Sensation is "the direct result of the present stimulation of the sense organs, as distinguished from perception, which involves the combination of different sensations and the utilization of past experience in recognizing the objects and facts from which the present stimulation arises" (Webster's *New Collegiate Dictionary*, G. & C. Merriam Co., Springfield, Mass., 1961). Obviously comparison of current stimulations against prior sensations is a fundamental part of a person's means of acquiring knowledge. Campbell and Stanley (1963, p. 176) even state, "Basic . . . to all knowledge-diagnostic processes including the retina of the eye . . . is the process of comparison, of recording differences, or of contrast." The concept of research design is merely *a more systematic* and *less error-prone* method of perceiving and knowing the world.

Research Design. The fundamental concept of research design is that of ascertaining the strengths and weaknesses of various comparisons to determine the quality of knowledge gained in the observational processes. For example, it is known that young drivers who took driver education have fewer accidents than those who did not. However, the comparison of these two groups as such may be faulty because they may differ initially in other ways as well. For instance, do those who take driver education have a higher socioeconomic status than those students who do not? Insurance data show that the higher socioeconomic groups also tend to have few accidents. Since driver education is rather expensive, perhaps more schools in higher socioeconomic areas can afford to offer it. Do more girls than boys take driver education? Girls have fewer accidents than boys, and a confounding of these two variables, sex and driver education, would make driver education seem to produce fewer accidents. Such comparisons are the key to understanding research results. Control or comparison groups much like the groups taking driver education are needed to determine the real effectiveness of the course.

Comparison Groups. The concept of comparison groups, or control groups, is basic to research design. Indeed it is inherent in the relational nature of facts. A scientific statement cannot be made without comparisons, explicit or implicit. Since a great part of educational processes fall within the realm of science, statements about education, except those about value and worth, imply at least one comparison, and thus a consideration of research design.

Comparison groups are used as a check or control on the quality of knowledge learned. If this fact is recognized and the quality of the comparisons is examined, a better understanding of educational research processes and education will result. As an example, take the census figures which show that college graduates make more money *compared* to noncollege graduates. This does not mean, however, that by going to college a student will earn more money. A more meaningful comparison is not college graduates versus noncollege graduates, but noncollege people of intellectual ability equivalent to college graduates compared to college graduates. (Of course other criteria also may be of interest.) Here are two groups more nearly comparable, and comparisons made between these two groups would be much more meaningful.

Sometimes groups of people are used as their own control or comparison group in educational research. Here, seemingly, the comparison groups would be quite equivalent and the knowledge gained of excellent quality. Sometimes indeed it is. However, in other instances, where the researcher actively presents a treatment, there is a concern that the initial treatments will change the subjects somewhat so they are not the same. If the subjects differ systematically when subsequent treatments or conditions are applied and comparative observations made, the knowledge gained may be of less value than it could have been. This occurs in a study of instruction if a class is used as its own control in an experiment. When the quality of the comparisons is diluted, so is the knowledge gained.

For example, if an arithmetic class is taught a concept via modern mathematics, the class is not the same afterward when other concepts are taught. The class has learned (hopefully) during the initial presentations and may be more ready to learn subsequent assignments. Alternately, there could be a conflict between the two procedures which would inhibit rather than facilitate learning. Further, in a study in which considerable time passes between the first and second instructional presentations, many other conditions also impinge on the class both within the classroom and outside the school. The students are learning in other classes, their home lives change, and they grow intellectually and develop. Again the quality of the comparisons and the quality of the knowledge derived would be infringed upon.

Comparison groups are often called control groups because they offer a check or a control against which to compare the observations made in the treatment or experimental group. A control group may have nothing done to it, or only standard treatments applied. Sometimes more than one experimental group will be used, as well as a formal control group. Then comparisons can be made among all the groups—experimental and control—and knowledge can be gained at a faster rate than in a simple experimental versus control group study. It is the *comparability* of the groups, both initially and when the comparisons take place, that determines the quality of the knowledge gained in the study. Since comparisons are so important to knowledge, the logic of these comparisons and comparison groups needs to be examined carefully.

If two groups of people are identical in their characteristics, then any identical conditions imposed on these groups would leave the groups still identical. The two groups of people might both be changed from their original state, but they would still be identical to each other. The treatments would be equally effective if nothing were done to the groups of people; they would still be identical. As in the axioms of geometry, if equals are added to equals, the results are equal. So, too, are equal subtractions, products, and divisions. If nothing is done to equal groups, the resulting groups are still equal.

In fact, this is a way to determine if two seemingly different things done to groups of people are equal or unequal in their effect. Knowledge can be gained about treatments via comparisons such as these. Identical groups of people are chosen, and two seemingly different conditions are imposed on them. If, using the criteria chosen to compare the groups, there are no differences, then it can be said that the conditions applied to the groups have no effect on them, with the use of these criteria: with these criteria, the conditions are identical in their effect on these groups. Note that there are always three aspects to the study: groups of subjects, treatments (or conditions), and criteria.

Conversely, it can be determined if two or more conditions do have a differential effect on groups of subjects. If, with the chosen criteria (of heretofore identical groups), the comparisons show differences after exposure of each of the groups to seemingly different treatments, it can be declared that the treatments did differ. Facts about the natural world of education can be established through these logical procedures, and thus a powerful lever is provided to pry loose the secrets of man's behavior in educational situations. Through such methods a factual behavioral and social science foundation for education can be laid.

There are only two problems. The first is how to determine possible differences from lack of differences in the observation of the criteria variables. The second is the impossible one, how to produce groups of people which are identical on all variables.

Speculation leads one at best to fantasizing solutions for this second problem. Caesarian sections could be used at the delivery of multiple births, and then roughly the quarter of these—twins, triplets, and so forth—who are genetically identical, taken for study. These infants would then be raised under as close to identical environmental conditions as possible. This identical up-bringing would require "equating" even the nurses who would have to be employed to change, feed, wash, soothe, love, and stimulate the infants until they reached the age where *the* experiment was to be conducted. Then one infant would receive the experimental condition and the other nothing. (One is reminded of the empirically oriented, mythical minister who fathered identical twins. He baptized one and kept the other as a control to see what would happen!)

Man has attempted since the dawn of the scientific age to solve the problem of equating groups of individuals and, in fact, has by the power of his intellect led himself into methods which now are known to be worse than the naturally occurring approximations to equality. As in many of his endeavors, though, man's intricate, difficult, time-consuming solutions that did not work have led to a simple, easy, neat solution with an overarching rationale that makes it exceedingly powerful and which also fits readily into a resolution of the first problem—how to determine differences from no differences.

RANDOMIZATION

This solution to equating groups is called randomization, and the concept was developed and elaborated upon by Sir Ronald A. Fisher in the several editions of his now famous book, *The Design of Experiments* (1935). Fisher's fundamental contribution was the method of achieving the unbiased equating of groups on all variables, except as they may differ by chance, via the randomization process. Further, when the equating of the groups is done by randomization, chance is defined in such a way that well-known decision rules are applicable to aid in determining differences on the criteria from no differences.

Randomization in experimentation is a relatively simple procedure. All of the subjects that will be observed in the experiment are listed and given individual numbers usually from one to however many subjects will be used. Then a table of random numbers is used and entered at a predetermined spot. (See Table I in Appendix C.) A table of random numbers contains lists of numerals determined in such a way that there is no discernible pattern to them. In other words, knowing any one or set of the digits is of no value in predicting what the next digit or set of digits will be.

Random numbers (each of a sufficient number of digits to cover the largest listed number) are then read in an order arbitrarily determined in advance. This can be down, up, sideways, or even diagonally. Subjects with the first-read numbers can be assigned to a first group, subjects with the second group of numbers can be assigned to the second group, and so forth. The subjects also can be assigned alternately—the first one to the first group, the second to the second group, the third to the third group, etc., until a subject is assigned to every group—whereupon the process is repeated until all groups are full or the list of subjects exhausted.

After subjects have been assigned to groups, then the groups are assigned, again at random, to the various experimental and control group treatments (or vice versa). The important point is that whenever there is a choice point in the allocation process, the allocation is made by chance, e.g., using a random process.

As an example, twenty people are to be assigned to an experimental or control group in an experiment. They are listed and assigned the numbers 01 through 20. A table of random numbers is consulted and entered at a predetermined point, say at the intersection of the 21st and 22nd columns and the 16th row on the first page of the table. Two digit numbers are needed (thus from 00 to 99), and it is preferred to read a double column of digits down the column and to continue, if needed, by reading at the top of the next column of double digits adjacent to the right of the column just read.

The process can be made simple but inefficient by ignoring all the numbers above the ones that can be used (01 to 20), or the process can be made sophisticated but more complex by using what is known as modulo 20 (where there are twenty subjects). In this case, multiples of 20 are subtracted from numbers over 20, and the remainder used as the random number. For example, number 21 is used as 01, as is 41, 61, and 81. Thus 75 is used as 15, 25 as 5, 30 as 10, etc. Any number that has already been used is ignored.

It is simpler, almost as fast, and probably more accurate for relatively small groups of subjects simply to skip numbers unusable in the listing process. Thus the numbers 13, 16, 20, 02, 11, 07, 04, 01, 12, and 10 chosen from the table would be assigned to one group and the residuals to the other group. One group would be called "heads" and

the other "tails," and a coin flipped. The "winner" is the experimental
group.

These two groups do not differ on any variable *(socially, psychologically, or biologically) greater than would be expected by chance.* Further,
chance is defined such that the assumptions underlying decision
processes of statistics are applicable. Thus one can be secure in the
conclusions drawn about the results of the analyses. The criteria
variables can be declared different or not different after the treatments
and, by inference, whether or not the treatment and no-treatment
conditions indeed were different in their effects on these criteria. (For
those who reject statistical analysis, it is not a necessary aspect of the
random allocation and experimental processes.) As sample sizes grow
larger, chance differences among the groups grow smaller, the expected
equating is better, and therefore the knowledge gained is also of better
quality.

The logic of the experiment and the experimental inferences
therein can be summarized in tabulated form:

1.   equals acted on by equals produces equals;
2.   equals acted on by unequals produces unequals.

Note, however, the difficulties under a third and fourth condition:

3.   unequals, acted on by equals, produces unequals;
4.   unequals, acted on by unequals, in general produces unequals.

In the first two sequences, by an examination of the end result, an
inference can be made about the equality or inequality of the acting
agents, treatments, or conditions. However, in the second two sequences (numbers three and four) in general both kinds of treatments,
equal and unequal, produce unequal results, and thus no logical
inference can be made about the equality or inequality of the treatments
from examination of the state of the criteria.

In an actual experiment there are, as indicated, also three
elements: 1) subjects' groups, 2) treatments, and 3) criteria. It is not
possible to say with certainty that groups of people would ever be
equal. The precise statement is, they are expected to be equal in the
long run. However, it is possible through the processes of random
allocation to declare that groups of people are *not unequal,* and further,
that they are not unequal on all variables.

Thus, while the perfection of the abstract model which requires
equality of groups cannot be met, a good approximation can be
obtained if the groups are not unequal. This is something like the
verdicts in criminal court trials. The defendent is declared either

"guilty" or "not guilty." Note carefully that he is not declared "innocent," even though his lawyers may report this to him. In Scotland, the courts may come a little closer to describing the real world situation with the verdict of "not proved."

In an experiment, then, subjects would be randomly allocated to groups, and experimental and control conditions allocated at random to the various groups. (There is no need to limit the groups to two except for convenience of illustration.)

As the result of the random allocation of subjects to groups, with the resulting expected equality of the groups on all variables, it should be noted that the patterns of relationship often found in naturally formed groups are broken up. All variables, hereditary and environmental, among the groups are expected to be equal. Physical and psychological differences resulting from parental inheritance, childhood surroundings, and prior education are generally reduced so that the groups resemble one another quite closely. This is especially true in the larger sets of randomized groups. Further, if no differing experimental treatments are applied, all future events are expected to occur with equal proportion and with equal force among all groups. Thus the average age of death and the number of children which the people in the groups will have are expected to be equal (as will the number who smoke and the amount of tobacco used, for example). The number of days spent in jail in each group, the amount of effort spent in support of religious activities among the groups, the number of years of college completed, and the quality of the college attended will be expected to be the same since all persons were placed in the randomized groups *by chance alone.* In a scientific experiment, although it is believed ("hypothesized" is the scientific word) that the treatment and no-treatment conditions will affect the groups of subjects differently, no one knows for sure. An inference about this will have to be drawn from the observation of the results of the application of the treatments in the experiment. This inference is named *experimental inference,* and it rests both on the logical conditions of the equality of the groups prior to the experimental treatments and the ability to declare the groups equal or unequal on the criteria.

Again, a tabulation of the possible conditions of the three elements of experiments will be made, this time using real world descriptions (see Figure 2-1):

1. Not unequal groups and not unequal treatments produces not unequal criteria; and
2. not unequal groups and unequal treatments produces unequal criteria.

	Groups	Treatments	Criteria
Condition 1.	=	=	=
Condition 2.	=	≠	≠

but

	Groups	Treatments	Criteria
Condition 3.	≠	=	≠
Condition 4.	≠	≠	≠ (in general)

FIGURE 2-1   The Logic of Experimental Comparisons

Again, note the difficulties imposed by unequal groups:

3. unequal groups and not unequal treatments produces unequal groups; and

4. unequal groups and unequal treatments produces groups generally either more unequal or less unequal.

This last condition removes the logic from a simple equal-unequal decision form and moves both the experimenter and the reader of experimental results into a gray area that requires considerable sophistication to interpret. It is best to stay with randomized experiments where possible. The world of education is best studied experimentally by the first two illustrations. Educational researchers can make only approximations to the real world at best, and random allocation does not guarantee identity, only expected equality. Accurate as these approximations may be, it is awkward to talk about "not unequals." Thus the words "equal" and "unequal" will be used, even though they are not quite a precise use of the language.

The next concern will be to examine the experimental inference process as such, and again a tabulation of the possible inferences is used.

	Subjects' Groups	*Conditions of Treatments*	*Criteria*
1.	equal	equal or unequal?	equal
2.	equal	equal or unequal?	unequal

In the first case, it can be *inferred* from the results based on the criteria in the experiment, that for these criteria, the treatment conditions are essentially equivalent. In the second case, it can be *inferred* from the differences based on the criteria used, that the treatments did make a difference. (See Figure 2-2.)

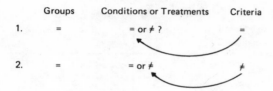

FIGURE 2-2   The Logic of Experimental Inference

As has been indicated, all scientific knowledge, including basic perception through the senses, uses this comparative process and the quality of the knowledge gained is directly related to the initial equality of the comparison groups. As also indicated, while exact equality of groups of people cannot be attained, an unbiased approximation to equality can be obtained through the rather simple process of random allocation. Other methods of obtaining equality of groups are not as good, and some methods used by researchers actually ensure unequal groups!

The grouping and treatment processes of research are not unlike a school's operations. Allocation of subjects to groups, maintaining the groups under differing learning conditions, and assessment of the condition of the subjects after a period of time is a part of standard practice in formal educational systems. Students are assigned to classes, they are instructed or they learn under the conditions of various curricula and educational methods, and they regularly are examined, tested, observed, and rated. To assign students to classes or conditions at random is often not very different than their assignment to classes by alphabetical order or by computer (if there are no competing conditions). The whole idea of school is formal instruction and creating appropriate conditions for learning. Development of education objectives, grading, rating, testing, and observation of performance are all a part of standard educational procedures. Education then is especially amenable to experimental evaluation and investigation. In large part, education can be considered one of the more experimental sciences. Thus the field has a major advantage in gaining knowledge about its processes and engineering them to the benefit of students, over such primarily descriptive scientific areas as geology, astronomy, seismology, and economics.

A TRUE EXPERIMENT IN EDUCATION

An examination of an educational experiment done by a high school teacher and doctoral student may help in defining terms and will illustrate much of the logic of experimentation that has been presented, as well as serve as an aid in defining terms. Later, comparisons of experimental research in education with other types of research designs that are used in educational research will be made.

Nedwidek, in searching for an area in which to do his dissertation (1965), had started generally in the area of attitudes of educational administrators toward high school athletics. He proposed to describe these attitudes by using a questionnaire. In a doctoral research seminar, however, the students were advised to pick a topic in which they personally had a keen interest and a topic which could be studied experimentally because of the more clear-cut nature of the findings and interpretations. The next week Nedwidek indicated that he was far more interested in a different kind of football heel cleat than he was in school administrators' attitudes, but was having difficulty in determining how the heel cleats could be studied experimentally. High school football in Western Pennsylvania is hardly played under the relatively neat, controlled conditions of a classroom, to say nothing of a laboratory, where experimental conditions can be imposed, one treatment variable changed at a time, and observations made.

Four conditions which are generalizable to most educational research have to be favorable to make an educational research experiment feasible. First, there has to be sufficient time to design and set up the study and sufficient opportunity for the treatment to show its effectiveness. There was time. The seminar met in the spring, football is played in the fall, and Nedwidek was not planning to finish before the following summer.

Second, financial, physical, and personnel resources must be available to carry out the study. The new type of heel cleats were not expensive; Nedwidek and his friends could install them and maintain the communications needed to make observations and records of the results. In addition, he had many friends among his fellow coaches who indicated a willingness to cooperate by having their teams participate in the study.

Third, there has to be a criterion measure which can be observed consistently among observers and which it is hypothesized that the treatment will affect. Fourth, and most important, for a randomized experiment the subjects must be able to be allocated to treatment groups and treatments to subjects' groups.

There was some laboratory evidence that the new type heel cleat would reduce ankle and knee injuries, a variable that is certainly subject to ready, replicable counting. The football team members can be randomly assigned to experimental and control groups. Further, Nedwidek indicated that, since football players are supposed to run on their toes, there should be no loss of traction or effectiveness of the players as the result of the experimental condition.

It was decided to do the randomization within teams, since in this way, if one or more schools found they could not participate or if they dropped out during the season, this would not totally upset the research design. Two factors enter into this decision, one practical and the other theoretical. First, a conscious determination of the sampling unit needs to be made. In this case, the sampling unit is players (or more accurately players within teams).

It would be possible to have the teams as the sampling units. Twenty-two schools could participate and eleven schools could be chosen at random in which all the players wore the new type heel cleat. The problem would be that because there are, at most, only twenty-two sampling units (teams) with relatively small numbers, there is a possible larger chance of variability between the two groups, making it more difficult to determine the effects of the experimental treatment, if any. (It should be noted, however, that since each school observation is based on a relatively large number of boys, this would stabilize the school averages somewhat.)

Alternatively, it would be possible to randomize the new type heel cleats to players within each team, leaving the rest of the players with their standard cleats. Here the sampling unit upon which the randomization is performed is the player within each school. The total number of sampling units (players) is relatively large, which means that any differences between the equated (not unequal) groups would be relatively minor. Inability of one or even several teams to cooperate, or worse, not be able to continue after the experiment was underway, would not be catastrophic.

However, there might be problems with players on the same teams wearing different types of shoe cleats. What if the process of randomization assigns the star halfback the new type heel cleats, and he decides he just can not cut as well in them? What if a starter last year loses his starting position this year after he was assigned to the new type cleats? What if the coach is having a below-average season and loses a crucial game because a defensive back with the new type cleats slips in the mud and lets a touchdown pass go over his head? With man's ability to rationalize, he may very well attach the blame to the one major changed element in the situation.

Problems such as these require that informed cooperation of both the educational system and participants be available. This type of problem could have arisen easily in this study. After all, football is not some relatively minor aspect of the educational system in which the supporting taxpayers are relatively uninterested (like English literature or biology). This area of education has a large public following and weak aspects are hard to hide. The newspapers are not likely to put the standardized test scores of schools' Title III or Carnegie Foundation programs in the headlines every week, but in this educational experiment they did publish the teams' scores (fortunately not associated with the new type heel cleats).

While a number of teams either dropped out or had to be dropped for various reasons, eight teams of the original twenty-two did cooperate fully. With over thirty players per team, well over 200 players were available for the study. This was more than enough to assure rather closely equated experimental and control groups and for rather definitive results, even after the inevitable dropouts during the course of the season.

For simplicity, the prior examples of randomization presented have been limited generally to random assignment to two groups of equal size, an experimental and a control. However, there is no reason why the random allocation could not be made to three or four or many more groups if enough students are available. Further, they do not have to be of equal size. Varying ratios, such as two to one, or three to one, or even filling a quota for an experimental group, and then assigning all others to control groups, are quite permissible. In these cases, the groups would still be expected to be equated on all variables except the group size.

Nedwidek randomized to three groups, two experimental and one control. The first experimental group used, in place of the two standard seven-eighths inch conical cleats on the heel, two commercially available, oblong cleats set at a slight angle to each other so that they formed an over-extended "V."

The second experimental group used, in place of the standard heel and sole cleats, a commercially available five-eighths inch cleat with a surface contact diameter of seven-sixteenths of an inch. The control group's shoes were examined to make sure that the players did use the standard cleats.

The coaches were asked to name the 33 players who were likely to play most during the season. These were the sample. With eight high schools participating, some 228 players were the subjects of this study. Over 500 of the oblong heel cleats were placed on the shoes during the year, four for each of the 70 players in Group A, plus replacements for lost and worn cleats. Group B required approximately 1,400 of the short cleats, seven per shoe times two times the 79 players in this group. The researcher had to get the list of 33 players at each school, make his randomization on the spot, get the shoes for these players, and attach the assigned cleats for two-thirds of them. This had to be done at all

eight schools within a matter of days since the rules regulating the date
when practice begins are strict. Further, means of communicating with
the experimenter and instructions for maintaining the experimental
conditions, broken cleats, loose cleats, and worn cleats had to be given
to coaches, players, and student managers.

Finally, and quite important, there were the records and communications necessary to collect accurate ankle and knee injury records.
A data sheet was prepared and a scale of severity of injury (mild,
moderate, or severe) was developed, based on the descriptions found in
the literature. Injuries were defined on that basis as well as on the basis
of the number of days the player missed either practice or games.
Descriptions and estimates of coaches, players, and physicians based
on the definitions, were obtained for the criterion data.

The experiment was about to begin. Subjects were available and
were assigned to equivalent groups, differing treatments were imposed, and observations of a criterion could be made. Important
questions about a major aspect of an educational system were being
asked and a means of answering them set forth with the clarity available
within the limits of a first experiment. Would clearcut answers be
available at the end of the study? No one knew. All that Nedwidek
could do was his best. Would the research design stay together under
the stress of the season's play and lack of perfect communication
between researcher and coaches, players, managers, physicians, and so
forth? There was hope that it would since the foundations for the
research had been carefully laid. Was the experiment a perfect one? The
answer is clearly "no." Almost by definition, no experiment in science
can be perfect.

Were all variables except the experimental treatment variable
controlled and kept constant? Obviously not, and further, this version
of control in research methodology, sometimes presented to school
children and occasionally others, is totally obsolete for huge areas of
science and particularly the social and behavioral sciences where it is
almost worthless.

Note that a more sophisticated version of control was used. Rather
than the researcher actively holding variables constant in the experiment, the variables are brought under control (in a passive sense) but
allowed to vary much as they operate in the real world outside the
laboratory. This allows the generalizations from the study to be made to
the world at large far more readily than by actively suppressing
variability by holding conditions constant.

There are other variables of concern in football knee and ankle
injuries. Ankle wrapping, physical conditioning of the legs, type and
condition of practice and playing fields, age of the players, other types

of cleats and types of shoes are some of these concerns. Were these variables studied and possible unique interrelationships among them and the types of cleats studied? Again the answer is, in general, "no." Nedwidek did record data about weather and field conditions, taping practices, training methods, number of coaches, and their experience, and these data were to some extent examined in relationship to the number of ankle and knee injuries. No unique interrelationships were studied between conditions on these variables and type of cleat.

Why not? First, size of the study must be a consideration. Note the sheer number of combinations that must be observed to obtain data on the simple conditions of just three types of cleats, times three kinds of field conditions (say wet, moderate, and dry), times three kinds of ankle taping (no taping, all taped, only prior injury taping), times three kinds of physical conditioning, times three levels of years of coaching experience (number of coaches and trainer support), times three age groups (say, grade school, high school, and college), times two types of shoes (high vs. low cut). This totals 1458 conditions. If only ten boys are observed in a given condition, this is almost 15,000 subjects.

Second, consider the set-up time involved, the number of cleats to be changed, and the number of coaches, managers, doctors, and so forth, with whom communications must be maintained. It is quite likely that, despite the much more representative study that could be done and the increased information that would be available from it, the quality of the implementation of the treatment conditions and the observations would drop drastically unless a huge research staff were involved. (This, too, generates its own problems.)

Finally, it should be noted that several of these "treatment" variables such as condition of field and the quality-quantity of the coaching staff varible cannot be randomly applied or not applied. They are intrinsic to the conditions: for example, it either rained before or during the game, or it didn't; the school emphasized football and assigned a large number of experienced coaches to the team, or it didn't. These variables are more or less a part of the research situation. While they indeed may cause certain outcomes on the criteria variables (such as more or fewer ankle and knee injuries), they are much more difficult to study than treatment variables such as cleats, tapings, and training conditions, which can be assigned at random to randomized groups. There may be natural patterns in the naturally occurring situations which are difficult if not impossible to extricate from one another.

Naturally, this mixing of treatments makes definitive statements about cause-and-effect relationships difficult. The quality of the comparisons among groups would be imperiled because of likely nonequivalent groups. The randomization process breaks up natual patterns, sets up equivalent groups, and readily allows cause-and-effect statements to be made among treatment conditions (within the limitations of science).

Assumptions were being made about what is known and what is not known about knee and ankle injuries in football. The review of the literature found some laboratory studies, and personal communications found some game condition studies where a whole collegiate team was using nonstandard heel cleats. In some instances, all the players on a team who had a history of ankle and knee injuries had special cleats or heels. However, none of these studies utilized randomization (even though it could have been used with the heel cleat variable), and thus the quality of the comparisons and the statements of results were more tenuous than were desirable.

It is not profitable generally in a research study to conduct complex, formal, randomized experiments in education until a solid foundation of knowledge has been gained through observation and analyses on a number of variables in naturally occurring situations. Large, formal experiments can be expensive, and it may just turn out that the treatment and/or criteria variables studied were not of as much interest as other variables surrounding the study and possibly inherent in it. On the other hand, with the assignment of students, conditions of instruction, and assessment of learning in educational systems so parallel to simple randomized experiments, far more randomized experimental research studies should be done.

Finally, even in the best and simplified small world of this randomized experiment, there were some problems. One school bought the whole squad new shoes four weeks after the study started. These shoes could not accommodate either the short cleats or the special heel cleats. Thus, all the players at this school had to be dropped from the study. Note, however, that the randomized groups still were intact at the other schools, and the quality of the comparisons overall was not damaged, just some of the administrative overhead effort lost. Also lost was a little bit of the power to detect observable differences among groups because of the loss of an eighth of the subjects.

Decisions within the educational system go on in the real world, sometimes destroying an experiment or a part of it. If the school has agreed to cooperate in an educational research study on an informed basis, professional educators will make major efforts to accommodate, if they feel the study truly is of educational value and thus of value to them. However, there are times when other values come first, and no researcher should test all their hypotheses in a situation in which they are overly dependent on one or a few schools. Nor should an experiment take place over too long a period of time during which changes may have to be made.

In another school in the study, the coach agreed to accept only the short-cleat shoe as an experimental condition. Thus, randomization there was made for two conditions only. The quality of the comparisons and thus the knowledge gained was not disturbed in any of the other schools, nor in this school for these two conditions.

The ability of a researcher to design his study to accommodate to the school conditions is important and often can be done if the researcher and administrator thoroughly understand randomization procedure and what it will do for them. By randomizing within the naturally occurring conditions of a school system, the researcher can gain much knowledge of excellent quality and usefulness.

In another school, the players had to walk down a concrete road almost half a mile a day to get back and forth to their practice field. This wore down the special heel cleats worn by Group A by the end of eight weeks. Regular heel cleats had to be used for three days until new sets of the special heel cleats could be procured. Good researchers maintain their communications, see and hear more than they came to observe, and realize that doing new and different things in a school occasionally will cause unusual things to happen. They must be prepared to accommodate to these responses, keep a contingency fund handy, and learn from the situation. These problems are valuable.

If researchers knew everything that was going to happen in a study, there would be no reason to do the research. Serendipity is finding valuable things by chance, but chance favors the prepared mind. One of the best things that occurs when research is done in the real world of the schools is that, by probing in the opaqueness of what seems to be happening, many other things than those specifically searched for are found that are of interest to the researcher and of value to the school. Randomized research designs help make these findings interpretable.

What did Nedwidek find in his thesis study? In Group A (with the special, wide V heel cleats) there were six ankle and knee injuries in the 70 players in this group completing the season (including players who were injured and could not continue). In Group B, the players who wore shoes with all short cleats, there were eleven ankle and knee injuries among the 79 players. In Group C, who were the players wearing the standard football cleat, there were 26 ankle and knee injuries among,

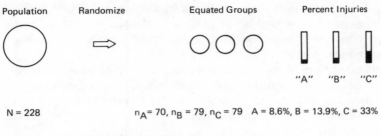

Population   Randomize   Equated Groups   Percent Injuries

"A"   "B"   "C"

N = 228 n_A= 70, n_B = 79, n_C = 79   A = 8.6%, B = 13.9%, C = 33%

Cleat Type: "V" Heel, Short, Standard

FIGURE 2-3   The Logical Structure and Results of the Nedwidek Football Cleat Experiment

again, 79 boys. The percentages are 8.6 percent, 13.9 percent and 33 percent of each group, or a 74 percent reduction in ankle and knee injuries in Group A from the standard cleat users in Group C.

These are remarkable results, not only from the humanitarian view of reduction in wear and tear and pain on the part of the boys, but also in the considerable strengthening of the teams during the year and cumulatively over the years of high school play. Further, many of the larger colleges and universities playing football are reluctant to offer grants-in-aid to players with a history of ankle and knee injuries. It would seem that a result such as this would lead to a change in the type of heel cleat used.

As those who follow the game know, this is not the case. After all, does educational research ever really prove anything? No, no researchers can ever say they are absolutely certain about their results.

How does this study compare with other studies of injuries? The organizations concerned with football regularly conduct descriptive surveys on the number, type, and conditions under which football injuries occur. From these, kick-offs and punt returns are known to be hazardous. Also, it is known that fewer ankle and knee injuries seem to occur on the artificial grass fields. These studies are done on huge samples using data from all over the country. Why should too much credence be placed in one small study, done once, on only eight high school teams, in one small area, in which several things went wrong during the study?

It is hoped that by now readers have enough knowledge to partially answer these questions, or at least be able to make a decision about what kind of cleats their school's team should wear, or they should wear. The question is not whether this study was perfect or even near perfect. The only real evidence to answer the questions about

Nedwidek's conclusions is from further experimentation. If there are some doubts as to some of his procedures, or if there are other questions of the "yes, but what if" variety, fine. These are the very types of questions, really hypotheses, that can be used in further research in this area. When this happens, a well-developed theory about football cleats and ankle and knee injuries will become available. One or two studies do not a scientific law make. However, one study, especially a randomized experiment with results as startling as these, does aid materially in educational decision-making, especially when the costs of the new heel cleats are equivalent to the costs of the standard cleats.

INTERNAL AND EXTERNAL VALIDITY

A number of lessons, definitions, and concepts about educational research generally and experimental design in particular can be learned from this rather simple research study. First, there is the concept of internal validity. *Internal validity* is the sum of the characteristics of research design from which the researcher is able to make causal inferences about the effect of research treatments on outcome of criteria variables.

Variables. Next, there is the concept of a variable. *Variables* are the names used in science to define the concepts, properties, or dimensions of the objects and functions that are studied. They are always quantifiable, even if on the primitive level of a dichotomy, simply labeled 0 and 1, presence or absence, of the concept or property. Numerals can be assigned to a variable.

In the football cleat study, the *criteria variable* measures were number of practices and games missed, and the physicians', coaches', researchers', and subjects' estimates of severity of the ankle or knee injuries. The *treatment variable* in an experiment is the variable that is imposed or withheld from, or presented in varying degrees of strength or quality, to the subjects. Alternatively, varying groups of subjects may be exposed to several conditions which collectively would make up the treatment variables. (Sometimes the criteria variables are called the dependent variables and the treatment variables the independent variables.) In this study the treatment variable was the special short cleats, the special heel cleats, and the standard cleats.

Interactions. Just as it is possible to have several bases for judging the outcomes of an experiment, which may or may not be related among themselves, so is it possible to impose several simultaneous treatments or conditions on subjects. These treatments and conditions may be used in specific combinations such that it is possible to extricate the effects of each treatment variable on the criteria. In addition, it is also possible to determine any unique effects of one or more particular treatment's relationship on other treatment variables. This would have been done if, at random, ankle taping or no taping had been imposed across half of each of the three cleat treatments. These unique interrelationships among treatment variables technically are called *interactions*. The concept also is important for considering inadvertent influences of extraneous variables on the subjects, treatments, and criteria in a research study.

As extraneous factors, interactions contribute to uncertainty or difficulties in interpreting the cause-and-effect results of treatments on criteria in research. These extraneous interactions and other uncertainties are called *threats to internal validity*. The lack of such threats to internal validity improves the ability of the interpreter of research to make true cause-and-effect statements. In a fully randomized experiment, such as the cleat study, the threats to internal validity are minimized, and thus the fully randomized experiment is called a *true experiment*.

Subjects and Samples. The units to which the treatments are applied are called the *subjects* of the research. These were the football players in the presented study. Some are called *experimental subjects* if one of the experimental treatments is presented to them (or they to it), as with the experimental cleats. Some are called *control subjects* if nothing is done to the subjects or if only standard conditions are continued, as with the standard football cleats. All together, the subjects are called the *sample*. All of the football players to whom the researcher makes generalizations about the results of the research are called the subjects' *population*.

Just as there are three aspects of an experimental research study—the subjects, the treatments, and the criteria—so there are three aspects of the generalizations about the research: populations of subjects, populations of treatments, and populations of criteria. These generalizations are to subjects, treatments, and criteria like those used in the study.

The characteristics of a study that allow the researcher and others to generalize from the specific study to other populations, settings, treatment variables, and criteria are referred to as *external validity*. It is noted that without internal validity, no generalizations can be made;

therefore, there could be no external validity in a study with no internal validity.

THEORY AND THE LITERATURE REVIEW

Generalizations involve inductive reasoning, making generalizations from the specific to the general or from the particular to the universe. The inductive reasoning in this case is making statements about subjects, treatments, and criteria not observed. Making inductive statements is logically impossible and a much riskier business than the simpler deductive logical processes (from the general case to the specific case), but generalizations and inductive reasoning about the natural world are what science is all about. These generalizations about a number of phenomena are called *theory*.

Scientific theory is the generalization of a system of interrelated facts, definitions, and propositions about the natural world. Scientific theory specifies relationships among variables in an attempt to explain their interrelationship. Note that scientific theory is founded on facts: it arises from facts and attempts to predict other facts. It is definitely not idle speculation or fanciful presentation of what some aspect of life would be like in a utopian world. Theory does go beyond *current* facts in that it attempts to predict observations and interrelationships that have not yet been observed. Theory attempts to make generalizations and overarching statements of what might be expected to occur. The observations and interrelationships predicted from theory technically are called hypotheses.

Theory about a topic is developed by examining the results of prior studies in the area, as well as applying to the topic predictions and generalizations from adjacent or related areas of science. This process of examining the results of prior studies is known as *reviewing the literature*. Original scientific studies are read, as well as prior efforts to assemble and organize scientific findings in articles, monographs, and books.

Generalizations, small ones as well as large ones, are made by the researcher and collected and applied to the phenomena under study. Sets of predictions and hypotheses are made and data collected to test their accuracy. If the predictions are reasonably good, then much greater faith is held in the quality of the prior generalizations and theories.

The process continues endlessly in this pattern. It also works in reverse. When observations are made about the functioning of the world which do not seem to fit into predicted relationships or patterns, then additional hypotheses are generated about why the observed situation differs from prior situations, and further observations are made based on the hypotheses from these observations.

Good theory suggests many hypotheses testable by observations, and astute observations in practical situations suggest good theories. In fact, one practical criterion of a good theory is the number of new, testable hypotheses that can be generated from it.

In the Nedwidek study, the literature review plus communication with other researchers was used to generate theory. The theory generated was that the anchoring of the heel by the heel cleats during a blow from the side caused ankle and knee injuries. During such a blow, the heel is held fast, as opposite forces are applied to the ankles and knees, and the thrust is outward while the lower leg is being pushed toward the midline of the body. Laboratory tests had demonstrated that special heels or heel cleats would reduce these forces. Observations, not under good experimental conditions, had tended to confirm this thinking (really a minor theory).

The problem also was a practical one in education. Thus the problem was educational research and the further development of theory about an educational problem. The problem developed from the practical situation of football injuries. Although a possible solution from prior developmental work was available, it had not been well tested, and common sense seemed not to be working too well in the acceptance, diffusion, or the development of the proposed solution. There was a need to convince educational practitioners by performing a demonstration, if indeed the development was as successful as claimed.

Two special types of shoe cleating were used which would help explain further why the development worked, and this would aid in confirming or not confirming, elaborating, or changing the theory. The theories in the case were the generalizations about the biophysical phenomena of the situation and how they arose.

EXTERNAL VALIDITY, FURTHER CONSIDERATIONS

Considerations of external validity, the ability to generalize, might be made about other types of heel and cleat arrangements, about other ways of describing and assessing ankle and knee injuries, and about players other than the ones involved in the study. It would seem reasonable to generalize to other players on the teams even if they weren't on the first three squads. It would seem quite safe to generalize to the players on next year's teams and even to a year or so after that.

Could the findings be generalized to other high school teams in the Pittsburgh area? This would seem acceptable even though they were not specifically declared part of the population of teams from which the sample teams were picked. Nedwidek had contacted twenty-two coaches of teams in the area and after explanation of the study had had no refusals. He finally selected thirteen to participate, purely on the basis of geographical contiguity so that he could personally monitor the research. There would therefore seem to be no selection bias thus far that would rule out generalizations to other Pittsburgh area high school teams.

The dropping of the remaining five schools might give a scientist cause for some concern. One school wanted to use only junior varsity players in the sample. Another school wanted to try out several types of recently developed shoes. Two schools changed from long, conical cleats to polyurethane cleats, and one school wanted to use the special oblong cleats on the sole of the shoe as well as the heel. All of these could have been experimentally evaluated, but this would have necessitated handling as separate studies, and Nedwidek was already more than busy. Without randomization and careful records, it must be assumed that these nonselected schools used commonsense to evaluate the effects of their changes.

Good quality schools initiate changes, better quality schools systematically evaluate changes, and the best schools review the research literature carefully before making changes and then evaluate via comparable groups' research designs.

However, the question here is the ability to generalize the results of one set of school teams to another set of school teams. Can it be done? Technically the answer is "no." The second set of school teams were not a part of the sampled population. Further, there was something special about these schools that made them different from the experimental schools. After all, the experimental schools accepted the research impositions and the nonexperimental schools did not. Technically and logically, true induction is not possible.

However, a coach, player, administrator, or parent, knowing the basic thinking of experimental design and Nedwidek's results, would be unwise not to implement the use of the special heel cleats. Even if there is skepticism of the results because of the several flaws in the research, the response should be to redo the study, taking into account the alternative hypotheses the skeptic generates, studying the effect of these hypotheses in an experiment, and thus building theory and improving educational practice.

INTERACTIONS, GENERALIZATIONS, AND DECISIONS

Should generalization of the results be made to high school teams in California, Texas, Minnesota, and Florida? Teams in these states were obviously not in the sample, nor were they even considered. How about collegiate teams? Would the injury rates be about the same? Perhaps not, but a better question would be, "Is there an important interaction between the variables suggested and the experimental treatment variable over other teams in other states and at other age levels?" This is the question, *not* of the same percentage rate or level of injury among the samples, but of no *different* rate of injuries occurring among samples over several experimental conditions.

With observations over all the samples, this hypothesis of a nonsignificant interrelationship interaction can be specifically tested. Without specific data, the generalization must be done via a theory. Broad theory or generalizations, in fact, can be said to be due to a lack of important interrelationships or interactions among treatment variables and other variables (including types of populations). An illustration may help (see Figure 2-4).

Note that the lines connecting the points are parallel to one another, denoting no interaction. Note also that the average injury rate between the two types of teams does not have to be equal, or even of interest, in making a generalization about this type of interaction. It was speculated here that the collegiate injury rate would be less. It might very well be higher. That is not the point. The educational decision would still be the same: choose the type of shoe with lowest ankle and knee injury rate if costs are about the same. The same is true in Florida, California, and Minnesota. Assume not that the injury rate would have to be roughly equivalent to generalize the results, but that there is no significant interrelationship or interaction between states or geographical location and type of shoe cleats.

An acceptable administrative decision-making process can proceed one stage further in the thinking. The interactions could be significant (nonparallel lines would connect the points on the figure), but if the lines did not cross each other between the points, the decision would be the same: use the special cleats. Thus the special heel-cleated shoe might not be quite as good at reducing injuries at the collegiate level or in Florida, but so long as the special heel-cleated shoe still was

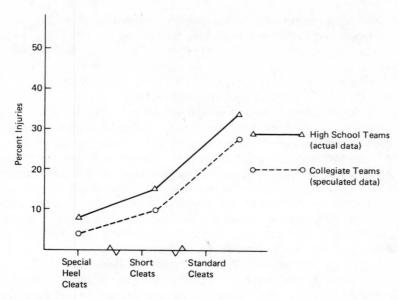

FIGURE 2-4   Illustration of No Interaction Between Educational Level of Teams

superior to the other shoes, as compared to the Pennsylvania high school data, it still would be the best decision.

Here then is a distinction between the scientist and the professional educator. This last example presents a rather restricted scientific generalization. There is (in speculation) no broad overarching theory but only statements of facts that must be changed somewhat with changing conditions. However, the administrative decision remains the same for all three types of possible interactions or noninteractions.

The concept of significant interactions (nonparallel connecting lines among classifications) and nonsignificant interactions (parallel connecting lines among classifications) is important in the study of research design, particularly in the area of external validity. External validity, as stated earlier, deals with the ability to make generalizations to other similar populations, settings, and variables. Lack of speculated significant interactions among various populations and settings with the treatment aids in making these generalizations.

Note in the football cleat experiment that Nedwidek did not match individuals on the basis of prior injuries, lineman or back, or prior playing experience and did not pretest or make pre-experimental observations for strength, shoe size, and so forth. He had faith that the randomization procedures would produce equivalent groups on all variables including all previous experiences and variables, all current variables, and all future variables (including an equivalent number of ankle and knee injuries during the course of the season). If no systematic treatment changes were applied to the groups, this would be true. Furthermore, it requires less effort and expense to be able to dispense with pretesting and matching.

As a matter of fact, Nedwidek's faith did waver slightly, at least enough to peek at the data afterward to check on the equivalency of the groups. For instance, he found the percent of linemen about the same in each of the three groups, 59 percent in Group A, 65 percent in Group B, and 61 percent in Group C. This near-equivalency is to be expected as the result of the random allocation, as it would be on any variable, important or unimportant. For *any* resulting differences *after* the treatment among the experimental and control groups in a true, fully randomized experiment, the most plausible explanation is that the effect was caused by the differing treatments.

There are hedges to this statement based on such factors as knowledge of treatments by the observers of the criteria variables, the effect on the subjects simply of the knowledge that they were in an experiment, chance variations in the randomization process, and biased errors of measurement in the criteria variables. Hopefully, the researchers will hypothesize *before* the research about possible differences rather than hunt exhaustively after the fact. Finally, it is advised that seemingly good things found by chance in research will be checked in another experimental sample before they are announced publicly. At the least, the findings in such instances should be identified as tentative.

STATISTICS AND RESEARCH DESIGN

Note that very little has been said about statistical tests for observed differences found among the three football players groups. This is deliberate. The general interpretation of good experimental designs and the logical thinking behind them does not depend on statistics. Campbell and Stanley (1963, p. 192) state, "Good experimental design is separable from the use of statistical tests of significance. It is the art of achieving interpretable comparisons and as such would be required even if the end product were to be graphed percentages, parallel prose case studies, photographs of groups in action, etc. . . . Use of significance tests presumes but does not prove or supply the comparability of the comparison groups or the interpretability of the difference found."

It is also noted that even one of the outstanding mathematical statisticians and research design men of this century, Sir Ronald Fisher, felt the need to write a book, *The Design of Experiments* (1935), which was quite distinct from his early book (1925), *Statistical Methods for Research Workers.*

However, in order for professionals to read critically, it is necessary for them to know some statistical terms and procedures. A minimum base in statistics will be presented in the next chapter. In the true experiment already presented, the comparability of the groups is the key to interpreting and understanding the results, which were of such magnitude that statistical tests were almost superfluous.

The research example presented also shows that true experiments can be used rather widely in education. Many educational problems involve assignment of students, teacher, instructional methods, school, classes, clinics, or services to one group or another. Frequently, if planning is done in advance, random assignment, which is strictly by chance, is the fairest and least politically involved method of allocating resources or facilities which are not available to all. Accelerated or honors classes, special classes for the retarded, driver education courses, intensive guidance programs, and new curricular materials are only a few of the areas and services where allocation on a random basis could be made. For once, what is politically safest is also simple, easy, and most of all, by far the best research and evaluation procedure. Any other procedure requires direct evidence of some type of comparability of the various groups, and this sometimes requires a rather complex measurement and statistical method to accomplish. However, consultation before the study begins should be obtained either from within or outside the educational system.

SUMMARY

This chapter has presented the basic processes for the determination of knowledge and the logic of research design which parallels them. Comparisons were shown to be the key concept in both of these procedures. The parts of an experiment were presented as was their relationship to the logic of research. The concept of randomization, how to apply it, and the results of its use in relation to research logic was presented. The similarity between research methods and the organizational processes of educational systems was noted, and a true experiment applied to the valuation of a practical educational problem, football injuries, conducted by a professional educator, was used as an example. The study was also used to define concepts used in educational research such as internal validity, external validity, theory, hypothesis, literature review, interaction, and generalization. Finally, implications of the research for scientific statements and for educational decisions were made.

STUDY AND DISCUSSION PROBLEMS

1. Design a simple educational experiment. Explain what precautions you used to ensure its internal validity.
2. Briefly explain or give example of the following educational research concepts: randomization, internal validity, external validity, variables, experimental subjects, control subjects, sample, theory, and hypotheses.
3. Distinguish between sensation and perception.
4. What are the three major components of a research study?
5. What are the three aspects of generalizations from a research study?
6. See if you can find a true experiment in the education literature. Report what the subjects, treatments, and criteria were. Explain how the research was designed. Report the results.
7. What is the value of randomization in educational research?
8. How is the external validity of educational research developed?
9. Why is comparison so vital in educational research?
10. Randomly assign 20 numbers to two groups using the table of random numbers in Appendix B. Are the groups equal?
11. Is it possible to produce two groups of subjects who are identical on all variables?
12. Present the four conditions necessary to make a true educational research experiment possible.
13. In the Nedwidek study, which groups were experimental and which were control? What was the treatment variable? What was the criterion variable?
14. Show the logic of experimental inference.
15. Use the table of random numbers in Appendix B to allocate the members of your class to two groups. Are the two groups equal? Present some evidence to support your contention.
16. As a school administrator, indicate where you could use the randomization process to advantage.
17. What role do comparisons play in developing knowledge?
18. Can cause-and-effect statements be made about educational programs?
19. What are threats to the internal validity of an educational research study?
20. Is inductive reasoning possible in educational research?
21. What is an "interaction" in educational research?

REFERENCES

Campbell, D.T., and Stanley, J.C. Experimental and quasi-experimental designs for research. In N.L. Gage (Ed.) *Handbook of research on teaching.* Chicago, Ill.: Rand McNally, 1963, 171-246.

Fisher, R. A. *The design of experiments.* Edinburgh, London: Oliver & Boyd, 1935 to 1966, editions 1 through 8.

Fisher, R. A. *Statistical methods for research workers.* Edinburgh; London: Oliver & Boyd, 1925 to 1970, editions 1 through 14.

Nedwidek, R. A. Football cleats and knee and ankle injuries. Unpublished doctoral dissertation, University of Pittsburgh, 1965.

Webster's new collegiate dictionary. Springfield, Mass.: G. & C. Merriam Co., 1961.

An Introduction to Statistics for Educational Research

Chapter 3

Statistics is the primary method of analysis used in educational research. All educational research variables are quantifiable (or they are not variables) and thus are subject to quantitative analysis. As was indicated in the previous chapter, if all educational research could be done using true, randomized experiments with large samples and frequencies by criterion category for evidence of effectiveness, then perhaps most modern statistical analyses would be less necessary. The results of the research would be stable, clear cut, and readily interpretable. Unfortunately, this is not the case. Educational systems are such that ethical and cost considerations require more than randomized experiments to be used in research.

Efficient research uses statistical analysis in part as a substitute for very large samples. Much assessment in education, observed and recorded, is done with instruments that yield reasonably close approximations to number systems that can be analyzed via statistics. The professional educator reading educational research must be familiar with statistical analysis. Computers and electronic calculators have relieved researchers from the need to be highly facile arithmeticians, but they have imposed the burden of being able to interpret an even broader range of analyses now far more extensively found in the professional literature.

As previously indicated, probably a minimum of three courses is required for the basis of a reasonable understanding in statistics.

Research design is a topic that interweaves with statistics but has sufficient content to be a topic in itself. It is on understanding research design that this book concentrates, but an introduction to basic statistics is required for an understanding of educational research. The basic concepts which are needed will be presented in this chapter.

CLASSIFICATIONS OF STATISTICAL PROCESSES

A series of almost dichotomous classifications exists in educational research areas involving statistics. Two predominant kinds of variables are used: nominal (or classification) and interval. There are two broad classifications of statistics: those used to summarize and describe data (descriptive statistics), and those used to aid in the determination of whether the observed phenomena might have occurred simply by chance process (inferential statistics).

Two major kinds of graphs depict relationships. The first, a frequency distribution, shows the relationship of the variables to the number of cases at various categories of the variable. The second kind of graph, a scatter diagram, shows the relationship between two variables.

There are also two major purposes of statistical analyses: those which attempt to demonstrate differences (or no differences) between or among groups of people (or other sample units) on one variable at a time, and those which attempt to show degrees of relationship among two or more variables within one group of people at a time. (There is also a summarizing or descriptive, aspect to statistics which generally precedes these two major uses.)

Given the type of data, nominal or interval, and the purpose of the analysis, to show differences among groups on a variable or to show degree of relationship among variables within a group, the particular type of statistical procedure is determined.

First in this chapter, methods for summarizing data—descriptive statistics—will be presented, and second, some methods of making decisions about possible chance differences among groups and relationships among variables. This will not be an extensive coverage because such coverage is the concern of books on statistics not research design.

DESCRIPTIVE STATISTICS

Descriptive studies are used primarily to aid the researcher and reader in bringing together large amounts of data so that they can be presented and comprehended with minimum effort.

When over 500,000 U.S. high school students are measured on some 500 variables, as occurred in Project TALENT, 250 million scores result. No individual could read, much less comprehend in a lifetime, the meaning of this amount of data without aid. With the use of statistics, averages can be presented on all 500 variables for various groupings of students. Indications of the students' individual differences, as well as the interrelationships of the variables, also are available quickly. With the minimum violations of the assumptions encountered in much educational data, the descriptions are quite good.

THE FREQUENCY DISTRIBUTION

A convenient number that will divide the data into ten to twenty groups is called a "class interval." Ten to twenty class intervals added successively to the lowest score, until all of the data are included, will allow all the data to be accounted for in one of the class intervals. The results, a frequency distribution, can be graphed as a "frequency polygon."

An example will be helpful. If there are 40 students in a class, their scores on a test might look like those in Table 3-1.

The highest score in Table 3-1 is 55 and the lowest 10, a difference of 45. A class-interval size of 4 would yield about 12 classes for the construction of a frequency distribution. It is customary to use as the lower limit of the lowest class interval a multiple of the size of class interval. In this case, the class intervals and their associated frequencies are given in Table 3-2.

THE FREQUENCY POLYGON

The graph of the frequency distribution, which shows numbers of cases on one dimension of the graph and score on the variable on the other dimension, is given in Figure 3-1.

Graphs are widely used in educational research, and it will be valuable to learn some of their characteristics. They are labeled at the

TABLE 3-1   An Array of Data

35	29	55	27	40	33	39	28
44	36	22	51	29	21	28	29
15	36	41	20	25	38	47	32
27	33	48	10	16	34	18	14
19	26	20	17	24	21	27	16

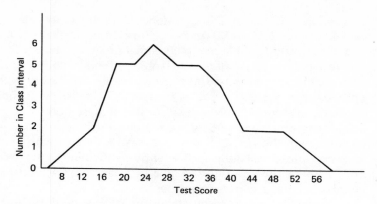

FIGURE 3-1   Frequency Polygon of Test Scores

bottom. The title should explain what it is that is being illustrated. Next, the graph should complement the text, and vice versa. The text should explain the concepts illustrated by the graph and the graphs should further illustrate the ideas presented in the text. The zero or low end of variables in graphs is at the left of the horizontal axis and at the bottom of the vertical axis. The high end of the variables is at the right and at the top of a graph.

Some writers in statistics and educational research methods use the class interval method of organizing data as a basis for calculating other statistics on an array of data. This procedure, in the age of inexpensive, portable electronic calculators, desk calculators, and com-

TABLE 3-2   A Frequency Distribution of the Data in Table 3-1

Class Interval	Frequency Count
52-55	1
48-51	11
44-47	11
40-43	11
36-39	1111
32-35	1111
28-31	1111
24-27	1111 1
20-23	1111
16-19	1111
12-15	11
8-11	1

puters, is a waste of a professional's time. Hand calculation, even calculator aided, is useful primarily for first indications of relationships and descriptions or for relatively small analyses. Educational systems and research projects often have large numbers of subjects, 100 or more, and a relatively large number of variables to describe them. With perhaps five or more variables for typical samples, it is cheaper, more accurate, and more thorough to do the analyses on a computer.

Computers are widely accessible and inexpensive to use, far cheaper than the cost of hand analyses. A person who knows how to analyze educational data is sufficiently costly that the time walking back and forth to the computer center is often more expensive than the charges for the computer analyses.

Thus the rule for statistical analyses should be: use only one formula to calculate statistics. Variations of equations for simplifying the work for different kinds of examples are a waste of time and complicate the learning of statistics. Concentrate on the interpretation and understanding of applied statistics. Too many students are taught arithmetical methods which are soon lost if they are not used regularly. Instead arithmetic should be minimized, computer usage maximized, and particular emphasis given to statistical interpretation. This latter is more than enough to keep students occupied, and it is only too obvious that this task has not been well done. Note, again for this purpose courses in statistics should be taken. The statistics presented here are primarily as an aid in understanding research design concepts. Thus only very small groups of data will be used and little about assumptions or full statistical interpretations will be included.

CENTRAL TENDENCY: MEAN, MEDIAN, AND MODE

Averages or indications of the middle of a distribution of scores on a variable are of interest in describing data. There are three types of averages: the mean, the median, and the mode. The mean is the type of average that is often taught in grade school arithmetic. It is the sum of all the scores divided by the number of scores. The median is the middle score when the data are ordered by score from low to high. The mode makes use of the class interval concept again and is the class interval with the most cases in it. As an example, IQ scores could be divided into five class intervals, 83 and below, 84-94, 95-105, 106-116, and 117 and above. For a sample, the class interval 95 to 105 might have more scores in it than any of the rest. Therefore the level 95-105 would be the modal interval.

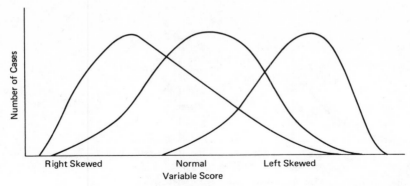

FIGURE 3-2   Illustration of Skewed and Normal Distributions

MODALITY, SKEWNESS, NORMALITY, AND KURTOSIS OF DISTRIBUTIONS

Some data are two humped, like a side view of a Bactrian camel, and are said to be "bimodal." Other data have the mode at the far right of the frequency distribution, and the frequencies tail off to the left. These frequency distributions are described as "left skewed." Data with the mode to the left and the tail to the right are described as "right skewed." It is the direction of the tail that determines the direction of the skewness (see Figure 3-2).

If a frequency distribution is the same on both sides of the mean, the distribution is said to be symmetrical. If the distribution has a particular shape that could have been determined by a line describing the equation of a normal curve, it is said to be "normally" distributed. This distribution is often described as bell-shaped. Many analytical methods in statistics have as an assumption in their mathematical development that the data being analyzed are normally distributed. It is now known that data which approximate this distribution are reasonably analyzed with these statistical methods.

In fact, as sample sizes increase, data which have only one mode somewhere near the center of the distribution and become increasingly less frequent as the scores approach the extremes of the distribution can be handled rather well by most standard, so called parametric, statistical procedures.

A parametric statistical test commonly is defined as one which assumes certain frequency distributions about the data, usually a normal distribution (see Figure 3-3). Descriptions of other types of

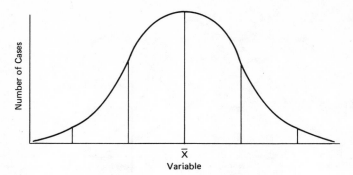

FIGURE 3-3   Variable: the Normal Distribution

distributions are of interest. Data which are markedly peaked, that is closely clustered about the mean of the distribution, are described as "leptokurtic." Markedly flatter than normally distributed frequency distributions are called "platykurtic distributions." (See Figure 3-4.) Kurtosis is a description of the peakedness or flatness of a distribution of scores on a variable.

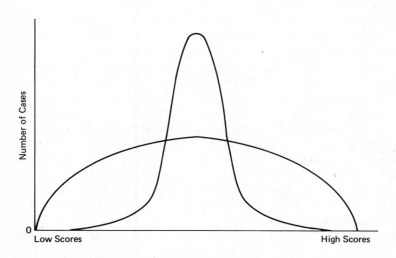

FIGURE 3-4   Illustration of Kurtosis

MEASURES OF VARIABILITY AND THE RANGE

To find the range for interval data, the lowest score is subtracted from the highest score and then one is added to the remainder. For the data in Table 3-1, the highest score is 55 and the lowest is 10. The range is $55 - 10 + 1 = 46$. In addition to the range measure of the variability of a distribution, there are more commonly used measures. Measures of variability can be considered by educators as indicators of individual differences among students on a variable. The most common of these is the "standard deviation." A standard deviation usually is about one-fifth of the range in small samples. In larger samples, it will be about one-sixth as large as the range of a distribution of scores. The standard deviation statistic is exceedingly important in education because it is used as a basic unit for measurement purposes. Scores on many standardized tests, such as college boards, military, and intelligence tests, use functions of the standard deviation statistic as the reporting score. The square of the standard deviation is also used and is called the "variance." Obviously the square root of the variance of a distribution is the standard deviation of that distribution.

With the use of data, some of these concepts as well as some common statistical notations can be defined more fully. Scores for two groups on a test are presented in Table 3-3.

A large "X" in Table 3-3 stands for a score on a variable. The symbol Σ, capital Greek letter sigma, is an operator—like a plus,

TABLE 3-3   An Array of Data for Two Groups of Subjects

	Group One Scores			Group Two Scores	
	X_1	$X_1{}^2$		X_2	$X_2{}^2$
Added	2	4	and	1	1
	3	9		3	9
	6	36		4	16
	4	16		2	4
	5	25		5	25
	2	4		5	25
	5	25		2	4
	4	16		4	16
	3	9		3	9
	6	36		1	1
	$\Sigma X_1 = 40 \quad \Sigma X_1{}^2 = 180$			$\Sigma X_2 = 30 \quad \Sigma X_2{}^2 = 110$	
	$n_1 = 10$			$n_2 = 10 \quad N = 20$	

minus, multiply, or divide sign. The two symbols $\sum X$ stand for "the sum of the scores on the variable." X^2 stands for a score squared. $\sum X^2$ stands for "each score squared and the squared scores summed." The small letter "n" stands for "number," usually number of scores. If more than one set of scores is being considered, the total number of scores is sometimes written as "N". The mean is denoted as "$\bar{X}$" in one notation and as "M" in another. (One of the problems in reading statistics is the use of more than one symbol to denote a concept.) Dividing the sum of the scores, $\sum X$, by their number, n, gives the mean, $\bar{X}$ or M, $\bar{X} = \sum X / n$. In the first set of scores in Table 3-3, $\sum X_1 = 40$ and $n_1 = 10$; thus $\bar{X}_1 = 4.00$.

The variance, denoted by the symbol small Greek letter sigma squared, is equal to,

$$\sigma^2 = \frac{\sum X^2 - \dfrac{(\sum X)^2}{n}}{n - 1}$$

Note the new symbol here $(\sum X)^2$. This denotes that all the scores in the set are summed and then that sum is squared. (Note also that this is a different number than $\sum X^2$ which is squaring each score and then summing.) Insert the values into the formula.

$$\sigma_1^2 = \frac{180 - \dfrac{(40)^2}{10}}{10 - 1}$$

$$\sigma_1^2 = \frac{180 - \dfrac{1600}{10}}{10 - 1}$$

$$\sigma_1^2 = \frac{180 - 160}{9}$$

$$\sigma_1^2 = \frac{20}{9}$$

$$\sigma_1^2 = 2.22$$

The standard deviation is the square root of this value, $\sigma = 1.49$. For the second set of scores similarly, $\bar{X}_2 = \dfrac{\sum X_2^2}{n_2} = \dfrac{30}{10} = 3.00$.

The variance of the second set of scores is,

$$\sigma_2^2 = \frac{\sum X_2^2 - \dfrac{(\sum X_2)^2}{n}}{n_2 - 1} = \frac{118 - \dfrac{(30)^2}{10}}{10 - 1}$$

$$= \frac{118 - \dfrac{900}{10}}{10 - 1} = \frac{118 - 90}{9} = \frac{28}{9} = 3.11.$$

The standard deviation is the square root of the variance, or 1.77. The mean (and other measures of central tendency), the standard deviation, and the variance are all descriptive statistics. They describe summaries of data.

INFERENTIAL STATISTICS

The logic of experimental research requires comparisons and inferences about differences. Statistics, in part, is a method of making a decision about whether differences probably do or do not exist between two sets of observations. This type of decision is one of the major purposes of statistics, to differentiate between or among groups on a variable. It is also a beginning aspect of "inferential statistics" since inferences are being made about true differences. If two sets of scores had been observed on a variable on a group of children who had been randomly assigned to one of two groups and an experimental treatment had been given to one group and not the other, the stage would be set to make an experimental inference about the equality of the treatments. The averages, or means of the two sets of observations on the criterion, could, as was indicated, differ by chance alone. In this case, these are two groups measured on one variable. The problem now is to determine the probability that these two means differ. These means, it will be recalled, are representative of the averages of the criterion variable of the two randomly assigned groups.

TESTS OF DIFFERENCES: THE "t" TEST

The statistical solution is the "t" test. The formula is:

$$t = \frac{\bar{X}_1 - \bar{X}_2}{\sqrt[2]{\dfrac{\sigma_1^2}{n_1} + \dfrac{\sigma_2^2}{n_2}}}$$

Substituting from the data analyses from Table 3-3:

$$t = \frac{4.00 - 3.00}{\sqrt[2]{\dfrac{2.22}{10} + \dfrac{3.11}{10}}}$$

$$= \frac{1.00}{\sqrt[2]{.222 + .311}}$$

$$= \frac{1.00}{\sqrt[2]{.533}}$$

$$= \frac{1.00}{.729}$$

$$= 1.37$$

This calculated value of "t" is evaluated by examining a "t" table. The "t" table is entered, as are many other statistical tables, with the degrees of freedom (df) available for these data. (See Appendix C, Table III.)

The degrees of freedom in a set of data are an indication of the freedom of the scores to vary. In these two sets of data in Table 3-3, there are ten scores in each set with two means calculated. If the investigator attempted to guess the scores in each set, he could make nine guesses in each set, and the tenth score in each group could be set at a given value to still obtain the same means. Thus, in a sense, nine scores in each of the two groups are free to vary, and one is not, once a means has been determined. In other words, one degree of freedom is lost from an array of observations when their mean is calculated. Formulas for determining degrees of freedom are used with many types of statistics and are needed to enter the tables to determine the levels of probability, or rarity, of the statistic.

The degrees of freedom for a "t" test in these data are equal to the number of individual observations minus two, or $df = n_1 + n_2 - 2$. Substituting $df = 10 + 10 - 2 = 18$. The value of t with 18 df at the 5 percent level of probability in the t table (Table III in Appendix C) is 2.101. The general rule in statistics is to compare the calculated value of the statistic with the tabled value of the statistic. In general (but not quite always for all statistics), if the calculated value is larger (that is the absolute value, or value without a positive or negative sign attached), the difference between the values is said to be "significant." That does *not* indicate that the difference is socially or educationally important, merely that probably this observed difference is not likely to have been a chance result. The probability level selected was 5 percent, or odds of 1 chance in 20, that the statistic would evolve as the result of a chance or random events alone.

In this example, the calculated value is not larger than the 5 percent tabled value of t, and the observed difference is therefore well within the limits that could have occurred by chance factors alone as the result of the initial randomization of subjects. The two means are considered not different in this example.

THE NULL HYPOTHESIS

Technically, this process of calculating the statistic and comparing it against the tabled values, which indicate what chance alone would produce, is called "testing the null hypothesis." A null hypothesis is one which declares that there is no difference among two or more groups on a variable, or that there is no relationship between two variables within a group. A null hypothesis, sometimes symbolized as H_0, is either rejected or not rejected, depending on the results of the comparison of the calculated statistic against the appropriate table value, which is determined by the degrees of freedom available for the calculated statistic. In this case, the calculated t statistic value is 1.37 with 18 degrees of freedom. The 5 percent level table value of t for 18 degrees of freedom is 2.101. (See Appendix C, Table III.) The calculated value does not exceed the 5 percent tabled value; therefore the null hypothesis, H_0, of no true difference between the means, is not rejected.

ERRORS OF STATISTICAL LOGIC

There are two possible errors of logic in the test of the calculated statistic against the tabled, chance values. The first is that the null hypothesis is really true, there truly is no difference, but the chance variability between the means was such that the test statistic was larger than the tabled value, and the null hypothesis of no differences was rejected. Technically in statistical practice, this result is known as a Type I error. It occurs when a statistical test of differences is declared "significant" when in truth there is no difference. (The inference in an experiment would then be that the treatment made a difference when in fact it did not.)

The second possible error in the logic of a statistical test is that the calculated statistic does not exceed the tabled, chance value of the statistic, and the null hypothesis of no difference (or no relationship) is not rejected, when, in truth, there is a difference between the means. Technically this is known as a Type II error. The statistic is declared "not significant," and the statistical inference made is that the results could readily have occurred by chance processes alone. The inference in an experiment would then be that the treatment made no difference. Here a promising innovational educational procedure would be shuttled aside unless further evidence as to its effectiveness evolved.

Science itself approximates the real world, and statistical procedures are also a convergence technique which in the long run will be a good approximation to the real world. Thus the evidence from a series of independent statistical tests and research studies must be weighed and generalizations made which are the theories that are the best approximations of the real world. Type I errors of statistical inference can be reduced by using small probabilities or levels of rejection of the null hypothesis, e.g., the 1 percent probability level or even the 0.1 percent probability level. This is done, however, at the cost of increasing the probability of a Type II error—not detecting a true difference (and thus a true experimental effect). The best way to reduce both types of statistical inference errors is to have large samples and precise observations. These, too, are costly, but in a different way. This is some of the thinking behind probability levels, null hypotheses, Type I and Type II errors, and statistical inference—all basic concepts in statistics.

Note that statistical inference and experimental inference are *not* the same. When statistics are examined, they aid in decisions about the probability of populations being different or not different. Experimental inference, on the other hand, is concerned with the logic of the design, the statements about the equality or difference between two or more treatments as the result of observations on criteria. The two are linked because first it must be determined whether indeed there are any differences on the criterion that could be considered unlikely by chance processes; and second, if there is a likely difference, is the research design one from which an inference can be made about the treatment conditions. In the *t* test example, the research inferences are acceptable because the research setting was a true, randomized experiment.

Both types of inference are used in educational research. With other types of research designs the research reasoning may not be the simple inferences used in randomized experimental designs, and in some cases the statistical tests of differences or no differences on the criteria may be useless unless the research conditions are such that research inferences can be made.

RELATIONSHIPS AMONG VARIABLES IN A SINGLE GROUP: CORRELATION

A second major purpose of statistics, in addition to the one of attempting to show differences on a variable among groups, is to attempt to show relationships among variables on one group of subjects at a time. For this purpose the correlation coefficient is often used.

The correlation coefficient is an expression of a degree and direction of relationship. The correlational statistic is an index that technically can have values from −1.00 through .00 and up to +1.00. Correlation in its simplest form requires two scores, one on each of two variables, for each person in a group. The index of correlation suggests the degree and the direction of the relationship between two variables within a single group of people.

THE SCATTER DIAGRAM

Correlation in graphic form is a second major type of graph, the scatter diagram. It has, instead of a variable for the horizontal axis and the number of subjects plotted on the vertical axis, again a variable for the horizontal axis, but another variable (other than number of subjects) for the vertical axis. For instance, if there is interest in the relationship between height and weight, weight could be the variable represented on the horizontal axis and height the variable represented on the vertical axis. Again, the zero score for both axes is to the left or down. High scores are to the right or up. In this case, either variable can be placed on either axis as long as it is properly labeled. In a predictive relationship, the vertical axis would be used for the predicted variable.

Some descriptive illustrations of relationships and correlations will be of help in understanding the concept. In these illustrations, as in all graphic representations of correlation, each person in the group is represented by a point on the graph. The person's score on the first variable can be determined by dropping a vertical line to the horizontal axis and reading the score at that point. The person's score on the second variable can be determined by extending a horizontal line from the point representing the person to the vertical axis. Readers of research should realize that in general there are only two basic kinds of graphs in educational research. One is a frequency polygon with axes representing the number of subjects and a variable or category. The other is a graph of a correlational relationship in which both the axes are variables and the subjects are represented by points. Further, zero scores and low scores are always to the left and down.

Some illustrations of positive, negative, and zero correlations and various strengths of relationships will be of value (see Figure 3-5). In the first pictured relationship, the correlation would be positive and moderate, perhaps on the order of +.60. This correlation is one that might be found between grade-point average for college freshmen and their grade-point averages in high school. The second pictured relationship (top right) is about equal in strength to the first relationship except

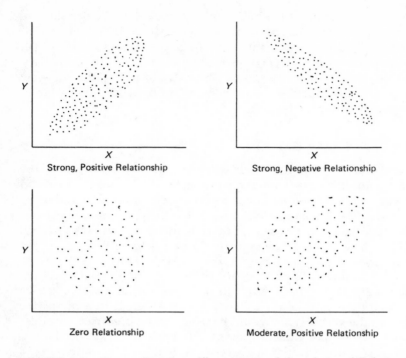

FIGURE 3-5   Scatter Diagram. Illustrations of Correlational Relationships

that it is negative, perhaps −.60. This could well be the degree and the direction of the relationship between scores on test of anxiety and grade-point average in a grade. Thus, a high grade-point average and a low anxiety score are associated with each other in this sample, as are a low grade-point average and a high score on the anxiety test. A zero relationship might be found between weight and high school grade-point average. There is no particular relationship between people's weight and their grade-point average.

A moderately positive relationship might be found between grades in band, orchestra, or choir and grade in a social studies course. Students who want to do well in grades in school are likely to work for grades in both of these types of courses and vice versa.

A brief example of the method of calculating a coefficient of correlation will be given. If a group of subjects has scores on each of two variables, tests, observations, and the like, then a correlation coefficient can be calculated. The scores for variable X and variable Y and the data for the correlation are found in Table 3-4.

TABLE 3-4   Data for the Calculation of a
Coefficient of Correlation

Person	Variable X Score	Variable Y Score	X²	Y²	X times Y
A	1	6	1	36	6
B	3	6	9	36	18
C	4	4	16	16	16
D	5	2	25	4	10
E	5	1	25	1	5
F	7	1	49	1	7

$\Sigma X = 25$ $\Sigma Y = 20$ $\Sigma X^2 = 125$ $\Sigma Y^2 = 94$ $\Sigma XY = 62$ $n = 6$,
$(\Sigma X)^2 = 625$ and $(\Sigma Y)^2 = 400$
$r_{4df} \geq .811$ to reject the null hypothesis (See Table IV in Appendix C.)

As before, by "ΣX" is meant "sum all the scores in the group on variable X," and by "ΣY" is meant "sum all the scores in the group on variable Y." By "ΣX^2" is meant "square each X score and then sum the squared scores," and by "ΣY^2" is meant "square each Y score and then sum these squared scores." Each person's X variable score is multiplied by his Y variable score to obtain the product, "XY." The product of each person's X score times his Y score is summed for all persons in the group yielding the "ΣXY." The number of pairs of observations is given by "n."

With these eight pieces of data, the coefficient of correlation for this readily understood example can be calculated. A basic formula for correlation, r, is as follows.

$$r_{xy} = \frac{n(\Sigma XY) - (\Sigma X)(\Sigma Y)}{\sqrt[2]{[n(\Sigma X^2) - (\Sigma X)^2][n(\Sigma Y^2) - (\Sigma Y)^2]}}$$

Substituting in the formula and reducing:

$$r_{xy} = \frac{6(62) - (25)(20)}{\sqrt[2]{[6(125) - 625][6(94) - 400]}}$$

$$r_{xy} = \frac{372 - 500}{\sqrt[2]{(750 - 625)(564 - 400)}}$$

$$r_{xy} = \frac{-128}{\sqrt[2]{(125)(164)}}$$

$$r_{xy} = \frac{-128}{\sqrt[2]{20,500}}$$

$$r_{xy} = \frac{-128}{143.18}$$

$$r_{xy} = -.894$$

degrees of freedom $(df) = 4$

table $r_{4df} = .811$ at the .05 level (See Table IV in Appendix C.)

Therefore an r_{xy} of $-.894$ with 4 df is significant at the .05 level.

The first question that might be asked is whether this correlation is significantly different from zero; in other words, might it be the result of chance processes alone? This is testing the null hypothesis that the correlation is really equal to zero (or no relationship). It is tested most simply by entering a table of the significance of correlations with, again, the appropriate degrees of freedom. For the test of significance of a correlation coefficient, the degrees of freedom (df) are the number of pairs of observations on variables X and Y minus two, or $df = N - 2$. In this case $N = 6$, and the $df = 6 - 2 = 4$. To be significant beyond the chance level with only six pairs of observations requires statistical values of r (absolute or unsigned) of .811 or larger at the 5 percent level of statistical significance and .917 or larger at the 1 percent level of significance, both given in the statistical tables of significance levels of correlation coefficients. (See Appendix C, Table IV.) The absolute value of the test statistic is greater than .811 but not as great as .917. Thus the null hypothesis of no demonstrated relationship is rejected at the 5 percent level, but accepted at the 1 percent level.

There is other information which can be produced from the data summaries in the correlation problem. The mean of the X scores, $\overline{X}$, is $\Sigma X / n$, or 25/6. $\overline{X} = 4.17$. Similarly, the mean of $\overline{Y}$ is 20/6, or $\overline{Y} = 3.33$. The standard deviation of X is:

$$\sigma_x^2 = \frac{X^2 - \frac{(\Sigma X)^2}{n}}{n - 1}$$

$$= \frac{125 - \frac{625}{6}}{5}$$

$$= \frac{125 - 104.17}{5}$$

$$= \frac{20.83}{5}$$

$$\sigma_x^2 = 4.17$$

$$\sigma_x = 2.04$$

For $\sigma_y{}^2 = \dfrac{\sum Y^2 - \dfrac{(\sum Y)^2}{n}}{n-1}$

$= \dfrac{94 - \dfrac{400}{6}}{5}$

$= \dfrac{94 - 66.67}{5}$

$= \dfrac{27.33}{5}$

$\sigma_y{}^2 = 5.47$

$\sigma_y = 2.38$

The correlation could be plotted in a scatter diagram (see Fig. 3-6). Note that the general slope of the data is from upper left to lower right, indicating a negative relationship.

This relationship can be plotted more explicitly through the use of *regression lines*. These are lines fitted through the data and have a linear (or straight line) algebraic equation of the form $Y = bX + a$. The Y is the

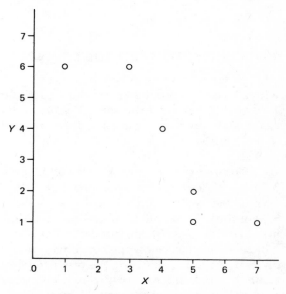

FIGURE 3-6   Scatter Diagram of a Correlation

score on variable Y, and X is the score on variable X. The "b" indicates the slope of the line and the "a" is a constant which adjusts the general level of the line to the differing measurement scales. The formula for "b_{yx}" for predicting Y from X is, $b_{yx} = r\frac{\sigma_y}{\sigma_x}$. The "$a_{yx}$" for this prediction is, $\overline{Y} - (\overline{X})\,b_{yx}$.

From the data presented then, $b_{yx} = -.89 \left(\frac{2.38}{2.04}\right)$, or $b_{yx} = -1.04$. The "a_{yx}" is equal to, $\overline{Y} - (\overline{X})b_{yx}$, or $3.33 - (4.17)(-1.04)$, or $3.33 + 4.34$, or 7.67. The full equation then for predicting Y scores from X scores in this example is:

$$Y = -1.04X + 7.67.$$

To predict X scores from Y scores, the reverse of the above, however, is a somewhat different situation and requires a different prediction equation. For this case, the subscripts on the "b" will be reversed b_{xy}. The formula for calculating b_{xy} is, $b_{xy} = r = \frac{\sigma_x}{\sigma_y}$.

For the given data $b_{xy} = -.811\left(\frac{2.04}{2.38}\right)$, or $b_{xy} = -.70$. The "a_{xy}" formula is $a_{xy} = \overline{X} - (\overline{Y})(b_{xy})$. Substituting in this, $a_{xy} = 4.17 - (3.33)(-.70)$. Thus $a_{xy} = 4.17 + 2.33$, or $a_{xy} = 6.50$.

The equation then for predicting X scores from Y scores on the basis of the presented data is,

$$X = -.70Y + 6.50.$$

REGRESSION TOWARD THE MEAN

Note that, unlike most equations in the physical sciences, starting with a Y score to predict X, and then using the predicted X to estimate a Y score will *not* yield the same Y score as the original Y score. As an example, to predict X from a Y score of 5, insert the 5.00 in the equation, $X = -.70(Y) + 6.50$. $X = -.70(5.00) + 6.50$. Thus $X = -3.50 + 6.50$, or $X = 3.00$.

To predict Y from an X score of 3.00 requires that this X score of 3.00 be placed in the equation, $Y = -1.04X + 7.67$. This is $Y = -1.04(3.00) + 7.67$. Thus Y equals $-3.12 + 7.67$, or $Y = 4.55$; not the 5.00 of the original prediction. Since the original Y score was *above* the mean of Y ($\overline{Y} = 3.33$), the prediction of the X score on its distribution will be somewhat below the seemingly comparable point of the Y score on its distribution. In using the predicted X score, in turn, to predict Y, again the predicted Y score is somewhat more towards the mean of the Y scores. This is part of the phenomenon called *regression toward the mean* that is intrinsic to almost all behavioral and social science data and predictions. If the original score used in the predictions had been *below* the mean, the regression phenomenon would have been *up* toward the mean of the predicted variable. Regression toward the mean must occur when the correlation between two variables is less than perfect, e.g., $r < 1.00$, or $r > -1.00$. Further, the nearer r is to zero, the greater the regression.

Lack of recognition of this phenomenon is the cause of much misinterpretation of educational data. It is rather common to read that an investigator has tested a group of children, taken a low-scoring percentage of the group, given them some sort of educational treatment or curriculum, retested them, and has been delighted that the children now test higher than they had previously. The investigator believes his treatment is effective. It may have been, but regression toward the mean by a sample of low-scoring children on a test must occur and severely confounds, or clouds, the investigator's interpretation of the data. This type of study is not often reported for high-scoring students. Upon retesting, they regress downward and seemingly no curriculum developer and administrator wants to take credit for this situation as they do the upward regression.

Note further than the *lower* the correlation between variables, the *more* pronounced the regression phenomenon. Thus, children retarded in their cognitive development generally are relatively more advanced in their motor development. The correlation between motor development and cognitive development generally is not high. Conversely, the intellectually brightest students would not be as superior relatively in their motor development. Regression toward the mean operates in both directions.

TYPES OF CORRELATION

As was indicated, there are in general two types of data in education, nominal and interval. The correlation and regression data presented were interval data. There are also correlations for the nominal data and mixed data, nominal and interval. While there are special formulas for these special types of correlations, the formulas are simplified forms of the correlation formula already presented. Any major correlational analyses will be done with computers, and there is no point either in simplifying a formula for the computer or in the student learning it. These correlations do have special tests of significance though, but these should be studied in a course devoted primarily to statistics.

If one variable is dichotomous (nominal) and the other interval, the statistic is called a point biserial correlation. (Note that a *t* test also involves a dichotomous variable, group one and group two, and an interval variable, score on a test. The point biserial correlation and the *t* test statistic are identical in the hypotheses that they test. A sophisticated user of statistics can often do an analysis either in a correlational format or in a format such as the *t* test. In general, when the assumptions underlying two analyses are the same, the results of the statistical tests must be identical.) If both variables are dichotomous, the correlation is called a "phi coefficient." (This statistic is identical to another statistic used with two nominal variables discussed in Appendix A, the X^2 statistic. The symbol is the small Greek letter Chi and the statistic is pronounced "Chi square.") If the two variables are rank ordered, the correlational statistic is called "rho," the Greek letter for "r." The formula used for hand calculation is still a simplified version of the formula presented. Thus, the formula assumes that the interval between the ranks are equal intervals.

There are also two coefficients of correlation which are estimates of standard correlations, the tetrachoric and biserial correlations. If both variables used in the correlation estimate are, or can be considered, artificially dichotomized, the correlation estimate is the tetrachoric correlation and a special formula is used in its computation. For biserial correlations, one variable is an interval variable, but the other of the two variables comprising the correlation is, or can be considered, artificially dichotomized. Again, a special formula is used to compute this estimate.

With modern computing equipment available, the use of these estimates of standard correlations is declining.

SUMMARY

This chapter has presented an overview of some basic and widely used statistical methods and some related concepts which are important in understanding the professional literature in education and interpreting research findings. It was noted that there are two general purposes of statistics: to show differences among groups on a variable, or to show relationships among variables within a group. Further, it was noted that there are two general types of variables, nominal and interval. Given the purpose for a statistic and the type of variables used in it, a specific statistical test can be determined. Given a statistical test and generally the number and types of variables used, the purpose of the analysis can be determined. It was indicated also that in general there are two kinds of graphs: those that show the relationship between two variables with the subject plotted as a point on the graph—a scatter diagram; and those which show the distribution of the number of subjects at a given interval of a variable—a frequency polygon. The descriptive statistics of frequency distribution, of central tendency (mean, median and mode), and of variability (the range, standard deviation, and variance) were presented. The concepts of skewness, kurtosis, and the normal distribution were explained and illustrated. Examples of methods of calculating means, standard deviations, and variances were given, as was the *t* statistic's purpose and calculation. The concepts of the null hypothesis and Type I and Type II errors associated with statistical decision-making were briefly discussed. Correlation coefficients and regression lines, their calculation, and interpretation were presented in somewhat greater detail.

STUDY AND DISCUSSION PROBLEMS

1. What is the role of statistics in educational research?
2. How many types of variables are there? Name them.
3. How many kinds of graphs are used to portray relationships? Describe them.
4. What are two major purposes of statistics?
5. Make a frequency distribution of the students' heights in your class.
6. Make a frequency polygon of your frequency distribution.
7. Calculate the mean and median height in your class.
8. Are the height data skewed, or do they have a kurtosis?
9. Use the data in Table 3-3 and reanalyze them with local computer programs. Find the means of the two groups and their standard deviations and variances. Redo the *t* test of the means' difference. Interpret your result.
10. What is a null hypothesis in statistics? Identify one in a journal article.
11. What are Type I and Type II errors in statistics?
12. What is the relationship between statistical inference and experimental or research inference?
13. Plot the data from your class of students' height vs. weight on a scatter diagram.
14. Use a computer and a locally available program to recalculate the coefficient of correlation from the data in Table 3-4.
15. Use the computer to calculate the correlation between students' height and weight in your class. Interpret the result. Develop the regression equation to predict weight from height. Take a height of 67 inches and predict the weight for a person this tall using your equation.
16. List the several different types of correlation and the types of variables producing them.
17. Find a *t* test in the educational literature. Tell what the two groups are, what the interpretation of the result is.

18.   Find a correlation in the educational literature. Tell what the two variables
       are, what the sample group is, and what the interpretation is.

REFERENCES

Downie, N.M., and Heath, R.W. *Basic statistical method* (4th ed.). New York:
       Harper & Row, 1974.
Guilford, J.P., and Fruchter, B. *Fundamental statistics in psychology and education*
       (5th ed.). New York: McGraw-Hill, 1973.

Chapter 4   Measurement in Educational Research

Levels of quantification of measurement, principles of measurement, discussions of the measurement concept of reliability and validity, and sources of data, tests, and measurement procedures will be discussed in this chapter. Further, the concepts of standard scores, percentile scales, and the relation of measurement procedures to research design concepts of internal and external validity will be presented.

The quantification of variables, operational definitions of variables, and making objective measurements of variables are of major importance in studying educational problems. As was indicated, all variables are quantifiable, or they are not variables. It is not possible to have subject, treatment, or object variables which do not have some characteristics or concepts in common. At a minimum, these characteristics are either present or absent in the objects, subjects, or treatments at a given time. To be called a variable, something at a minimum is either present or absent. A variable can be quantified as either one or zero. To be a variable something must vary; if it is constant, by definition it has no variation.

To be a variable there also must be some kind of common measurable element. If two objects or concepts are so grossly unrelated as not to be considered as falling into a common class, or having some similarities, or being able to be compared, then they do not form a variable. The old question "What's the difference between an elephant and spinach?" (if you don't know, I'm not going to send you to the store for spinach) holds true for variables also. If there is no basis for comparison, there can be no variable. Without comparison, there is no scientific knowledge.

The best that can be done, if it were felt that the elephant-spinach question might define a variable, is to classify the variable under the rubric "elephant" and "nonelephant." To quantify the variable nominally, let "elephant" equal *one* and "nonelephant" equal *zero* (or vice versa). This variable would be of interest to other elephants, and at least the variable would have some elements in common.

LEVELS OF MEASUREMENT

Four levels of measurement are commonly cited.

Nominal Measurement.   This is the lowest level, and is simply the assignment of labels or numerals (without a number meaning) to objects, like the "one" and "zero" assigned to elephant and nonelephant. There is no need to restrict the classification process to dichotomies. For example, the letters *M, P,* or *B* could be assigned to Methodist, Presbyterian, or Baptist groups. There need be no ordering, alphabetically or in any other way. Other letters or symbols could have been assigned.

Another example of nominal measurement is the classification of college majors into the Schools of Fine Arts, Science, Humanities, Engineering, Agriculture, Business, and so forth. In a given university, a student would be enrolled primarily in only one school. Again, there is no ordering or ranking, simply a labeling. The statistics used for this level of measurement would only be nominal or categorical enumeration.

Counting, percentages, and Chi Square are the major statistical methods of analysis of nominal data. (Discriminant analysis is a rarer, but useful, procedure used in classification or categorical studies.)

Ordinal Measurement.   This measurement requires that the properties of objects that constitute the variable be ordered—from least to most of the variable property. All the levels in between are classified as greater than the preceding, superior to the preceding, or more than the preceding. There can of course be ties, but all the levels of the ranking must be such that if "a" is lesser than "b," which in turn is lesser than "c," then "a" must be lesser than "c." The numerals that are assigned are ordered from one through "n" categories such that "one" is less than "two," is less than "three," etc. The ordered numerals indicate a ranking of the objects on the variable and nothing more.

Ordinal measurement is a serial arrangement of things. There should be no assumption of equal differences between adjacent levels of the rankings. In general (d − c) is unequal to (b − a). Beauty or height ordering are examples of ordered measurement. A zero numeral assigned on a rank-order scale is merely the category between plus one and minus one in the ranking system. It does not mean necessarily that the labeled zero level has none of the property being measured.

The analyses used for ordered data should be order statistics. Medians, modes, and coefficients of concordance are legitimate statistical methods to be used with ordered data.

Interval Measurement. This has all the properties of rank order measurement. In addition, the interval levels can be numbered and can be considered equal (or at least man's best estimates of equality). Thus the levels can be numbered, in order, from one to seven, and it can be assumed that the average value of the variable in the level seven minus the average value of the variable in level six is equal to the difference between the average values in any other two adjacent levels, such as three minus two. An interval labeled "zero" is the number of the interval between minus one and plus one and does not mean the absence of the property.

Appropriate statistical analyses are product moment correlation, *t* tests, analysis of variance, and various analyses using several variables (multivariate methods). Further, it is desirable to use this level of measurement and multivariate statistics since education is a multivariate phenomenon. The scope of the analyses that can be done, and the testing of the higher-order interrelationships among variables are most valuable to understanding educational processes and systems. It should be the goal of the educational researcher to use measurement instruments which produce interval scales, or these should be constructed if possible.

Ratio Measurement. It is here that a zero score does mean the absence of the property being measured. The zero score point is called absolute zero. Ratio scales are generally not used in education except in connection with physical or biological variables. For example, there is no meaningful concept, as such, of a zero IQ or a zero socioeconomic status. Ratio scales allow a statement such as this: one category on the variable scale has three times as much of the variable property as another category.

Scale and Test Development. The development of good quality equal interval scales for paper- and-pencil tests, for observations, and for interview responses is a major undertaking, almost as much work as some research efforts. Further, this development takes formal training and a reasonable amount of experience in the field of instrument construction and analysis before proficiency develops. Therefore, it is suggested that would-be researchers in education take measurement courses (in addition to courses in classroom testing for teachers) and do field work to gain experience prior to developing such instruments. They are advised also to use instruments and measurement systems of demonstrated good quality which are already available.

AVAILABLE MEASUREMENTS

Many measurements in educational systems are already available in the records of the system. In fact, there may be more measurement records in the files than are really necessary. One of the more productive practical goals of educational research is to determine which among the many records of a school system are highly related, are not predictive of educational criteria, overlap with other measurement information, or perhaps do not predict or describe much of anything. The cost of testing, rating, marking, and scoring these measures, and then recording and interpreting them, is rather high.

One of the uses of educational research is to take samples of the student records kept in a school, intercorrelate the variables, and see which among them correlate. One investigator did this for a school system and concluded that all the academic records and test scores were mainly a number of different ways of measuring one major underlying variable (Lohnes and Marshall, 1965). Barnes, in a project for a research methods course, found that an algebra prognosis test given in the eighth grade was not needed (Barnes and Asher, 1962). Research of this type can pay for itself rapidly.

One of the prime concerns of those who measure for educational research purposes is what to measure. As was indicated, the selection of criterion measurement procedures for assessment of an educational process suggests a philosophy of education and what the goals of the educational system or class "should be." "Should" implies values and falls within the realm of philosophy. Yet too often educational researchers, trained in the behavioral and social sciences, will observe an educational procedure, use one or more measures as criteria variables in their study, and unwittingly fall into the trap of believing that the selected criteria measures are major goals of the educational process. Not everyone in education may accept the measures as such.

Among the first steps in research is to determine explicitly the goals of an educational system held by various educators—teachers, principals, supervisors, administrators, and students. There generally is a core of agreement, but often there will be some special considerations to be taken into account. The researcher needs to find and document what these various educational goals are, the degree of agreement, and, to some extent, the unique or conflicting goals of those involved.

One of the reasons for this is the possible shifting nature of these goals as the research or evaluation progresses. As evaluation reports are submitted, it may become apparent that the widely vaunted, new educational method is not working too well, and the desired goals are not being accomplished. The innovators and administrators are human like everyone else (and perhaps a little more so). Among their best rationalizations and lines of retreat are the claims (sometimes quite valid ones) that the evaluator's criteria are not really the ones of greatest interest. A classic example is the now often heard statement (after evidence of the ineffectiveness of driver education for reducing accidents started to accumulate) that a major aim of driver education is to teach good citizenship!

In recent years the movement toward behavioral objectives, statements of purpose, more explicit statements of the philosophy of education in an educational system, and taxonomies of educational objectives has focused education goals much more sharply. Among the accomplishments this has brought is that the job of educational evaluator and researcher is made somewhat easier by defining the criteria of the educational program.

Classroom tests and standardized tests of educational achievement are the most obvious and widely used measures of educational goals. They must be considered among the criteria chosen for analysis by a researcher in a school. In fact, it is not wise for those whose major focus is on the standard educational criteria in educational systems to spend much time developing measurement instruments. Generally, supplementary instruments, to add to the breadth and depth and to check on the measurements already being done, should be about all that are considered by educators for the usual classroom evaluations.

If assistance is needed in choosing standardized instruments, the use of the latest edition of Buros' *Mental Measurements Yearbook* (1972) is recommended. Lists of most of the educational achievement tests (as well as many other kinds of tests) are presented, along with publication dates, prices, publisher, and extensive reviews of the tests. To extend the range of assessment somewhat, Buros' *Tests in Print*, Volume 2 (1974) can be used, along with other data available from the classroom records such as attendance, discipline, written papers, homework, and seating patterns.

Simple checklists of various accomplishments listed in the objectives of instruction can be developed such as, "Can locate the continents on a map, Yes ___ , Generally ___ , No ___ ." The two handbooks of the *Taxonomy of Educational Objectives* (Bloom, 1956, and Krathwohl, 1964) present a range of behaviors in the cognitive and affective domains. Six levels of accomplishment are given for the cognitive domain: Knowledge, Comprehension, Application, Analysis, Synthesis, and Evaluation.

It is important, as a first concern, for the educational researcher in developing criteria in the cognitive achievement area to consider moving beyond the simple and even complex knowledge areas to the higher levels in the domain. In addition to the cognitive and affective areas, sometimes psychomotor and social domains are added to the list of areas, although social accomplishments might be considered a combination of affective, psychomotor, and cognitive dimensions. The important thing for the educational researcher to remember is to consider possible achievement in all of these areas and all of the levels of accomplishment within each domain, to assure himself and his employers that no major dimension of human behavior has been inadvertently overlooked in the review of educational criteria to be assessed. The statements of educational objectives, goals, philosophies, and purposes of the system being assessed can be compared then against the domains and levels of the taxonomies.

A second concern is to use more than machine-scored paper-and-pencil instruments. Observations, records (other than achievement), interviews, social measures, and ratings by students and others are perfectly worthwhile methods to use in assessing a wide range of behavior and dimensions of educational processes and systems. Non-multiple choice instruments should be used more often than they are. These procedures are somewhat more expensive to use than the machine-scored achievement tests, but the goals of education are often broader than those which are generally measured through the use of multiple-choice devices alone. There are procedures which reduce the number of observations or samples needed for such interviews and will yield at least some indicators of important variables at a reasonable cost.

What types of data will be found in school records? Standardized achievement tests and various kinds of paper-and-pencil intelligence tests may form the bulk of the test data in a typical school's cumulative record folders. On these, test scores are often reported in terms of grade equivalents, that is, in terms of what the average student in a given grade can accomplish on the test.

Grade equivalent scores can be used as a basis for either comparisons among groups or for showing relationships among variables within groups, as long as the grade equivalent scores being used all come from the same levels of the test. In general, it is not reasonable to say that a grade equivalent of 4.5 on a primary level battery is equal to a grade equivalent of 4.5 on the intermediate grade school battery. Also, the analyses cannot mean too much more than the grade equivalent norms upon which they are based.

There are some problems of interpretation of grade equivalent scores. For instance, a grade equivalent score of 9.5 in mathematics for a seventh-grade child does not mean that the child knows mathematics through the first semester of ninth-grade algebra. It merely means that this seventh-grader is very good in arithmetic. This is expressed as an extrapolation of the child's raw score into a grade equivalency score. (There are other problems of interpretation with grade equivalent scores and with other types of educational test scores, but these are covered in more detail in texts on educational measurement, such as Thorndike, 1971; Thorndike and Hagen, 1969; Downie, 1958; Remmers, Gage, and Rummel, 1965.)

Raw scores are sometimes reported in the school's records. These may be simply the number of items right that the child scored on the test, or perhaps the number right minus a correction for guessing. The score may be a teacher's rating. Generally, schools have test manuals or standard procedures for scoring tests or observations which describe the level of behavior that is to be rated as a "3," "5," or whatever. These manuals and scoring systems should be studied carefully before data are recorded for further analyses so that the meaning of the data, and thus the results of analyses, will be clearer. Are the scores comparable to a normative group's scores, for instance? They can only be comparable if at least the scoring methods used were the same.

Criterion-referenced testing is a concept in educational measurement that is becoming more widely used and is tied much more closely to the stated goals of an educational procedure in a local school system than to performance comparison. Criterion-referenced testing, unlike many of the norm-referenced testing devices just described, concentrates on documenting the successful accomplishment of each phase of the educational goals of a program by at least 90 percent or more of the students involved. Thus, generally, no grade equivalent scores or other normative data are developed from national samples for comparative purposes. Instead, criterion-referenced testing is concerned with a highly successful accomplishment by the students of the educational goals of the particular program or curriculum. The concepts of standard scores and percentiles which follow will not apply as readily to the data produced from criterion-referenced testing as do the scores from norm-referenced testing. A number of measurement specialists feel, however, that most of the other traditional standards of measurement do apply.

STANDARD SCORES

Raw scores are often transformed into standard scores which perhaps are easier to interpret. However, first the process of arriving at these transformed standard scores must be understood.

Most standard scores and their several equivalents are based on a normal curve frequency distribution, that is, a bell-shaped curve. This distribution is believed, on the basis of considerable evidence, to be a reasonable estimate of the distribution of many biological, psychological, sociological, and educational traits of people.

Recall from Figure 3-3 that the center of the normal distribution is indicated by its mean, and a measure of individual differences is the standard deviation. About six standard deviations encompass the range of the bell-shaped distribution, from the highest score to the lowest score. There is no absolute zero (the absence of a trait) in most measurement systems in the behavioral sciences. A score of zero is used by convention to represent the mean. The score of plus one marks the first standard deviation distance above the mean, and minus one marks the first standard deviation distance below the mean. A plus two score is set two standard deviation units above the mean, plus three at three standard deviation units above the mean, and minus two at two standard deviation units below the mean. In a normal distribution, the range from minus three standard deviation units to plus three standard deviation units covers 99.74 percent of the area under the distribution. These units can be further divided into smaller units, say tenths of a standard deviation unit, yielding possibly sixty scores in the scale's range.

However, many people find the use of plus and minus signs confusing and unwieldy clerically. They prefer a measurement system without them. Others dislike decimals, and there is really no need for them in a number system that is scored only in intervals. Thus, several closely related systems of *standard scores* have been developed for use in reporting data in educational records. (See Figure 4-1.) In one set of standard scores, the mean is set at 500 and one standard deviation unit equals 100. Thus a score of 600 is one standard deviation above the average score in that distribution. College Entrance Examination Board tests, STEP tests, and Graduate Record Examination scores are reported in this manner. The top of the usual range would be a score of about 800 (three standard deviation units times 100 above the mean, 500) and the lowest score about 200 (three standard deviation units times 100 below the mean, 500).

The middle of the group, between minus one to plus one standard

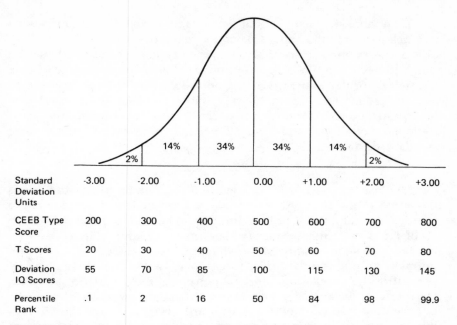

	2%	14%	34%	34%	14%	2%

Standard Deviation Units	-3.00	-2.00	-1.00	0.00	+1.00	+2.00	+3.00
CEEB Type Score	200	300	400	500	600	700	800
T Scores	20	30	40	50	60	70	80
Deviation IQ Scores	55	70	85	100	115	130	145
Percentile Rank	.1	2	16	50	84	98	99.9

FIGURE 4-1   Comparisons of Standard Score Measurement Units and CEEB Type, T Scores, IQ Scores, and Percentile Rank Scores

deviation above the mean, or scores of from 400 to 600, constitutes about 68 percent of the total distribution. About 14 percent more of the distribution is found between plus one and plus two standard deviations, or scores of 600 to 700; and another 14 percent between minus one and minus two standard deviations, or scores of 300 to 400, in this standard score system. Scores above plus two standard deviations are slightly over 2 percent of a normal distribution, as are those scores below two standard deviations. Scores above two standard deviations and below two standard deviations are scores of over 700 or below 300 in this standard score system.

Another scoring system found in educational records merely reduces the 500 and 100 system by a factor of 10. These are sometimes called "T" scores. Thus the range of plus and minus three standard deviation units is about 30 scoring units up and 30 scoring units down from the mean of 50, or scores from about 20 to 80. Plus and minus one standard deviation unit scores are at 60 and 40, respectively, while plus and minus two standard deviation unit scores are at 70 and 30 in this standard score system.

The same statements about percentages of the distribution above and below a certain standard deviation score point follow just as they did in the example using 500 for the average score, with 100 as the standard deviation, if the distributions are bell-shaped. A score of 40 is ten points, or one standard deviation unit, below the mean in the 50 and 10 system. Thus about 16 percent of a distribution of scores falls below this point, 14 percent between minus two and minus three standard deviations, and about 2 percent more below minus three standard deviations.

IQ Scores.   Scores of intelligence tests often are presented in this deviation form. These IQ scores use a mean of 100 as average and a standard deviation unit of 15 points (for some tests 16 points). Thus an IQ of 115 is 15 points, or one standard deviation unit, above the mean. In the typical standardized intelligence test, where the scores are normalized, one standard deviation above the mean exceeds about 84 percent of the population, since 50 percent of the population is below the mean (or the average), and 34 percent of a normal distribution falls between the mean and plus one standard deviation. An IQ of 100 is at the center of the distribution and an IQ of 85 is one standard deviation (or 15 points) below the mean. This score of 85 exceeds 16 percent of the population (assuming a normal distribution of scores). There are 14 percent of the IQs between minus one standard deviation units (85) and minus two standard deviation units (an IQ of 70). Those below an IQ of 70 are about two percent of the distribution.

Stanine Score.   In order to avoid numbers of two and three digits, such as some of those illustrated above, a normalized standard score system ranging from one to nine was developed called the "stanine" (short for "standard nine"). The stanine standard score system uses a mean of 5 and a standard deviation unit of slightly less than two. The odd-numbered set of scores has a middle score, 5, with a range from about a quarter of a standard deviation unit above the mean to about a quarter of a standard deviation unit below the mean. Above and below the middle stanine score of 5, each stanine score encompasses about one half of a standard deviation score unit, except the stanine scores of one and nine. A stanine score of 9 encompasses all the raw scores above approximately +1.75 standard deviation score units, and a stanine score of 1 includes all the scores below approximately −1.75 standard score units.

PERCENTILES

Most of the scores and their variations found in school records can be considered equal interval scores. One other type of score, often found in school records, can cause problems in research analyses. These are percentile ranks. Percentile ranks are widely used because they are easily calculated and, in one sense, readily interpreted in terms of knowing what percent of the normative group is below a given percentile score. However, in another more fundamental sense, percentile scores are difficult to interpret and to use.

Percentile ranks are rank-ordered scores and have, by definition, an equal number of subjects per score. This means that the scores in a percentile rank scoring system have a flat, rectangular distribution. For most variables, this appears to be at odds with all the other scoring systems, particularly those based on standard deviation unit systems.

For instance, the score distance between the 50th and the 51st percentile and the 98th and 99th percentile are considered and treated as if they are equivalent in the percentile rank scoring system. In the standard deviation unit system, these scores would be .000 and +.025 standard score units for the 50th and 51st percentiles and +2.060 and +2.330 for the 98th and 99th percentiles. For the first, the difference is .025 standard units apart, but is .270 standard units for the second difference, more than ten times as large a difference as the seemingly equal units in the percentile system.

The percentile rank scoring system systematically distorts differences between scores near the center of a distribution, making them appear larger, while also distorting differences between scores at either extreme by making them appear much smaller than when they are scored in most other measurement systems. In general, when only percentile rank scores are available for a variable, it is good practice to use a conversion table to change them back to raw scores. They can also be converted directly to standard scores.

Figure 4-1 showed the interrelationships among the normal distribution, several types of standard score units, and percentile rank scores, and will be of help in understanding them.

SUCCESSIVE CATEGORY MEASUREMENT

Other scores used in educational research may be ratings, responses to questionnaire categories, or interview categorizations. Generally, statistical analyses of counted data (enumeration statistics) should be used for these measurement procedures, unless the researcher first developed an interval measurement system for scoring. This involves prior judgment by an independent sample that the labels describing the categories of responses are equal-appearing intervals on a social or psychological dimension. (The scales could have been developed and tested for equality by others.)

Likert and Thurstone in the late 1920s and 30s did basic work in developing procedures and language that can be used for equal interval measurement systems. The words to describe each of the Likert five successive categories are "strongly agree," "agree," "uncertain," "disagree," and "strongly disagree." Other labels and responses to successive categories of responses could be placed by scaling techniques into equal-appearing intervals and an interval number system applied. (These methods are given in courses in measurement in education, psychology, sociology, and other social and behavioral science fields.) If equal intervals for the categories have not been developed, then only nominal, enumeration analyses should be used.

RELIABILITY AND OBJECTIVITY

Reliability is the basic requirement for any measurement procedure. Reliability is repeatability, or more formally, replicability. Since one of the requirements of science is replication, reliability is basic to the study of the scientific aspects of education. Reliability also aids in determining that an observation is not just a private experience but a public one. Part of the definition of science is that its information and observations be public as well as replicable. Agreement among observers, reliability, is thus essential also to educational research. While genius in part is the ability to see what others have not seen, it is imperative that the genius report his observations and insights so that others can see them also.

One of the ways to separate the geniuses from the hallucinators and the neurotics (who fulfill emotional needs by projecting their personalities into an indeterminate structure) is to check on the reliability of the observation. The concern about overlooking genius is minimized in science because one person with replicable, reliable evidence is given more credence than hundreds without such evidence.

Objectivity is Reliability, and Reliability is Objectivity. Objectivity can be defined as impersonal, unprejudiced, impartial, and unbiased. Kerlinger (1973, p. 491) defines an objective procedure as "one in which agreement among observers is at a maximum." He also agrees "that it is possible to objectify the subjective. If, in fact, it were not possible to do so, it would not be possible to have scientific psychological procedures" (Kerlinger, 1964, p. 480).

Title I of the Elementary and Secondary Education Act of 1965 requires, "That effective procedures, including provisions for appropriate objective measurements of educational achievement, will be adopted for evaluating, at least annually, the effectiveness of the programs in meeting the special educational needs of educationally deprived children" (see a compilation of Federal Education Laws by the Committee on Education and Labor, House of Representatives, U.S. Government Printing Office, Washington, October 1971, pp. 32 and 33). It should also be noted that annual reports must be made containing these "effective procedures," "objective measurements," and "evaluations" by the local school agency and that these evaluations shall be public information.

This requirement for objective measurement has focused the attention of school systems on standardized tests. As was indicated, educational goals generally are somewhat broader than those assessed by paper-and-pencil instruments, but those goals too can be objectively measured.

Reliability also is agreement between tests and among observers. Generally, if a test is given to a single group on two separate occasions, there should be agreement between the two sets of observations. Essentially, the test acts as two variables, one now and another later. The statistical method of reporting these kinds of relationships is through the use of a correlation coefficient (if the test or observational scores are interval). For the reliability (and objectivity) to be high, the correlation coefficient must be high.

The degree of reliability and objectivity which is needed changes with the purpose of the educational activity. For early stages for basic research purposes, where only the statement is needed that variables are related, low reliability correlations are acceptable. In fact, Nunnally (1967, p. 226) declares that for basic research, reliabilities of .50 to .60 will suffice and reliabilities above .80 are wasteful. But he indicates that for applied research, a reliability of .90 is a minimum and .95 a desirable standard.

Stability. Where a test or observation is made and then the test is given again, or the observer repeats the observation, the correlation coefficients generated are known as test-retest indices of reliability. They indicate the ability of the testing devices or observers to be able to replicate their measurements. If the object or process being observed changes somewhat over a period of time, this reliability coefficient will reflect these changes also. In this sense, the reliability is a measure of *stability*.

Equivalency.   Because of problems of subjects remembering items, or learning as the result of exposure to items or a limited set of items presented, two or more tests may need to be constructed as equivalents or alternatives to one another (except in the actual items used). These alternate forms are used for successive measurements of groups of individuals. Alternate-forms reliability is established by correlating the scores on two or more forms of the test on one group of people. This alternate-form reliability, or measure of the *equivalency* of the content or processes assessed by the two forms of the test, is useful in educational research where before-instruction and after-instruction measurements are needed. If the tests are equivalent, there is assurance that scores on one of the tests will not be systematically higher or lower than on the other. Learning gains then can be inferred to be the result of the instruction and not differences in the tests because of subjects' memory of items or learning of specific items.

One of the better ways to construct equivalent forms of a test is to develop a large number of items in the domain of the test and randomly to assign the items to form one or form two, rather than try to construct a second test like the one that is available. If the items can be paired by content area and level of difficulty and if one item of each pair is randomly assigned to each test, the equivalence of the forms will be even better.

Internal Consistency.   A third and very important type of reliability is the result of the interrelationship of items among themselves in a test (or of the interrelationship among observations) on a dimension of behavior. This type of reliability is called *internal consistency* reliability.

One type of this reliability is called *split-half reliability*. Think of a set of items on a test which are allocated to measure "A" or measure "B." These could be the first half of the items on a test and the second half of the items, or the odd items and the even items, and so forth. Then, if for each student his two scores on each of the two halves of the split test are correlated with each other, a correlation coefficient could be calculated which is a function of the reliability of the total test. This splitting of the test can be into thirds, quarters, fifths, or whatever, all the way down to where each item in the test is considered a separate test in itself! All of these splits are possible, but the split half is widely used, as is the individual-item split.

Using the individual-item split and an overall average of the correlations among the items (when they are scored simply "right" or "wrong") is known as the Kuder-Richardson reliability, or more often in the literature as a K-R reliability. KR_{20} is the most general of the several varieties of K-R reliability.

Another variety of individual-item internal consistency reliability is Hoyt's analysis of variance approach, while Cronbach's alpha coefficient is the most general internal consistency reliability measure and is used for items and observations scored as intervals, as well as items or observations scored simply "right" or "wrong" (dichotomously). Internal consistency reliability estimates can be made with one presentation of the test, or one observer making only one set of observations.

The internal consistency reliability coefficient yields information which is particularly important to research in education because it is an index of the *unidimensionality* of the measure being used. It helps answer such quesitons as: Are the items or observations measuring only one phenomenon? Are the items measuring the same underlying varible? Internal consistency reliability coefficients tell the researcher the precision of his measurement and if an aspect of behavior is really a single variable.

For example, if on an observational scale the observer is asked to to rate a series of objects on the dimension of "authority" and the objects are spinach, chairs, sidewalks, and farms, the internal consistency reliability of this scale for these objects undoubedly would be low. Most judges do not see "authority" as basic to these entities; there would be only minimal consistency among the ratings. However, these words as vocabulary items given to students would show a high interrelationship. Those who answer any one item right are more likely to respond correctly than incorrectly to any other item. There is a high internal consistency among the items. Thus, vocabulary word meaning is a unidimensional scale. The scale measures one, and perhaps only one, aspect of human behavior; certainly it does not measure a series of rather diverse behaviors. It is a unidimensional variable.

Influences on Reliability. Reliabilities can be high and low for other reasons as well. Reliability correlation coefficients (as well as all correlations) are rather dependent upon the dispersion of the variable being measured, the spread of scores, and the individual differences in the group being measured. Intelligence tests, when used in a general population, will have a higher reliability than when used in a group which is more restricted in the range of intelligence represented, such as college students, for instance, particularly those in graduate school. Tests given in selective honors courses in high school, measuring dimensions of talent related to the basis for selection, will not show exceptionally high reliability. Similarly, the restriction in the range of talent could be toward the low end of the dimension, such as reading ability in a school attended by the culturally deprived. Restriction can occur also in the middle of a dimension such as a "general" class in high school English where both the college-bound students and students who are slow learners take other courses.

Reliabilities are greatly influenced by the number of items in a test or the number of observations made. Using very short tests, or making only a few observations, simply does not produce high reliability. Very early in behavioral science measurement, the relationship of number of items (or observations) to reliability was determined independently by two researchers, Spearman and Brown. Their equation, since named the Spearman-Brown formula, is

$$r_k = \frac{kr}{1 + (K - 1)\, r}$$

where r is the observed reliability, r_k is the reliability of a proposed test k times as long, and k is the length of the proposed test as compared to the available test. Low reliabilities can be increased by making more observations, including more items in a test, or using more observers. If an observation system or test is too expensive or too time consuming, the reliabilities can be reduced to a predetermined level estimated quickly through the use of the Spearman-Brown formula.

Reliability can be understood better if an analogy is made to the diameter of a lens: the larger the lens, the sharper the focus and the easier it is to detect images in dim light. So it is with reliability indicators. Good test items, like high-quality glass, will aid in producing high reliability, but they cannot overcome restrictions in length of the test. Reliability can be increased by adding more items (or more observers) of the same or better quality to those which are being used.

Further, the reliability of tests (and measures) distinctly limits the size of the correlations between the measurement instruments. Generally, a predictor measure cannot correlate with a criterion measure higher than the criterion measure can predict itself. This self-prediction of the criterion measure is its reliability.

The rule in general is that a test cannot have a correlation associated with it higher than its reliability. The mathematical statement is as follows: the upper limit of the correlation between two variables is the square root of the product of their reliabilities, or

$$\sqrt[2]{r_{11} \times r_{22}} \quad .$$

Attempting to detect moderately reliable variables is like attempting to determine the shape of an object in a haze, through a pebbled glass window, or behind a screen. The detection of the object can be done and is valuable, but it takes effort. With low reliability, one views the world "as seen through a glass darkly." Since reliability coefficients are seldom perfect, the view of the behavioral and social science world is imprecise, but it is an assumption of all science that natural world variables and relationships are approximate at best. Reliability indicators suggest the degree of the approximation.

One of the best and most authoritative chapters on reliability is that by Stanley (1971). All of the concepts discussed here briefly are developed much more fully in his work and the examples are in the context of education.

VALIDITY OF MEASUREMENT

To be valid is to be *bona fide,* genuine, authentic, truthful, and effective. Validity of measurement is the extent to which tasks, observational systems, questionnaires, and ratings are effective, truthful, and genuine, in serving their stated purposes. A measurement system is valid to the extent to which it predicts other measures (except alternative forms of itself—which is reliability). Validity of measurement is the soundness of the interpretations of a test or observational system. One way to validate a test is to demonstrate its worth empirically. Validity also indicates the degree to which a measurement system is capable of achieving certain aims. To determine the usefulness of a measurement system is to determine its validity. However, validity is a matter of degree and is a never-ending process. All behavioral and social science measurements must undergo scrutiny continually; they must be checked in numerous situations. Even in seemingly constant social environments, assurance must be made that the measurement procedures retain validity, and their validities are expanded and contracted as the empirical evidence warrants.

The one characteristic which a measurement procedure must have is validity. Without validity a test or observational procedure is of little value. Validity and reliability are related in that if a test or observational procedure can be demonstrated to be valid, it must have some degree of reliability. However, procedures can be highly *reliable* and have little or no *validity*.

Probable validity is defined best by the operations which are used to produce it. There are generally four types of validity described: content, concurrent, predictive, and construct.

Content Validity. This is the representativeness of the behaviors, topics, or substances being measured, and is of particular importance in education for curriculum content achievement measures. For a test to have content validity, it must have items that are representative of the scope and content of the study area and should be definitive of the achievement to be measured. Content validity to a large extent is a matter of judgment about objectives and evidence, not statistical indices. Content validity would be important for a history test or one in literature.

Concurrent Validity. The degree of relationship (often expressed by a coefficient of correlation) between an available, known valid measure of a trait or behavior and the test or measurement procedure under study is called concurrent validity. The two measurement procedures must be independent of one another in their methods, items, tasks, and observations. The data used in concurrent validity are empirical, that is, scores from both sets of measures on a group of people. A high correlation between the sets of scores indicates high concurrent validity. Often this procedure is used to establish the validity of a less costly measurement procedure, like a group intelligence tests, with a more expensive measure, such as an individually administered intelligence test. Sometimes concurrent validity needs to be demonstrated between an older, known valid test and a recently constructed test believed to measure the same general abilities. (For instance, a new intelligence test would be correlated with the older Stanford-Binet or the Wechsler-Bellevue.)

Predictive Validity. As the name suggests, predictive validity attempts to forecast some state of being or measurement in the future (other than the same measure again) from a current test or observation. A typical example in education is the prediction of grades in school. A test is said to have predictive validity for grades if the scores on a test given now correlate with grades that are given at some future time.

Prediction is one of the major goals of science, and predictive validity is one of the severest trials of a measurement procedure. A test either can or cannot predict a phenomenon. Predictive validity is thus one of the most desirable forms of validity for a test or observational procedure in an applied situation.

Construct Validity. This is concerned with the scientific variables (constructs) a test is measuring. It helps determine the adequacy of the test's explanatory constructs (which are scientific concepts or ideas). Construct validity attempts to explain the behavior exhibited when persons take a test or are observed with systematic procedures. Construct validity is concerned with the further understanding of behavior in the context of scientific theory.

The persons validating a construct must have a thorough understanding of the scientific theories from which the construct is emerging. They make predictions about what subjects are like, or would do, if they obtained high scores or low scores on a measure of the construct. Next, the investigators must collect evidence to examine the accuracy of their theory's predictions and from this evidence make inferences about the adequacy of the construct. Actually, the investigators are attempting to validate the theories from which the constructs evolved. Construct validity processes come closest to basic research models, and there is a constant cycling between the development of theory and testing data about the theory. Construct validity is important when the validator accepts no existing measures as fully defining the variable which is conceptualized or believed to be perceived by the researcher.

Validity is convergent, a confirmation of theory by variables which are measured independently of one another. For construct validity, however, there is a need for discrimination among variables as well. Construct validity can be destroyed by having an hypothesized new variable correlate too highly with an older measure of a supposedly different construct. Campbell and Fiske (1959) call this method of construct validation the *multitrait-multimethod procedure*. With this method, each new construct measure to be validated must be included with other measured traits which might be related (multitrait). Each trait must be measured in at least two different ways in a group of subjects (multimethod). To attain construct validity, it must be shown that each trait correlates highly with itself, between methods of assessment (e.g., that it has reliability) and, further, that each set of trait measurements correlates near zero with all other traits in the study. This latter shows that indeed the variable is a new one that does not overlap highly with prior measures.

This method of demonstrating construct validity also illustrates an aspect of the scientific *principle of parsimony*. Parsimony in this instance is using only one name to describe a single variable or construct. For instance, to measure creativity validly the measures must be reliable. To assure best validity, creativity should be measured by more than one method, such as multiple choice tests, judgment of created work, and so forth. Further, the measures of creativity must not correlate highly with measures of general intelligence. If they do, the creativity tests could really be just another measure of intelligence. In the case of a high correlation between the two measures, it is not parsimonious to call each measure by a different name as if they were two separate entities.

For an excellent overview of test validity see the chapter by Cronbach in *Educational Measurement* (1971).

OPERATIONAL DEFINITIONS

Operational definitions are related to the concepts of parsimony and validity. An operational definition defines a variable strictly in terms of the procedures through which a score or measure is produced. "Intelligence is what a test of intelligence measures" is a type of operational definition. This operational definition is rather simplistic and circular, yet few worthwhile constructs or variables can be cited that do not have at least a definition like this one and, hopefully, a set of measurement procedures which will aid in defining the constructs. To an extent, an operational definition is a restatement of the thinking that all variables are quantifiable. If a so-called variable cannot be operationally defined, there is considerable doubt that it is a variable.

Intelligence is indeed in part what an intelligence test measures, but the construct of intelligence is more than that. Intelligence is what all valid intelligence tests measure and what all intelligence tests would measure if all the facets of the construct of intelligence were operationally defined. This is the idea of multiple operational definition which modern science now generally accepts. It goes far beyond the older, more limiting definition of a single operational procedure.

The most conclusive evidence that a construct actually does exist is a convergence, or a triangulation, of various measures of the construct. In the process, further evidence enriches the construct and aids in developing the theory from which it emerged. When multiple operational definitions converge and provide consistent results, chances of slippage between the conceptual definition and the operational definitions are greatly reduced. With a number of defining operations demonstrated by intercorrelations, the construct becomes richer in its theoretical implications and at the same time far more objective and real.

INTERNAL AND EXTERNAL RESEARCH DESIGN
VALIDITY AND MEASUREMENT

Four major sources of lack of validity in research design in the realm of measurement have been identified by Campbell (1957) and later expanded in Campbell and Stanley (1963): Instrumentation, Testing, Regression, and Reactive Arrangements. The unique, possible interrelationships (interactions) of these effects with treatment effects are also discussed in Campbell and Stanley.

Instrumentation.   The instrumentation source of internal invalidity of research is that in which changes of calibration of the measuring instrumentation are involved. These can be changes in the observers, yielding changing ratings when the subjects have not actually changed. Instrumentation problems also arise when different forms of a test are used, and one is easier or harder than the other. If two different post-test measures are used, one for each randomized group, and one is more difficult than the other, observed differences between the two groups could be due solely to differences in the tests and not to the effect of a treatment or no treatment. The observed pseudo-difference would be confounded with any treatment differences, and thus any effects of the treatments would be difficult to interpret.

Raters' scores may change from time to time for a variety of reasons. The observers become tired, shift standards, or become more blasé or familiar with the situation or persons being observed. Instrument invalidity results when these observers' changes result in differences in criterion scores which are interpreted as actual changes caused by the treatments. Also observers' knowledge of the treatment conditions of the subjects may cause them to change their ratings. The observer "knows" the treatment works and rates the subject accordingly. An observer involved in the experiment may wish the treatment to be effective so much that his wish is "fulfilled" by his ratings.

Testing.   The research design internal validity problem of *Testing* involves the effects on subjects of a prior testing or observation which the subjects have undergone. It is known that in a second testing (such as in a pre- and post-testing situation), the subjects have done better the second time perhaps from practice, learning, or familiarity. Even on intelligence tests, these gains are as much as three to five points on a short-term basis. For personality tests generally, the subjects appear better adjusted.

For typical classroom educational achievement variables, however, this Testing effect may have been greatly exaggerated. Bracht and Glass (1968) indicate that the effect of pretesting on academic achievement is found less often than once believed, particularly if more than a week intervenes between the pretest and the post-test and the criteria variables are not self-report measures of personality, attitude, or opinion.

Welch and Walberg (1970), in a national sample in secondary schools, found no pretest effects at all for three cognitive, one behavioral, and two affective criteria. The tests were given in a normal classroom situation over the academic year, and test taking was a part of the daily routine. They conclude that the effects of pretesting alone were not important, and that there is little empirical evidence that a pretesting effect exists in most typical school situations, even less than it exists in curriculum research. If effects of *Testing* do exist, they would be interpreted most likely as the effects of the treatments which were applied to the subjects. Obviously such a conclusion would be invalid given the pretest, post-test research design.

Statistical Regression.   These effects were alluded to in the previous chapter on statistical analyses. When measurement systems are not perfectly reliable (which includes almost all of them in education) and selection of high or low groups on scores is made, Regression effects toward the mean inevitably occur. The more extreme the groups' scores, the greater the regression-toward-the-mean effect. The lower the correlation (or reliability) between two measures, the more pronounced the regression-to-the-mean effect. When the correlation between two variables is zero, the best prediction from one variable to the other is at the mean of the criterion variable. Some investigators consider this an intrinsic effect of the Regression phenomenon.

For instance, they carefully investigate the motor abilities of the intellectually retarded and announce that the retardates' motor abilities are relatively well above their intellectual capacity. These "differences" or "gains," if preceded by a training treatment of some sort, are sometimes cited as being "caused" by the training treatment. This is an invalid conclusion because of the regression-toward-the-mean phenomenon—(in this case a regression-toward-the-mean of the general population's motor abilities).

Reactivity.   Sometimes referred to as reactive arrangements, reactivity is the research design validity problem caused by the process of the testing or observation procedures themselves making enough of a difference in the educational environment to cause a change in the tested subjects. This change takes place even if no educational treatment occurs. This change is likely to be mistaken for changes caused by the treatments introduced in the research design.

As every experienced teacher knows, the mere process of observers in a classroom may change the behavior of the students over a short period of time. The students know they are being watched; something else is happening in addition to whatever educational treatment differences are being introduced. These two sets of differences may well confound one another, making it difficult or impossible to determine cause-and-effect relationships. This source of experimental research invalidity is called Reactivity.

These effects are sometimes called the Hawthorne effect, after a famous industrial experiment in which the lighting in a plant was systematically varied. When it was determined that the plant personnel could hardly see and yet production still increased, it was realized that the personal interest of management in the workers' jobs was the likely cause of the increased output.

The introduction of a TV camera, equipment, change of rooms, out-of-town visitors, and visits by principals, supervisors, and professors can change behavior on a short-term basis. This can wreak havoc with the internal validity of the research.

Specific accommodations should be made to blend the treatments in with the school routine, acclimatize the students to these factors, and spread the treatments and observations over an extended period. The effect of these extraneous, reactive factors alone can be studied, if desired, by using a separate comparison group in addition to the group given the experimental educational effect.

The additional comparison group, a reactivity or Hawthorne group, is a separate control group in which the suspected reactive elements are introduced but not a new educational treatment. As was indicated, Welch and Walberg (1970) in their educational research found no sensitization effects on any of their several domains of criteria. They used typical educational routines over a long period of time.

Cook (1967) studied the Hawthorne effect specifically in elementary schools, both with direct and indirect cues that the children were in an experiment. The differing cues were to tell the children they were participating in an experiment, were being introduced to a new curriculum, or were having a different mathematics teacher for only the math period. Cook concluded there were no differences between the presence or absence of either direct or indirect cues at the end of one and two years of the study. He further concluded, on the basis of an extensive literature review, that the Hawthorne effect does not contaminate the experimental results on measures of academic performance.

Interaction Effects.   The interaction effects of these four sources of internal validity problems are also possible, but two that particularly were thought to be problems are evidently not of nearly as much concern in education now that evidence is appearing on the topic. The interaction effect of Testing and many kinds of treatment effects were found to be negligible. Also the interaction effects of Reactivity and other effects are also not major problems.

Welch and Walberg (1970) were specifically concerned with pretest treatment interactions on their six criteria variables and found none. Even Campbell and Stanley (1963, p. 188) had indicated at the time of their summary that there were few published research results on these interaction effects, and those published showed either no effect or an actual reduction in post-test scores as the result of pretest exposure. (One of the two reaction studies cited was in spelling, but the pretest and post-test in that study were given the same day. There also is some doubt about the method of equating the groups).

In summary then, pretesting reactive arrangements seem not to be a major problem in educational research if reasonable precautions are taken to rush the research into the educational routine, keep the criteria tests much like those typically given in schools, give the students a chance to accommodate to the new aspects of the procedure, and run the study for more than a week. However, Instrumentation and particularly Regression-toward-the-mean effects are major problems in misinterpretation of measurements.

SOURCES OF TESTS AND MEASUREMENT INSTRUMENTS

To this point, the only major reference to specific sources of scales, tests, and observational instruments has been to Buros' *Mental Measurements Yearbook* and this in relation to achievement tests. Educational research quality has suffered from the constraint that the only educational variables thought to be usable were data found in students' record files and that the important variables are impossible to measure. On the basis of the presentations in this book, this latter thought should be dispelled. Important educational variables may be difficult to measure, but if they are found to be impossible to measure, the better question might be, do the concepts exist?

The book *Unobtrusive Measures: Nonreactive Research in the Social Sciences* (Webb, Campbell, Schwartz, and Sechrest, 1966) demonstrates the wide range of variables already measured, scales, observational systems, and questionnaires available, of value, and of interest to educators. This list was compiled: socioeconomic status, social distance, group cohesiveness, sociometric choice, employee satisfaction, job satisfaction, community attitudes, solidarity rating, social participation, leadership, supervisory behavior, leadership opinion, wear and markings on library books, and attention span. A quick review of colleagues', students', and associates' research leads this writer to add: teacher morale, lunchroom garbage counts, toilet usage (analyzed via line-standing theory), essay analyses, attendance records (absences by day of week, weather, etc.), disciplinary actions (and barometric pressure), graffiti, content analyses, appointment calendars, administration of in-basket problems, public library withdrawal rates near schools, newspaper reports, memo and phone counts, budget analyses of many kinds, child wiggling (and quality of lighting), pictures in school annuals, school participation information (with size of school), requests for transfers by teachers, teacher turnover, sick leave records, parent commendations and condemnations, and opinions of janitors. An ultimate criterion variable of major interest is, of course, votes on school bond issues and tax rates.

Every record related to education should be examined for possible use in building better educational theory and practice. These variables should be related and compared to many other variables. In the process it may be possible to stop some record-keeping, greatly improve the use of other records, and increase the understanding of sources of error of many of the rest. To learn how these variables were measured, studies about them in the education literature can be found and examined to see how the researchers quantified them.

Teacher-rating literature summaries and methods have been reported in a book by Ryans (1960) and in a chapter in the *Handbook of Research on Teaching* by Remmers (1963). Flanders' book (1970), *Analyzing Teaching Behavior;* Medley and Mitzel's chapter (also in the *Handbook of Research on Teaching),* and Amidon and Hough's (1967) book, *Interaction Analysis: Theory, Research, and Application,* are excellent sources of rating scales and methods of observation dealing with teachers and classroom behavior. For observations of behavior generally (but with an educational flavor), Whitehall's (1960) chapter in the journal *Review of Educational Research,* "Research Tools: Observing and Recording Behavior"; Simon's and Boyer's book (1970) *Mirrors for Behavior II;* and Boyd's and DeVault's chapter (1966) in the *Review of Educational Research* are all quite useful. Buros' *Mental Measurements*

Yearbook and his book *Tests in Print, Volume 2* (1974) give lists of measuring devices for almost every test known, and the first-listed volume gives excellent reviews as well. Other good source books of measurement devices are Bonjean, Hill, and McLemore's *Sociological Measurement; Inventory of Scales and Indices* (1967); Shaw's and Wright's *Scales for the Measurement of Attitudes* (1967), and Wylie's *The Self-Concept* (1961).

The student and researcher in these areas soon learns to buy books that are good sources of measurement, to subscribe to journals which report research using classroom and educational variables (such as the *Journal of Educational Measurement*), and to keep card files and lists. He avoids constructing a new instrument if possible because of the extensive effort involved in developing reliable and valid measuring devices. Professionals in education should be doubly wary of research involving test construction. They should take at least one course in the theory and practice of measurement and realize that the construction of a good, new test, scale, questionnaire, or interview format is often as much work as doing the research project, and perhaps more. In fact, the development of a good, new measurement device is a research project in itself.

As a concluding note on measurement, the tale might be told of the art museum director who used attendance counts in his pleas for funds from philanthropic foundations. One year the inevitable chart showing gains in yearly attendance was conspicuous by its absence, and a foundation trustee asked about it. It emerged that the attendance had dropped considerably because the city had built a comfort station in the park across the street! The moral of this story is that all measurement is comparative. No measurement is absolute. Meaningful and useful measurement cannot occur in isolation. An implicit measurement comparison exists even when explicit measurement comparison does not.

SUMMARY

In this chapter some basic principles of measurement were presented, together with some thinking about objectivity, multiple operational definitions, and quantification of variables. Four levels of measurement, kinds of measurements available in educational records, and sources of other tests and measurement procedures of interest to educators were described. Standard scores, percentiles, and successive category scales were discussed, and longer presentations made on the reliability and validity of measurements—two fundamental concepts. Some threats to internal and external research design validity as the result of measurement were discussed, as were sources of reliable and valid measurement procedures in the educational literature.

STUDY AND DISCUSSION PROBLEMS

1. What are four major sources of problems of research design interpretation related to measurement? Describe each one.
2. Tell what reliability is.
3. Tell what validity is.
4. How can the reliability of a measurement device be increased?
5. Why are standard scores better than percentile scores in education?
6. Does reliability presuppose validity?
7. Does validity presuppose reliability?
8. Find and describe how several variables were quantified in an article in the educational literature.
9. List several ways of assessing educational objectives via measurement procedures.
10. Operationally define several of the educational objectives of a given school system.
11. What is a variable?
12. List several educational research variables and indicate how they could be quantified.
13. What are the four levels of measurement in science? Given an example of each in education.
14. Suggest a number of available measurements useful in educational research other than test scores.
15. What is the relationship between educational measurement and the philosophy of education of a school system?
16. Find the Buros *Mental Measurement Yearbook* and report what it says about a particular test.
17. List three kinds of standard scores and show the relationships among them.
18. What is objectivity? What is its relationship to reliability?
19. List three types of reliability and indicate how each could be obtained.
20. What is an operational definition? Give three operational definitions of some variables.
21. What is the upper limit that a correlation between two variables can have in relationship to the reliabilities of the two variables?
22. What are four types of validity? How is each developed or used?
23. Describe how the multitrait-multimethod procedure is used to develop construct validity.
24. What is the scientific principle of parsimony?

REFERENCES

Amidon, E.J., and Hough, J.B. *Interaction analysis: Theory, reserach, and application*. Reading, Mass.: Addison-Wesley, 1967.

Bloom, B.S. *Taxonomy of educational objectives*. New York: Longmans, Green, 1956.

Bonjean, C.M., Hill, R.J., and McLemore, S.D. *Sociological measurement*. San Francisco: Chandler, 1967.

Boyd, R.D., and DeVault, M.V. The observation and recording of behavior. *Review of Educational Research*, 1966, *36*, 529–551.

Bracht, G.H., and Glass, G.V. The external validity of experiments. *American Educational Research Journal*, 1968, *5*, 437–474.

Buros, O.K. (Ed.) *Seventh mental measurements yearbook*. Highland Park, N.J.: Gryphon Press, 1972.

Buros, O.K. (Ed.) *Tests in print, Volume 2*. Highland Park, N.J.: Gryphon Press, 1974.

Campbell, D.T. Factors relevant to the validity of experiments in social settings. *Psychological Bulletin*, 1957, *54*, 297–312.

Campbell, D.T., and Fiske, D.W. Convergent and discriminant validity by the multitrait-multimethod matrix. *Psychological Bulletin*, 1959, *65*, 81–105.

Campbell, D.T., and Stanley, J.C. Experimental and quasi-experimental designs for research on teaching. In N.L. Gage (Ed.), *Handbook of research on teaching*. Chicago: Rand McNally, 1963, 171–246.

Cook, D.L. *The impact of the Hawthorne effect in experimental designs in educational research*. Columbus, Ohio: Ohio State University, 1967.

Cronbach, L.J. Test Validation. In R.L. Thorndike (Ed.), *Educational measurement*. Washington: American Council on Education, 1971, 443–507.

Downie, N.M. *Fundamentals of measurement*. New York: Oxford University Press, 1958.

Elementary and Secondary Education Act of 1965, Title 1, Part D, Section 141 (a) (6).

Flanders, N.A. *Analyzing teaching behavior*. Reading, Mass.: Addison-Wesley, 1970.

Kerlinger, F.N. *Foundations of behavioral research*. New York: Holt, Rinehart, and Winston, 1964.

Kerlinger, F.N. *Foundations of behavioral research* (2nd ed.). New York: Holt, Rinehart, and Winston, 1973.

Krathwohl, D.R., Bloom, B.S., and Masia, B. *Taxonomy of educational objectives. Handbook II. The affective domain*. New York: McKay, 1964.

Lohnes, P.R., and Marshall, T.O. Redundancy in student records. *American Educational Research Journal*, 1965, *2*, 19–23.

Medley, D.M., and Mitzel, H.E. Measuring classroom behavior by systematic observation. In N.L. Gage (Ed.), *Handbook of research on teaching*. Chicago: Rand McNally, 1963, 247–328.

Nunnally, J.C. *Psychometric theory*. New York: McGraw-Hill, 1967.

Remmers, H.H. Rating methods in research on teaching. In N.L. Gage (Ed.), *Handbook of research on teaching*. Chicago: Rand McNally, 1963, 329–378.

Remmers, H.H., Gage, N.L., and Rummel, J.F. *A practical introduction to measurement and evaluation* (2nd ed.). New York: Harper & Row, 1965.

Ryans, D.G. *Characteristics of teachers.* Washington: American Council of Education, 1960.

Shaw, M.E., and Wright, J.M. *Scales for the measurement of attitudes.* New York: McGraw-Hill, 1967.

Simon, A., and Boyer, E.G. *Mirrors for behavior II.* Philadelphia: Research for Better Schools, 1970.

Stanley, J.C. Reliability. In R.L. Thorndike (Ed.), *Educational measurement.* Washington: American Council on Education, 1971, 356–442.

Thorndike, R.L. (Ed.) *Educational measurement* (2nd ed.). Washington: American Council on Education, 1971.

Thorndike, R.L., and Hagen, E. *Measurement and evaluation in psychology and education* (3rd ed.). New York: Wiley, 1969.

Webb, E.J., Campbell, D.T., Schwartz, R.D., and Sechrest, L. *Unobtrusive measures: Nonreactive research in the social sciences.* Chicago: Rand McNally, 1966.

Welch, W.W., and Walberg, H.J. Pretest and sensitization effects in curriculum evaluation. *American Educational Research Journal,* 1970, *7,* 605–614.

Whitehall, J. Research tools: Observing and recording behavior. *Review of Educational Research,* 1960, *30,* 496–512.

Wylie, Ruth C. *The self-concept.* Lincoln: University of Nebraska Press, 1961.

Quasi-Experiments

Chapter 5

While it is generally preferable from a researcher's viewpoint to have randomized groups and groups randomly assigned to conditions such as those in the football cleat study in Chapter 2, sometimes it is not possible to do so, even in educational situations where relatively great flexibility exists. There are also some types of research problems, of course, that do not require experimentation to answer the questions asked.

When the conditions cannot be met for a true experiment, such as random assignment of students to groups and groups to experimental methods or conditions, quasi-experiments are used for experimental research and evaluation in education. In a quasi-experiment, one or more, even all, of the randomization procedures are missing, yet there are elements of differences or change in instruction or educational conditions which can be examined to determine their effects. A quasi-experiment, though, is not based purely on the description of one group that occurs at a given point in time. Rather, it attempts to assess the effects of changes over time via comparisons among various treatments. In the better quasi-experiments, there will be an untreated control group or a group which is given typical instructions or conditions. In the best quasi-experiments, these control (or typical condition) groups and the various experimental treatment groups will not be distinguishable from randomized groups.

110

The results of quasi-experiments, because of the lack of complete randomization of subjects to groups and treatment conditions to groups, generally are more difficult to interpret than in true experiments. Problems of measurement and statistical analysis interpretations arise more frequently in quasi-experiments that are of little concern in true experiments. Thus, the concepts in Chapter 2 portraying true experiments could be presented before Chapters 3 and 4 on statistics and measurement. Chapters 3 and 4, however, were necessary before this chapter on quasi-experiments could be read with understanding. The special problems of measurement in the behavioral sciences and education in quasi-experiments, which add to the difficulty of interpreting the effects of the treatments, are further threats to the internal and external validity of research which uses quasi-experimental designs.

While only a small portion of all research and evaluation in education uses true experimental design, not all studies are quasi-experimental either. All quasi-experimental designs must meet three requirements: (a) there must be a nontreatment as well as a treatment group; (b) there must be pretreatment and post-treatment measures; and (c) there must be a statement of the differences between the treatment and nontreatment groups, even if there is *no treatment* effect (Kenny, 1975).

The true experimental conditions of randomized groups are preferable, but ethics and naturally occurring forces sometimes prevent full randomization. Can a school ethically withhold offering drivers' education courses where seemingly life-sparing and injury-prevention techniques are taught? Can a school system stand up to the social and political power sources in its community and not allow certain children to be taught to read via a new teaching alphabet or learn under a Montessori system when these children may be the youngsters from some of the more vocal and socially active parents in the community? Stanley (1966, pp. 79 and 80) has said, "nature, the great experimenter, abhors randomness." Many factors impinging on educational systems are seemingly adverse to being randomized even though in many ways education is an area in which perhaps more randomized, true experiments can be done than in many of the other social and behavioral settings.

Information and the interpretation of the results of a study still depend on the quality of the comparisons in an experiment. For best quality information it is desirable to have randomized experiments, yet reasonably accurate information is better than none at all. Thus, a quasi-experiment is better than no experiment at all. In a quasi-experiment the experimenter lacks complete control over the study but does have some control. There will be imperfections, as compared to a true experiment; nevertheless, quasi-experiments are advocated where better experiments are not feasible. It should be noted that a true experiment does not mean a perfect, crucial, or definitive experiment in terms of the subject matter with which it deals. It is simply the best experimental method of gaining knowledge.

A QUASI-EXPERIMENTAL READING STUDY

A quasi-experimental situation occurred in the school system of a county not far from a university where a senior honors student was enrolled in a course in educational research methods. As part of her educational experience, she also worked as a research trainee with a faculty member. She noticed in the newspapers in the spring that, beginning in the fall, the school system would have two classes in the fourth grade that would be segregated by sex, one class totally of boys and the other only girls. The school system was proud of its innovative stance and reported widely the proposed change. The young lady graduated that spring and continued for her master's degree. She wanted to take advantage of the naturally forming experiment in the school system for her master's thesis. She contacted the school system's administration and, after the usual precautionary inquiries as to her purpose, methods, and possible interference with classroom activity, her proposal to study the effectiveness of the changes in the class composition on reading and self-concept was accepted.

The school system was not large and the only available classes of any comparability were two more nonsegregated, typical classes in another grade school in the community. All the classes were self-contained and the schools had good libraries and remedial reading programs. The two teachers in the experimental fourth grades had been the instigators of the innovation and had asked permission to segregate their classes. This permission was granted by the school authorities and ultimately by the school board. The two classes used as controls were chosen by the school superintendent as being equivalent to the segregated classes in intelligence, socioeconomic background, and achievement, certainly the variables most highly correlated with reading achievement. The classes were not high or low ability classes. The segregated classes had thirty-four boys in one class and thirty-five girls in the other class. In the mixed classes, there were twenty-six students in one class and twenty-seven in the other.

One of the most important factors in any educational study is the teachers. All four teachers were highly recommended by the superintendent (which probably is why the two teachers were allowed to change such publicly visible procedures in the first place). Three teachers then had master's degrees and the fourth her bachelor's. All were women with at least nine years of teaching experience, the mean experience being sixteen years. Questionnaires completed by the teachers before the study started indicated that all used the same basal reading series, followed the teacher's manual accompanying it, and grouped the children for reading instruction according to ability and past achievement.

Thus it seemed as if many of the considerations about the groups of importance to a study of reading were reasonably similar in the four classes. Further, the researcher would collect data on the students at the beginning of school to check in more detail on the seeming equality of the groups so vital to the good comparisons needed for informative research.

Intelligence test scores and ages in months were available from the school files for the segregated and nonsegregated boys and girls, and their averages were as found in Table 5-1.

Statistical analyses (via standard computer programs) revealed no significant differences among the groups. Thus it could be seen that the classes were rather similar and at minimum had no differences initially that were statistically significant. Pretests of reading and self-concept were given in September, since the children had not been randomly assigned to classes, and further assurance of similarity on the variables of major interest was needed. The pretesting was done in an educational context, the study would last for more than one week, and at least one test was of educational achievement. Thus there was no major concern that the results of the study would be invalidated by a threat to internal or external research design validity from the effect of testing. The researcher had queried the professor and searched the sources of

TABLE 5-1   Intelligence Test Scores and Ages for the Groups in the Sex-segregated Study

	Boys		Girls		Overall	
	IQ	Age (Months)	IQ	Age (Months)	IQ	Age (Months)
Segregated	106	123.8	104	124.6	105	124.2
Nonsegregated	104	125.3	108	124.0	106	124.6
Overall	105	124.5	106	124.3		

Groups =?, Yes	Treatments = or ≠?	Criteria = and ≠
Self Concept? Yes	Treatments	Self Concept, =
Teachers equal? Yes	n_{1_A} = 34 boys	Reading, =
IQ's equal? Yes	n_{1_B} = 35 girls	Behavior Problems, ≠
Chronological age? Yes	n_{2_C} = 26 mixed	Classroom Verbality, ≠
Reading? Yes	n_{2_D} = 27 mixed students	Esprit de Corps, ≠

FIGURE 5-1   The Logical Structure and Results of the Sheppard Sex-Segregation Study

tests to find the two that she selected. She assured herself that they were both reliable and valid from sources in the educational literature and from the test manuals. The reading test was the Rand-Bulow-Hoyt, and the Self-Concept Test was the Piers-Harris.

The analyses of the criteria variables were by the two treatment variables class type and sex. The reading criteria variables used as post-test scores were vocabulary, information, relationships, appreciation, literal comprehension, creative comprehension, and general comprehension. The criterion scores for self-concept were also analyzed. The analysis took into account the pretest/post-test nature of the data and again was done via computer and standard analytical programs. Intercorrelations of all the eight reading subtest scores and the self-concept scores were also computed in a single computer run with a standard program. Some 71 statistical null hypotheses of no differences were tested with the data. The results (Sheppard, 1972) of the analyses indicated no set of major significant differences on the sex-segregated group on the reading and self-concept measures. There were some significant interactions between sex and class type on a few of the pre- and post-test measures of reading, but these may have been artifacts of the pretesting procedures for one group of boys. (See Figure 5-1.)

The researcher was able to find some half-dozen other studies with data in areas corresponding to hers. She related her findings to theirs by indicating the similarities and differences among the findings. She also noted problems of interpretation of the data in her study: the lack of randomization as such, the slightly unequal class sizes, the rural versus small-town backgrounds of the students in the experimental and control groups, respectively, and the small number of teachers and their high motivation. Although not part of the design or theoretical foundation of the study, fortuitous statements by both teachers about their segregated classes were interesting. They both indicated they had more behavior problems than in previous years. Neither of the teachers in the regular classes felt there were other differences from past years. The classroom observations by the researcher and responses by the parents of the sex-segregated classrooms indicated that the quasi-experiment was successful. The segregated classroom students were more verbal and displayed more *esprit de corps*. A number of suggestions were made which would enrich future studies made in this interesting and important area of elementary education.

Obviously the professional world of education did not wait with bated breath for the findings of this study, and the pure researchers (and even not so pure ones) can find numerous reasons why the results should not be accepted fully and immediately implemented. Yet the study does represent the usefulness of a quasi-experimental design in investigating practical educational problems in the public schools. There is much speculation in the professional education literature about sex differences and sex-segregated classes. There are a few studies with solid data at various grades with several types of criteria variables. This research by Sheppard adds to those studies and suggests further interesting cues about the behavior of students in classes. Further, the school system has a much better basis for administrative decisions about sex-segregated classes. Finally, the student-researcher, who after graduating began her own teaching career in the public schools, will be a far more knowledgeable professional as she reads the educational literature, listens to "experts," and builds her own teaching strategies and methods. She may even assist her school system in evaluating innovative programs systematically with the use of meaningful research designs and data.

She demonstrated again that professional (and even preprofessional) educators with an understanding of research design and with expert consultant help can do good research on worthwhile educational problems of some scope. Further, they collect major amounts of reliable and valid data beneficial in moving educational problems generally toward resolution. They can analyze and interpret their data without major effort. The results of these analyses are valuable locally in decision-making by administrators and are of some worth to the broader research effort nationally and internationally. Certainly research of this type is more valuable than the weakly substantiated writings in many educational magazines and books that merely speculate and conjecture about the issues.

THREATS TO RESEARCH DESIGN VALIDITY

There are at least seven threats to valid inferences about cause-and-effect relationships in research generally and in the sex-segregated reading research study in particular. The presentation of these and other threats will be useful in understanding interpretations of modern research designs. The internal validity threat of *Testing* has already been discussed. *Instrumentation* is not a threat in the reading study since all the major tests used were standardized measures with objective scoring procedures. Also there were no observers collecting data who would tire, adapt, learn, know which group was experimental or which was control, or have any of the other problems associated with the use of observers. Observers are valuable and necessary to record data vital to understanding educational processes but care must be taken in their use.

Regression-toward-the-mean effects are not plausible alternative explanations of observed effects of the treatments in the reading study either. The classes chosen were about at the average for the school system. More importantly, no classes or students were selected on the basis of test scores, nor were any considered and then not used because their scores or observations were too high or too low. All students in all four classes were used as subjects unless they moved out of the school district or were ill for long periods of time during the pre- or post-testing. (This loss ran to about 20 percent of the classes.) The children who had extended illnesses or whose parents moved probably were not different on the average from the rest of their classmates; therefore the remaining students were also about at the average, and there can be no Regression-toward-the-mean effects. (They were already at the mean.)

Mortality. This reduction of the groups in the classes being observed is a *Mortality* threat to the validity of the interpretations of cause-and-effect relationships in a quasi-experimental design. If two groups were equivalent at some prior time, and there was a dropping out or changing of individual members of the groups over a period of time, the two groups could be quite different at the time of observation of the criteria as the result of the changes in group membership alone. Under these circumstances, an interpretation that changes were the result of an educational treatment or condition could be quite erroneous and the research design interpretation invalid.

A typical example of this threat of Mortality to research design validity is the comparison of the attitudes of freshmen and seniors in college. A college administration, upon determining distinct attitudinal differences in a graduating class after four years in college, might proclaim that the curriculum and learning environment are the causes of the apparent difference. These factors may very well account for the change. However, students who cannot tolerate an indoctrination that passes for education at a particular college leave to go elsewhere. The residual students stay, and their attitudes, similar to those assessed during the senior year, could be exactly the same as they were when they were freshmen. Yet by the differential processes of Mortality, the senior class attitudes seem quite different from their freshman class attitudes four years ago.

Occasionally the experimental treatment itself on a group of children, such as influencing parents' decisions to move, will cause a subject Mortality. In innovative special education programs that may promise some hope for handicapped children, parents of the children in the experimental group may make sacrifices and not leave the city or a school district in order to keep their child in the new treatment. Parents may also move into a city or a school district that has developed a special program. This, too, is a type of differential "Mortality."

History.   Another threat to the internal validity of cause-and-effect interpretations between experimental treatments and criteria variables in quasi-experiments is *History*. The threat of History is the intervention into the study, or a change in the external conditions surrounding a study, such that another extra-experimental stimulus occurs in addition to the experimental treatment variable. A part of this threat can be controlled by isolating the subjects from these variables. This is not always possible and to an extent requires some luck to avoid. A curriculum study using materials to reduce tensions in race relationships may be difficult to evaluate systematically if a racial incident occurs in the school or community between the set of pretest observations and the post-test observations. In addition, all effects of seasonal (winter absences vs. spring) or institutional event schedules (winning athletic teams, major faculty shifts) are classified as threats to History. The researcher in the sex-segregated reading study found no such events occurring during the course of the year for her research.

Maturation.   All of the effects on the research which occur systematically with the passage of time, such as maturing, developing, getting older, hungry, or more tired, rather independently from specific external causes, are called *Maturation*. They are primarily biological but can be psychological in nature. Remedial education of all types is particularly prone to misinterpretation of the relationship between remission and remedial treatments. Children do mature, develop psychologically, and have more neurological synapses connect as they develop. At the start of the sex-segregated reading study, both groups of children were the same average age. Thus Maturation does not seem a viable alternative hypothesis to explain the results of the research. However, misinterpretation of Maturation effects has caused rather major misdirections of effort in school remedial programs.

Selection.   Generally cited as the seventh threat to internal validity is *Selection*, and Selection could be a problem in the interpretation of the sex-segregated reading study. The threat of Selection is concerned with initial differences among the experimental and control groups in a quasi-experiment. Where groups are used that already exist (intact groups), there may be differences among them. Children who watch television over forty hours a week are different from children who do not, in more ways than in their TV viewing habits. These differences probably existed before the children even started to watch TV for that number of hours. These differences would still exist even if TV had not been invented, and it is a major error to ascribe these differences solely as effects of TV viewing. People who go to college are different from those who do not, and when these differences are still found after the young men and women graduate from college, there is no reason to attribute the differences to the effects of the educational treatment (four years of college) alone. To do so is to have more than the research invalidity threat of Selection questioned; it is to have it occur.

Superintendents in high socioeconomic school districts may take pride in the number of National Merit Scholars their schools produce, but they are like Albert the alligator in the cartoon strip ''Pogo'' who while running for President for his second term, declared that there had been lots of rain during his first term of office. Pogo asked Albert if he was going to take credit for the rain. Alligator indignantly replied that it had happened during his administration, hadn't it? The error of Selection was committed here also.

In the sex-segregated reading study, the classes were formed before the advent of the researcher. Probably there was no way in which she could convince the superintendent, the school board, the parents (or the children) that, if they really wanted to know whether sex segregation made a difference in reading achievement or not, the best way was to randomize children to classes (within sex groups). Thus, despite her efforts to demonstrate equality of the classes at the start of the study, she could never be sure that it was accomplished. In fact, as the readers may recall, the sex-segregated groups were mainly from rural backgrounds while the regular classes were from a small town. Did this difference in backgrounds confound (the nontechnical word is confuse) the experimental treatments? It is not believed to be of major importance, but it does make the reader of the research report think. It is possible but probably not plausible. Only further replications of this study in other areas will give us the evidence to answer the question. The threat of validity of Selection is one of the more common errors in commonsense thinking about cause-and-effect relationships.

There have been seven threats to internal validity presented: History, Maturation, Testing, Instrumentation, Regression, Selection, and Mortality. These are the seven threats to internal validity most often presented (Campbell and Stanley, 1963) and undoubtedly cover the major scope of the problems involved in interpreting and determining cause-and-effect relationships. These relationships are fundamental to the thinking and decisions made by professionals in education about which curricula and programs to use, remedial treatments to give, and changes in methods of instruction, selection, and guidance. The evidence for the efficacy of these decisions and decisions generally in the behavioral and social sciences lie mostly in quasi-experiments or research of a type rather closely related to quasi-experiments. These seven threats to the validity interpretation of the cause and effect relationships, when well understood, are invaluable aids to careful thinking and decision-making by professionals.

There are two other threats to internal validity. One of these is a group of several unique effects, *Interactions* of one threat with another, such as Selection and Maturation, Testing and the treatments presented, and so forth. There is also one more threat to internal validity presented by Campbell (1969), *Instability*.

Instability. Another threat that is concerned with unreliability of measurements, fluctuations in samplings, and the inequality of "equivalent" measures is Instability. Campbell notes that this is the only threat to which statistical tests are relevant! These are the Type I and Type II errors in statistical anlalyses (See Chapter 3). In these errors of statistical interpretation, by chance alone, rare events do sometimes happen and are declared statistically significant. In some other statistical analyses there is not enough power (in terms of number of observations, etc.) to detect differences which may exist. If the internal consistency reliability of a criterion measure is low, or if the instability of a measure from time to time is rather great, these also will lead to errors of interpretation of cause-and-effect relationships. These types of occurrences fall within the research design internal validity problem of Instability.

External Validity.   If any of the threats to internal validity are present so that it is impossible to determine the nature of the relationship between the experimental treatment and the criteria variables, then obviously no general cause-and-effect statements about the treatments, groups, and curriculum can be made. However, to attempt to generalize to other groups of students, other similar curricula, and other measures is essentially to consider the *external validity* of a study. Logically, in a strict sense, these generalizations, which are a theory of social behavior, are impossible. Practically, however, generalizations are a necessity. Nevertheless, if there is no internal validity of a quasi-experiment, there simply can be no external validity. Conversely, as was suggested, external validity can never be fully demonstrated.

There are six threats to external validity now listed by Campbell (1969), two more than the list in Campbell and Stanley (1963). Of these, *Reactive Arrangements* has been described in the chapter on measurement, where the concern was the effect of special testing and observers on the group being studied. The effect of the knowledge by the group that they were in an experiment and being given special attention, the Hawthorne effect, also was discussed briefly in that chapter. The external validity problem of Reactive Arrangements is that other children and other teachers in other classes may not react in the same way when there is no experiment being conducted, as the research students and teachers reacted.

In the sex-segregated reading study, two of the teachers (those teaching the experimental classes) were intimately involved in instigating the experimental arrangements. The principal and the superintendent had indicated to the school board and to the public that they did not feel the changes would be detrimental to the children. They were committed to the successful outcome of the study. However, as was indicated in the prior discussion of Reactivity in educational studies, it seems to make little difference if most of the activities are done in the usual educational settings and over an extended period of time. In this reading study in fact, if there was Reactivity, the results would be predicted to increase the reading ability of the experimental group. This was not the case. Thus it would appear that the extensive review of the literature and the research by Cook (1967) concluding that the Hawthorne effects in education do not contaminate research to the extent claimed, is supported again by these results.

Interaction of Testing and Treatment. The external validity threat of *Interaction of Testing and Treatment* was also discussed in the chapter on measurement. This interaction seems not generally applicable to educational research where school-like tests are used and treatments extend over a week. In the reading study, there was no way to test this external validity threat directly but, with the exception of the self-concept test, the research would seem to meet all the concerns expressed about the external validity threat of Interaction of Testing and Treatment.

Interaction of Selection and Treatment. The third external validity threat is the *Interaction of Selection and Treatment.* This threat concerns an unrepresentative responsiveness of an experimental group because the group is unique in some way. Research done in a university laboratory school, where enrollment is a sought-after privilege and a significant proportion of the children are from faculty families, has results suggested as being not generalizable. This reading research was not done in a school that was influenced unduly by a university; however, it was done in only two elementary schools in one school system. Thus there may have been something unusual about the students, although this seems unlikely. However, the usual precautions of generalizing to other types of pupils are reasonable. To accept the results of one small study as typical of students everywhere, including those in central cities, in non-English-speaking groups, etc., is foolish. On the other hand, if no research, such as this reasonably valid reading study, is done by professional educators in schools with other kinds of students, then the professionals ethically have little choice but to make decisions on the basis of what valid data and results are available. Data and results of some validity are better than no data. The hope is, of course, that educational professionals will be more involved in in-school research and that dozens of internally valid sex-segregated class studies would be done in many types of schools. The core of the theory resulting from such work would establish the external validity of the educational method.

Multiple-treatment Interference. A fourth threat to external validity is *Multiple-treatment Interference.* This threat is seen when a number of simultaneous or successive experimental conditions are presented and result in interfering with each other. Further, the several treatments may make the subjects atypical responders; the effects of earlier conditions and treatments stay with the students and are only slowly forgotten.

Irrelevant Responses of Measures and Irrelevant Replicability of Treatments.   The last two threats to external validity listed by Campbell are *Irrelevant Responses of Measures and Irrelevant Replicability of Treatments.* For Irrelevant Response of Measures, Campbell (1969, p. 411) indicates that, "All measures are complex, and all include irrelevant components that may produce apparent effects." An observation or test may measure more than one dimension of behavior at a time. A group intelligence test requires the ability to read; if a child has difficulty reading (test dimension one), he will not score well on a group test of intelligence (test dimension two). Yet both are measured simultaneously by the test. Any educational treatment that improves the ability of a low-scoring child to read may help the child score better on the intelligence test, and this improvement might be interpreted as a gain in intelligence. (After all, the test is labeled "Intelligence Test.")

This threat to external validity can be alleviated somewhat by determining that the students have the basic skills to respond to a test and that the internal consistency index of reliability of a measure is high. These precautions should be assurance that only one dimension of human behavior is being measured by the test. The best defense against this threat is the use of several types of measures to assess a criterion dimension.

Irrelevant Replicability of Treatment.   This threat to external validity is essentially the same concern as expressed above, except instead of being applied to criteria measures, it is applied to treatments. As Campbell (1971, p. 412) says, "Treatments are complex, and replications of them may fail to include those components actually responsible for the effects." Treatments and experimental conditions also need to be considered in the attempts to generalize to other treatments and conditions "such as these," just as there are concerns about generalizing to other groups of students "such as these" in a research study.

Again, repetition and implementation of the treatments and conditions by professionals in their own schools is important. They need to attempt both to duplicate exactly the experimental treatments and conditions and to vary them as necessary to adapt to local conditions. These repetitions of the studies will yield a core of results and theory about the educational treatments and conditions from which other professionals can make decisions.

OTHER TYPES OF QUASI-EXPERIMENTS

Not all research in schools can make use of simultaneous groups of students. These are quasi-experiments which include groups that can be shown to be equated approximately, even though they are not available at the same time.

Regression-Discontinuity. For this quasi-experimental research design, for example, remedial care facilities, available openings into an educational curriculum or system, amount of scholarship, student aid, or Title I money, or some other facility or program is insufficient to accommodate all of the eligible students. This is a common occurrence in education. There are few administrators who will say that their funds and facilities are sufficient to meet all of the legitimate demands on them. All that is needed for this research design is to have a strict cut-off point on only one variable (or possibly a pooled variable developed from several variables) above which, or below which, the award, treatment, condition, or entry for the student is made. A follow-up study is done, using as measures of success the criteria variables for the two groups established above and below the cut-off point (one receiving the award or treatment and one not). If indeed there has been an effect, there will be a break (a discontinuity) on a plotting of later accomplishments of the two groups. This plotting of both groups should be against the score which was the basis for the award treatment originally being granted (see Figure 5-2). If there is no such break, it can be interpreted that the award or condition was of no particular value in enhancing scores on the criterion.

This sort of analysis is needed because if one picks scholarship or award winners on a variable (i.e., intelligence) which is known to produce later high scores on criteria (i.e., income) variables, then picking persons with high scores on the predictors for awards (i.e., intelligence) produces persons who indeed will be high on the criteria (i.e., income)—whether or not they were given the award. The regression-discontinuity design aids in sorting out the partially con- founded effect of score on which award was based from the particular effect of the award itself.

Another design, that is valuable sometimes in instances such as the above, is simpler to analyze and interpret. If there is a shortage of treatment facilities, honors programs, or awards of Title I money, it may be possible to establish a tentative cut-off point for admittance or presentation of the award and then establish a zone above and below this point such that an ambivalency area of acceptance-nonacceptance is created. This zone must be large enough so the group included in it is sufficient for research purposes. The tentatively accepted group indi- viduals can then be randomly assigned to either the accept or nonaccept group for exposure to the condition or award of the treatment. The

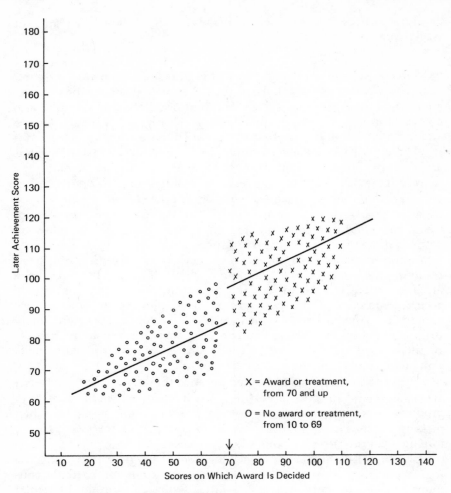

FIGURE 5-2   Regression-Discontinuity Analysis

standard randomized group interpretations can then be made about cause-and-effect relationships of the treatments or the criteria.

A problem of interpretation may come in external validity. Is it reasonable to generalize from this borderline accepted group to groups above and below it? This question is best answered by further research with those groups after the initial studies are completed.

Interrupted Time Series. When there are no readily available, comparable groups, the *Interrupted Time Series* design can be used. The best comparison available is to study the prior classes or groups that

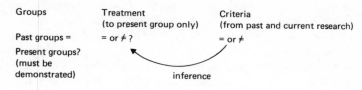

Groups   Treatment   Criteria
(to present group only) (from past and current research)

Past groups =   = or ≠ ?   = or ≠
Present groups?
(must be
demonstrated)   inference

FIGURE 5-3   Interrupted Time Series Design Logic

appear to be like this one. If a school district is rather stable in its socioeconomic level and other social psychological characteristics, and the criteria data to be used in the current year are available for the prior year's groups, then current year/prior year comparisons may be made. Sometimes there are also data available in the schools' records to check on the equivalency of the prior year/current year groups. Are the mothers' years of education and fathers' occupational levels about the same? Are the intelligence quotients, chronological ages, and percent of boys and girls about the same? These variables can be tested for equivalency, as was done in the sex-segregated reading study. The researcher used intelligence scores and pretest reading scores, which happened to be available in the same year, to test the equivalency of her two groups. However, there are added problems in interpreting an Interrupted Time Series design over the equivalent groups in the same year. All the data desirable to check equivalency may not be available for the prior-year group. The internal threats to validity of History and perhaps Instrumentation may make conclusions difficult to draw. The external validity of the Interrupted Time Series is also somewhat more open to question than is the simultaneous equivalent (though nonrandomized) groups design.

Control Series. The last design to be discussed will be the *Control Series* design. The most common of these is the nonequivalent control group design. Here, two or more intact, naturally formed groups are available for research after an educational treatment or condition already has been imposed on one group. The researcher may attempt to establish the equivalency of the groups but fails. What to do? The problem is difficult because the quality of the information gained is dependent on the quality of the comparison. The basic logic of research design is recalled: With equal groups, unequal criterion groups are produced only by unequal treatments. However, with unequal groups, both equal or unequal treatments generally produce unequal groups. Thus inferences about the experimental treatments' equality or inequality with a standard treatment are difficult to make.

One possible method does exist. That method is to determine, after the treatments, whether the initially unequal groups are now more unequal or less unequal than when the groups started. In the physical sciences, and often the biological sciences, this is not too difficult. In the behavioral and social sciences, this determination of greater or lesser inequality can be a problem. The major concern is in the area of measurement. If one of two groups is not the same as the other, then both cannot be at the average of some one larger group. Thus there may be Regression-toward-the-Mean effects. These likely will be larger or smaller for one group than the other on a later measurement, *even if no treatment or condition intervened between the pretest measurements and the post-treatment measurements!* The inequality of the groups before and after measurement can increase or decrease even *without* experimental intervention. A major quandary exists.

However, if the location of the groups above or below the larger normative group is known, at least the direction of the Regression-toward-the-Mean effects can be ascertained. If the treatment or condition moves the groups in directions opposite to these Regression effects (and overcomes them), then the effectiveness of the treatments is established. If the Regression effects confound (add to) the theoretical effects of the treatments, little can be learned. (Gain scores and differences between pretest scores and post-test scores on intact groups may suffer from the same difficulty and, in addition, have a few more problems.)

Matching of individuals from unequal groups on the basis of scores that are not close to perfect reliability almost always will get the novice researcher into more trouble than it avoids. Unless the researcher can randomize the subjects into experimental and control

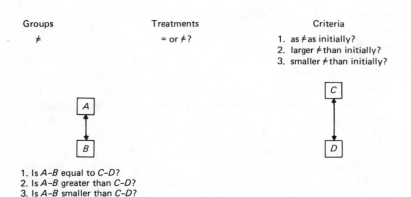

Groups   Treatments   Criteria

$\neq$ = or $\neq$?   1. as $\neq$ as initially?
                                       2. larger $\neq$ than initially?
                                       3. smaller $\neq$ than initially?

1. Is *A–B* equal to *C–D*?
2. Is *A–B* greater than *C–D*?
3. Is *A–B* smaller than *C–D*?

FIGURE 5-4   Control Series Design Logic

groups from each pair after the matching, the researcher can expect to mislead himself and his colleagues and is likely to be the target of some sharp criticism. Matching from intact, unequal groups has been known to be a methodological error since the early 1940s, yet the practice is only slowly dying, perhaps because it is still advocated in some beginning educational research texts.

Analysis of Covariance. One method long advocated, which recently has come under closer scrutiny and is now known to cause problems of interpretation, is *analysis of covariance.* Analysis of covariance is an extension of analysis of variance. The difference is that the criterion variable (the one upon which the analysis is made) is adjusted mathematically by means of a variable (intervally measured) which reflects the initial differences in the groups. (There are other purposes for which analysis of covariance is used, but these are not of concern here.) This covariate variable (a covariable) must correlate with the criterion variable for covariance to be effective. Many analyses of covariance are done and reported in the educational literature to adjust (among other purposes) for initially unequal groups. The logic of covariance approximates this statement: If the unequal groups were adjusted, via the variables which reflect the inequality, so that the groups were equal, what would the comparison of the groups on the criterion variable show now, equal or unequal? (Note the use of the subjunctive mood and the conditional tense to make this statement.)

A problem is that analyses of covariance generally underadjust, as used now throughout the behavioral and social sciences. Analysis of

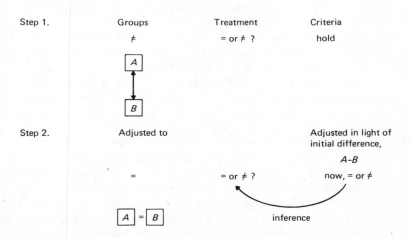

FIGURE 5-5   Analysis of Covariance Design Logic

covariance adjusts for unequal initial differences only to the extent that
the covariate and the criterion correlate with each other. Because of the
upper limits placed on this correlation by the reliabilities of the two
measures, $\sqrt[2]{r_{11} \cdot r_{22}}$, the covariance adjustment is unduly conservative
to accommodate for the initial inequality of the groups. (An adjusted
analysis of covariance has been most fully developed by Porter, 1967;
a full discussion of the method and its restrictions can be found in
Campbell's and Erlebacher's chapter in *Disadvantaged Child*, 1970, p.
201.)

Because of the many problems and concerns with unequal groups
research, it should be avoided if possible. Top-level consultants in
statistics, measurement, and research design theory who know educational processes well should be used from the beginning to the end of
such research, if it is attempted. In reading research articles about
initially unequal groups reported in the literature, the student is
advised to discount the conclusions somewhat until expert advice on
the article can be obtained.

Pseudo- and Pre-experiments.   There is a group of studies which
Stanley (1966) classifies as pseudo-experiments or pre-experiments. The
general rule to remember for these studies is that there must always be a
comparison to have information. In a pseudo-experiment there is none,
or at least not a good one. In pseudo-experimental and pre-
experimental studies, a group is designated and observed, a treatment
is applied, and the group is then observed again. Any result which
occurs after the application of the treatment is said to be the result of
that treatment. Sometimes the group is observed prior to the administration of the treatment and then again afterward. Changes are
ascribed, generally naively, to the effect of the treatment. At other
times, a group that has experienced a treatment is observed and
compared to another group that has been observed. In all these pseudo-
and pre-experiments, a comparison is made or implied, but the
comparisons made have little solid, initial base of equality. Any
information gained is open to considerable question, indeed if it can be
considered information at all.

Campbell (1969, p. 426) says that in the real world there is little
competition between true, randomized experiments and fairly interpretable quasi-experiments. "Both stand together as rare excellencies in
contrast with a morass of obfuscation and self-deception." The general
ethic for professional educators in drawing conclusions about the
effectiveness of programs and innovations is to use the best research
method possible under the circumstances for their systematic evaluations. The possibility of a threat to internal validity is not enough to

negate a cause-and-effect conclusion. There must be a plausible threat in the quasi-experimental design and data to invalidate the interpretation of the results.

Alternative Hypotheses. The testing with data of *alternative hypotheses* about possible threats to internal and external validity is the best way to approach a research problem. These alternative hypotheses are generated best by theorizing about possible cause-and-effect relationships and correlations among the variables from a study of prior literature in the field under perusal.

Throughout all of these quasi-experimental descriptions, it is assumed that the researcher does have the opportunity to make observations and to collect data on the subjects within reasonable limits. In the case of the Interrupted Time Series where the comparison groups are from prior years, only the current year's classes are accessible. The weakness of the Interrupted Time Series in design is the inability of the researcher to test alternative hypotheses about the various threats to internal validity. If the researcher reviews a projected study in terms of what threats and errors of interpretation might exist, then additional measures—pre-observations, post post-tests (ones done well after the experiment is finished), and additional control groups and partial experimental groups—sometimes can be added to the study to test explicitly whether the alternative hypothesis threats do exist. Another way to generate good alternative hypotheses is to think about how the quasi-experimental groups might be different from groups that would exist if they had been formed randomly. All of this presupposes that the researcher has at least one group available, and most generally two or more groups, from which data can be collected.

Ex post Facto Designs. If studies are made entirely from the records of what has already happened, the research is labeled *ex post facto,* after the fact. Frequently, an innovative educational method is introduced amid appropriate publicity in the news media and continues during the school year. Near the end of the year, or even after school is out for the summer, someone asks the question, How do you know the innovation was effective? At that point it is difficult to know. Sometimes interesting postmortems can be held to see what the cause of the demise of the innovative evaluation was. Campbell (1969) suggests that *ex post facto* designs be totally rejected. This writer, though, suggests that they do have some value in education in designing future research, since they may give insights into the kinds of alternative hypotheses that can be developed and the kinds of data needed to test them. They are readily done in educational systems as considerable data are in the school files.

SUMMARY

In this chapter the concept of quasi-experimentation, as contrasted to a true experiment, was developed. The true experiment is rather immune to threats to internal validity, that is, inability to determine cause-and-effect relationships between induced treatments or conditions and outcome produced on criteria variables. A simple quasi-experiment was presented to demonstrate that important research in education can be done by able professionals using expert consultation to direct analyses, guide the development of research design, and be of assistance, if needed, in the interpretation of the results.

Nine threats to internal validity were discussed: History, Maturation, Instability, Testing, Instrumentation, Regression, Selection, Mortality, and Selection-Maturation Interactions. Six threats to external validity were presented: Testing Interactions, Selection by Treatment Interactions, Reactive and Hawthorne Effects, Multiple-treatment Interference, Irrelevant Response Measures, and Irrelevant Replicability of Treatments. Other types of quasi-experiments than those which approximate the true experiments, the Regression-Discontinuity, Interrupted Time Series, and Control Series designs were described. Mentioned were special concerns about measurement, regression, measurement of gain, a covariance analysis, difference scores, matching, and adjusted analysis of covariance. Finally pseudo-experiments, pre-experiments, and *ex post facto* designs were discussed.

STUDY AND DISCUSSION PROBLEMS

1. What is a quasi-experiment? How does it differ from a true experiment?
2. What are some of the problems encountered in a quasi-experiment? How can they be overcome?
3. Find in the educational literature an example of a quasi-experiment. Indicate possible threats to the internal validity of the study and how they influence your interpretation of the results.
4. Design a quasi-experiment that would be useful in a local school system.
5. List the major threats to the internal validity of quasi-experiments.
6. Suggest some quasi-experimental designs for educational situations where true experiments are not possible.
7. Find an *ex post facto* quasi-experiment in the educational literature. Indicate what the groups, treatments, and criteria were. Suggest the possible threats to the internal validity of the study and what your conclusions from it are.
8. Design an educational study using an interrupted time series design.

9. What is the experimental design purpose of analysis of covariance?
10. What is regression toward the mean?
11. If you selected the slow learners from a classroom on the basis of a test and gave them special attention, in which direction would you anticipate the regression toward the mean to operate? If the group improved their test scores after special instruction, how would you interpret this?
12. Give an example of a possible study in which Mortality is a threat to its interpretation.
13. Give an example of a possible study in which History is a threat to its internal validity.
14. Give an example of a study in which Maturation is an internal validity threat.
15. Give an example of a study in which Selection is an internal validity threat.
16. List the most common threats to internal validity.
17. How is the threat to internal validity of Instability related to statistical analysis?
18. What is external validity?
19. List the six threats to external validity and indicate what each is.
20. Design a simple Regression-Discontinuity study in education.
21. Design a Control Series study in education.
22. What is a pseudo-experiment? Find one in the education literature. What did the author conclude from it? What do you conclude?
23. What is an alternative hypothesis?
24. How are good alternative hypotheses generated?
25. Of what value are alternative hypotheses?
26. What is the conclusion that is drawn about Hawthorne effects in educational research?

REFERENCES

Campbell, D.T. Reforms as experiments. *American Psychologist*, 1969, 24(4), 409–429.

Campbell, D.T., and Erlebacher, A. How regression artifacts in quasi-experimental evaluations can mistakenly make compensatory education look harmful. In J. Hellmuth (Ed.), *Disadvantaged child*. New York: Brunner/Mazel, 1970, 3, 201.

Campbell, D.T., and Stanley, J.C. Experimental and quasi-experimental designs for research. In N.L. Gage (Ed.), *Handbook of research on teaching*. Chicago: Rand McNally, 1963, 171–246.

Cook, D. The impact of the Hawthorne effect in experimental designs in educational research. Columbus, Ohio: Ohio State University, June 1967, ERIC ED 021 308, 213 pp.

Kenny, D.A. Quasi-experimental approach to assessing treatment effects in the nonequivalent control group design. *Psychological Bulletin*, 1975, 82(3), 345–362.

Porter, A. C. The effects of using fallible variables in the analysis of covariance. Ph.D. Dissertation, University of Wisconsin, June 1967.

Sheppard, Sharon C. A comparison of the effects of sex-segregated and nonsex-segregated classes on reading achievement and self-concept. Unpublished Masters Thesis, Purdue University, 1972.

Stanley, J. C. A common class of pseudo-experiments. *American Educational Research Journal,* 1966, 3(2), 79, 80.

Tatsuoka, M. M., and Tiedeman, D. V. Statistics as an aspect of scientific method in research on teaching. In N. L. Gage (Ed.), *Handbook of research on teaching.* Chicago: Rand McNally, 1963, 142–170.

Chapter 6

Descriptive Research

There are times when even quasi-experiments, to say nothing of true experiments, are not available to the researcher as a method of studying educational problems. There may be no systematic changes in treatments or conditions made in an educational setting, but simply things which are being done with students, teachers, administrators, and the public which may affect them in different ways.

An educational process may be simply ongoing, and the investigator tries to determine the relationship of the teaching or administrative inputs to the criteria variables. This is done by describing the interrelationships of the many input and criteria dimensions in the educational system. (These types of problems are somewhat like those of systems analysis.)

In other instances, the cost of implementing a change in an educational process and evaluating it with an experimental or quasi-experimental design may be high. These costs can be too large financially, or socially, without first making a preliminary descriptive study (or a series of descriptive studies). The decision to conduct a formal experiment may be made only when the administrator feels that the risks are small, compared to the educational benefits that are foreseen as the result of preliminary, descriptive studies. There may be no period of time over which the effects of a proposed educational change can be evaluated, and an administrative decision must be made rather quickly.

On the other hand, a study of the development of children or adolescents, for example, may investigate the relationship of changes in students over a period of years to determine the antecedents of behavior. No particular treatment is imposed on the students. The researcher studies the consequences of the natural variation in behavior among the individuals and how the many various ways of working with students may influence them. At other times, sometimes a careful description of an aspect of the education process is needed to refute or allay false or inaccurate statements that are being made.

All of these types of descriptive studies may use systematic data collection—in other words, research. In all these cases, while a study of systematic changes with formal comparison groups would be the ideal solution in the search for cause-and-effect relationships, for many reasons, some just suggested, true experiments or quasi-experiments are not possible.

Research was once described as doing your best to understand a situation with the tools available to you. Descriptive research is often the only research tool available; it can be quite worthwhile when well used. However, descriptive research places greater demands on the statistics, measurement, and research design skills of the researchers, as well as on their knowledge of the theory of behavioral and social sciences and the substantive field being studied, than other types of research. For these reasons, descriptive research should be approached cautiously by beginners. It is sufficiently difficult that experts often fail in attempting to interpret their results accurately.

It is recommended that descriptive research problems be undertaken with caution by new researchers and those with only an average preparation in statistics and measurement. Further, an expert can throw the data in the wastebasket and start on another problem, should his study go awry. However, a graduate student may find it difficult to extricate himself from the formal commitment to work on a problem. A new researcher may have less expertise than needed for a descriptive research study.

Descriptive research is aimed at discovering the interrelationships among the dimensions of a problem, describing them, and determining the cause-and-effect direction of the relationships if possible. The broader the scope and depth of the inquiry, the better the descriptive research. Many sources of data will give a more detailed and sharper focus to the picture being obtained of the educational system. The reliability and validity of the instrumentation must be of high quality or aspects of the picture will be missing or distorted.

Types of descriptive research to be discussed will include studies of current school problems, *ex post facto* studies (developed from the files of educational institutions), longitudinal studies, case studies, ecological and anthropological studies, and historical research. The exceptional need for theory to guide and interpret the research will be discussed, as well as the need for high-quality data of many types. The need for experts in measurement, statistics, and research design, as well as their role in descriptive research, will become more easily seen.

THE ROLE OF THEORY

A well-developed theory is important to all research, but it is the key to the best-quality descriptive research. The researchers' careful, personal explorations of the problem are essential. By becoming involved in the system to be investigated, they will be able to answer the following questions: What is seen and heard from those already involved in the system? What really are the problems? What do those involved think the solution may be? What are the stated aims versus perhaps the real objectives of the system? What professional and scientific literature sources do those involved feel are useful to them?

With answers to these questions, the researchers themselves are ready to make a thorough review of the problem, the related literature, and their proposed attack on it. The proposed solutions should be recycled back through those people directly concerned with the problem for their further comment.

Essentially, what the researchers must do first is to develop a rich, even elaborate, and well-organized explanation or theory describing the problem and its ramifications as thoroughly as possible from the evidence of those persons directly involved and those who have written about the problem and its related aspects. The researcher's own observations, thinking, and ingenuity play a crucial role in this process. A good theory attempts to explain what the problem is, what the variables are that constitute it, and how they are interrelated. With this theoretical framework as a guide, the investigators can select the dimensions of the problem which need to be observed, described, and reported. The theory tells the researchers what measuring instruments will be needed and what analyses will be made.

A good theory also suggests to them what results might be expected and gives them a basis for interpretation of the analyses and alternative explanations that may be suggested. These *alternative hypotheses,* developed from the theory about the problem, are the key to the quality of descriptive research. Although well-developed theory and alternative hypotheses enhance the quality of any research investigation, still the role of theory is particularly important for research which is wholly or almost completely descriptive.

Doing descriptive research with a minimum of theorizing is like putting a jigsaw puzzle together with the blank side up. The "picture" obtained from nontheory-oriented research usually makes about as much sense as the lines delineating the pieces on the blank cardboard side of a puzzle.

Descriptive research is much like removing the face from a grandfather clock and taking a series of pictures of small portions of the mechanism. To comprehend what mechanism is driving which gear requires an organization of the picture-taking and a system of arranging the pictures afterward. If sense is to be made from them for further picture-taking, the guidance of a theory is desirable to find where the gaps are and what parts need further viewing.

Similarly, descriptions of an educational procedure or organization require such an arrangement, structuring, and guidance. This structure and organization in research is called theory—a broad overarching explanation based on prior evidence but going somewhat beyond it. Theory is used to guide, interpret, and explain what is being described in the research. To attempt to describe and understand a dynamic educational situation through a static description, even successive static descriptions, is difficult. Theory facilitates the researcher's task.

AN EXAMPLE OF DESCRIPTIVE RESEARCH

A young woman enrolled in a master's degree program in education undertook a descriptive research study using some of the extensive placement records kept on the teaching graduates at her former university. Among the records were five ratings by the school administrators of various facets of the new teacher's ability in teaching, lesson preparation, and in cooperating with other staff. (These ratings were obtained by follow-up questionnaires to school administrators and used by the university in reviewing, revising, and up-dating its teacher preparation programs.) The collegiate and placement record variables plus follow-up variables obtained from the records were in such areas as the following: sex, type of residence, age, marital status, judged participation in campus activities and off-campus activities, scholarship aid, percent college expenses paid by jobs held by the student, and faculty ratings of such personal variables as appearance,

TABLE 6-1   Simulated Data Setup for a Descriptive Study of Teacher
            Education

Student	Sex	Residence	Marital . . . GPA . . .Teaching . . .Staff Status Ability Cooperation			
Able 001	1	2	2			
Baker 002	2	1	1			
Charles 003	1	2	2			
.						
.						
.						
Fox 010	2	1	1			
George 011	1	1	1			
.						
.						
.						
King 099	1	1	1			
Love 100	2	2	2			
Michael 101	1	2	1			
.						
.						
.						
Peter 111	1	2	1			

Code: Sex: 1 = male, 2 = female; Type of Residence: 1 = on campus, 2 = off campus;
  Marital Status: 1 = not married, 2 = married; GPA 4.00 = A; Teaching Ability, 5 =
  excellent; Staff Cooperation, 5 = excellent.

poise, initiative, professional competence, judgment, and reliability.
Grade-point average, coursework grades in introduction to education,
educational psychology, and student teaching, in addition to the
prior-mentioned information, were obtained by the graduate student
(see Table 6-1).

The student's research questions concerned the influence of the
dimensions of the collegiate environment, particularly the teacher
education curriculum and the student's personality and activities, that
contributed to the student's success in teaching. Obviously these are
complex and difficult questions to answer. To do a randomized, true
experiment or quasi-experimental research would require perhaps a
period of two or three years and could be very expensive. Further, little

feedback into the educational system would be available during that time. A descriptive study is useful in such a case.

The research can interrelate the variables available in the rather extensive records, and it can be done rather rapidly. It yields information that is of immediate use. It can also indicate other information being kept that is of negligible value and which can be eliminated in future placement operations. Additional research on the teacher education system may be suggested by this first, overall descriptive study. Then, too, descriptive research in such a case can indicate where more detailed information would be useful, along with possible biases in current measurement techniques. Finally, descriptive research theorization and literature reviews will focus attention of the curriculum activities and operations that prepared the teacher in the university. The impact of this review can be useful in itself.

The student reviewed the literature on teacher preparation, methods of rating teaching, predicting the success of teachers, and placement office practices. For this study, thirty variables were developed from the placement office records. One hundred twenty-one certified teaching candidates were the subjects for whom the data were recorded. An immediate problem with much descriptive research, particularly that based in part on file records, is missing data. Of these 121 teacher candidates' records, ten could not be used because of lack of information. Some of this group did not teach in public school, others had no administrator's ratings of their on-the-job teaching, and so forth. Further, eight more of them lacked some of the university-related data. However, statistical procedures taking into account missing data were used so that these records could be included in the study.

Note that there really was only one major group involved in this research and so no direct comparisons among groups could be made. Thus, relationships among the variables within the group was the appropriate analytical procedure. This method is correlation.

Some of the variables were dichotomous, such as sex, and marital status, etc. Others were scaled into interval data. It is conceivable that separate groups based on the splits of the dichotomies and trichotomies could have been used. Instead of one large group of 111, two groups, one of males and the other females, could have been studied separately and compared. Similarly, marital status and residence could have been used as the basis for divisions into groups, or all three variables could have been used to obtain eight groups (two sex groups times two marital status groups times two types of residence groups). Note, however, that these groups would average only about fifteen subjects each, too small for definitive analyses.

Trichotomous variables, or even a multi-category nominal variable, can be used to study the effects of grouping by converting the multi-category variable into several nominal variables. For the multi-category instance (and nominal variable), major in college could be converted into the variables of *Art Major,* yes or no; *Home Economics Major,* yes or no; *Business Education Major,* yes or no, and so forth. In this way, overall group size is maintained. This is a convenient way, in many instances, to keep the subjects in several large groups or only one group, as was done in this study. (Without this procedure, each college major would have to be a group in itself and the small groups would be difficult to study.)

The analysis with only one group is the interrelating (correlation) of all the thirty variables with one another.

In this case, the matrix is square and symmetrical. Each of the thirty variables are represented across the top of the square and also along the side of the square. Thus 900 cells are formed in the square by the combination of each of the thirty row variables with each of the thirty column variables (30 × 30 = 900). In each of these 900 cells is a possible correlation between every two sets of variables in the study. These 900 correlations are each based on the 111 teachers. Each of the 111 teachers had a score (or rating) on variable "1" and on variable "2." Thus a correlation between variable "1" and "2" could be determined. A correlation could also be calculated for variables "1" and "3" and "1" and "4" and for all of the other variables with "1." Further, the correlations of variables "2" and "1" and "2" with "3" and "2" with "4" and for all of the other variables with "2" could be calcualted. The same could be done for variable "3" and variable "4," etc., to complete all 900 cells in the 30 variable by 30 variable correlation matrix.

Note, however, that thirty of the cells would have to be correlations of a variable with itself: "1" with "1," and "2" with "2," and so forth. These are, by definition, reliability coefficients for which the data are not available in this study. Thus 30 cells of the 900 would be empty. Note also that the correlation of variable "1" with variable "2" is the same as the correlation of variable "2" with variable "1," etc. Thus half of the remaining 870 cells in the correlation matrix are identical to the other half. In practice, only 435 correlations would be calculated along with the means and standard deviations of the thirty variables.

The data input to the computer was 111 cards, one for each subject (plus some computer systems cards). Each data card contained the thirty scores on each of the variables for each subject. A standard computer program was used which required only that the user be identified to the computer system, the standard analytical program entered from stor-

TABLE 6-2   Selected Correlations Among 25 College and Personality Variables and Five on the Job Rating Variables of Teachers*

	Student Teacher Grade 25	Teaching Ability 26	Prep. Subject 27	Discipline 28	Tact. Students 29	Coop. Staff 30
1–12 College & Personal Background Variables		Negligible (not significant, most near zero)				
13–21 Personality Ratings Median Correlations	.27	.16	.22	.17	.10	.05
22 Grade Point Average	.25	.29	.28	.20	.13	.09
23 Intro. to Ed. Grade	.24	.05	.03	−.07	−.13	−.09
24 Ed. Psych. Grade	.16	.01	.05	.03	.00	−.03
25 Student Teach. Grade	—	.34	.36	.28	.20	.11
26 On the Job Ratings		—	.77	.71	.62	.65
27 Prep. Subject			—	.59	.56	.52
28 Discipline				—	.60	.56
29 Tact. Students					—	.53
30 Coop. Staff						—

n = 111

Significance Level (100 df) 5%, $r \geqslant .195$; 1%, $r \geqslant .254$

*From P.B. Simon and W. Asher. The relationship of variables in undergraduate school and school administrators' ratings of first-year teachers. *Journal of Teacher Education*, 1964, 15, 293–302.

age, the size of the problem be entered (in this case 30 variables times 111 subjects), and the way the data were entered into the cards (the card data format) be indicated. (Some additional analytical work was done that is not of importance here; see Simon and Asher [1964] for a more extensive report.)

Some of the results of the study were quite interesting generally. Specifically, they were valuable to the university and the educational systems (see Table 6-2). The only academic course grade which correlated with successful on-the-job teaching was the student-teaching grade. None of the other professional education course grades correlated significantly with on-the-job ratings, nor, in turn, did these prestudent-teaching course grades correlate well with student teaching grades. The nine faculty ratings could be termed simply variations of one overall judgment. Neither these ratings nor the twelve variables gleaned from the placement office file predicted successful teaching nearly as well as the simple student-teaching grade.

A number of tentative conclusions could be drawn from the results of this study. First, a great deal of data was being collected by the placement office which was of little value to those who were hiring teachers. The best decisions could be made on the basis of the student-teaching grade alone. In fact, this descriptive research suggests that more extensive data be collected about the quality of the student teaching experience, and further suggests that it could be used as an intermediate criterion variable pending more longitudinal data or experimental research. Second, the nine personal characteristic ratings of the students by the faculty can be reduced considerably. This would save a lot of faculty time and placement office clerical effort. Next, it is apparent that professional education courses other than student teaching are of little value in facilitating performance on the job (confirming the informal observations of thousands of teachers). At least those who do well or poorly in the professional courses in terms of grades (and presumably knowledge or at least tests of that knowledge) do no better or worse than one another in rated teaching competence on the job.

Here, then, is the beginning of a formal systems analysis, since many components of the system are described; all of them interrelated. This first approach suggests where descriptive measurements should be increased and decreased and where it might be profitable to gather data on additional dimensions of the system. Essentially what has been done is to further extend and develop information about effective teaching, its prediction, and the professional educational requirements for it. There also are definitely some cues in the study for school administrators who can select and hire new teachers from a number of candidates. It is also interesting to note, in retrospect, that the research report considered the need for a true experiment with half of the students being randomly assigned to the standard sequence of required professional education courses, and the other half required to take only practice teaching with minimum preparation for it. Descriptive research serves as a valuable basis for experimental research. In this case, the true experiment was not done, and it may still remain to be done. It would be a valuable study to do if assurances could be obtained that the graduates of the experimental program would be certified.

Again, a professional with minimum technical training in research, aided by a consultant with statistical and measurement skills, made a definite contribution to educational knowledge and practice. The key was the professional's ability to discern how an important problem might be moved toward better resolution and to obtain help in collecting, analyzing, and interpreting the data. More research could be done on this problem and should be done in many schools to further develop theory and aid in problem-solving.

The internal validity of such a study is not strong. There are many alternative hypotheses that could be suggested to explain the results, and readers undoubtedly have thought of several. (They are invited to test them with their own data.) However, the external validity probably comes close to approaching the maximum limits set on it by the limitations of the internal validity. The research was done with real students who were living their lives, going to school, taking courses, becoming certified to teach, and actually becoming teachers. This study was in the real world, not the artificial one of a laboratory. However, it was done in just one university and the teachers were in schools primarily in Pennsylvania. The theory developed prior to the research came from many sources and areas, and studies testing it should be done in many many areas with many kinds of students, faculties, and teacher ratings using other methods. The study could be redone studying the newer teacher education methods and with current teachers who have different value systems about appearance, course work, and campus activities. Data such as these in teacher education are often available in schools of education.

A SECOND DESCRIPTIVE STUDY

At the elementary and secondary school levels there are also many practical problems which can be moved toward resolution, or at least better solutions, by descriptive research. An example of a problem such as this was one studied by a high school teacher on the use of cars by high school students and the effect on their academic accomplishments (Schusler and Asher, 1967).

This topic hits the newspaper headlines with some regularity when an administrator is so rash as to attempt to restrict the use of cars by students to drive to school. Secondary school administrators discuss this problem when they convene (NASSP, 1959) and occasionally the topic is the subject of an article in national magazines (White, 1958). Sometimes data are collected on students' driving time, driving to school, or ownership of a car, as one variable, and grades as another. These car access data are then related to the students' grades and conclusions drawn. If low grades are shown to be related to high access to cars, the conclusion often is that too much driving (or possibly leaving school to work to support a car) is detrimental to studying and achievement in school. In other cases, no relationship is found and the conclusion is that driving a car or owning one is not detrimental to scholarship. (No instances of high access to cars and high school achievement are known. This fact alone may suggest certain conclusions.)

There are a number of possible errors in relationship to this problem of grades and students' access to cars. First, no data might be gathered at all. The authoritative eyeball analysis method might prevail with conclusions being emitted from a position of power. Action might be taken, but in these days of rejection of authority *per se,* this is a dangerous administrative stance. Second, data could be collected, as was suggested, on car access and grades and these correlated. The determined degree of relationship or no relationship then would be taken as a cause-and-effect relationship (between cars and grades) and presented for consideration for action and public support. Since few of the public believe in the certainty of cause-and-effect relationships in the social and behavioral sciences, they might obfuscate the issue further and no decisions would be made. In neither procedure would professional leadership be exercised based on good evidence.

The problem should be thought about in terms of variables which are correlated with the criteria variables, or might be, since the problem probably must be approached via descriptive research methods. (To do a true experiment, the researcher would have to randomize students to two groups and provide one group with cars, expense accounts to drive them, and driving lessons for those unable to drive. For the other group, there would be a number who would have to be persuaded to give up the access to cars that they already have. Both these conditions and impositions usually are beyond the resources, ethics, and control of a researcher.) Thinking about the variables possibly correlated with the criteria leads to alternative hypotheses that often can be tested by gathering additional data.

A variable known to be associated with automobile usage is family socioeconomic status (from accident-insurance rate differentials for different occupations). Socioeconomic status is also known to relate to school achievement and intelligence test scores. Sex is related to automobile accident insurance rates (adolescent girls' rates are lower than boys). There are also suggestions in the scientific literature that boys may work part time to support a car. The possible intercorrelations among all of these related variables—socioeconomic status, sex, intelligence, and part-time employment—help form a theory about automobile access and grades. Further, these correlations suggest that additional data be collected to test the alternative hypotheses so crucial to best quality descriptive research. In a descriptive research study, these then should be the groups and variables on which data should be gathered to study their influence. They form the alternative hypotheses generated from the theory relating to the problem.

The incidence of car ownership in the working group can be compared to the incidence in the nonworking group. The socioeconomic level of both groups, working and nonworking, within high and low access groups needs to be studied also. Interview data about the use of cars and the emotional meaning of the cars to the adolescent would give insight into why the adolescents are driving or feel the need for a car. Are the boys neglected or ignored socially in school, especially by girls, and are the boys buying cars to overcome this handicap? Are the families with the high economic resources buying cars for their adolescents' use? Is family's socioeconomic status positively related to grades in school? If any one of these questions are answered "yes," then the ownership of a car may be positively related to grades in school for these reasons. If the latter is not the case, then there is some evidence that actually obtaining a car for one's high school adolescent may be detrimental to scholastic achievement.

Further, the situation is made more complex by variables specific to a school. If the school is located in a rural area, students may need to drive to jobs after school, to participate in afterschool activities, or simply to save considerable time riding school buses every day. In an inner city in a large metropolitan area, few students may have cars and little opportunity to drive. The ones that do may be rather unique.

Broad generalizations and policy decisions are inappropriate. In school situations there is conflicting evidence about the effect of car access on grades; this might be expected.

In the actual study, data were collected in a semi-suburban community that had many of the characteristics of the major central city to which it was adjacent. However, it was not an inner city area. The socioeconomic range of the students was rather broad. As was suggested by many of the questions just asked and the theory resulting from the review of the literature, the variables of interest were intelligence test scores, access to automobiles, sex, and grade-point average. The grade-point averages were collected both at the end of the freshman year in the high school and also at the end of five semesters of work. These two points span the first time at which almost no one could legally drive and the time at which almost everyone could obtain a driver's license. Thus, there was a longitudinal aspect to the study, even though all the data except that about the students' access to cars were taken from school files and thus are *ex post facto* (after the fact).

It was found that boys do indeed differ from girls in their use of cars, boys having more access to them. For the boys there seemed to be only a minor relationship, if any, between intelligence and car access, but for girls there was a marked relationship. However, contrary to some expectations, girls of low intellectual ability seemed to be given (or they demanded) access to cars more than the girls of higher ability. There was no differential influence on before-and-after grades by either having or not having access to cars. The grade-point average did increase between the two marker points, but this upward trend of grades over the school years is typical of many educational systems. It would be a difference in the upward slopes (an interaction effect) that would be of importance here. There was none. Even when the influence of intelligence was taken into account, there was no residual relationship which would suggest any effect of increased access to cars influencing grades in either sex group in this school.

Thus, considerable question was raised about prior reports of relationships between grades and car access. Had these administrators who reported them fallen into the trap of believing that simple correlation is equivalent to causation? Strong cause-and-effect relationship statements can only be made in experimental research. Carefully hedged cause-and-effect statements about descriptive research should be made only after a thorough testing of many alternative hypotheses and in a number of different situations: schools, student bodies, regions, and so forth. To make statements inferring cause-and-effect relationships to public news sources or to attempt to make administrative decisions on the basis of simple descriptive, correlational research is unbecoming for a professional.

A little knowledge of educational research methods, the collection of additional data on related variables, both coupled with consultation with an educational research specialist, constitute the professional approach and can contribute importantly to increasing the effectiveness of an educational system.

LONGITUDINAL DESCRIPTIVE STUDIES

The studies just presented described educational phenomena at one point in time or with only the records available that described any prior states of the students involved. They were limited by the nature of the records. If a particular aspect of personality was of theoretic interest to test an alternative hypothesis, it was either available in the records or it was not. There is no easy way, or perhaps no way at all, to get descriptions of personality and similar variables on students in classes from two or three years ago. The solution to problems such as these is to look ahead, instead of backward, and to start descriptive research that begins at the present time, collecting data on students, teachers, and systems as time passes. In this way, the data that are desired can be collected now, and immediate, intermediate, and more ultimate criteria data collected at later times as the people and systems evolve in their educational roles.

Thus, in the teacher education study, perhaps more objective personality tests rather than ratings could be obtained, and the tests might be selected for their theoretical relevance to the criterion, "success in teaching," as known from a number of prior studies. These tests could be selected also for their independence from one another and their reliability. Grades or, less formally, ratings of success in student teaching other than the usual "A" or "B" would be collected. An attempt should be made to devise a "success in student teaching" rating in which the typical student is near the middle of the scale so that the really outstanding student teachers and the above average ones are not both simply graded as "A." (The standard deviations of the grades thus would be increased.) The five criteria of success to the expert's eye in the presented teacher education study appear to be assessing primarily only one dimension of teaching ability. (They intercorrelate among themselves near the maximum levels possible.) There are several general dimensions of teaching success known, and there may be specific aspects of the acceptability of new teachers by the school systems in addition to these. Further, judgments about teachers are desired by the university for feedback to revise their teacher education curriculum. In a longitudinal study extending over three, four, or more years, these accommodations can be made.

In the access to cars' study, not just the seniors in the school could be studied and their present access to cars reported, but, starting with the sophomores, yearly or every semester reports could be taken on actual car use at that time. Further, the effects on dropouts could be studied, which could be an important aspect of such a study.

Longitudinal studies, sometimes called developmental studies when the subjects are children or adolescents, have a distinct advantage over descriptive studies that observe subjects at one point in time or over relatively short periods of time. They are much superior to the *ex post facto* study, which is somewhat of a longitudinal study in reverse. Longitudinal studies can show the development of subjects continuously over a period of time and the relationship of what occurs earlier with happenings at later times.

Such longitudinal studies in education are too rare. Perhaps they are rare partly because of the problems in doing them. First, they are a great deal of work for a researcher. The researcher must plan to spend the number of years covered in the longitudinal span plus the planning time and the analyses and reporting time. The researcher is thus locked into the study and to the area for that period. Longitudinal studies are expensive, and funding that is guaranteed for the whole time span is hard to obtain. Illness or other incapacity of the investigator can make the research incomplete. Further, new measures and theories for the behavior of the subjects may emerge from others' research after the start of a longitudinal study, and these measures will not be a part of the early data on the subjects. The dropout rate of subjects increases as the time span increases and can be disastrous over a long time span unless very large numbers of subjects are used at the start or large sums are available for locating and testing subjects individually at distant places.

A substitute plan for research on subjects over a developmental span is to describe a series of age or developmental groups over the time span of interest, perhaps each age group in the time span, but all during the same year. Here some trend information is available, but of course, the interlocking developmental phases are difficult, perhaps impossible, to determine. A compromise plan between these two extremes can be used in which there is a shorter overall research time but more than the series of cross-sectional data available, such as indicated previously. In these designs, perhaps a series of three-year overlapping spans are selected within a larger development period, e.g., seven years. Five age groups, starting with the youngest age and increasing one year in age for successive groups, could be studied. At the end of three years, observations would be available for all age groups in the overall time span, and interlocking data would be available across all ages in the span.

With all the problems of longitudinal studies and their costs in school time, student time, and investigator energy, perhaps independently conducted longitudinal studies should be markedly reduced in number, and major, regional or national longitudinal studies done. The data from these major studies can be exceptionally broad, cover major time spans, and be used for research not contemplated when the original data were gathered. Data banks can be established with individual subject identities concealed and access to the data available only for authentic research projects. Such a data bank has been established already in Project TALENT. The variables available, samples, costs, prior studies done, and so forth, can be readily ascertained from a review of the *Project TALENT Data Bank: A Handbook* (Flanagan, 1972). For research on adolescents and secondary education, the TALENT data bank is invaluable and should be used far more than it is. It is a much better source of data and problems for dissertation researchers than the data that can be collected on a limited sample by one person doing his or her first major research project. Its use is recommended.

CASE STUDIES

Another major type of descriptive research is the case study. While most scientific descriptive research deals with a number of subjects or educational systems and collects systematic data on each one for a reasonably broad spectrum of variables, the case study is generally confined to one or just a few subjects or educational organizations. In the case study, the focus is exceedingly broad in the types and quantities of variables which are observed, and as many of the interrelationships are studied as possible. Interviews, documents, social and academic interrelationships, feelings, perceptions, test scores, and physical data are all of interest. In fact, there may be little that is not of interest regarding the subject.

This is both the strength and the weakness of the case study. A great deal of effort and observation goes into the study of only one or two subjects or educational units. The concern is to seek out every possible cause lying behind current behavior or status. A well-done case study will uncover most if not all of the causal antecedents, but they may be so buried in the mass of information that they may be impossible to separate from the irrelevant variables. A case study must be capsulated within a very thorough and wide-ranging theory of behavior and society to give the data focus. If done without reference to theory, the understandings developed will be superficial or of value for the one or two cases alone. At best, it is difficult to generalize from just a few subjects.

The scientific value of case studies is for the development of hypotheses which can be tested with greater rigor with standard observational systems on larger numbers of representative groups of subjects. All research of better quality, either of an experimental or purely descriptive nature, involves a great deal of theory, but in case studies, it is imperative to have good theory if any organization of data and meaning is to evolve.

As in all research, the observers in case studies must be cautious in letting personal biases and judgments influence their observations. The rule in all research is to record facts and only facts at the time of observation and later to interpret the facts in light of theory. Facts should be replicable by other observers. Interpretations of facts may differ, but the facts remain the same. In case studies, the observer must be careful of subjects' deceptive, unaided memories of past events and biases in recall and interpretations.

Almost all research should have some small case studies done prior to the collection of data, indeed even before the research design becomes final. The investigator should observe the research subjects to learn what the dynamics of the situation are. Some of the questions asked at that time should derive from theory as indicated earlier. What really is the problem? What do the teachers, administrators, and students believe is happening? What do the data in the records and files really represent? What are the artifacts in the situation? Are these research subjects different in substantial ways from others who are seemingly the same? These are some of the questions that might be answered by a small case study by the researcher before the major research effort begins.

ECOLOGICAL AND ANTHROPOLOGICAL RESEARCH

Ecological and anthropological research methods are used to study and describe education. Ecology is the area of science concerned with the interrelationships or patterns of relations between organisms and their environment. In education, ecological studies are concerned with such things as ways teachers generate learning environments; the classroom milieu that produces learning; and the media, equipment, formats, and occupants of the classroom. In particular, how do these aspects of the learning environment relate to the behavior of the children and teacher in a classroom or school? This is the focus of the ecology of learning and education. Educational ecologists observe classrooms as they occur naturally, and as free as possible from the influence of the investigator.

Anthropologists do somewhat similar work in that they observe directly the flow of life surrounding them. However, frequently they become participants in the situation which they are observing and immerse themselves in a particular culture. Anthropologists are concerned also with the interdependence of phenomena and cultural patterns and configurations. They are interested in how their observations fit into the total matrix of the sociocultural situation. They have a holistic orientation. Anthropologists in education want to relate each classroom, school, and school system to the broad social and cultural contexts as they exist. Educational anthropologists determine the cultural and social patterns which influence pupils, teachers, and administrators in their relationships with others. Major variables for anthropologists are social and culturally conditioned values, attitudes, styles, conceptions, role expectations, and modes of personal relationships.

Anthropological studies of education have focused on three areas: schools and how they relate to their social and cultural environment, the description and analyses of classroom processes, and the study of individual students and educators. Data collection involves the community surrounding the school as well as in the school itself. The relationship between the two is studied in detail. The studies are broad and range from family socialization to urbanization and change. Generally, educational anthropologists build ethnographic descriptions of educational processes, but more recently have started to generate hypotheses which can be tested.

Ecologists and anthropologists working in educational settings generally are doing basic research—attempting to discover new dimensions of behavior and the environment and new relationships among facets of behavior and the setting in which it occurs. Their approach might be likened to a scientifically focused case study, but one which is concerned primarily with the relationship between an individual or educational unit and the larger cultural and environmental setting in which they are placed. Both ecologists and anthropologists in education bring to their work the thinking and structuring of phenomena of their scientific fields. They thus may gain insights of value to educators which can be used in their day-to-day work. These insights can be invaluable starting points for applied educational research and evaluation work done by the professional educators themselves.

HISTORICAL RESEARCH

Historical research is descriptive research and to an extent uses case study methods in its approach. It is also longitudinal and the quintessence of *ex post facto* research. Historical research is an account of past events generally of major magnitude. It is also an art in that, in presenting history, the writer uses a literary format. As such, the presentation should be well written in a polished style, with logical organization and careful phrasing.

Historical research has some common methodological bases with scientific research. Both historical and scientific research describe the natural world. In both, prior knowledge of a topic should be brought to bear in an organized fashion to form a theory to guide the research efforts. They should both set forth hypotheses for testing which will aid in generalizations, and they should both be concerned with the interpretability of the evidence collected with regard to a problem. Historical knowledge like scientific knowledge is never complete. Both scientific and historical research methods are concerned with cause-and-effect relationships, and both are critical searches for the truth.

There are differences between scientific research and historical research. Historical research attacks problems of some scope and magnitude. The day-to-day, problem-solving research approach often used in the behavioral sciences, which can serve a useful educational purpose, often is too narrow to be of interest to the historian. The historian is interested in an accurate presentation of the major forces operating in past societies as an aid in understanding present pressures and conflicts and as a means of formulating policy for decisions about the future. In historical research there are generally few ways in which the writer can make personal observations. Historical knowledge is limited to the facts derived from known, surviving records of only a limited number of events of the past. Any observations that were made at the time of the event have either been recorded or are not available.

The historian's collection of data is a search to find and collect observations of past events and to authenticate them. This authentication of the validity of documents is called technically, *external criticism*. It answers questions such as: When was the document produced? Who was its author? Why was it written? In contrast to external criticism, *internal criticism* is concerned with the interpretation of the contents of an externally acceptable document. What biases did the author have? Was the writer a competent observer? Was the writer an observer of the events portrayed, or were they described from second-hand accounts or hearsay? These are the questions asked to develop evidence about internal criticism. Were the events recorded immediately, somewhat after the fact, or after many years.

As with any other rules of evidence, if independent sources agree about a fact, greater faith can be put in the fact's acceptance. Official testimony should be more accurate than unofficial statements, but probably both are necessary for an accurate picture. Evidence which has been shown to be dependable and authenticated in one part of a document leads to greater acceptance of other data in the document and acceptance of that observer.

Historical research of best quality requires the use of primary sources, first-hand accounts, and records such as letters, newspapers, minutes of meetings, court decisions, remains, relics, school texts, catalogues, diaries, and information recorded or filmed at the time of the event. Without primary sources, an historian is almost helpless. Primary sources are the basic data of historical research.

Secondary sources are sometimes used in historical research, but the evidence in such efforts is much less trustworthy. Facts have a way of becoming distorted in transmission. The rules of evidence in law generally prohibit hearsay evidence, and reputable historians avoid secondary sources if at all possible. Readers of educational history should recognize the difference between primary and secondary sources in determining the authenticity of what they read.

Doing historical research in education is difficult for those not skilled in its procedures. To be of general use, the scope of the topic must be broad and primary sources must be available. Training in historiography is a must. Extensive knowledge of general history, history of the area, the era of the topic, and history of education are prerequisites if good quality historical research in education is to be done. A thorough understanding of educational philosophy, society, technology, and comparative education are also useful and in most instances essential. These are not skills, interests, faculties, and problems learned in a year's course work. Those committed to the scholarly study of educational processes and problems are best advised to avoid historical research problems unless they have been thoroughly trained as historians, have the diligence to go to the sources of primary documents, will dig them out, and have the skills to write facilely.

However, every professional in education should be a reader of history, or, to rephrase the carvings on the wall of the National

Archives, he will be condemned to relive it. In reading the history of education, professionals must be able to distinguish good historical research from that which is sometimes done about education. Charlatans are only too ready to distort history for their own purposes, and all too often enrich themselves by writing in the public press to "enlighten" the masses about education. Good historians write, but all who write about the past are not good historians.

Historians of education have much to offer in the attempts to resolve current educational problems. They can try to prevent the mistakes of the past from being repeated. The accountability of teachers via their students' standardized tests, as advocated by government officials and others, is a case in point. A historian of English education writing in *The Phi Delta Kappan* (Small, 1972) stated the evidence succinctly and concluded that teachers' accountability in Victorian England was a device used by the national government to reduce the cost of education substantially. There are many historical precedents for today's educational problems and proposed solutions. Professional educators must be aware of them.

SUMMARY

Purely descriptive research is widespread throughout education in several general forms. The study of interrelationships among a number of variables, longitudinal studies, case studies, ecological, anthropological, and historical studies are types of descriptive research. Restrictions in the educational systems leading to the use of descriptive studies were discussed, as was the very important role that theory must play to guide and aid in the interpretation of descriptive research. Two examples of descriptive research approaches to educational problems were used to illustrate the scope of the educational problems which could be moved toward resolution with this method. Concerns about *ex post facto* research were expressed. The values, types, and problems of longitudinal studies were indicated with the suggestion that data banks be used as the source of longitudinal data. The prerequisite of a minor case study before more formal research is done was suggested, as was the methodology of case studies. The holistic view of education in its cultural and social environment is the emphasis of ecologists and anthropologists working in education. The scope and value of historical educational research was presented, together with the high standards, education, and dedication needed by those who propose to engage in it. The necessity of professional educators to read and be able to evaluate historical educational research was emphasized.

STUDY AND DISCUSSION PROBLEMS

1. Select a problem in your area of education that lends itself to descriptive research. List the variables that would be included, the method of analysis and possible findings.
2. Describe an educational area where a case study would be valuable.
3. Find a descriptive research article in the education literature. List the variables, the method of analysis, and possible problems of interpretation.
4. List common problems in cause-and-effect interpretations of descriptive research studies.
5. In what ways is theory important in descriptive research?
6. List several types of descriptive research and the characteristics of each.
7. List the problems that are typical of the various types of descriptive research.
8. List some of the similarities and differences between scientific and historical research.
9. Describe and give examples of internal and external criticism in historical research.
10. Develop in brief form an historical research study in your area of education.
11. Why might experimental and even quasi-experimental studies *not* be available to a researcher in education.
12. What are the demands on the researcher doing descriptive research in terms of knowledge of statistics, measurement, and research design?
13. What are alternative hypotheses? How are they used in descriptive research?
14. What does the descriptive study of teacher education suggest about changes needed in the preparation of teachers?
15. What alternative hypotheses would you suggest be tested in an extension of the teacher-education study or in the students'-access-to-cars study?
16. What data would you collect to test your alternative hypotheses in a teacher-education study or in the students'-access-to-cars study?
17. What types of educational administration decisions are not as good as doing descriptive research about a problem?
18. What are the problems of testing alternative hypotheses in an *ex post facto* study?
19. Look up information about *Project TALENT* in the educational literature. Design a study using the TALENT data bank to answer a question you have about educational processes. Could you actually do this study for a thesis?
20. Your school system hires ten to twenty teachers a year. Indicate the types of data that would be available or could be developed that could be used in the hiring process.

REFERENCES

National Association of Secondary School Principals. Do automobiles and scholarship mix? *Spotlight on junior and senior high schools,* 1959, No. 36.

Project TALENT data bank: A Handbook. American Institutes for Research. Project talent. David V. Tiedeman, P. O. Box 1113, Palo Alto, Calif., April 1972.

Schusler, M. M., and Asher, W. Students' grades and access to cars. *Journal of Ecuational Research,* 1967, *60,* 435–437.

Simon, P. B., and Asher, W. The relationship of variables in undergraduate school and school administrators' ratings of first-year teachers. *Journal of Teacher Education,* 1964, *15,* 293–302.

Sindell, P. S. Anthropological approaches to the study of education. *Review of Eduational Research,* 1969, *39*(5), 593–606.

Small, A. A. Accountability in Victorian England. *Phi Delta Kappan,* 1972, L III(7), 438–439.

White, W. Owning and operating a car in high school can dull the students' zest for learning. *Saturday Evening Post,* Feb. 15, 1958, *CCXXX,* 10.

Willems, E. P., and Raush, H. L. (Eds.). *Naturalistic viewpoints in psychological research.* New York: Holt, Rinehart and Winston, 1969.

Sampling Surveys and Instruments

Chapter 7

Survey studies are a special form of the descriptive research presented in the last chapter. Survey studies are quite useful to education. While precautions have been noted in this book about professionals doing research without consultation, survey research methods are a valuable means of making some large administrative jobs smaller. When rather straightforward, descriptive information is needed about a large number of people, schools, or other groups, a sampling survey should be considered.

A sampling survey describes a large group by studying a relatively small number of the group. This is done by using sampling methods. A *sample* is a portion of the whole group taken to represent the whole group. The whole group is spoken of as the *population*. The easiest way to assure that the sample represents the population is through the use of randomization procedures. A table of random numbers to select individual units, called "sampling units," from a listing of the population assures that the *random sample* represents the population within certain limits. These limits, called *confidence limits* or a *confidence interval*, can be used to estimate how closely a sample represents the population. Generally, the description of the group desired is not one based on psychological or educational interval measurement. Instead, simple counted measurements yielding percentages on rather clearcut attributes usually are used. Thus the descriptive information is often obtained through the use of self-report devices, questionnaires, or an interview schedule. Information generally obtained is for variables such as sex, formal educational achievements, family background, job characteristics, habits, and brief indicators of attitudes, thinking, and opinion. Estimates of information available in files also can be obtained quickly with the use of sampling procedures.

This chapter will indicate how sampling procedures can be used, problems involved in using sampling, the calculations involved in determining sample size, examples of problems in which sampling can be used, and principles involved in developing survey instruments.

SAMPLING PROBLEMS AND PROCEDURES

The two main principles of sampling survey methods are: (1) that small samples can accurately represent large populations, and (2) that the precision of this representation is a function of the square root of the sample size. That is, a study sample of 400 is only twice as precise as a sample of 100 even though a sample of 400 involves four times the number of observations as a sample of 100. (400/100 = 4. The square root of 4 is 2.)

Similarly, using the square root of the sample size rule, a sample of 25 loses only half of the precision available from a sample of 100. ($^{25}/_{100}$ = $^1/_4$. $\sqrt{^1/_4}$ = $^1/_2$.) Here then is a way to describe people, events, activities, or other units in education with an acceptable precision and with considerably less effort than attempting to describe the entire population, or even a very large part of it. Many decisions in education are based on estimates of descriptive information on populations of students, parents, teachers, voters, professional organization members, and so forth. With 5,000 students in a college, it may be difficult to ascertain the percentage who want the library hours extended until midnight or who have some other concern about the college. The decision to extend the hours can be costly, and perhaps just a vociferous few are making this request. Other questions might be: What is the percentage of a college student body that votes in the state but not at the college? What are the various educational opinions of the 1,000 teachers in a school system? To ask questions of all 5,000 students or 1,000 teachers is an expensive and time-consuming process. To inquire generally among those who meet with administrators or among those contacted over the course of a few weeks risks obtaining information which is not representative of the total group.

As an example, in the days when undergraduate college women had hours, a Dean of Women suggested that perhaps college women could handle unrestricted hours. The assembled university's administrative officers considered the problem at some length, talked with a number of women, and finally agreed. One person, though, suggested that they should ask the women to express their opinions, since the ruling affected them the most. Instead of a mass meeting, or inquiry of the officers of women's organizations, or a questionnaire sent to all women, the easiest way in this case to gather accurate information would be to select a small sample of the women. They then could be queried, probably using a short questionnaire, about what they want to do about their hours. A random sample of just 200 would yield answers that, at worst, will be within about plus or minus seven percent of the true percentage for all women in the school. This is probably a figure close enough to the truth to base most decisions, unless there is a special concern over a 50–50 split in the thinking. It also is better than the expense of asking all women in the college to respond.

Random Sampling. It was indicated that random sampling methods can be used to draw a sample so that it will be representative of the population. The random sampling is done much like that described in Chapter 2 where tables of random numbers were used to randomly allocate subjects to groups in an experiment. In random sampling, each sampling unit in the population must have an equal chance to appear in the sample. The population is numbered, usually in sequence, and numbers drawn from a table of random numbers until the desired sample size is available. The units in the population corresponding to these random numbers will then constitute the sample. The *sampling unit* in most educational work will usually be people: students, teachers, principals, administrators. However, the sampling unit could be elementary schools, school systems with over 50,000 students in grades one through twelve in the United States, bibliographical entries in the references of the 1969 *Encyclopedia of Educational Research,* classes in a school system, and so forth.

The sampling unit should be made explicit in the definition of the problem of interest. It is important not to obtain a sample based on one unit of classification and then describe a different sampling unit. For instance, it is *not* random sampling to be interested in individual students (as the sampling unit) and randomly sample whole *classes* of students from all the classes in schools or entire schools within a school system. Sampling by classes, when the interest is in individual students, is called cluster sampling and will be discussed later. This is a different type of sampling than using a random sampling of the students themselves as the sampling unit. If high schools are the sampling unit, generalizations cannot be made readily about high school students. Some high schools are several times larger than others and the data on students in the small high schools would be overweighted in simple summaries. (There are other problems as well.) The concern is to define just what it is that is to be observed, i.e., the sampling unit. Then the population of interest must be defined. Finally, a representative sample of those sampling units must be drawn from the population.

As was indicated, the simplest way to draw a representative sample from a population is to do it at random. The major problems in drawing a random sample are, first, to select the population and the sampling unit, and second, to number the population. The problem of enumerating the population is often already resolved by prior numberings of the group for other reasons, in our number-happy society. In many educational systems the students have numbers. They may be sequential or have a pattern which can be used for identification. Teachers have payroll numbers. The number of high schools in a state is usually listed in the office of the state educational agency. (If not, the state high school athletic association can be contacted.) Once a numbered list or file, or a listing which can be numbered, is available, random samples can be drawn using the table of random numbers. If 1,000 sampling units or people form the population, sets of three-digit random numbers from 001 to 000 (representing 1,000) will be needed. For 100 or fewer in the population, sets of two-digit random numbers could be used, from 01 to 00 (representing 100). The table of random numbers is entered, three-digit numbers read, and their sampling units (students, schools, teachers, administrators) identified until the sample size needed is available. This is simple random sampling.

Systematic Sampling. A variation of random sampling is *systematic sampling*. Actually, the process is first random, then systematic. In many populations there is a great deal of clerical work involved in listing the random numbers from the tables and finding the identified sampling unit in the population. It is easier, but not quite as defensible, to pick a random number between one and ten, for example, "three," and then take every tenth number after that, e.g., 3, 13, 23, 33, etc. Thus a 10 percent sample is drawn readily from a sequentially numbered file. There is one simple precaution. The file cannot have been set up in such a way that the last digit has a special meaning. For instance, there might be a special code existing that all credit card numbers ending in three are limited to purchases of less than fifty dollars. Telephone numbers ending in zero are more likely to be businesses, and so forth. Also, the interval chosen cannot be a function of a recurring cycle in the file. (This writer once picked a one-third systematic sample of dwelling units in a city by taking every third one. When he got tired of climbing to the top floor in several blocks of three-story buildings and flats, he realized that the dwelling units (apartments) ran in a cycle of threes. Further, families who live on the top floor of three-story buildings are different from those on the first and second floors.) The sampling interval chosen cannot be a function of any cycles in the population.

Stratified Sampling. A third type of sampling is *stratified sampling*. Sometimes populations can be broken into subgroups which, for sampling purposes, are called "strata." The strata might be "class in school": for instance, freshman, sophomore, junior, or senior. The strata could be "type of higher-education school": four-year liberal arts, two-year liberal arts junior college, four-year technical, two-year technical, vocational school, or community college. For some purposes, precise information about seniors may be of more interest than information about freshmen and sophomores; or perhaps the reverse is the case and lower classmen may be of more interest than upper classmen. Large high school data for some purposes are more important than data for high schools with graduating classes of less than twenty-five. Those doing follow-up studies of high school graduates may have more interest in the thinking of students who graduated more than ten years ago than those who graduated within the last few years. The principle to follow for stratified sampling is to identify the groups of greatest interest and obtain more precise data for them by taking larger samples of them.

For a regional study of professional staff of schools, three strata could be used: superintendents, principals, and teachers. A 100 percent sample of 25 superintendents might be taken, a 50 percent sample of 80 principals, and a 10 percent sample of 2400 teachers. Each separate stratum is considered as a population in itself, and random selection is done within each of the strata to pick the sample representing that particular stratum. There is little point to stratifying a population unless different percentages of samples are drawn from each. Thus, in making statements about the total high school population, the researcher must be careful to weigh the data in each class stratum proportionate to the sampling percentage in order to describe the total population accurately. In other words, if only half as many freshmen as seniors are sampled, then ultimately the freshmen data will have to be weighted about twice that of the seniors in the total data in order to present an accurate picture of the total school.

Quota Sampling. This is a fourth method of sampling and is used where it is difficult to enumerate the population. For a tax rate or school bond referendum, the voters of a city might be the population of interest. From census records, the characteristics of those of voting age can be established, the percent of men and women, the percent of various racial groups, the percent in various areas of the city, the percent of homeowners, and the percent in various occupational and industrial groups. The precision needed in the data is determined and the sample size calculated. This sample is then broken down into quotas based on the several characteristics of the population as given by the census or other data. Thus, a certain number of black, female, clerical, or salespersons living in a given area of the city would be required, as would white male laborers and white male semiprofessionals. Then it is the task of the data gatherer to obtain the sample to fit the several quotas so that the result will be representative of the city. Once the quotas have been filled, the sample is treated as if it were random.

Cluster Sampling. This is a fifth general type of sampling procedure. While any of the first four methods of sampling—random, systematic random, stratified, and quota—are recommended as useful for professional, administrative, and general research work in education, cluster sampling is not. Cluster sampling draws the sampling units in groups or clusters, and thus the usual random sampling logic and procedures do not apply precisely. The description of cluster sampling is presented here only so that professional educational practitioners will recognize and avoid it.

For example, if the subject of a study is the behavior of individual students, then the sampling unit is an individual student. All the students in the population of interest, for example the school system, must be accounted for and a sample of individual students drawn by any one of the methods presented above. It is the individual students who are to be observed, not whole classes of students. This means that each student in the sample must be sought out and studied. Since the students will be spread out all over the school system and in various classes in a school, there is some effort involved in finding each student in the sample.

Occasionally, a person will decide to do such a study by drawing a sample of classes in the system, although he intends to study the individual behavior of specific students in the sampled classes. After all, it is much easier to find 20 classes of 25 students each than it is to find even 200 individual students in perhaps that many classes. Further, these persons reason that, while it is not strictly a random sample of students, there would be a lot more students (500) in the class sampling method than the 200 in the individual student sampling method. They reason, faultily, that big samples are better than small samples and thus use the class-sampling method. However, by using the class as the sampling unit, but the student as the observational unit, the sampling procedure falls into the category of cluster sampling.

The calculation of sampling limits and the assurance of samples representative of the populations is a much more difficult task in cluster sampling than it is in random, systematic, stratified, or quota sampling. For these latter sampling methods, a professional educator interested in the procedure and reasonably adept with arithmetic can handle the sampling methods and calculate the confidence intervals. For cluster sampling, a mathematical statistician with a knowledge of sample survey theory is often required. Even then, certain prior knowledge is required about the effects of the clustering (into classes, schools, school systems, and so forth) on the standard deviations (representing individual differences) of the variables of interest. These effects of clustering technically are called *intraclass* correlations. They generally have not been calculated for educational variables, at least in any available form. Even though cluster sampling appears to be labor-saving for educational professionals and most educational researchers, it is best to avoid cluster sampling and using sampling units which are not the units being observed.

SAMPLING IN EDUCATION

There are also many combinations of the sampling methods just presented. Experts in the field of sampling and survey methods, particularly in the U.S. Bureau of the Census, have devised many procedures which maximize information gained while minimizing the costs of collecting data. These may involve combinations, such as a stratified and systematic cluster sample, for example. If one is not in the full-time business of sampling, the costs of assembling a team of experts to do the job in the very best way will not be offset by the savings in the sampling plans they devise. For most administrative information gathering in a school system (or even for much state and regional work), it is adequate to use the principles and confidence intervals to be presented here. The slight additional gains in precision or cost savings with the complex sampling plans are lost in the additional planning overhead and analysis costs. Also, the local expertise that develops in doing a sampling study is valuable. Finally, usually the data are needed quickly. It is better to get the data (at less than best efficiency) and make the administrative decisions, than to await an expert's complex sampling plan before being able to obtain data necessary to make a costly decision.

Sampling plans involve the estimation of sample sizes, costs involved in obtaining the sample, and precision of estimates from the sample of the population's descriptions. The major problem to resolve in developing a sampling plan is precision versus cost. With large samples, although the estimates of the population characteristics are rather precise, the cost of obtaining such a sample is high. When costs are reduced by using small samples, the estimates of population characteristics are less precise. However, the alternative to not using a sampling plan to obtain information on a population is either to study the entire population or to make decisions on the basis of an authoritative eyeball analysis. Both of these alternatives are costly, though in different ways.

The first step in an educational problem involving descriptions of fairly large groups is to identify areas in the educational system about which decisions are being made. If the total population's records are being analyzed to obtain data for decision-making, a sampling procedure certainly should be considered. More frequently the problems are less obvious. The question should be asked: Where are decisions being made about groups for whom there is little information? This tries to avoid the error of omission of data.

Consider some educational problems. How many retired teachers are there in the state whose only resource is their pension (which now is near the poverty level)? How many teachers are teaching high school mathematics in the state who were not majors in this subject? How many students who graduated from high school in the school system five years ago actually finished two years of academic education beyond the high school? These are very large data-gathering problems if the whole population were to be studied, yet decisions involving these kinds of data are made regularly. The best data-gathering solution is a sampling plan in which precision of information is balanced against the costs of collecting the data and the costs of the effects of the decisions.

An educational administrator needs to recognize the need for precision, or lack of it, before making a decision. A guessed estimate of the percentage of the population with the characteristics is also needed. If the guessed estimate of the percent of the population having the incidence is near the 50 percent point and the administrator has to be very sure that a majority exists in the population, a very large sample will be needed. If the administrators making the decision feel that an observed *sample* value estimate could be different by plus or minus 10 percent from the true *population* value and the same decision would still be made, a rather small sample will be sufficient.

SAMPLE SIZES

A first appraisal of the precision of a sample value incidence is simply $100/\sqrt[2]{n}$ percent with a 95 percent confidence interval. The letter "n" is the size (i.e., number) of the sample. Thus a sample of 100 will yield sample estimates of true population percentage values within a precision of plus or minus 10 percent. This calculation is $100/\sqrt{100} = 100/10 = \pm 10$ percent. Thus, if the population value is guessed to be 50 percent in the administrator's judgment, a sample of 100 will be expected to give a sampling incidence value within plus or minus 10 percent of the true population value incidence.

A sample of 49 yields a first estimate value of slightly more than plus or minus 14 percent, $100/\sqrt[2]{49} = 100/7 = \pm 14+$ percent. Larger samples yield smaller percent limits. A sample of 225 gives a first estimate value of about plus or minus $6\frac{2}{3}$ percent. The calculations are $100/\sqrt[2]{225} = 100/15 = \pm 6\frac{2}{3}$ percent. Samples of 400 reduce these limits to about plus or minus 5 percent, $100/\sqrt{400} = 100/20 = \pm 5$ percent. It is emphasized that these are first appraisals of precision because they are reduced, in some cases considerably, (1) if the population percentage to be estimated is other than 50 percent, and (2) if the sample size is a large proportion of the total population from which it is a sample.

A *confidence interval* is defined by these plus and minus limits. These plus and minus limits are placed around the actual percent incidence value found in the sample. *Then* the reasoning is that the true percent incidence in the population would fall within the confidence interval (estimated from the sample value) in 95 percent of all such samples.

The confidence intervals estimated previously are ones typically used by statisticians. They are the interval estimates around the sample's calculated average percent of incidence of the characteristic. Within them is expected to be the population's true percent incidence in 95 percent of all the random samples that could be drawn. (Note that in random sampling almost anything is *possible*, including very extreme samples from a population. Extreme samples are not *probable*, however.) This 95 percent confidence interval used in these examples covers 95 percent of all the possible samples from a population, except the 2.5

percent of the possible sample values at the upper extreme and the 2.5 percent of the possible sample values at the lower extreme of the sampling distribution. Thus, the data resulting from a sample using the plus and minus confidence limits given indicates the limits of the accuracy of the sample data nineteen times out of twenty.

In studying only a fraction of the total population via a sample, some accuracy will be lost. The statement that the population value lies beyond the indicated plus or minus confidence interval limits only one time in twenty, or 5 percent of the time (100% − 95% = 5%) is the typical statement made using sampling procedures. Actually, the confidence interval will be within half of the indicated plus or minus confidence limits around the obtained average more than two times out of three. In the example with 95 percent confidence limits of ±10 percent, this means that in two out of three samples, the sample values obtained actually would be within ±5 percent of the true population value. This lack of absolute accuracy then is not a great cost, particularly if many more studies can be made because of the use of sampling. If the whole population had to be studied, it might be done only infrequently.

Some statisticians use a 99 percent confidence interval. The 99 percent confidence limits are about one-fourth larger than the ones which will be presented here. While the 99 percent confidence intervals are larger estimates, the true population value falls outside of the indicated plus and minus values only one time in one hundred.

Instead of calculating the rough first appraisals of the sample size needed, the plus and minus confidence interval values can be obtained from Table 7–1. For a given plus and minus limit desired (using the 95 percent confidence interval size), the sample size can be read. Conversely for a given sample size, which is feasible in terms of time or costs involved, the plus and minus confidence interval limits in the table can, be read.

To estimate the money available for data collection, first subtract from the total funds the costs of analyses and report preparation. The funds remaining are those available for data collection. The cost of collecting one sampling unit observation could then be divided into the funds available for data collection. This yields a first estimate of sample size. This is the reverse method of estimating sample sizes than that of working with estimated needs for data precision, but it often helps in arriving at a decision about sample size.

With this sample size, enter Table 7–1 and determine the first estimate of plus or minus confidence interval limits. Present these plus or minus limits to the administrator who will be using the information with a statement something like, "With such and such (amount) dollars,

TABLE 7-1   First Estimate of Sample Size and Confidence Interval Limits

95% Confidence Interval Based on a Population Estimate of 50% and a Population Quite Large Relative to Sample Size

Sample Size	Plus and Minus Confidence Interval Limit
0	(Guess a population value of 50%. You can't be in error more than ± 50%.)
10	± 31%
20	± 22%
30	± 18%
40	± 16%
50	± 14%
60	± 13%
70	± 12%
80	± 11%
90	± 10.3%
100	± 9.8%
125	± 8.8%
150	± 8.0%
175	± 7.4%
200	± 6.9%
225	± 6.5%
250	± 6.2%
275	± 5.9%
300	± 5.6%
400	± 4.9%
500	± 4.4%
750	± 3.6%
1000	± 3.1%
2000	± 2.2%
5000	± 1.4%

Based on $\dfrac{1.96\ \sqrt{2500}}{\sqrt{n}}$

I believe we can get estimates of the percentage of various characteristics in the population group within ± X percent. This is for the total group only, not for subgroup breakdowns. Is this close enough for you to make a decision?" If not, then ask how close an estimate is needed. Enter Table 7-1 with this value and get an estimate of the sample size needed. Multiply this sample size by the cost per sampling unit and add the analysis and report preparation costs. Indicate the total of these costs to the administrator (and perhaps the cost of collecting the data from every unit in the population, if feasible). Within these two sets of estimates, usually a reasonable compromise of sample size, costs, and acceptable plus and minus confidence limits can be achieved.

Actually, the plus and minus confidence intervals generally will be somewhat better, that is, smaller. This is true because it happens that the largest set of confidence limits are those for a population characteristic incidence of 50 percent. This is the incidence of greatest sampling variability. Any population characteristic incidence percent other than 50 percent (higher or lower) will have a smaller confidence interval for a given sample size. For instance, if the percentage of males in a population of high school teachers is estimated at 50 percent, then the plus or minus confidence intervals for a given sample size will be at a maximum. However, if the percentage of male elementary school teachers in the population of elementary teachers is to be estimated, the plus or minus limits will be much smaller for the same size sample. This is because it is known that the percentage of male elementary school teachers in most schools is further from 50 percent than the percent of male teachers in high schools. With a 10 percent estimated average for males in the grade school teacher population, the plus and minus confidence interval limits are less than two-thirds the size of the limits for the 50 percent incidence high school teacher population. (The same statement would be true also of the plus and minus confidence interval limits if the population incidence were 90 percent.)

The principle is that equal size samples of characteristics that are at or near 50 percent in a population have larger confidence interval limits than characteristics that are far more common or much rarer in a population, e.g., 80 percent or 20 percent, 90 percent or 10 percent.

Thus, a second step can be made in estimating sample size and confidence interval limits. Take the first estimate of confidence limit size from Table 7-1 and multiply it by a correction factor from Table 7-2. This will take into account the reduction in confidence interval limit size because of common or rare incidence of the characteristic being studied.

An example is a sample size of 80. From Table 7-1, confidence limits of plus and minus 11 percent are read from the table. However, the percentage incidence estimated in the population is not 50 percent but 20 percent. From Table 7-2, the correction factor is found to be .80. Thus the Table 7-1 confidence limit of plus and minus 11 percent is multiplied by .80 or 11 percent × .80 = 8.8 percent. The confidence limits now are estimated at plus or minus 8.8 percent.

One last correction can be made if the sample size estimated is an important part of total population size (or stratum size in the case of

TABLE 7-2   Correction Factor for Table 7-1 Values for Common and Rare
              Percentage Incidence of Characteristics

Percent Incidence	Correction Factor
50%	none
40%, 60%	.98
35%, 65%	.95
30%, 70%	.92
25%, 75%	.87
20%, 80%	.80
15%, 85%	.71
10%, 90%	.60
5%, 95%	.44
2.5%, 97.5%	.31

Correction factor based on ratio of $\sqrt{\dfrac{(P)(1-P)}{2500}}$, where P = the estimated percent of incidence.

stratified sampling), as would be the case in many local school situations. If a graduating class is 250 and a sample of 100 is to be used in a follow-up study five years after graduation, the sample of 100 is a large part of the population of 250. As a result of this, the confidence interval limits estimated at plus and minus 9.8 percent from Table 7-1, and perhaps reduced by the correction factor found in Table 7-2, would be reduced still further. Table 7-3 gives the confidence limit correction factors when sample size is an important part of the population size.

TABLE 7-3   Correction Factor for Confidence Limits When Sample Size is an
              Important Part of Population Size (Population Size over 100)

Percent Sample/Population	Correction Factor
5%	.98
10%	.95
20%	.89
30%	.84
40%	.78
50%	.71
60%	.63
70%	.55
(over 70%, generally takes a 100% sample)	

Correction factor based on $\sqrt{\dfrac{N-n}{N-1}}$, where N = population size, and n = sample size.

In the example of the graduating class follow-up, the sample of 100 is 40 percent of the population of 250. Consulting Table 7-3, we find that the confidence interval plus and minus limits estimated from Table 7-1 (and, if desired, corrected by the factors in Table 7-2) can be reduced by multiplying them by .78. Thus the plus and minus 9.8 percent estimated confidence limits for a sample of 100 (found from Table 7-1), when corrected for the important sample size fraction of the population, are now 7.6 percent.

It may be noted that when the sample size is over about two-thirds, or 70 percent of a population, it is easier to study the whole population. The advantages of sampling procedures are offset by the extra administrative labor of drawing a sample, identifying the sample in the population, and doing the arithmetic of computing the confidence limits.

The three tables presented give the estimates and correction factors for the confidence intervals in sampling studies. The tables are useful as quick, working values, but those adept at arithmetic may wish to make more exact estimates of the confidence interval limits obtained after the sampling study data have been collected. These are not difficult and are useful for more formal scientific research, though they may be more than the educational administrator needs. The complete 95 percent confidence limit equation is as follows:

$$1.96 \sqrt[2]{\frac{P \times (1-P)}{n} \times \frac{N - n}{n - 1}}$$

Where, P = percent of incidence

n = sample size

N = population size

This value is added and subtracted from the observed percentage in the sample to form the confidence limit. It is expected that the true percentage value in the population will lie within these limits in 95 out of 100 samples in the long run.

(The 99 percent confidence limit equation substitutes the constant 2.58 for the 1.96 of the 95 percent confidence limit examples presented in this chapter. The 90 percent confidence limits use a constant of 1.65. Use of a constant of 1.00 yields a confidence limit of 68 percent, slightly larger than two-thirds.)

ACCURACY AND PRECISION IN SAMPLING

The preceding discussion of confidence interval limits was in terms of *precision*. A confidence interval is more precise when it is small and less precise when it is large. However, it is assumed that the sample value around which the confidence interval is placed is not a biased estimate of the value in the population. If the sample value for any reason is not representative of the population value, the sample is said to be inaccurate. *Precision* of a sample refers to the "tightness" of the confidence interval limits, and *accuracy* to a lack of bias. With random sampling or any of its variants, an unbiased, accurate estimate of the population incidence is expected. A biased estimate may be present with deviations from a random sample because of a lack of response in the sample group, out-of-date population list, lack of file data available for some sampled units, use of the wrong sampling unit for the population of interest, or a biased population listing for the population of interest.

Any of these problems can lead to a biased, inaccurate estimate of the population incidence, despite very precise confidence interval limits as the result of a very large sample. Very precise confidence interval limits around an inaccurate estimate of a population value (as the result of a biased sample) are not very helpful. To avoid biased samples, use random samples based on up-to-date population listings. It is helpful to consider what the population of interest is so that the correct sampling unit from the population will be chosen.

One of the major problems in much educational work is the lack of response to a sample contacted by mail. Returns of 40 to 50 percent of the designated sample are not uncommon in the literature. A return rate at those levels should be a source of great concern. One of the ways to avoid a major lack of response is to pick small samples such that each sampling unit in the sample can be vigorously pursued. Several follow-up cycles to bring in the missing responses usually will be required. These follow-ups may have to be done by telegraph and telephone, as well as by several mailings, if a thorough job is to be done. This means that the financial resources available for the study will need to be allocated in advance to accommodate for follow-up costs. Better still, perhaps the information is best collected by interview or by phone in the first place rather than by mailed response. It is suggested that an 80 to 90 percent response rate is needed from the identified sample for reasonable assurance that the samples' estimates of the populations' values and incidences will be reasonably accurate.

Even with a 90 percent rate of response, some idea of the characteristics of the nonresponders should be available, along with considerations of how these characteristics might influence the reported data. This can be done by having a small set of population or sample characteristics that are known and against which the characteristics of the responding group can be compared. This comparison should give clues to the direction of biases and their extent in the responding sample. It should be noted that the confidence interval limits set should be based on the size of the *responding* sample. This should be taken into account when the sample sizes needed are estimated from the tables and equations.

CROSS CLASSIFICATION AND SUBSAMPLE ANALYSES

One more precaution on confidence interval limits needs to be given. There is great temptation, once the data of a survey are collected, to analyze them by a number of cross-classification variables. Confidence interval limits based on sample size (or stratum size) have been suggested. To attempt to make statements about subsamples, e.g., girls within the Senior class, or worse, Senior girls who went on to a noncollegiate type of technical or occupational training beyond their high school education, cross-classifies the sample into such small groups that the confidence interval limits are quite large. It is important to estimate the subsample sizes needed by taking any cross-classification analyses into account. This is done in order to accommodate for the subsample analyses. The procedures are as given previously, but the survey designer will find that the overall size of the sample must increase by several magnitudes if rather precise confidence limits are to be made for subsamples based on cross classification of identification variables. Care should be taken in reporting analyses based on cross-classification samples to indicate the enlarged confidence interval limits and the greater uncertainty of the statements made about the subsample data.

One alternative way to handle this problem is to use the cross-classification variables in defining strata within the overall population, then to use these strata as the groups within which samples of varying size will be taken. For instance, in the school survey example, the male-female and collegiate-technical school-work dimensions could be used as the stratifying variables producing six separate samples. Then, various sampling plans could be used within each of these six strata depending upon the precision needed of the estimates in each cell.

SCHOOL SURVEYS·

Educational survey research also has another meaning and use that needs clarification. This is the school survey method. The school survey method has developed separately from sampling and survey research methods. The school survey is really a case study of a single school system by experts who make recommendations based on their review and study of the system. They compare what they find with what, in their expert opinion, is good practice within the limits of the resources available, and they make their recommendations on these judgments. A school survey could make use of sampling methods in the collection of information for this purpose. More often, however, the experts generally use available data plus their own data based on nonsystematic observation.

SAMPLING SURVEY INSTRUMENTS

As was indicated, sampling survey methods can be quite useful for collecting valuable information upon which educational decisions can be based. Generally the information collected for this purpose is not the kind for which standardized instruments are readily available. Each survey instrument is more or less tailor-made for the particular data collection purpose at hand. It is likely not to be an entirely new instrument, however, in that other investigators will have asked similar questions before. It is recommended that those questions be used, if possible.

All the general rules and suggestions of the chapter on measurement hold true for survey instruments as well. Instruments must be developed individually. It is valuable if an item or sets of items can be found which have been used previously in similar situations. The strengths and weaknesses of these items can be studied in rephrasing the items for use in the current survey instrument. It is suggested that any instrument construction for a survey be guided by a rationale, that is, a set of tentative explanations of the operation of the situation to be described: What are the probable interrelationships among the variables? What alternative possibilities are there? These are also the questions to be answered by the items which will be used in a survey instrument. Once the area of the problem has been identified and the rationale relating to it developed, questions to be used in the survey instrument can be developed which will yield information about the overall questions in addition to the standardized instruments.

METHODS OF PRESENTATION

In addition to the survey instrument to be used, the method of presentation of the survey instrument needs to be considered. The questions can be asked orally in a face-to-face interview. This has the advantage of following interesting areas of observations as they come to light in response to the initial survey questions. The interview format allows greater rapport to be established and more sensitive questions to be asked. Some information may be offered by the respondent which is off-the-record but which is invaluable for interpreting the dynamics of a situation. A disadvantage of the interview is that the range of standard, directly comparable questions that can be asked is reduced from those which can be asked in written form in a questionnaire. The interview does make the information of illiterate and nonfacile readers and writers available, and these are often important populations of interest to educators. The interview is costly in interviewer time, but it allows a range of responses which is not obtainable in any other way.

The telephone interview is less costly in time, but the depth of response in the telephone interview is not as great as the face-to-face interview can be. Another problem is the socioeconomic stratification of those who have telephones which may reduce the representation of lower socioeconomic groups. While not as severe a problem as it has been in the past, the concern may still exist for certain types of problems. Of great concern is the number of unlisted phone numbers, if one uses a telephone book as the source of the population list.

QUESTIONNAIRES

The mailed questionnaire is one of the more ubiquitous forms of data collection in education. It can be quite valuable when well used, but frequently it is used so poorly that the statement is heard that questionnaires should be banned for ten years to see if there is any real loss in the quality of educational information available. Most question-naires in education are too long, have a percentage of returns that is inadequate, attempt to study high level, scientific problems from an inadequate theoretical base, or tend to underanalyze the data.

When used to make smaller jobs out of large jobs and involve the simpler forms of description of educational resources or processes, the questionnaire can be a useful and valuable research method. When used to study the more abstract forms of human social behavior and interactions, its use requires a finesse and approach based upon years of experience in the behavioral and social sciences, if it is to be used well.

Survey research, with its emphasis on the representative descrip-tion at a fairly straightforward level of large populations, can be handled by mailed questionnaires. However, these questionnaires must be well used, or they are worse than useless. Poorly used, they are a waste of effort for both the researcher and those who fill them out.

The construction of a questionnaire is time-consuming business and is an art as well as a science. If the information requested is more than routine file data, it is probably wise to seek the consultation of an expert with extensive experience in the development of questionnaires. Sociologists and social psychologists, whose scientific problems often require the use of questionnaires, are often experienced in this activity.

The questionnaire attempts to obtain information which will describe educational phenomena. Generally there will be prior information about the phenomena in the educational literature which will give suggestions about relative incidence and organization of the variables to be described. This incidence and organization should be used as the basic information in the construction of the questionnaire. The structure of the questionnaire must be well organized. There must be a set of specific objectives which can be translated into questions which, in turn, can be answered by a respondent. These questions must be designed to elicit a response which will describe accurately the information being sought. The questionnaire organization should flow logically from the objectives and be such that an analysis of the data can be made which will yield the answers to the questions asked. There are a number of suggestions which can be made that will assist in this task.

First, a questionnaire and its accompanying cover letter and materials must be brief unless the respondents are to be paid for their time. (Payment of the respondents always should be considered in research involving questionnaires. If the information to be obtained is valuable to education, is it not worth paying the respondents so that the data are complete and accurate?) One of the main purposes of brevity and paid respondents is to make every effort to achieve a high rate of response, hopefully the 80 to 90 percent or better return rate suggested. Long, rambling questionnaires sent to a convenient population are not conducive to a high rate of response, nor do they often yield significant information.

A well-developed rationale for the study, when conveyed to a carefully selected sample, will motivate the group to respond. Each topic in a questionnaire must be introduced with questions which take into account the frame of reference of the respondents. The relationships among the questions, and the respondent's view of the importance of the objectives of the research and the questionnaire are important. Thus the questions must be in a sequence that follows an organization that makes sense to the respondents. The well-designed questionnaire leads the respondent from one question to the next.

In the broad scope, most general questions are asked first, followed by an increase in focused and more restricted questions in each area. The language used in the questions should be chosen so that the vocabulary and sentence structure are simple. The words used should be well within the range of ready understanding by the respondents. Slang and clichés should be avoided. The questions should relate to the respondents' current level of information so that they can respond easily.

As in all measurement procedures in the behavioral and social sciences, only facts and behavior should be requested as responses. Interpretations of facts and behavior should be done later by the researcher. In general, no questions should be asked, especially in a mailed questionnaire, which might require a socially unacceptable answer or which might be a threat to the self-concept of the responder. Such a situation encourages inaccurate answers or nonreturns of the questionnaire. Also, leading questions should not be asked, i.e., those that suggest an appropriate response or make it easier to respond in one way rather than another. Use of words in the questions which are emotionally loaded, favorably or unfavorably, should also be avoided. Associating a particular response with a desirable goal, such as the end of war, lower taxes, and elimination of disease and suffering, should also be avoided. Each question should be restricted to a single concept. To link a question about vocational education with universal employment intertwines these concepts to the extent that it is difficult to interpret the responses.

Questions can be of two general forms, open-ended or multiple response. In the open-ended response, the respondents reply in their own words. In the multiple-response format, a range of replies are given and the respondent selects the one (or several) that are most appropriate. The open-ended response can yield a wide range of information and indicate the respondent's level of knowledge. Thus, it can be more clearly ascertained whether the question was understood by the respondent. However, the open-ended response can be difficult to code for analysis purposes. Content analysis techniques are appropriate for this purpose but require a scientific expertise not usually acquired by users of questionnaires for the purposes suggested in this chapter. Open-ended questions are valuable as a means of ascertaining, in a pretest of a questionnaire, the range and dimensions of responses to a question. These responses can then be categorized for the development of closed-end responses to a question.

All questionnaires should be pretested, usually several times. After the original structure is set up and questions framed, instrument and language should "cool" for several days; they should then be reread. Ambiguities pop up where the wording seemed perfectly clear before. When this revising and editing is done, the draft of the questionnaire may be given to several friends for response to the items and to the questionnaire in general. More imprecise language and concepts will become apparent. After these changes are made, a trial run with subjects from the population should be made without the researcher being present. However, comments and suggestions should be solicited from the respondents. After all of these changes, reorganizations, revisions, and editing have been done, the questionnaire is ready for use.

However, even at this stage, instead of one grand data collection, consideration should be given to a two, or three, or four-stage sequence of several questionnaires and samples in order to gain deeper insight into the nature of the phenomena described and to test alternative hypotheses about the data. If ambiguities arise, or further questions seem necessary for clarity or explanation, these can be handled in later phases of the series of questionnaires. Several stages of inquiry reduce the need to attempt to obtain all the answers in one questionnaire and help keep each one brief, an all-important consideration. This sequential inquiry procedure grows out of the continuing concern for checking alternative hypotheses and explanations that is so important in all descriptive research. Information will be learned and questions arise in the course of administering the first questionnaires in the sequence which can be further probed and examined by later instruments in new samples.

RESPONDENT RAPPORT

All data collection requiring the cooperation of subjects should be explained to the subjects to gain their cooperation and aid in establishing rapport. *Rapport* is the atmosphere of accord, harmony, and good feeling between the researcher and the respondents. The purpose is to assure the respondents of the mutual interests they and the researcher hold and of the value of the data to be collected for achieving goals which the respondent holds. The thoughtfulness, care, and sincerity of the researcher should be evident in the cover letter and in the questionnaire. The whole atmosphere of any data collection process should be one of receptive understanding, a warm responsiveness, acceptance of expressed feelings, and freedom from pressure or coercion. A cover letter for a questionnaire, while brief, should explain the purpose of the study, why and how the respondent was selected, and the sponsors of the research, if any. (Note that for much federally supported educational research, the federal agency regulations forbid the use of their name. They may also require agency clearance of nonstandard instruments such as questionnaires.) The cover letter should aid in establishing the credentials of the study and the researcher.

If the research involves recording data from files, there should be little problem in obtaining accurate data. Dry runs of the procedures can be made to assure that instructions are well understood and all contingencies covered. If something is not included, the file can be marked and the researcher can instruct the assisting data-gatherer as to the correct response. However, for questionnaires and interviewing, the situation often will not "hold" until a decision can be made. Thorough pretesting of questionnaires and training of interviewers is a must.

DATA HANDLING AND ANALYSES

Thinking ahead is also a good slogan for anyone collecting large amounts of data. Data handling, transfer, and analyses must be carefully considered before a final commitment on a data collection instrument is made. Consider how answers will be scored, how this scoring will be done, how the scores will be recorded, how they will be put into analyzable form, and what the analysis and its possible interpretations will be. The scientific aspects are important, but the data handling and analyses can be overwhelming to those who have not thought ahead and planned for these procedures. Special machine-scored computer cards, mark sense cards (cards which can be machine punched from the markings on them), machine scoring, or optical scoring of responses via photosensitive methods should be considered if the samples are large. Postcards and IBM cards used as the response record should be considered. Further, the size of these cards forces brevity, a worthy achievement, upon the researcher. Payment of the responder aids in establishing sincerity and importance of the data. Return, stamped envelopes and a cleanly typed or printed instrument are basic requirements. Responses to closed-end questions should be made by a simple checking or marking.

If the researcher starts to get beyond the study of rather straightforward administrative data and the limits given here, a consultant should be sought who has experience in sampling survey studies (as has been recommended with other types of research). Survey research, particularly with questionnaires, can range from the simple, quite useful, and labor-saving to highly complex sampling procedures and analyses, the latter in scientific studies of social and personal relationships. The first are recommended to the professional educator; the latter reserved to the domain of scientists.

SUMMARY

The material included in this chapter has indicated the value and procedures of sampling studies in making large jobs smaller, particularly for decision-making by educational administrators. Types of information amenable to data collection via surveys and types of sampling methods were presented. Definitions and examples of precision and accuracy of sampling were given, and their relationship to the square root of the sample size and random sampling presented. Problems of missing data, sampling plans other than random, questionnaire construction, and return of data compared to indicated sample size were given. Sample, sampling unit, and population were defined. Both tables and formulas for estimating confidence interval limits were put forward. Finally, rules for the construction of questionnaires were offered, and the types of problems for which questionnaires are useful, cover letters, data handling, "do's" and "don'ts" of question construction, preliminary tryouts, brevity, organization, bias, and open- and closed-end questions were discussed.

STUDY AND DISCUSSION PROBLEMS

1. Describe an educational problem where a sampling survey would be most useful.
2. Can you think of survey studies done recently in education that could have been done better and cheaper using sampling procedures?
3. List several types of sampling procedures. Which would you use and not use?
4. Pick a sample size from a population of size 1,000. Determine a confidence interval for your sample size.
5. Define some educational populations of interest to you. Suggest methods of sampling from these populations.
6. Develop a brief questionnaire for an educational study. Pretest it and suggest revisions for it.
7. List some of the considerations that must be taken into account when planning a questionnaire survey.
8. Estimate the costs of a mailed questionnaire to 250 persons. Included should be the costs of development, typing, questionnaire reproduction,

mailing, payment of respondents, return mail, clerical efforts, analyses, report writing, and report reproduction.

9. Differentiate between precision and bias in sampling studies.
10. What effect does the rate of response have on the usefulness of a questionnaire study?
11. What is a school survey? How does it differ from a sample survey study?
12. Find a questionnaire study in the educational literature and comment on it in light of what you have learned in this chapter.
13. List several methods for collecting survey data other than questionnaires.
14. List characteristics of a well-constructed questionnaire survey study.
15. What is rapport? How is it established?

REFERENCES

Cochran, W. G. *Sampling techniques* (2nd ed.). New York: Wiley, 1963.

Hansen, M. H., Hurwitz, W. N., and Madow, W. G. *Sample survey methods and theory*. New York: Wiley, 1953.

Parten, M. B. *Surveys, polls, and samples: Practical procedures.* New York: Harper Brothers, 1950.

Warwick, D. P., and Lissinger, C. A. *The sample survey: Theory and practice.* New York: McGraw-Hill, 1975.

Prediction, Classification, and Related Issues in Education

Chapter 8

The last two major types of purely descriptive research methods in education are prediction and classification. To predict and to classify are the main purposes of science; however, this chapter will be devoted to applied prediction and classification in day-to-day educational situations.

PREDICTION

Prediction is description of the future status of a student, teacher, enrollment, and so forth. Classification as presented here will be primarily that of student classification—attempting to determine what group a student looks most like in terms of test scores, abilities, interests, and background. Prediction and classification of students (and others) are among the major decision-making areas of education. These functions form a large part of the activities of guidance personnel in schools, but they are not limited to guidance people. Principals, teachers, supervisors, directors, and school psychologists are among those who will recognize, upon examination, that some of their decisions are in the categories of prediction and classification.

The problem of prediction of individual behavior has long been of major interest in the behavioral sciences. In general, there are two major approaches to the problem. One approach is to have a trained expert, well versed in some area of behavior, examine the available records. The information can be test scores, interviews, and observational data for one individual at a time. The expert then makes a judgment of what that individual might do in some future situation. The second general approach is to examine a standard set of record data of a group which has performed a task and then determine which of the prior records correlate highest with successful performance of the task.

Meehl (1954) made one of the first major examinations of the relative effectiveness of these two general approaches. He searched the literature of the behavioral sciences for examples where both of these procedures had been tried and compared one against the other. There were sixteen to twenty comparative examples available in the literature at that time, and Meehl found that in all but one of the comparisons, the standard weights of the statistical predictions were either superior or, at worst, equal to the overall judgment of an expert. Later it was determined that even this one deviant case had been a misclassification and that it, too, followed the general conclusion. Meehl also noted that it was far less expensive and a better use of experts' time not to have them make broad predictive judgments when statistical methods would do as well.

As with almost all good research, one of the important outcomes of Meehl's work was that better questions could be asked. Sawyer asked them in 1966 when he reexamined the Meehl data and brought together a number of additional comparative studies of the same type. His questions were not simply which general approach was more efficient, but what kind of data was more effective, expert judgments or standard records, when combined in which of the two ways: (1) a global, overall interpretation, or (2) a more or less mechanical procedure (statistical weighting). Essentially, Sawyer was using the accumulated, comparative data of the behavioral sciences over the span of their relatively short history to gain insight into this problem of such importance to educators, especially to guidance personnel. He was able to find and examine forty-five studies covering a range of topics from success in many types of training and school situations, to parole violations, length of hospitalization of psychotics, marriage success, job statisfaction, leadership improvement in therapy, and number of live births from a marriage. Considering the worldwide sources and the range of topics, the consistency of the results is remarkable. Again, in not one case did the global, overall expert's opinion exceed the quality of the decision made by a purely mechanical statistical weighting of the data, as in a regression analysis. (See Regression in Chapter 3). For the second part of the question, that of the use of experts' judgments in collecting data about the subjects, it was clear that these judgments were of distinct value and aided the predictions. In fact, many of the observations were data that could have been collected in no other way; namely, interviews, and ratings of behavior using projective tests.

This summary of the methods for prediction and the types of data of value has major implications for educational prediction. First, all predictions should be based on a standard weighting of variables developed through statistical methods. Second, all types of data, standardized tests, prior grades, judgments, observations, and anecdotal records should be used as variables in making these predictions.

There are other considerations in the use of these suggested methods for educational prediction. Among these is that statistical prediction is cheaper than any other method. Further, with computers, it is a simple matter to collect the records of a group that has passed through an educational process of some kind and determine which of the prior-collected data variables predicts the educational accomplishment. These are differentially weighted by the correlational analysis so that the weighting of overlapping predictors is minimized. The total number of variables that have to be observed, collected, recorded, stored in files, and actually used in the system can be reduced to a minimum. Thus, the administrative costs of data collection, scoring, recording, and filing are reduced.

Another consideration is the legal one. Federal laws, as well as the laws of many states and cities, forbid discrimination in hiring, firing, advancement, placement, or awarding benefits on the basis of race, creed, color, sex, or national origin. If casual observation or general thinking is used as a basis for prediction of success in educational and training activities, those procedures may very well be shown: (1) to discriminate on one of these bases, and (2) not to be empirically related to the measures of educational success. At this point the educational system can be immersed in grave legal problems. Even if the educational system is a part of the state or local government and not covered specifically in the law, this is still a tenuous ethical situation. It is best to demonstrate, through correlation and regression equations, that the bases for prediction of educational and training success are empirically determined.

Another legal concern is the possible applicability of the Supreme Court decision of Griggs, *et al.* vs. The Duke Power Company (1971). In this case, which has had far-reaching implications for personnel management practices in business and industry, the Court specifically indicated that no general test or measurement device can be used which has not been shown to be related empirically to success on the job. It may seem strange that those who use psychological tests had to be forced into an effective use of them as the result of a Supreme Court ruling, but it has been noted already that people are not always rational. If the ruling were extended to education, there might well be some panic, and much selection and testing would cease. Consider teacher-selection testing as an example. Further, the number of repeated, specific validations of psychological tests in school systems against school criteria is not exceptionally high compared to the opportunities for such validity studies.

Upon the announcement of the Supreme Court decision, one of the major scientific and professional groups in the behavioral sciences, the American Psychological Association, indicated that the Association fully concurred with the court's thinking and further, that there was nothing in the decision that was not already a part of their code of ethics relative to the use of psychological tests. The code of ethics (1970, xxii) for members of the Association indicates that "The psychologist . . . does not . . . use techniques that fail to meet professional standards established in particular fields."

Finally, the general public is becoming disenchanted with tests that are poorly used. Even some professional groups in education are concerned. At least one National Education Association affiliate has called for an immediate moratorium on standardized testing and for the previous scores to be removed from the cumulative record files.

If tests, observational data, and other records in cumulative record files are to be used for prediction purposes, they should be used with maximum effectiveness. In fact, one might ask, of what use are cumulative file records other than for predictive purposes unless they are kept for historical purposes? Maximum effectiveness is established through the determination of empirical relationships between the test, observational and record data, and those behaviors which are to be predicted. Before the advent of computers, this could be done only on a now-and-then basis with the results extrapolated to other grades, other schools, and other groups in broad but rather tenuous generalizations. With computers and standard analytical programs for correlation and regression procedures, the empirical validity among possible predictor variables and the measures of educational accomplishment can be determined readily. The importance of each predictor variable can be ascertained also, and each student's predicted score can be estimated for numerous criteria. This should be done and can be done simply, easily, and at minimum cost for every student or possible student in a class, school, or system.

TYPES OF PREDICTION AND CLASSIFICATION

There are two general types of prediction. First, recall from the chapter on measurement (Chapter 4) that there are two general classifications of variables: interval measures and nominal (or categorical) variables. The first general type of prediction is used when the criterion variable being predicted is interval measurement, such as grades in school or scores on a standard achievement test. The question asked is: How well will this person do on this criterion? The reader will recall from Chapter 4 that many standardized educational achievement tests, grades, and some observation scales and ratings tend to be scored as interval measures. Thus, this type of prediction has wide applicability in education. If there is only one predictor variable, the correlation and regression weights are developed as they were in the chapter on statistics (Chapter 3). If there is more than one predictor variable available, as is usually the case in educational prediction, then *multiple correlation* is involved.

Multiple correlation is merely an extension of simple correlation. In multiple correlation, a set of potential predictor variables are analyzed for their value in predicting a single criterion variable (which is measured in intervals). The maximum relationship between the set of predictor variables and the criterion variable is determined by weighting each of the predictor variables according to its relationship with the criterion variable and with its relationships with the other predictor variables.

In the usual educational situation, the file is full of data collected prior to the students' entry into the particular learning period or course. All of the data might as well be used in the initial determination of the multiple correlation and the appropriate regression weights. The variables that are weighted essentially zero as the result of the analysis then can be dropped from further consideration. Statistical tests should be made of these, the multiple correlation, and increases in the multiple correlation as additional predictors are added.

The weightings given to the predictor variables are called "B" weights. The several B weights are used as multipliers for each person's predictor variable scores. Then the products of these multiplications are added. A constant, labeled "A," is added to this sum to adjust the total prediction to the criterion variable's measurement system. The process of prediction is this simple. However, there are "tricks in the trade" of interpretation of multiple correlations which can be rather complex. The reader is referred to any statistics book that covers multiple correlation, and there are many of them. One which might be found particularly useful is by J.P. Guilford and B. Fruchter (*Fundamental Statistics in Psychology and Education,* McGraw-Hill, 1973, New York, Chapter 16 "Multiple Prediction"). Wherry's (1975) discussion of multiple correlation based on his extensive use will also aid in avoiding inappropriate use and interpretations. Again, the services of a consultant should be sought unless a staff member in the educational system has knowledge and experience in statistics.

The second general type of prediction involves the question: What group is the student or person like? A major way in which this type of prediction, really a classification, differs from simple and multiple correlation prediction is that the criterion variable is a nominal, or categorical, variable. Thus, a typical criterion on which students might be classified is type of scientific interest: theoretical-research, engineer, or teacher of science. Educators might be classified as administrative, student-oriented, or subject-matter-oriented. College students might be classified by subject major or school in which they are enrolled. These schools could be the humanities, social science, behavioral science, biological science, physical science, business, agriculture, and so forth. The criterion classification variable is a nominal variable, nonordered. Again, because of the student-centered approach and the broader orientation of this classification process, classification prediction may be of particular interest to guidance and personnel staff.

The statistical method of classification prediction is called *discriminant analysis.* Discriminant analysis is one of the newer multivariate analysis techniques and often is not studied in shorter sequences of courses in statistics. Discriminant analysis attempts to maximize the individual differences *among* the classification groups while minimizing the individual differences *within* each classification group. The method is quite useful in its application in education, is readily available in standard statistical program packages for computers, and should be used more frequently than it is. It will require the consultant services of one familiar with the method, though, to interpret the analyses and to help initiate its use in a school. Once this is done, it is as useful as multiple correlation. (For interpretation and use of discriminant analysis and classification procedures in an educational problem, see Chapters 9 and 10 of Cooley and Lohnes, 1971.)

The major emphasis in the discussion here, again, is for professional educators to recognize problem areas where a discriminant analysis approach would be useful in coming to a resolution of the concerns. A second accent at this point is a recognition of the types of questions for which discriminant analysis is used. This multivariate analytical technique is being more widely used in educational journals and reports. To recognize its approach and answers will make the scientific and professional literature more meaningful to the reader.

AN EXAMPLE OF MULTIPLE CORRELATION
PREDICTION

A high school was concerned about predicting the success of its students in college. In reviewing the professional literature, the guidance faculty found numerous studies of success in *a* college for students from *many* high schools. This information is valuable, but even more valuable for a school would be the weighting of variables in the records of students from *a* high school who are going to *many* colleges. These studies are rarer. The most valuable data for a high school would be the weightings of variables for its prior students which will maximally predict their college grade point average.

McCormick (McCormick & Asher, 1964) did this type of study for his high school as a class project. He requested the first semester grade point average from the colleges of all the students who had gone to college from his high school the previous year. He then used the school's cumulative record files to record the students' high school grade point average, grade point averages in each of five curriculum areas (English, Social Studies, Mathematics, Science, and Foreign Languages), three School and College Aptitude Test scores, and two Scholastic Aptitude Test Scores. There were thirteen variables in all for 116 graduates. Correlations among all the variables were computed (using a standard computer program) along with all means and standard deviations. A multiple correlation analysis also was performed to determine the weights for the twelve predictor variables (from the high school cumulative record folders) which maximized the prediction of the college grade point average. Once these weights were obtained, then it was possible to take the few important variables (and further those which are not yielding redundant information) for the current senior class, and apply the obtained regression weights to obtain the prediction of the first semester college grades. This listing of the predicted college grade point averages for the entire current senior class then can be used as a factual base from which counseling can start. It is known that these predictions are the best estimates that can be made.

Upon learning their predicted college grade point average, some students who were not thinking about going to college might think again about their decision. Others who are being pressured into going to college might have their parents brought closer to reality by examination of the predictions. The high school counselors would not have to mull over extensive records and consider at length every statement they make about a student's possible success. The predictions, while a long way from perfect, are as good as can be expected from the set of predictors and the criterion employed.

The result for this high school was that a combination of a test of intelligence and the overall high school grade point average produced a rather good prediction. The actual equation which predicted the first semester college grade point average was .20 times the intelligence test score added to .63 times the grade point average added to a constant (of adjustment) of −17.0. Readjusting the intelligence test score weight and adding the weighted Social Studies grade point average to the equation aided the prediction somewhat. Other additions and combinations gave insight into the educational and testing systems but were not of major value for the practical purpose of producing guidance information regarding college decisions for the senior class.

Given the 78 computed correlations in the 13-variable by 13-variable correlation matrix and the several multiple correlation equations, there was further information available to aid administrative decisions. For instance, there was considerable overlap of information among the standardized tests being given in the school. Perhaps it would be worthwhile to reduce the amount of standardized testing, give longer and more reliable tests when standardized tests are used, and give some of the tests later in the student's attendance in school, for example, just before the college decision is to be made. The variables already in the cumulative record, i.e., curriculum area grade point averages, may yield much the same information as some of the standardized tests. Thus, these standardized tests could be eliminated. Here the careful weighting of two or more variables increased the prediction of the overall college grade point average markedly. For other schools with different populations and different records and tests, the results could be rather different.

This methodology is readily available for every school and should be used as an engineering method to do the best job with the materials available at a reasonable cost. If some insight is gained into interrelationships among various aspects of the school's operations, so much the better. The educational professional will want both kinds of information and will recognize that these are areas where analytical methods are available for assisting with problems. They also will be able to make standard interpretations of the analyses. Experts in behavioral science methodology with experience in educational problems should form part of this team to give assistance where necessary. However, this particular study does show that the best prediction systems in the behavioral sciences are readily available to school systems. Further, it is well within the scope of every school system to analyze the data in each school to gain insight into its functioning in a systematic, thorough manner.

The cost of the clerical time to copy the twelve variables from the cumulative record folders onto a data sheet can be estimated quickly. The preparation of the data and preparing for the computer run by the educator doing the study was about one hour. The computing time for the 13×13 correlational matrix and the multiple correlation for the 116 students was considerably less than one minute. At the time the study was done, the out-of-the-school system costs were estimated at less than ten dollars, plus communication and travel time. (Today the computing time would be negligible.) Even the resultant information that one standardized test being given in the system was of rather negligible value certainly is worth this small cost. The cost of giving, scoring, and recording the scores of that test alone is far greater than this cost of analysis. The additional knowledge gained is pure "profit."

Every educational professional should take advantage of these technological innovations which are readily available to them. Professionals can devote part of their time to great advantage by doing practical educational research of this sort.

AN EXAMPLE OF DISCRIMINANT ANALYSIS CLASSIFICATION

Discriminant analysis has as a purpose the prediction of group membership. It helps answer the question: Which group's members does this person most resemble? Molnar and DeLauretis (1973), working in a freshman engineering department of a major engineering school, became interested in the way freshmen engineers chose which engineering or industrial management curriculum they would enter.

Curriculum choice is a major educational problem. In engineering, much of the specialized course work beyond the freshman level does not meet the graduation requirements of another engineering major. The already overloaded students sometimes had to spend much additional time obtaining a degree if they changed from one curriculum to another. The additional time is costly to the university and delays students from starting work in their professional field.

The freshmen are exposed to lectures and courses which indicate to them the various engineering areas. They can talk to upper classmen about their interests, and there are extensive counseling services available within the Schools of Engineering, but this advice cannot be as accurate as discriminant analysis classification.

Although this example is from a technical field, the educational problem is not too different from that which many students and schools encounter. It is not so much a case of a student succeeding in an area of study or an occupation as not really liking it or not feeling comfortable in it. These particular engineering freshmen were all able students or they would not have entered engineering school, yet it is known that 60 percent of them would change majors. They simply did not enjoy the same activities as do others in the curriculum or occupation. Changes are costly fiscally and personally, yet not to change may be worse. One answer to the dilemma is better information upon which to make decisions prior to the commitment, and discriminant analysis is the method by which the data are organized to produce usable information for these decisions.

In the example used here, there were five fields of engineering: Aeronautical (AE), Civil (CE), Chemical (CHE), Electrical (EE), and Mechanical (ME); and Industrial Management (IM) used as the nominal classification criterion available. Senior college year students' majors were used. The predictor variables were first semester college grade point average, an interest questionnaire with seven separate scales (all relating to engineering and management interests), a measure of high school grades, a standardized verbal and mathematics aptitude test, and two standardized college entrance achievement tests in English and Mathematics, or thirteen predictors in all. Over 900 engineering students' freshman data were used in the analysis.

The discriminant analysis was run, and it was determined that the noncognitive interest questionnaire scores were of greatest value in making the classification discriminations. However, the first semester college grades did aid in separating those who entered industrial management from those who stayed in engineering. None of the cognitive standardized tests or high school data were useful for this rather homogeneous group. (The average of these students on the standardized mathematics aptitude and achievement tests was one standard deviation above the mean, in the top third of the normative college group.) Even within this rather narrow range of fields, almost 50 percent were correctly classified.

A typical way in which successful classification is judged is the "hit-or-miss table" which is generated by the computer. The hit-or-miss table shows how many subjects could be classified into their correct category. Note, for example, that 35 of the 74 Aeronautical

TABLE 8-1   Hit-or-Miss Table*

| | | *Predicted Classification* | | | | | |
		AE	CE	CHEM	EE	ME	IM
A	AE	35	4	10	14	6	5
C							
T	CE	2	23	3	4	2	7
U							
A	CHE	3	1	31	2	2	2
L							
	EE	16	5	13	42	7	8
C	ME	13	16	10	12	14	22
L							
A	IM	3	19	7	18	12	68
S							
S							
I							
F							
I							
C							
A							
T							
I							
O							
N							
Actual Classification Totals		74	41	41	91	87	127

*From G. Molnar and R. J. DeLauretis, Predicting the curriculum mobility of engineering students: A comparison of discriminant procedures. *Journal of Counseling Psychology*, 1973, 20(1), 50–59.

Engineers were correctly classified, but that 14 were misclassified as Electrical Engineers. Only four looked like Civil Engineers and five as Industrial Management majors.

The equations and calculations used in reducing the intervariable correlational matrix to the distinguishing variables are too complex to be presented here. They are important though to the classification system and in assigning persons to classification either in the original research or for educational practice. Matrix algebra is used, and the equations are given in Cooley and Lohnes (1971) for those who wish to examine the methods. Both the discriminant analysis and applied classification procedures must be done on computers in any practical situation. However, this should not be a deterrent. The programs are widely available, and consultants with good educational backgrounds can use them for school systems readily. The information they yield is quite valuable.

Molnar and DeLauretis (1973) also studied transfers, persisters, and dropouts from engineering, using discriminant analysis techniques. However, one of the more valuable studies they have done involves the broader transferring of engineering students into other schools in the university. Many entering engineering students eventually transfer to areas such as schools of science, humanities, pharmacy, agriculture, and so forth. These investigators were concerned about how these decisions were made, and the methods by which the information from the educational research they were doing could be used by the freshmen students and in counseling.

One possible solution was to use the freshman testing scores and questionnaire data in a discriminant analysis, using all of the schools in the university as the criterion classification variable. Then the discriminant analysis weights could be used in a classification hit-or-miss table printout for each of some 6000 freshman students. These computer printouts would indicate to the students (and their counselors) their probability of being a member of each school group, based on their abilities and interests. On this basis perhaps more rational educational and vocational decisions would be made.

While this might seem to be a huge, expensive task, actually the computer time, including all the printing, is estimated to be on the order of an hour or so. If only one student saved one semester's additional time in the university, the cost-benefit ratio would be favorable. The reduction of university failures (where the student drops out), of student failures (where they are dropped out), and of the psychological stresses on both students and the university certainly could be reduced.

High schools also should be doing studies of this type with students' post-high-school plans as the criterion. Does the student psychologically look like the college-going groups, community collge groups, other post-high-school education and training groups, or vocational and industrial job groups? Do any of these groups overlap in their characteristics in a particular high school? Why should not all students have available their personal hit-or-miss table with an explanation of the probabilities of their group membership in the table? As Cooley and Lohnes suggest (1971, p. 327), "These are the young people who need information about their multipotentialities for education and careers that *splhdr* [second phase longitudinal human development research] can make available to them."

The first phase of the research is for the behavioral or social scientist to find the variables which are important to the adolescent's development. The professional educator's task is to use these results well in practice. To do this, educators need to understand the objectives and results of the analytical methods and first phase research, and then make administrative and teaching decisions to implement them in schools. The counselor's role, in part, can be one of providing alternative, more realistic, educational and vocational goals.

APPLIED PREDICTION CONSIDERATIONS

To make predictions about success, or lack of it, for a person in a group (using regression and multiple regression methods) suggests that the person is indeed a member of the group. Discriminant analysis helps determine whether a person looks like a member of a group. Thus, it is suggested that these two broad methods of prediction—regression analysis and discriminant analysis—be used together, discriminant analysis to suggest group membership and regression analysis to predict achievement in a task the group is undertaking. Further, in this chapter it is assumed that there is a need for prediction. In some education situations this is not true. If there is, for example, an honors course in Senior English capable of enrolling up to twenty students and only fifteen students (after due publicity) request to take the course, there is little point to making predictions about whether they look like previous Honors English students or their probable achievement in the course. Generally, decisions have to be made only when selection occurs, that is, when more people or students are available than can be taken or managed. Decisions can also be made when there are several choices available for the students. Thus, if there are a number of occupational or educational choices available to graduating seniors and they might be accommodated in any of their choices, still a decision has to be made about what to do first.

Both of these situations, limited availability of accommodation and choice among possibilities, suggest selection and a *selection ratio*. A selection ratio refers to the number of people to be chosen compared to the number available to be chosen. This is a useful situation when the ratio is less than 1.00 and where typical psychological and sociological measures are used in prediction systems. The accuracy of these measures is seldom close to perfection and, as a result, the predictions made can be only in general terms. With a selection ratio of less than

1.00, the success of the students accepted via regression equations will be higher than if all students were admitted. (It is assumed there is a relationship between the measures used in the selection procedures and the criteria of success. If there is no such demonstrated relationship between the selection procedure and the criteria of success, then the methods at best are wasteful. They may also be unethical and in some instances illegal.) Even rather small correlations are useful if the selection ratio is also small. Extensive tables are available for indicating the expected proportion of students who would be considered "satisfactory" where selection procedures were used. Information used as the basis for these procedures included proportion of applicants now considered satisfactory, the selection ratio available, and the correlation between selection measures and criterion measures. With this information, the tables will indicate the expected proportion of students who would be considered satisfactory if the selection procedures were used.

These tables are called the Taylor-Russell tables and can be found in many personnel psychology textbooks. The original work is presented in Taylor and Russell's article (1939). As an example, if 70 percent of the students in a course can be considered to be doing satisfactory work, and a correlation of only .50 can be obtained between selection measures and the criterion of success, with a selection ratio of 30 percent (either through restriction or other allocation), it is estimated from the Taylor-Russell tables that 80 percent of the selected students would now be rated satisfactory. Even small relationships can be made useful in this way.

SUMMARY

Two methods of broadly applicable descriptive research in education, prediction, and classification are the topics of this chapter. A general theory of prediction, taking into account global and variable-by-variable data, and an overall prediction, versus a standard weighting of variables, was presented. The value of the use of all types of data for prediction was indicated, but only statistical weighting of the variables is useful for the predictions themselves. Legal and ethical problems of selection and prediction were discussed. The use of prediction and classification strategies in education was put forward.

The differences between prediction of success on a criterion variable for subjects and classification of students (or others) into categories was indicated. Multiple correlation and regression methods were presented as an extension of simple correlation and regression. Discriminant analysis was discussed as the method for classification prediction. Purposes and examples of the educational problems for which it could be useful were given. Educational examples using multiple correlation prediction and discriminant analysis were given also. The values of these procedures for educational decision-making were discussed, as were general costs and strategies. Types of educational questions which could be answered and some indications of what the methods might be able to do for students were proferred. The concepts of selection, a selection ratio, and the Taylor-Russell tables were also put forward.

STUDY AND DISCUSSION PROBLEMS

1. Pick a course in an educational system and determine the student variables which correlate with students' success in the course.
2. Suggest variables which might be useful in predicting students' success in a course for which you are (or will be) responsible.
3. Suggest other areas of education where discriminant analysis procedures would be useful in suggesting appropriate groups or classifications of students.
4. Indicate the role of expert judgment in educational prediction and classification.
5. What does the evidence suggest is the best combination of expert judgment and statistical prediction in educational forecasting?
6. What are the similarities and differences between educational prediction and classification?
7. Find in the educational literature an example of discriminant analysis and describe how it was used.
8. Find examples of multiple regression prediction procedures in education and describe how they are used.
9. You are on the administrative staff of a college and have responsibility for student admittance procedures. What types of data do you collect and how do you use them in your decisions?
10. As a teacher, you aid in making decisions about selecting students for various honors programs. This is the third year of the programs. Indicate the data to be collected to aid in the decisions, their analyses, and their use in the selection processes.
11. You are on the faculty of a School of Education and have been charged with reviewing the processes by which students are admitted to your school. Part of these data are clinical judgments from an appearance of the students before a panel of faculty. Comment on the procedure. Indicate the process of validating the procedures. What ethical and legal problems are suggested?
12. Describe how multiple correlation works. Are there computer programs available to do this analysis for you?

13. Estimate the costs of collecting data, preparing them for computer analyses, running the computer analysis, and writing a report for a correlational, predictive, decision-making situation in education.
14. What is a selection ratio? How is it useful in educational prediction and selection?
15. Give examples where selection ratios exist in educational systems. How can these existing selection ratios be used to improve the educational system?

REFERENCES

American Psychological Association biographical directory. Ethical standards of psychologists, 1970, xxii.

Cooley, W.W., and Lohnes, P.R. *Multivariate data analysis.* New York: John Wiley, 1971.

Griggs, Willie S., *et al.* vs. Duke Power Company. Number 124 The Supreme Court October term 1970, March 8, 1971 (*The U.S. Law Week*, 39LW 4317 Vol. 39 July 1, 1970 June 30, 1971.).

Guilford, J.P., and Fruchter, B. *Fundamental statistics in psychology and education.* New York: McGraw-Hill, 1973, 358–394.

McCormick, J.H., and Asher, W. Aspects of the high school record related to the first semester college grade point average. *Personnel and Guidance Journal*, 1964, XLII(7), 699–703.

Meehl, P.E. *Clinical versus statistical prediction.* Minneapolis: University of Minnesota Press, 1954.

Molnar, G., and DeLauretis, R.J. Predicting the curriculum mobility of engineering students: A comparison of discriminant procedures. *Journal of Counseling Psychology*, 1973, 20(1), 50–59.

Sawyer, J. Measurement and prediction, clinical and statistical. *Psychological Bulletin*, 1966, 66(3), 178–200.

Taylor, H.C., and Russell, J.T. The relationship of validity coefficients to the practical effectiveness of tests in selection: Discussion and tables. *Journal of Applied Psychology*, 1939, 23, 365–378.

Wherry, R.J. Underprediction from overfitting: 45 years of shrinkage. *Personnel Psychology*, 1975, 28(1), 1–18.

Evaluation   Chapter 9

Evaluation has become a much more important word in education since the passage of the Elementary and Secondary Education Act of 1965. The Congress insisted in that Act that evaluation procedures be required in order to determine whether the expenditure of federal funds for the purposes of the Act actually had made a difference. Thus the phrase, "The effective procedures, including provisions for appropriate objective measurements of educational achievement, will be adopted for evaluating at least annually the effectiveness of the programs. . . . ." [ESEA, Title I, Part D, Section 141 (a) (6)] was inserted into the bill which became law. Objective evaluation would seem to be rather straight forward in its meaning.

Objective measurement, as was indicated in Chapter 4, means the use of reliable instruments and agreement among observers. In a larger sense, the word objective also could mean agreement among experts on the interpretation of the possible cause-and-effect relationships observed in the data. Were the new and expanded teaching methods and materials supported by the Act causing improved learning in the target populations? This question is answerable in terms of the concepts of internal validity which have been presented earlier in this book. Establishing definitive cause-and-effect relationships is, of course, one of the aims of research, and thus objective evaluation could be included in a broad definition of applied educational research.

In addition to measurement and research definitions, it is possible to an extent to define objective evaluation in terms of administration. If a set of objectives is accepted and certain educational programs and procedures are developed for achieving the objectives, evaluation could consist of determining that indeed the program was instituted, the procedures implemented, and the objectives met; thus the words "objective" evaluation. It is unimportant whether the program and the procedures caused the achievement of the objectives or not. It is sufficient that they were achieved or, at a minimum, that everything was done in the program that was supposed to have been done. If the thinking (theory) behind the program was faulty and the objectives only partially achieved, at least an honest administrative attempt was made to achieve them.

A wide range of definitions and procedures have come to be acceptable in determining what evaluation is in the educational world. See, for instance, the *Encyclopedia of Educational Evaluation* (Anderson, Ball, & Murphy, 1975). Evaluation may encompass many of the procedures of research (broadly defined), can have an emphasis on measurement, or may be part of an administrative model. This chapter will cover definitions of evaluation, research models, summative and formative evaluation, the CIPP (Context, Input, Process, and Product) model, and discrepancy analysis.

EVALUATION CRITERIA AND DEFINITION

As was indicated in the section on Evaluation and Educational Research in Chapter 1, educational evaluation has a series of definitions that are rather broad in scope. Educational evaluation is obtaining and using information for judging which alternative should be selected in making an educational decision. Educational evaluation is also becoming thoroughly informed about an educational process. It can be a careful depicting of the educational situation. Since evaluation involves information about the natural world, the scientific criteria for information apply: for example, reliability and validity of measurement and internal and external validity of research methodology.

Stufflebeam and the Phi Delta Kappa National Study Committee on Evaluation (1971) also add several practical criteria necessary to the definition of evaluation. These are: relevance, importance, scope, credibility, timeliness, pervasiveness, and efficiency. The committee feels that, in addition to the scientific criteria for data, evaluation procedures and data must go beyond science and thus the additional criteria.

Relevance.   They feel that data for evaluation are collected for a purpose and the criterion of *relevance* asks whether the purpose of the educational evaluation is served by the data. The purposes of the evaluation hinge on two factors: the persons to be served by the evaluation and the criteria of the educational process. The people involved in administering and performing the educative services should be asked what questions they wish to have answered and to state their criteria and the education objectives of their program. *Relevance* is determined by comparing the proposed data to be collected with the purposes and criteria to be met.

Importance and Scope.   The evaluative criteria of *importance* and *scope* refer to priority and range of the data to be collected in the evaluation. Evaluative data collection can be rather broad, but broad data collection effort is costly. Further, not all data are equally valuable. Available evaluative data should be sorted to bring into major focus the most important information as determined by the relevance criterion of the evaluation. However, balancing the importance criterion is the criterion of scope. A set of data too narrow to meet the purposes of the users of the data lacks scope. The evaluator should work to develop data which will be of importance in making educational decisions. If these data are too broad, some of the variables may lack importance, the costs of the evaluation will be higher than necessary, and important data will be buried among data that are less important, perhaps trivial. On the other hand, if the data collected are too narrow, information may be lacking upon which to make sound decisions.

The first three practical criteria—relevance, importance, and scope—work in combination with each other to expand, contract, and focus the extent of the information to be collected for evaluative purposes. The stated criteria or objectives of the educational program are the bases upon which the judgments are made.

Credibility.   The *credibility* of an evaluation is the concern or belief in the evaluators and trust of them by the users of the evaluation data. This belief and trust are, in turn, developed by the nature of the relationship between the evaluator and the user of the data analyses and reports. The integrity of the evaluators, their concern for professional relationships, and their openness with the people in the educational system and the users of the evaluation are all important to the credibility of an evaluation. If the measurement and scientific bases of the data developed in an evaluation are excellent, yet the decision-making user does not trust the evaluators, then the credibility of the data is low. If differing values are held and are irreconcilable, this serves to reduce the credibility of the evaluation. A self-evaluation by the administrators and staff of a program or an evaluation by those associated with the educational process, while valuable for purposes within the system, often will have a reduced credibility for those outside and by those at a higher level in the system who have a more general administrative responsibility. In self-evaluation there is always the problem of self-interest. Thus, to aid in the maximization of credibility, emphasis should be given to outside evaluators who are independent of the system or institution.

　　Timeliness, Pervasiveness, and Efficiency.　　These are the last three criteria applied to evaluative information and methods. Timeliness is concerned with the presentation of evaluation information. Information that arrives too late to be used in making a decision is worthless. Educational systems frequently run on rather fixed schedules and cycles. Planning for the continuation or change of a program usually must be done well in advance of the next beginning date of the program. The evaluator should learn what these crucial dates are and make provision to have appropriate analyses and information available at those times. That information may not be complete. For instance, the final criteria observations and tests given in early summer at the end of a school year may not be analyzed and reported until several weeks later, yet some administrative and program decisions may have to be made prior to that data. Rather than wait for the last pieces of data to become available, it is far better to make interim reports based on intermediate criteria that can be used as guides to the incremental changes in the administrative decision process. The complete information can be taken into account at a later time. Presentation of reports when due and called for is an exceptionally important aspect of evaluation.

　　Pervasiveness is the concern that the dissemination of the evaluation reports is complete and in such a form that the varying audiences can use the information. The criterion of pervasiveness in evaluation is met if it can be shown that those who need the information and are affected by it do indeed know about and are using it. Pervasiveness is one of the easier evaluation criteria to meet. However, one concern is that administrators have a tendency to publicize positive information while down-playing or burying negative findings.

　　Efficiency in evaluation involves being prudent in terms of costs, personnel, and time. Evaluation can be done in many degrees of thoroughness, ranging from the superficial to extensive individual observations running over several periods of time and complete with several control groups of varying natures. It is foolish, though, to have the evaluation costs approach the implementation costs of a project. The emphasis should be on the program itself.

Of course, to have worthwhile data upon which to make decisions does require money. Suggested guidelines for evaluation costs might be on the order of ten percent of total costs of the project. Smaller projects might have evaluation costs somewhat higher than this, while very large projects with tight budgeting might run somewhat below this figure. Much depends, of course, on the nature and conditions under which the data must be collected. If much data will be collected by the educational system in the course of regular testing programs and in the course of the project by the staff of the project, then the outside evaluation costs can be less. On the other hand, certain data needs increase costs. Assurance that possible cause-and-effect relationships can be accepted as true requires careful data collecting that is expensive. Data describing emotional changes may require interviews over a period of time by highly trained personnel. These are expensive. Crucial decisions, like those required for large, high-cost changes in an educational system, demand a high quality of cause-and-effect information. Administrators' careers can be made or broken by such decisions, and they will want the best information available. One way to judge the cost requirements in an evaluation is to determine and compare the evaluation costs with the costs of the decision that will be made on the basis of the evaluation information.

Other definitions of evaluation relate to measurement. Certainly good measurement procedures underpin good evaluation. Evaluation in a measurement sense may involve a synthesis of various measurements, both formal and informal, including rather subjective impressions and judgments about the merit of a program which may be made as a result of these measurements. *There can be no evaluations made without data, and data imply that measurement criteria be applied to them. Evaluation, while including measurement, goes beyond it.*

Evaluation also has been defined as correspondence between the educational objectives and the accomplishments of the program or system. Evaluation, then, is a determination of the extent to which the educational objectives actually have been achieved during the course of the instruction. Evaluation is, under this definition, one of the basic tasks of curriculum development. The others are the selection of the objectives and the learning experiences by which the objectives will be acquired, including the organizational sequence and continuity of the experiences. Thus, evaluation of curriculum in this sense is concerned with student or system achievement and the procedures by which instruction took place.

Another definition of evaluation pertains to experts' judgments and the placing of values on data collected. A school system survey is such an evaluation, as is an accrediting team's evaluation of a school or college. In these procedures a team of experts visits the educational system or college, views the procedures, facilities, and organization, and makes judgments about quality. They also may make various recommendations. The experts' judgments are the evaluations. Their data are collected in broad, general categories, and the data and analysis are not very specific. It is their expertise that suggests what data are to be sought and how they are to be interpreted. Their judgments about the data are based on their cumulative and collective experiences. The evaluation in this sense is the judgment of the experts, based on whatever information they are able to collect and observe.

In all of the definitions, the term evaluation suggests decisions and judgments based on data and observations. The data may be rather sketchy and their internal research validity open to some question. On the other hand, highly reliable data over a broad range of variables in the educational situation may be collected under conditions of excellent internal validity. In all cases, the object of the data collection is to provide information for administrative decision-making. The emphasis in evaluation is on the utility of the information.

Evaluators are concerned with the immediate relevancy of the data and its information for decision-making. A particular program, curriculum lesson, or system is the focus of the work of the evaluators, not whether their answers are broadly generalizable, as they are in a research emphasis, or even generalizable to the next similar program. There are numerous similarities between evaluation and educational research, but evaluation and basic research have little if any overlap in purpose.

Both educational research and educational evaluation have a rather specific purpose or goal. The educational researcher's purpose is to provide broad generalizations about the process and status of education so that better general decisions can be made about education. The educational evaluator's purpose, as has been indicated, is to provide information so that specific decisions can be made to improve a particular program in education. The major purpose of basic research is to generate general knowledge. The products of basic research can be of significance to education, but basic research is not done to be of value to education specifically.

Basic and applied educational research and educational evaluation all use, to some extent, the same fundamental procedures of describing the real world, in this case primarily the methods of the behavioral and social sciences. These scientific methods are concerned with reliability (which is objectivity) and validity of data, and the internal validity of the conditions under which the data were collected is of concern so that valid interpretations and good decisions can be made.

Basic and applied educational research are concerned also about external validity—the ability to generalize beyond the specific situation in which the data were observed. Basic research places much more emphasis on broad generalizability than does applied educational research. Educational evaluation proponents are quite willing to place the reliability and validity of data and the internal validity of the observational situation in some jeopardy if the decisions to be made on the basis of the data are not major or costly. Data in educational evaluation are valued for their usefulness for decisions in a specific instance. In many cases, considerable information is already available about a program, major change decisions about the program are not contemplated, or only minimum current data are needed to maintain assurance that objectives still are being met. Costs must be considered in the collection of evaluation data, particularly in relationship to the costs of the program and the decisions being made using the data. Costs are of negligible concern to the basic researchers (as long as they have time to do research), and not of major concern to the applied educational researcher, although they are considered.

Reliability and validity of data and its internal research validity are important to basic and applied educational research, as well as to educational evaluation (if major decisions are to be made as the result of the evaluation). Thus, basic and applied researchers and evaluators use the same scientific methods in the collection of data, even if they do not have the same concerns for the use of the data. In fact, evaluation is a form of applied research but evaluation pertains to immediately relevant data of utility in making decisions. Many of the procedures that are used in evaluation are also used in research. In fact, in many instances no distinctions can be made between research and evaluation methods. In evaluations for major decisions, the best of the research methods available should be used with care and precision. The more relevant, precise, valid, unbiased, reliable, and complete the data and information available, the more utility they have for the educational decision-maker. Evaluation is far broader than research in its day-to-day utility, but both evaluation and research methods use many of the same criteria. Thus, it is in the utility of the information that differences may arise. Evaluation decisions *need* be no better than the costs of the consequences of the decision but *cannot* be better than the quality of the data upon which they rest.

Research models for evaluation use the same procedures as applied educational research. A practical problem exists, an attempt is made to resolve it, and a determination is made as to whether or not the attempted resolution actually worked. Research models for evaluation answer the general form of the question: Was the educational problem alleviated by the treatment? As has been indicated, the considerations of internal and external validity in true experiments, quasi-experiments, and purely descriptive studies, apply directly to this type of evaluation. However, the emphasis in evaluation is usually immediate decisions about the program; cause-and-effect relationships are of secondary concern. If sufficient funds are available for the development and assessment of control groups as well as the target group, excellent quality educational research can be conducted, in addition to the collection of data for evaluation purposes.

Systems analysis is the method of evaluation concerned with the interrelationships of the many variables in the educational process. As was indicated earlier in this book, those who use this approach attempt to determine in particular the relationships of input variables to educational achievement. In allocating resources in accord with the systems analysis results, maximum achievement ultimately can be obtained for the given costs involved within the existing confines of the systems resources. The ultimate development of the systems approach would be formal experimental research because in experimental research, cause-and-effect relationships and their strength can be determined. Thus, the best allocation of resources could be made on the best quality evidence. Often one suspects that what is labeled "systems analysis" in education is thorough administrative analysis.

Summative evaluation is a procedure that concentrates on the criteria of the educational process. In its more elementary forms, those who use it simply ask, Were the goals achieved? There is not too much concern as to how the goals were achieved. Formative evaluation is closely linked with summative evaluation as described by Scriven (1967).

Formative Evaluation.   From the concern in evaluation for process, as distinct from product, the distinction between formative evaluation and summative evaluation has evolved. *Formative evaluation* generally precedes summative evaluation (or outcome or product research), or formative evaluation may be done alone. Formative evaluation is focused on the programs or processes of education which, it is hoped, will produce certain accomplishments in the students, teachers, and organization. Scriven (p. 51) defines formative evaluation as "process research, but it is of course simply outcome evaluation of an intermediate stage in the development of the teaching instrument." Scriven goes on to say that "the role of formative evaluation is to discover deficiencies and successes in the intermediate versions of a new curriculum." Sometimes formative evaluation is done to assure that indeed the various parts of the curriculum, the teaching staff, the buildings, the students, the materials and the administrative actions actually have been procured, are operating, or just do exist. There is little point to doing formal, comparative evaluation of students' achievement on criteria instruments unless at least most of the educational activities and plans suggested in a program proposal actually were put into operation. Further, and one step beyond the implementation of an educational program, is that any changes and restructuring of the program be made where it is apparent that the educational program is not working. Where students are unable to cope with reading assignments or practice problems, where teachers are unprepared or unable to work with the materials, where community pressures are such that there is opposition to a program, there is little point in attempting to make comparative judgments or summative evaluations as to the students' accomplishments. It is apparent that there will be little accomplishment, or none.

One step above these formative evaluations, which use rather straightforward observations of a program, are formative evaluations of a quasi-administrative nature. The first time an educational program is put into action, there are likely to be some slips between the thinking and planning about the program and its unfolding in a concrete situation. Many governmental funding agencies requesting evaluations want formative evaluations. The agency wants to be assured that the bold thinking and planning, which caught their attention in the proposal requesting funds, has been translated into action. There is also little purpose in attempting to determine whether a proposed program made a difference or not if the program itself was only partially implemented.

An example of a need for formative evaluation with which this writer was concerned involved an alternative school to attract dropouts. The school was to start September 1. The agency waited for funds to be appropriated during the summer and finally notified the school system in the second week of September that the program could be implemented. Of course the procurement of faculty, facilities, and the advance publicity needed to start the program had not been done. The staff had to be hired from available graduate students from nearby universities. The principal was obtained a month late and then only due to the courtesy of another school system where she had gone to teach. Inadequate, temporary facilities were used before an acceptable building was acquired in Janauary. Finally, after several months, the confidence of a number of the dropouts was obtained, and sufficient students were attracted to get a semblance of the proposed program activated. To do an evaluation as to the summative effectiveness of a program undercut and crippled in these ways is near-nonsense. However, a formative evaluation to aid the administrators and teachers in developing a more effective program is quite worthwhile. Determining what the students like about the program, why other adolescent dropouts were not attending, elements of community support and nonsupport, problems in administrative relationships, and curriculum adequacy were most important. These are the types of questions answered and determinations made in formative evaluation.

Formative evaluation is designed to develop information about the adequacy of smaller curricular units and their learning and instructional materials while teaching is ongoing, but it should be beyond curriculum building (or rebuilding) to include appraisal of students' learning, teaching effectiveness, and administrative adequacy.

Summative Evaluation. Summative evaluation, on the other hand, is defined by Aisasian (1968, p. 128) as "that type of evaluation which is designed to yield terminal judgments about a curriculum as a whole." Summative evaluation is concerned with the outcomes of the educational program as a whole, often as compared to other programs. Summative evaluation is concerned with determining the effectiveness of the overall program, that is, the end product of instructional programs, not just the means of instruction, as in formative evaluation. Summative evaluation comes very close to being applied educational research.

Actually, the definitions of educational research and evaluation in the summative sense have gone almost full circle. Summative evaluators are not concerned now that their models do not fit the classical experimental models, but researchers also have long since used other than the classical research models. Much of the debate back and forth between educational researchers and educational evaluators died down when both sides realized that many of their concerns about the others' activities were based on out-of-date knowledge. When both groups realized that certain quite worthwhile things were being done by the other, given the context in which they were being done, much of the heat in the debate cooled. Both sides, as can be seen, are now borrowing techniques and methods from the others.

Summative evaluation determines whether the objectives of the educational system or methods have been accomplished. It involves the collection of data defining the educational criteria and comparing them with the standards set by the curriculum developers and administrators. It also may compare the achievements with other reasonably comparable groups, and thus, in this aspect, summative evaluation and applied educational research have an identical methodology. The reliability and validity of measurement and the internal research validity of the evaluation all play important roles in summative evaluations. Thus, summative evaluation methods are quite like applied educational research methods.

THE CIPP EVALUATION MODEL

One of the major evaluation models now used grew out of the formative and summative, process and product, evaluation models. The CIPP model was developed in great part by Stufflebeam in a paper prepared for the Association for Supervision and Curriculum Development (1968). The CIPP model name comes from the initial letters of the four types of evaluation functions which constitute the method: Context, Input, Process, and Product. As Stufflebeam discusses them in the book *Educational Evaluation and Decision Making* (1971), context evaluation provides the broad basis for stating the objectives of the evaluation and the surrounding conditions of a possible program. Input evaluation provides the specific data and considerations for the assessment of staffing, time, budget requirements, procedural barriers, operationally stated objectives, and educational and administrative strategies prior to the start of an educational program. Process evaluation is much like the prior definitions of this aspect of the evaluation models given earlier in this chapter. Process evaluation takes place during the implementation of an educational activity or program. It is concerned with the actual implementation of the program, its description, and the facilitating and impeding factors as the program proceeds. On the other hand, product evaluation is more concerned with the end result of the educational program on the students or participants in it, although there may be intermediate points at which product evaluation is needed. Thus, product evaluation is concerned primarily with the outcomes of a program in terms of accomplishments.

Input Evaluation.   This is more specific and immediately action-oriented than context evaluation. The purpose of *input evaluation* is to determine how to utilize the educational systems and the surrounding resources to accomplish the objectives of an educational program. The product of input evaluation is determination of the resources, costs, and possible benefits of a selected series of specific programs. Alternative methods of accomplishing certain educational objectives are assessed in terms of staffing, students, time, space, equipment, materials, budget, and possible procedural barriers. On a more abstract level, input evaluation is concerned with whether or not the proposed programs can indeed accomplish the objectives which have been identified.

The function of input evaluation is to determine the best way to achieve specific educational objectives and which curricula and programs to select. Input evaluation can be relatively simple or rather complex, depending on the size of the program to be implemented or the consequences of the changes in present programs. If the changes or new programs are not major departures from current activities in an educational system, then the input evaluation can be rather routine. Unanticipated problems are likely to be few and of minimum consequence. If major departures from past practices are contemplated though, input evaluation should be thorough and far-reaching. Similar programs in other settings should be visited and inquiries made about problems and how they were handled. All costs should be identified. On the theoretical side of the input evaluation, a careful review of the scientific and professional literature should be made, keeping in mind the possibility that the reported achievements of the implemented programs may not be, in fact, caused by the programs. Other factors in the populations, staff, or community may have been crucial or more important than the particular educational program or procedure itself.

A knowledge of educational research methods is important in input evaluation where major educational changes are contemplated that hinge on abstract concepts. A thorough knowledge of reliability and validity of data, internal and external validity of data collection settings, and common errors in educational research and professional literature are of major importance. In a situation where major educational change is contemplated, after the primary literature has been located and screened, it probably is good insurance to invite educational research experts to be consultants. They can review the selected articles and publications to determine further the adequacy of the cause-and-effect claims made for the prior programs. As the result of input evaluation, specification of procedures, facilities, equipment, staff, budgets, materials, schedules, and organization should be available for various programs so that appropriate decisions can be made.

Process Evaluation.   This involves the assessment of an educational program or system once it has been implemented. It provides periodic feedback to staff and administrators about the procedures, facilities, staff, equipment, materials, and organization of a program as it begins and operates. The objectives of *process evaluation* are to detect problems in the procedural design early in the program, to assure implementation of the procedure, to provide information for program decisions, and to keep records of what the actual procedures were so that they can be replicated or changed as desired.

Process evaluation monitors the activities of the program on a more or less continuous basis, and also monitors supporting activities and organization. It also describes the nature of the staff, materials, students, and so forth as they appeared and took part in the program. A description is kept of what actually took place during the program. Process evaluation further is concerned with projecting the decisions that will have to be made in implementing the program and providing data so that intelligent administrative and staff decisions can be made. Process evaluation information is useful in determining why the objectives were or were not achieved, and requires regular observations of all parts of the program and regular meetings with the administrators and other decision-makers in the program. Concerns and issues should be identified, but the process evaluator's main role is to describe, not to decide.

In addition to the more formal measurement and observation devices such as tests, interview protocols, rating scales, check lists, and interaction analyses, the process evaluator must see and hear much more. Diaries, minutes of meetings, suggestion boxes, nondirective listening in informal settings, open and receptive communication, and looking for unanticipated events are important activities and procedures for the process evaluator to use in learning about problems and investigating them in implementing the program.

Process evaluation is particularly important in the early stages of program implementation. If the program is not well started or if it bogs down, there will be difficulty in getting it functioning well again. Problems must be identified and remedied early. Continuous feedback of process evaluation information is vital to the effective functioning of a program. Process evaluation provides both a record of what happened in the implementation of a program and data during the program for administrators to make decisions, to anticipate problems, and to surmount the difficulties encountered.

Product Evaluation.   This is generally much like applied educational research. Operational definitions of objectives are developed, measurement instruments devised, the comparative groups or standards identified, internal validity of the comparisons considered, analyses performed, and interpretations of the results made. Product evaluation assesses the extent to which the objectives of the educational program or system have been met. It may focus somewhat on intermediate goals of a program if they are ends in themselves or must be acquired in order to learn later material in the program. Product evaluation reports indicate that objectives were or were not being achieved.

Product evaluation essentially hinges on whether the context, input, and process evaluations were done well. If they were, then, theoretically, the product evaluation should indicate successful educational achievement. If not, then the records of the prior evaluation procedures should be available to indicate the source of the trouble. The older sense of the word "evaluation" essentially meant an evaluation of the products of an educational program.

The CIPP model is much more of a service to the administrators of a school system than some evaluation models. It provides the general background (context) and the specific information (input) to identify problems and to choose among the possible methods of solution. The evaluation procedures in this model monitor the implementation of the chosen solution and alert administrators to problems, failures, and future decisions that will have to be made. The records of the manner in which an educational program was put into effect are also maintained. Finally, a CIPP evaluation procedure assesses the product of all the foregoing, and the evaluator reports the findings to the administrators.

This model of evaluation is extremely broad. The conceptualization of its functions range from the philosophy of education to educational research, and much in between. The CIPP evaluation model includes most of the educational developmental and implementation processes, except making the actual program decisions, directly administering the program, and performing the teaching in the programs. The evaluator assists the decision-makers.

The next evaluation model, while perhaps not as broadly conceived, moves even further into the realm of educational administration.

THE DISCREPANCY EVALUATION MODEL

Discrepancy evaluation was conceptualized and developed primarily by Provus (1971). It is the procedure whereby differences (discrepancies) between a standard of performance and the performance itself in an educational program are found and corrected. Discrepancy analysis is very much process-oriented but also is concerned ultimately with educational products. However, discrepancy evaluation does not limit itself to fixed goals and objectives. It is also concerned with philosophy—what should be produced—and administration—how the product is to be produced. The "what" and "how" are defined in terms of discrepancies between developed standards and actual performance in implementation. These standards and performances are compared for discrepancies in five stages of the evaluation: design, installation, process, product, and cost. Any differences found at any of these stages in the evaluation are given to the program staff by the administrator (or the evaluator) so that the staff has a sound basis to make program changes. These changes may be either in the standards or in the levels of performance of the program at the particular stage where the discrepancy was found, or at some prior stage.

The first three stages—design, installation, and process—are useful particularly in program development; the last two stages, product and cost, are valuable in more ultimate program achievement assessment. Stage One activities are program design and redefinition (much like context evaluation in the CIPP model). Stage Two, installation, and Stage Three, process, are concerned with the implementation and continuation of a program as it was designed. Stage Four, product, uses traditional classical evaluation and applied education research procedures to determine whether the program processes and conceptualizations indeed have produced the product or achieved the objectives of the program. Stage Five, cost, is concerned with cost and benefits of the program. However, Provus is apprehensive about a premature application of the cost stage. He indicates that it is almost impossible in this era of evaluation and research to compare programs with similar goals and differing costs until much greater information is available about program conditions and settings in schools. The discrepancy evaluation, with its emphasis on the achievement of program goals in line with administrative objectives, seems more likely to influence management practices than evaluation or research practices, although evaluation and research methods are incorporated in the discrepancy model.

AN EXAMPLE

Grades one through six in a moderate-sized city were desegregated by pairing schools. All children in grades one, two, and three were placed into one of the pairs of schools and all children in grades four, five, and six in the other school. The primary goals of the desegregation program were enhanced social relationships among the children and improved educational achievement, especially among the minority groups. After the desegregation program began, the school board became concerned about implementation and effectiveness of the program and asked that an evaluation be done.

In order to establish the credibility of the evaluation team, two outside experts were brought in, one a university professor specializing in research and evaluation methods and the other an administrator in a public school. In addition, a teacher from the system was released from her regular duties to spend full time observing, collecting data, and writing. The need for timeliness of the evaluation was made clear in that the evaluation report had to be available in time to be used in planning for the following school year. The scope of the problem and reasonable costs were established in advance via contractual letters specifying renumeration and activities.

Under the CIPP model the context of the activity was already a fact. The outside evaluators needed to learn the context of the administrative decision and summarize it as an introduction to their final report.

The input in the CIPP model is concerned with the resources of the school system used to implement the educational program being evaluated. What were the costs of the buses and drivers? What central administrative costs were there? Were additional resource staff needed, such as reading specialists or teachers' aides? Were new texts and curriculum materials needed to accommodate to the children's needs? What does the prior literature on this problem say? These were the kinds of questions asked about the resource input to the program.

Process questions were concerned with how well the program was being implemented in the schools. These were questions such as: Had problems developed? How are staff interacting? What facility changes are needed? What records are being kept of problems and achievements? How are communication channels to administrators being kept open? These kinds of questions were asked and observations made in the school system and in the elementary schools over a period of several months. These probes attempted to determine which educational and social processes were operating well and which needed attention. Were programs not being implemented as planned such that the objectives of the desegregation program could not be met? Did unanticipated problems arise?

For example, one such problem was that there were no sixth graders in the grade one-through-three schools to act as crossing guards. Another problem was that the grade school recreation program in basketball, under the direction of the park system, kept its team eligibility rules based on the old elementary school boundary lines. Split loyalties developed.

Teachers and principals were interviewed to learn how they felt the desegregation program was being implemented in their school and what the faculty and local administrators' achievements and problems were. Children were observed as they rode the school buses. Parents and other members of the community were interviewed, as was the school's Director of Transportation. The Minority Affairs Officer was interviewed at length about her experiences during the course of the year with teachers, administrators, parents, and community members.

All of these questions, observations, and concerns of process evaluation are a part of formative evaluation too. Summative evaluation with the discrepancy model is much like the product evaluation of the CIPP model.

Product, or summative, evaluation data on the elementary school integration program included observations of the children in class-rooms, halls, playgrounds, and on buses. Teachers' aides were asked to complete rating of their observations of children. A random selection of principals and teachers also were interviewed for their observations of social relationships among the children. The teachers' and principals' opinions were sought regarding rate and breadth of classroom achievement compared to prior years. Standardized tests were adminis-tered to the children who had adequate ability to read them, and one grade used a statewide testing program that had several years of prior comparative data.

Relative achievement by grade, compared to prior years' achieve-ments on the tests, was modified in its interpretation by long-term trends for each group. Conclusions were drawn. However, precautions were stated about alternative conclusions that might be drawn because of the special nature of educational and psychological measurement. Much greater concern was expressed by the evaluators about a question that had not been asked: What is the overall level of educational achievement relative to children in other, similar cities?

Finally, in the product evaluation phase, the fragmented and very diverse nature of the curriculum was noted, as were the problems that this caused in the system. Again evaluators, as well as researchers, see more than they are looking for. A second major finding was the exceptional quality and professionalism of the elementary school systems' faculties and principals. All of these findings fall within the realm of product or summative evaluation.

Discrepancy evaluation is directed at differences between what performance should be and what it actually is in an educational activity.

Feedback of information to administrators at all stages of the discrepancy model evaluation process is a key aspect of that model. Were there particular problems at a school to which the principals wished attention be given by the central administration? Could it be determined that, in general, the desegregation was going rather well? This information should be given to appropriate administrators as quickly as it is determined. Discrepancies between expected performance and actual activities can be noted and corrective action taken, if needed.

The first two stages of discrepancy evaluation—design and installation—had been done before this particular evaluation was requested. The two discrepancy model stages used here were the process and product phases. Cost, the final stage, was considered somewhat, but as Provus suggests, it is difficult to apply because of the need to compare this program with other similar ones in other schools. This was not done.

The importance of this evaluation to the community is indicated by the fact that the final report of the evaluation team was reprinted in its entirety in the community's newspaper.

It was noted that the context, C, aspect of the model was in part definitely outside the realm of science, since it was concerned with the philosophy of an educational setting and program. The input, I, and the process, P, parts of the CIPP model, refer to the process orientations of both management and evaluation. The product, P, phase is quite similar to modern educational research, as such, with its emphasis on the question: Did the program make a difference in the achievement or accomplishments of its students? The discrepancy model of evaluation is the most administratively oriented of those presented. It is concerned with differences (discrepancies) between standards and performances in five stages of the evaluation: design, installation, process, product, and cost. Similarities and differences of the various models to one another were discussed.

SUMMARY

This chapter has described a series of evaluation models and reported the several definitions of the term "evaluation." The main similarities of applied educational research to evaluation were noted, particularly the procedures used in collecting data and in measurement. Internal validity of evaluation designs and reliability and validity of data are of importance in most cases. An older definition was given in which the terms measurement and evaluation were used almost synonymously, and the current usefulness of this measurement definition was considered. A much broader conceptualization of evaluation, the CIPP model, which has received widespread attention, was described at some length. An example of an evaluation of a desegregation program was presented. The procedures involved in that evaluation were related to various phases of the evaluation models given in the chapter.

STUDY AND DISCUSSION PROBLEMS

1. What is evaluation? What are its similarities and differences compared to research?
2. What is formative evaluation? Summative evaluation? Discrepancy evaluation? Context, Input, Process, and Product evaluation?
3. What similarities are there among the various evaluation models?
4. List and briefly describe seven practical criteria of evaluation studies.
5. Pick a curriculum with which you are familiar. Make a brief evaluation of it, using the CIPP model.
6. Suggest areas of education in which formative evaluation is more appropriate than summative evaluation.
7. How does objective evaluation, as used in Title I programs, relate to measurement?
8. What is the purpose of educational evaluation?
9. Go to a school system with a Title I program and read the required annual evaluation report. Comment on it in terms of your knowledge of evaluation, measurement, analyses, and design procedures.
10. What are the five stages of the discrepancy evaluation model?
11. Give examples of educational evaluations in which you have been involved. Give their strengths and weaknesses.

REFERENCES

Airasian, P.W. Formative evaluation instruments. *The Irish Journal of Education*, 1968, *11*, 127–135.

Anderson, S.B., Ball, S., and Murphy, R.T. *Encyclopedia of educational evaluation*. San Francisco: Jossey-Bass, 1975.

Bloom, B.S., Hastings, J.T., and Madaus, G.F. *Handbook on formative and summative evaluation of student learning*. New York: McGraw-Hill, 1971.

Elementary and Secondary Education Act of 1965. Title I, Part D, Section 141(a)(6).

Provus, M. *Discrepancy evaluation*. Berkeley, Calif: McCutcheon, 1971.

Scriven, M. The methodology of evaluation. In R.W. Tyler, R.M. Gagné, and M. Scriven (Eds.), *Perspective of curriculum evaluation*. Chicago: Rand McNally, 1967, 39–83.

Stufflebeam, D.L., *Evaluation as enlightenment for decision-making.* Association for Supervision and Curriculum Development, 1968.

Stufflebeam, D. L. et al. *Educational evaluation and decision making.* Itasca, Ill: F. E. Peacock, 1971.

Reading and Writing Educational Research

If man is not aware of what has been learned in history, it is said he is bound to repeat the experiences. In the short run, too, professional educators will repeat the mistakes of others if they are not knowledgeable about previous work. Very few problems in education are totally new. There may be unique aspects to a problem, but usually someone somewhere has faced the problem before and written of the experiences. Professionals will find these reports, evaluate them, and use the information from them that they feel is worthwhile. This chapter will be concerned with providing guidance in finding these reports and later in writing them.

A professional has unique knowledge, but no one can be expected to have all of the knowledge at his fingertips in a field as large as education, nor can anyone keep abreast of all new developments. However, there are ways to attack the problem of learning about an area, a concern, or a topic. The aims here are to teach how to make the inquiry rapidly, to be comprehensive, and to acquire the information in an understandable manner. The information needed may be only for a quick review, or it may be needed in considerable depth. These considerations must be taken into account in acquiring professional information. The one thing that is needed in all information is accuracy. Accuracy of explanation is a problem in the educational literature.

LEARNING WHAT OTHERS HAVE DONE

A good way to proceed is to find a source which is broad in its overall coverage of education, yet is accurate, concise, and reasonably up-to-date on a given topic. General sources will give the reader a good overview of the dimensions of the problem. The reader can gain an overall picture of the problem area and then dig into the particular aspects that are of concern by following the general source citations back to the books, journal articles, and papers cited. In those book chapters and articles, more explicit information and additional citations to prior work upon which the current research is based will be found. This process can go back into the literature almost indefinitely as various areas of the problem are probed and then the areas accepted, broadened, or eliminated. This is the pyramiding technique in bibliographic work.

The pyramiding technique of searching for information has an advantage in that it can focus on explicit aspects of a problem after the broader topics have been concisely reviewed. However, this type of information search has the disadvantage of not bringing the reader up-to-date on the latest findings and thinking in an area.

One of the best single sources for an overall, yet concise view for initial searching purposes for problems in education is the most recent edition of the *Encyclopedia of Educational Research* (Ebel, 1969). This volume is sponsored by the American Educational Research Association (AERA), an organization with an excellent reputation and one whose publications can be trusted. *The Encyclopedia of Educational Research* covers a variety of topics over a wide range of educational concerns. It is well indexed (the index pages are in the center of the volume) and the articles are rich with citations to authoritative books, journal articles, and papers. However, when it is published, the *Encyclopedia* is about a year-and-a-half out of date, and most of the articles and books cited will be based on research work that is at least an additional six months to a year old. For most administrative decisions, these time lags are not important. However, for a person or educational system about to embark on a research project or major change, the time lag can be crucial.

There are other sources which are good in presenting in-depth pictures of various aspects of education. The National Society for the Study of Education (NSSE) produces one or two yearbooks annually on various topics. Recently, these have been in such areas as teacher education, educational evaluation, educational sociology, media, international education, gifted children, early childhood, youth, curriculum, art education, vocational education, linguistics, libraries, deviancy of youth, school testing programs and mathematics education. There is no set cycle of topics, and for any given topic the yearbook information might be somewhat dated. However, the chapters in each book are written and edited by able people and are authoritative. A big advantage of the NSSE yearbooks is that in the more than seventy years of their publication, almost every topic in education has been covered, and many libraries have twenty or thirty feet of shelf space devoted to housing them. A diligent reader can become knowledgeable about an educational topic in an afternoon and evening using nothing more than this resource.

The *Handbook of Research on Teaching* (Gage, 1963; Travers, 1973), also sponsored by the AERA, is another excellent basic source. As the name suggests, it is not as broad in its coverage of education as the *Encyclopedia of Educational Research,* but the coverage has greater depth. In addition to teaching as such, the *Handbook* also covers typical elementary and secondary education subjects such as reading, foreign language, mathematics, and science. Its first edition included a now-famous chapter (Chapter 5) on Experimental and Quasi-Experimental Designs for Research on Teaching by Campbell and Stanley (1963). That edition also has a brief, simple overview of a broad range of statistical methods used in educational research.

The annual *Review of Research in Education* (Kerlinger, 1973–) is a book series which publishes summary reviews of research topics. It replaces in part the older form of the journal *Review of Educational Research* which has now changed to a new format. (Both are sponsored by AERA.) The *Review of Educational Research* accepts reviews of a research area submitted on any topic. The older format of the journal covered six areas a year over a three-year cycle. Thus, eighteen topics were covered in some depth before they were repeated. These reviews covered the same eight to ten years between *Encyclopedias* and kept their readers up-to-date on recent developments. The *Review of Research in Education* books now will perform much this same function.

BOOK SEARCH METHODS

Finding books that are important in a problem area in education is no different than finding books in any field. Books are one of the basic assets of a library, and a good library is as invaluable to a researcher in scientific problems as it is to the philosopher, historian, and scholar in the humanities.

It is not the purpose here to teach all of the intricacies of library usage, but every researcher and professional should know how to use the library's card catalogue. It is alphabetically arranged and each book has a title card, an author card, and one or more subject cards.

It is the subject card that is of particular value in locating books in a field of research. Key words describing the topic are used as a start. For instance, in predicting success in ninth-grade mathematics for minority group students, the words "mathematics," and "minority group students" might be used to begin the search. Almost immediately the searcher would have to shift down to a more restricted area from "mathematics" to "mathematics education." The shift might have to be up to "students" and then to the category "students, minority groups." In a large library, it might be possible to find books on the particular kinds of minority group students, and maybe even books on mathematics instruction for minority groups which include chapters or sections on predicting levels of entry and success. Several trials of shifting up and down in the level of the topic may be needed. If Library of Congress cards are used, the subject phrases at the bottom of the cards may be used to discover the subject headings of the Library of Congress for a particular area. These, in turn, may lead to further subject cards and help map and define the topic area. As the scope of the books that are found is reviewed, call numbers must be kept. When books are located which are at the right level and breadth for the researcher's purposes, the shelves nearby may be scanned and their books examined for their value.

These search procedures are elementary to a habitual library user, but in the broader picture, information retrieval is itself a science with mechanized and computerized searches. Differing methods for storage and retrieval may be used, but basically the searching strategy is similar in all systems. Starting with search terms, synonyms may be found if the retrieval is scanty, or the searcher moves up to more inclusive categories. If the retrieval starts to become massive, the shift is down to narrower search words. When a reasonable balance between need and results is achieved, then the searcher looks for other information in the classification categories and other classifications similar to the ones in which the retrieved documents (books, etc.) were found. More sophisticated searches can be made by using several search terms simultaneously and accepting documents only where all the search terms are satisfied simultaneously, such as ninth-grade minority group mathematics. This searching strategy knowledge is becoming increasingly important because information retrieval in education is being made frequently by computers (see Asher and Kurfeerst, 1964).

The federal government, through its Educational Resources Information Center (ERIC), a part of the National Institute of Education, produces summaries of research information in various areas of education at the cutting edge of problems of major concern. Many of these have been compiled through automated retrieval systems. Substantive educational areas such as accountability, student involvement, systems building, class size, and differentiated staffing patterns are typical of these summaries produced in the ERIC system.

From time to time, professional organizations or even an individual will publish an extensive review of research in their area of education. The University Council on School Administration, the American Association of Health, Physical Education, and Recreation, The American Association of School Administrators, and The International Reading Association are the types of organizations which have done this in the past. Membership in one or more professional education organizations and a knowledge of the professional organizations of friends can be quite valuable in finding sources which give a good overview of a field of education.

This human element has another aspect which should not be overlooked. When students pay tuition at a college or university, one of the resources to which they have access is the faculty of the institution. Schools and departments of education have experts in many areas of education, as do many other departments. These experts in departments outside of education are of importance to educational research in areas such as administration, child development, computing, the academic areas taught in public schools, and psychology. The talents of the faculty in these areas should be tapped by asking them for recommended sources.

Once the overview of the broad problem area is gained, the narrower task is selected, and, if desired, a study of its recent history is made, the next task is to determine the current research on the problem. The bigger picture is usually not a recent picture (in a research sense) unless the reviewer happens to be fortunate enough to be in an area where a major summary and integration of the research has just been completed. Even then, very recent results and thinking will not be available in the work because of editing and publishing delays. The concern in this second phase of learning what others have done is to overcome the information lag, which might run anywhere from a year or so up to five or six years or more, if only research summaries are used.

JOURNALS

At this point, the search for information moves away from a primary reliance on books to journal publications, abstracting services, information retrieval systems, and personal contacts. In the sciences, including those aspects of educational research which are scientifically oriented, one of the primary ethics is that all knowledge be public and formal. Printed publication is the primary means of making one's results public and commonly occurs in journals in scientific and professional fields. (It is from these journal articles and other sources that the larger summaries and overviews are compiled.) Thus, to be current, persons searching the literature on a given problem must also search journals, abstracts, and so forth.

One of the clues as to which of the hundreds of journals to review is to note which of the journals are frequently cited in the cumulative summary books and pamphlets. Then the current issues of these journals can be scanned quickly to ascertain if there are recent articles in them of interest to the searcher.

The usual way to determine the extent of the journal articles possibly pertaining to a problem is to search through various abstracting and indexing publications. These abstracting services have as their business the searching of journals in their field of endeavor and related to it, briefly reporting the articles found, and indexing them under a series of headings and search terms which a searcher might be using. Further, these abstracting and indexing services will also cite books in the field, and one service, *Resources in Education,* collects, indexes, and makes available occasional papers, mimeographed materials, government reports, and documents which have not been formally published in journals or in book form. Often, in addition to regular monthly or bi-monthly publication of recent articles and books, the services usually will make summary publications at larger intervals (six months or a year), so that a whole series of smaller sets of abstracts and indices do not have to be searched to obtain thoroughness. Occasionally, summaries over a much longer period of time are made for reference purposes. For instance, *Psychological Abstracts* has indexed all its abstracts from 1927 to 1960 in one large volume with supplements in two- and four- year periods. There are also semi-annual indices to the abstracts. Thus, almost all the published work on a topic, or by one person, can be found readily without making multiple searches through numerous yearly volumes. However, recent literature on a problem also is available because of the frequent abstracts and indices published throughout the year.

The *Education Index*, the *Current Index to Journals in Education*, and *Resources in Education* are probably the three key abstracting and indexing services for education. These three journals will form the core area for the problem search for most educators. The *Education Index* has yearly volume summaries of all its indexed literature during the preceding year. The *Education Index* is *not* an abstracting service, simply a citation source. In addition, it publishes monthly citations (except for two of the summer months) so that the information service is quite up-to-date. It is a cumulative subject and author index of a broad range of educational periodical material. It also includes yearbooks, bulletins, and materials printed by the federal government. It is indexed by subject fields such as art, audiovisual education, special education, mathematics, and by educational areas such as administration, guidance curriculum, preschool, elementary, and so forth. In addition, it lists several hundred journals of interest to educators, together with their editors and their addresses.

The *Current Index to Journals in Education* also publishes cumulative summaries. In 1969 and 1970 these were yearly; more recently they have been semi-annually. Throughout the year, the index is published monthly and includes over 500 education and education-related journals. The Index has both author and subject indexes. The subject index is of more than passing importance because it uses a uniquely developed set of ERIC descriptors which are quite comprehensive. By use of the *Thesaurus of ERIC Descriptors* (1972), the professionals and students in education can gain great facility in searching the educational literature. There are suggestions for taking the searcher's original topic words and using broader or narrower terms, as well as related terms to facilitate the effort. Descriptor groups, their definitions, and the descriptor words displayed with commonly used modifiers, adjectives, and as adjectives for other words are given also. The ERIC system has become the best single source of entry into the educational literature.

The companion service to ERIC's *Current Index to Journals in Education* (CIJE) is *Resources in Education* (RIE). Patterned in much the same way as CIJE, the major difference is that the materials indexed and abstracted in RIE generally have not been published formally. RIE presents reports and documents of interest to educators. Since their materials are not available in journals and books, as a part of the ERIC service, a number of Clearinghouses located at universities and professional organizations are responsible for particular areas, such as the disadvantaged, teacher education, vocational and technical education, and reading and communication skills, and are used to acquire, review, abstract, and index these documents. In addition to the abstracts published in RIE, most of the full documents are available in 4″ × 6″ microfiche (microfilm cards) and on 8½″ × 11″ hard copy sheets. Many higher education libraries in institutions with major commitments to professional education have complete ERIC microfiche document collections and readers.

Both the CIJE and RIE reference data in the ERIC system can be searched via computer since all of the material is on computer tape for storage. The complete tapes can be purchased by an institution, but a simpler approach is to have searches done by organizations providing such services. The costs of these services are negligible compared to any semblance of a manual search. Probably not atypical is the "Probe" service of the School of Education at Indiana University. For $12.00 this service will search on descriptors and their combinations to find relevant studies in either RIE or CIJE; for $18.00 they will search both. The Probe service for RIE combines subject headings and prints the abstracts of the RIE reports that match the request. The cost includes up to 100 abstracts and up to 700 additional title-author citations. For the CIJE, a list of journal articles which match the descriptors will be listed. Once these are received, the most relevant articles in the journals or the ERIC microfiche of the RIE can be read.

One precaution must be observed in using the RIE abstracts and documents. Since they have not generally passed through an independent editorial acceptance and although there has been a selection made by the ERIC Clearinghouses, the quality of the information in the documents cannot always be accepted at face value. Vockell and Asher (1974) in their study found that 44 percent of the documents representing a one-year period of RIE documents were rated by research specialists as either poor or completely incompetent.

Other indexing services of a more specialized nature for educators include the *Educational Administration Abstracts*, the *Exceptional Child Education Abstracts*, *Child Development Abstracts and Bibliography*, *Psychological Abstracts*, and *Sociological Abstracts*. One particularly valuable source is *Dissertation Abstracts*, in which are included all the abstracts of doctoral dissertations done in participating universities in the United States. These include educational dissertations as well as those in related fields. While the topics tend to be diverse and the quality varies, if there does happen to be a recent well-done dissertation in the area of the problem being searched, it can be quite valuable.

For other fields in special areas, the thorough professional will make an effort to learn what reference services are available. A good reference librarian can be an invaluable asset for this purpose.

There is an additional, valuable procedure for aid in finding what others have done. When standardized instruments play an important role in the investigation of a problem, it may be useful to employ Buros' *Mental Measurement Yearbook* reference about the instruments as a major source of information concerning the test. For instance, in a prediction study of success in algebra, if an algebra prognostic test has been used, the citations in the *Yearbook* to prior studies suggesting its validity in educational situations would be an important source of related literature.

ADDITIONAL SEARCH METHODS

These previously cited sources will bring the searcher almost up-to-date on all the written statements concerning what is known about the problem of interest. There are some time lags between the publication of a journal or the selection of a document by RIE and the time the citation or abstract appears. This lag might range from a few months to much more, depending on whether or not an abstract has to be prepared and whether the abstractors are volunteer labor or not. There is also a time lag between the time a document is written in final form and its acceptance and publication by a journal. (In RIE, this time lag would be that which occurs before the document is found or brought to the attention of the RIE Clearinghouse staff.) Finally, there are varying delays between the time a researcher makes the final analyses of the data, mulls over them, and gradually arrives at conclusions and the time that they appear in final written form.

For the researcher doing a major study or investigation toward the basic end of the research spectrum, it may be worthwhile to obtain all the knowledge that is available, even though it has yet to appear in journals, abstracts, or in RIE. This can be done by contacting researchers who are working in the general problem area. Their names will appear in the list of documents that have been found in the searches described above. Colleagues in other educational systems and colleges and universities may know additional names of centers where this work is being done. In addition, researchers may check convention programs where research papers and symposia are given, go to convention meetings to be held in the near future, introduce themselves to the relevant speakers, and indicate an interest in their presentations. Researchers should also write to the investigators and make a knowledgeable inquiry by indicating an acquaintance with the presentor's work and asking for recent report papers. Several telephone calls doing the same thing are also usually a good investment if up-to-the-minute information is needed. Most researchers are flattered by carefully considered questions indicating that the inquirer has read their work. (Of course, the most flattering approach of all is to ask a person to be a paid consultant to the project!) If money is to be spent in developing or using knowledge, projects should be started right by developing a sound, well-organized, in-depth base from which to work. This pays in the long run.

Actually in the search of the literature, a basis is being formed for the development of a theory about the problem: how the parts of the problem may fit together, how they may be explained, how they work, what the problem is *not*, and, ultimately, the leap to the suggested answers to the question "Why?"

REPORTING RESEARCH

The professionals who learn and use the knowledge their colleagues have generated have the obligation to give to others what they, too, have learned. Ultimately this will be in written form. Even if the presentation is made orally, accuracy in science requires a written basis for the report. The purpose of this section will be to present the parts of a report, whether it be a formal, scientific presentation for a thesis, dissertation, journal, for a technical report, or for administrative action. A proposal for funding from a governmental agency or foundation also uses the majority of the same parts as a scientific report. Some attention will be given to style, format, and suggestions for writing for publication.

Style. The purpose of a report in science is to present the findings of an investigation and to give them in such a way that the methods, observations, and results can be replicated by others who are knowledgeable about the field. Public knowledge and public methods are an integral part of the ethics of the scientific method. In education, the concern is not that professionals would attempt to be secretive about their procedures but that they may lack clarity in description or omit detail about the methods they used.

To be well written, a report of any kind must be clear, but it also must be concise and complete. This report needs an organization and a manner of expression which have been generated from the experience of hundreds of years of communication in science.

The key to expression in scientific writing is simplicity. Simplicity is achieved through the use of short sentences and nontechnical words, but not jargon (jargon being the ill-defined words and phrases popular at the moment in the profession). In a technical report, technical terms are unavoidable. These terms should be defined starting with a dictionary (or a technical dictionary such as Good's [1973] *Dictionary of Education*) if necessary. Operational and theoretical definitions can be cited from authoritative works.

A simple sentence structure is also useful. Long, compound sentences with several subordinate clauses are best left to literary artists who can handle them. The purpose of scientific writing is to report findings and methods accurately and objectively. Scientific reporting is description of what was done, to whom or what, and the results. The reports should be written as intelligibly as possible so that they can be understood by another who is informed about the field but who is not an expert. Thus these reports will be precise, unambiguous, and economical. The chances that a reader will misunderstand must be reduced to a minimum.

For example, one way of avoiding ambiguity is to avoid sentences and paragraphs beginning with "this" or "that"; the antecedents of these words too often are vague or distant. Instead, repeat the name or the idea to assure comprehension; for example: "Jones' study found . . . . ," or "The sex-segregated group described . . . . ," *not*, "This study described . . . ."

The past tense should be used in scientific reports, since these reports are descriptive of what was done and what was found at some time prior to the date the report was written. The present tense can be used sparingly to indicate statements of findings that are broadly applicable and of continuing or timeless value. Definitions, well-defined scientific theory, and hypotheses (if used) also are stated in the present tense. The future tense is rarely used in scientific writing.

Scientific and technical reports generally are written in the third person. The use of "I" and "we" in such writing usually is avoided (at least until a list of several publications is achieved!). One way to avoid the first person style is to write as if someone else had done the research, and the writer is reporting what was done. The third person, "The investigator gave the tests . . . . " is used frequently. However, avoid references to "the writer" and "the author." The passive voice is also used: "The tests were given . . . ."

While the word "data" (with an initial long "a") is beginning to be used as a collective noun, the novice writer should be conservative and use plural verbs with it: "The data were . . . ." "Criteria" is also plural;

"criterion" is singular. The singular of data (datum) seldom is used. Finally, do not split infinitives, and never use a preposition to end a sentence "up with."

The facile use of quotations is of great help in scientific report writing. Building on prior work is an integral part of science. Quotations build authenticity, but extreme care should be taken to assure that the quotations are in context with the original writer's meaning, and the original wording, punctuation, spelling, and emphases must be preserved. All quotations in the final copy of a report must be checked to assure authenticity. If the original is in error, the scholar's jab, "sic," should be inserted in brackets (as are all insertions into quotations) after the word or parts in error.

To use a quotation where not all of the words or sentences are desired, ellipses, three spaced periods, ". . ." are used. If the omitted words appear after a complete sentence or complete a sentence, four periods rather than three are used.

The scientific citation style for quotations, and other material that is referenced, gives only the author's last name (enclosed in parentheses), if not given in the text, and the year of publication. If the reference is to joint authors, both last names are used. For multiple authors, the last names are used in the first citation, and the first author's last name and "et al." are used for all citations thereafter. For more than one publication in a year by an author, the year with "a," "b," "c," etc., can be used. For quotations, the page should be added to the parenthetical citation in the text.

This citation style practically eliminates footnotes and a reference numbering system, both of which are difficult for fledgling writers and typists to master. In effect, referencing by footnotes was a hindrance to public scientific communication. It is vanishing in the behavioral sciences, and almost all educational journals now either use manuscripts with this citation format or will accept them. (Again it is assumed that historical and philosophical scholars in education, writing for publication, have mastered long ago the footnoting documentation, citation, and referencing systems of the humanities.) See parts of the *Publication Manual* of the American Psychological Association (1974) for behavioral science format and style recommendations.

Writing is one of the more time-consuming tasks in the scientific and professional fields. It is exacting and frequently a task in which many graduate students are deficient. Yet almost anyone who can graduate from college can be an acceptable writer and a publishable writer, given editorial assistance. Good writing is an art which some people have developed. Professionals and researchers who have only a modicum of this ability and training in writing should use the talents of those who do. Fortunately, education is blessed with talent in many areas. Some educators are facile in quantitative skills and areas, some in social interaction, some in the use of language, and some in all of these areas. Consultation, advising, and trading the use of skills should be frequent in a multidisciplinary task such as educational research.

In the scientific and scholarly aspects of education, no one can really say that they are full-fledged members of the discipline unless they contribute to their field through writing. In the professional and administrative areas of education, those who write and speak frequently will rise faster and further than those who do not.

The hardest part of writing is the self-discipline of applying the seat of the pants to the seat of the chair and producing 200, 300, or 1,000 words or more at regular intervals. There is no doubt that for most people it is demanding work, but almost everyone can write, given the discipline, practice, and editorial assistance of others: friends, spouse, and professional users of the language.

Organization. One of the secrets in getting the picture of the overall task is organizing it sequentially for writing, and then breaking the task into a number of small manageable parts. In scientific writing, the organization and parts have been developed over several centuries, and it is now difficult to make scientific presentations in any other way. Even for the technical reports and reports for administrative actions after investigations, the same parts can be used, but placed in a different order to encourage implementation. These parts are: an abstract, a statement of the problem, a review of the literature, a methods and procedures section, a results section, a discussion section, and the conclusions. For technical report implementation in a school system, a recommendations section should also be included. Each of these sections has a different purpose. They generally are not read in this order, nor should they be written necessarily in this order. In fact, beginning writers and students are advised to start on the methods and procedures section, since they are most familiar with the methods by which they have collected the data for their study.

Methods Section. The methods (or procedures) section should describe the data collection and analysis procedures in enough detail so that readers reasonably knowledgeable in the field could repeat them if necessary. In this section, the abstract, theoretical variables are operationally defined. For instance, the theoretical variables *intelligence* and *school achievement*, can be observed operationally as the Stanford-Binet test score and grade point average.

The methods section is usually further broken into smaller parts such as subjects and groups, instruments, data, analyses, procedure, design of the study, sampling, controls, and treatments. (Only those headings which are applicable are used.) The description of each aspect of the methods section can usually be rather brief, although in some studies any part may be somewhat involved. For instance, in a sampling study with several subgroups, each studied somewhat differently, the "subjects," "groups," "sampling procedures," and "instruments" parts could be rather long. However, there might be no "treatment" or "control" headings used at all. In experimental studies, the "sampling" heading might not be used, but the "design," "treatment," and "control" parts would be important. In these sections, references are made to standard sources about analyses, prior similar procedures, instrument sources, and so forth.

Results Section. The results section immediately follows the methods section. In the methods section, data gathering and analysis procedures are described. In the results section, the results of the analyses of the data are indicated rather succinctly. There is little elaboration, just the facts. The organization follows that suggested in the methods section where certain groups were observed under certain conditions, and data were recorded. If this repetition sounds as if it makes dull reading, it does. The purpose of scientific writing is not entertainment but fast, accurate communication so that replication can take place readily. Keeping the structure of the sections the same facilitates this purpose. Little explanation is given other than to present the more unfamiliar aspects of the analytic method in some detail. (Interpretations of the results in light of the research methods used are included in the discussion section.)

Tables and figures presenting results in a collated form are often quite useful in the results section. While all the original data usually cannot be presented (except in some dissertation and technical report work), usually enough of the results should be presented so that the researcher's later interpretations of them can be checked. In order to avoid blocking the flow of the development of the presentation, where quantities of data can be included in a report, they should be placed in an appendix following the main body of the text.

A table is a presentation of various kinds of tabular data. The title, placed above the table describes the content of the table. A figure is all other graphic material that is not tabular presentation of data; figures are labeled at the bottom. Tables, figures, and text should compliment each other. Tables and figures should be placed in the text following their first reference and should be referenced in the text.

The novice writer of scientific reports would do well to write the results section immediately after the methods section, since finishing the analyses of the data usually is the end of the excuses not to start writing. Having these analyses fresh in mind and organized in a logical order for ease of understanding should simplify the task of reporting the results. There is no editorializing or apologizing in the results section, just the results of the analyses of the data collected from the subjects.

Discussion Section. The opportunity for budding authors and others among the scientific writers to interpret the results of the analyses of the data occurs in a discussion section. The purpose of the discussion is to indicate the limitations of the results as the consequence of unusual or different samples, methods, instruments, and occurrences that might have influenced the data-gathering procedures. The style can be somewhat more narrative than the preceding sections, and the interrelationship of the results within the study and relationships of the results with other prior work should be discussed. In dissertations and technical reports where space is not so limited, the style can be somewhat discursive and even slightly personal.

However, one of the major purposes of the discussion section is to tie the current results of the research into the larger body of theoretical knowledge in the field of the study. At this point, the extensive searching of the prior and current literature, as well as conversations and learning what others have done, is valuable. Relevant notes, photocopies, journals, and books should be consulted, and the interweaving of prior results with current results must be made. This, of course, is the extension of the theory of the research area. The formal presentation of the prior theory in the research report, the literature review, has yet to be presented in this chapter. However, the writing of the discussion section is not finished until the literature review has also been completed and perused for added information which can be used in interpretations of the current results. Limitations of the results, correspondences, and differences between the current findings and widely accepted viewpoints should be presented in this section.

Conclusions Section. Summary statements resulting from the discussion of the results of the research are presented in the conclusions section. What can the writer (and others) conclude generally as the result of the research effort? Frequently, the conclusions section can be written in a series of rather short, sequentially numbered statements— at least as a start. This section can be developed rather quickly by going through the results section and writing a statement of conclusions modified by the examination of every set of results found in the discussion section.

Once all of the conclusions have been identified and written, an integration and reordering of them may take place. Larger, more important, overall conclusions may emerge. The conclusions of greatest prominence should be placed first and minor conclusions later. A summarizing statement should end the section. Sometimes the concluding section is labeled *Summary and Conclusions,* and the opportunity is taken to recapitulate the study briefly. When the reports of others are read, the conclusions and the summary are often read first because they are brief and do summarize the study succinctly.

The Introduction. In every report, the old adage of preachers should be followed: "Tell 'em what you're going to tell 'em, tell 'em what you're telling 'em, and then tell 'em what you've told 'em." The methods, discussion, and results sections tell the readers what you're telling them. The summary and conclusions tell them what you've told them. The introductory aspect of the scientific report serves to tell the readers what you're going to tell them.

The introduction can be divided into three parts: the opening phases (unlabeled), the review of the literature, and the statement of the problem. These sections, though first in the report, are the most difficult to write for novices in scientific reporting; thus they are saved for last. Once the writer has gotten "off the ground" and has demonstrated to himself or herself that he or she can write, this is sufficient motivation to continue and finish. Further, the methods, results, and conclusions sections are of a rather concrete nature, organize themselves (to an extent), and so are easier for most to write. The discussion section does require more elaboration and an intertwining of themes, but the review of the literature causes many to have problems. It reports the theoretical and the abstract, and there is not usually a ready-made structure for it.

These introductory sections are important in that almost all of the study revolves around themes and knowledge reported in this phase of the report. Even if it is not written formally at first, the work preparatory to it must be done. This preparation is the development of a formal problem statement and the learning and understanding of the past research from which the formal problem statement arises. (In most professionally oriented educational research, it is assumed that the problems of interest generally are found informally in the day-to-day and year-in-year-out concerns and problems found in the profession.)

The development of a scientific, formal problem from an informal professional one is done by the search of the literature and communications with those who are working on the problem. While some people work well in this abstract framework and follow the traditional textbook approach to scientific investigation by taking an area of general interest, reviewing the literature in that area, and developing a formal problem from the literature, most do not.

Just because the review of the literature and statement of the problem appears first in a journal article does not mean that these parts of the article are written first or should be read first. (In fact, in reading articles it is recommended that the literature review be read last.) An article is of minor interest unless the research reported in it is rather close to one's problem area. Most experienced researchers have a fairly good idea of the major theories and variables relating to the problem on which they are working. If it is a new area to them, the researchers also will spend a considerable amount of time reviewing the literature. Generally, most researchers will not spend much time on prior literature except to read current journals in their area and alert colleagues to bring articles of interest to their attention. Then, when the research is done and the reports are being written, they will make a systematic search to aid in the further development of their interpretations of results. At this point, they will piece together an overview of the literature.

Except for articles and books devoted to theory development and bibliographic reviews, few published scientific reports have extensive, formal reviews of the literature. There simply is no room for them in the space-tight journals. The usual journal article writer develops briefly the theoretical setting in which the research takes place, summarizes the main literature in a few sentences, and cites the location of a number of the major prior works.

Dissertations and technical reports often will present much more. For one thing, there is more space available to the writer to make the report. In dissertation work in many instances, the faculty wants the students to demonstrate that they can find and organize the literature into viable theory as part of their doctoral work. When these dissertations and reports are published, frequently this section requires severe editing, leaving only the summary sentences and the citations, while adding the reference to the dissertation for the fuller exposition.

One of the better ways to organize the introduction is to indicate the general area of the problem and its importance to education. A quotation or two from an eminent authority aids in getting started. (One can find that someone, somewhere, feels that any particular educational problem is of major importance if one looks far enough!) However, typical education majors need to be restrained in writing the general opening. Educators often have been well schooled in writing extensively about a subject, sometimes at rather shallow levels. Scientific writing is concerned primarily with facts and fact-based theory. The review of the literature should be moved into quickly after a brief introduction.

The Literature Review Section. The review of the literature is just that, a review, not a summary, of the literature. It was indicated that some of the scientific literature in education is not of the highest quality. The writer should apply what has been learned in this book and elsewhere to examine critically the articles of importance in the area. The words, "to review critically the literature" are sometimes used to describe this process. To "review critically" is redundant, but often is necessary to communicate the task that is to be done in this section of a scientific report. To summarize the literature in education is not enough.

The organization of such an ill-defined job as reviewing the literature can be trying. One of the better ways, and almost always useful as a first approach, is to examine the major dimensions of the research by listing the subjects, groups, variables, instruments, data, analyses, sampling, criteria, treatments, and so forth. The literature review should cover these aspects of major importance for the research. Usually some parts are more important and will aid in organizing the overall picture for the writer. Since the review of the literature is often rather roving, an overview of the section is a must. Often the review of the literature is organized further for the reader by using subheadings within it. Thus the task is organized and broken into smaller parts for the writer also, making the composition task easier as the various articles and notes can be sorted into groups conforming to the structure.

Problem Section. The statement of the problem presents the formal problem and the specific questions to be answered or the hypotheses to be tested. Occasionally both the questions and the hypotheses are given, although the hypotheses are simply the questions in present tense, declarative form. Some universities insist that hypotheses in dissertations appear in the statistically testable, null form, i.e., stating in effect that no differences among groups or no relationship between variables exist. Since there are few other ways to test hypotheses in the behavioral and social sciences than by statistical procedures, most sophisticated readers of research assume that the

actual tests of the hypotheses will be in the null form statements.
(Students may need to be reminded of this though.) Whether the
problem statements culminate in specific questions to be answered or
hypotheses makes little practical difference in the research. New
researchers are sometimes more comfortable presenting questions to be
answered. If formality requires it, then these questions can be readily
transformed into declarative statements of positions tentatively taken
which are drawn from theory, which are to be tested, and which will
indicate the value of the theoretical position.

The statement of the problem flows rather naturally from the
general informal problem area as developed and elaborated upon by the
review of the elements of the problem area in the review of the
literature. Thus, for a logical sequence, the formal statement of the
problem would come after the literature review and just before the
methods section. This tends to bury it, however, in the exposition of
longer reports and especially dissertations. Thus it is sometimes
recommended that the formal statement of the problem with its
hypotheses or questions be placed just before the literature review.

The Abstract.   For efficient retrieval purposes it is useful for the
writer to produce an *abstract* of the research report. Abstracts are brief
summaries of the report that run from one sentence to five or six
hundred words, depending on the length of the original report and the
limitations placed on the abstract by the publishing source. Requirements and limitations on abstracts should be learned before they are
written. It is easier to write the abstract after the full report is
completed. Often it can be produced from a rewriting of the summary of
the report, if there is one. An abstract should contain, at a minimum,
the results of the study. It is also desirable, if there is room, to include
the kind of subjects involved, the type of research design, the method,
and the problem.

The Title.   The title of a report is exceptionally important. Usually
it is wise not to commit oneself to a title until after a study is completed.
(It is easier to change the title than to change the study!) The title should
be short, yet convey the exact topic of the report. However, it is not
necessary to specify all the variables involved in a study in the title.
Also, phrases such as "An investigation of" or "A study of" should be
avoided. Good titles usually can be limited to fifteen words or less.

References.   References are also important, and here again a
particular format is often required, depending upon the potential

publisher of the report. These requirements should be noted before the references are typed. Science depends upon the cumulative nature of evidence, and the references aid in maintaining this chain of knowledge.

Certain information is required in all references to allow others to find them in libraries and other information retrieval systems. For journal articles, these facts are author's surname and initials, the title of the article, the name of the journal, the year of publication, the volume number, and the pages in the journal where the article was published. For a book, in addition to the names of the authors, the title of the book is required along with the city and state where it was published, the publisher's name, and the year of publication. When the literature is being searched, it is wise to record this needed information at the time when articles, books, and materials are being collected. Those who neglect noting this information the first time have the task of searching for it all over again.

Note that the list of the citation sources is not labeled as the "bibliography" unless the literature search was exhaustive. Every reference that is cited in the text should be included in the list of references, but there should be no general compilation of references in the area unless the research report is primarily a review of the literature. A good source of reference style and format is the *Publication Manual* of the American Psychological Association (1974).

Tables, Figures, and Headings. For some of the larger publication formats, a list of tables, a list of figures, and a table of contents must be compiled. The listings of the tables and figures can be obtained from their titles. The table of contents essentially lists all of the headings of the major divisions and subdivisions of the report or article.

There are four types of headings that can be used, but most reports need use only three at the most. If these headings and their use are understood in advance, the task of writing a report is facilitated. The four headings are centered heads, second-order heads, side heads, and paragraph heads. Short reports need only one type of heading, and these can be headings which are centered on the page line. Centered heads are typed in capital and small letters.

Most articles in journals need only two levels of headings. These are the centered head and either the side heading or the paragraph heading. The side heading is typed flush to the left margin in capital and small letters. The text that follows starts on the next double-spaced line. The paragraph headings are typed with a paragraph indentation and have only the initial letter capitalized. They end with a period, and the text follows on the same line without extra spacing.

When three levels of headings are required for a report, they should be the centered head, the side heading, and the paragraph heading. The use of four levels of headings should be restricted to very lengthy reports and books. The additional heading, the second-order heading, should be centered and typed with only the initial words capitalized.

The major divisions requiring centered heads ordinarily would be the literature review (if there is one), the methods section, the results, the discussion, and the conclusion. (Note that there is never a heading for "introduction.") A side heading might be used for lengthy aspects of the methods section, such as sampling procedures, research design, or instrumentation. Paragraph side heads could also be used for this purpose or in longer articles could be used to aid in organizing paragraphs or sets of paragraphs within the side-headed or center headed divisions. For instance, within an extensive methods division, the description and organization of the subjects in a descriptive study could be rather detailed. It might clarify and organize the report to use "subjects" as a side head and a paragraph heading for each group being described. Essentially the headings form an outline of the report which is useful in writing it and in organizing it for the readers also.

Recommendations Section. A part of a report not found in basic scientific writing is the recommendations section. However, in reporting to professionals, a specific section should be included in the report indicating how the conclusions might be used or implemented in educational practice. The conceptual order of the recommendations section would suggest that it follows from the conclusions and therefore should be placed after them. For reports other than those in the scientific style, the order of the sections may be changed.

For reports to administrators for implementation, it is good procedure to place the recommendations first. Administrators may not have the time to read in the logical order of prior literature and theory, problem statement, methods, results, discussion, and conclusions. Administrators may want only the recommendations of their subordinates. Should the administrator feel the recommendations might not be warranted, then he or she will read the conclusions of the study next, and then possibly the methods, followed by the discussion. The literature review, if any, should be placed last. The recommendations and conclusions should not be buried at the end of a report.

Proposal Writing. Proposal writing is another very useful form of writing. In order to do research or initiate an educational program, a proposal indicating what the problem is, its background, and the proposed methods and procedures for doing the research of implementing the program must be written before it will be considered by funding agencies.

Proposal formats are very much like the report format just presented. The problem and its importance in education is stated. The literature on the theory of the problem or what others have done in attempting to resolve it, is then given. However, the last major section of a proposal is the methods section. Here the details of what is to be done are presented with sufficient specificity to indicate competence and to justify the budget requested. The budget request should be closely related to the activities to be implemented, which are suggested in the methods section. There are at this point, of course, no results, so no results can be discussed or conclusions drawn. In their place, usually there is an indication of what results might be expected, given the theoretical background and the procedures to be employed, and a discussion of the implications and importance of the possible results. The background of the initiators suggesting the project and the facilities available to implement it usually cover the rest of the information requested (except for the budget data). A Small Grant proposal to USOE, one which was subsequently funded, is given in Appendix B as an example.

Proposal writing can be a valuable skill to learn. Many people have ideas; few can present them easily and quickly in writing.

Scientific Communication.   Scientific writing does not use an essay style; it is far more than an expression of opinion and is not based on appeals to authorities. The essential idea of scientific report writing is that it is based on facts and includes conclusions based on facts, not just the writer's thinking. It should be impersonal, yet clear and forceful in expression. There should be no alibis or unsupported evidence in the reporting.

Scientific writing, like all writing, is aided by the early presentation of advanced organizers. Tell the readers succinctly what you are going to tell them. Give them an overview in every section of what the organization of the section will be and what it will contain. At the end of every major section summarize for the readers what has been presented to them. This gives the writer three "shots" at the reader. If the point is communicated on any one of them, the reader will learn.

Scientific communication is sufficiently detailed that its procedures can be replicated. In general, it is better strategy to overwrite than to underwrite. In the long run it is faster (and offers the writer fewer excuses to quit for the day) to write out the theory, explanation, and methods than to ask someone later if they are necessary. Further, in reworking a manuscript, it is easier to edit down to a size limit than to try to increase the descriptive material. Finally, journal editors are convinced more readily of a manuscript's acceptability if all the details are given than if they are left wondering if a particular procedure was used or an appropriate theoretical position was considered. They can delete easily parts of the manuscript or suggest reducing ten pages to one while conditionally accepting it. It is difficult to make the opposite decision—to accept the manuscript if more description of the research is added.

When writing, it is a good idea to use similar writing as a guide to follow (a dissertaion, journal article, report, and so forth). After the first draft, allow a "cooling" period before going back to edit, add, and delete aspects of it. Next, have friends, or a spouse, or a professional editor make comments and suggestions, especially in scientific writing, with regard to clarity. Scientific writing must be, above all, precisely understandable.

For those still in school, it is well to get practice in writing and publishing by starting with small research project reports for conventions and journals. Working with a faculty member as co-author is a good apprenticeship. Writing brief comments on journal articles is another way to get started. Use what has been learned from this book to detect errors. These comments usually are short, can be written relatively fast, and help improve the quality of the journals as well. (See Vockell and Asher, 1973; Asher, 1968a; Asher 1968b; Reed and Asher, 1971, as examples.) Writing a master's thesis is worth the effort in terms of time and experience gained toward doing a doctoral dissertation. On all of these writing efforts, offering to write a first draft in exchange for co-authorship in a publication is worthwhile. The ideas, format, approach, and later editing and advice from a publishing writer-researcher is well worth the trade. Last, but not least, get a good manuscript typist and an appropriate style manual. Writing is rewarded in the scholarly and professional worlds, and anyone who gets three articles or reports to his or her credit early in a career will be well on the way to continuing publication.

SUMMARY

This chapter has presented some fundamental concepts in the search for what others have done in the field of education and related areas. The structure of the information system and the various ways it is entered and used in practice were given. Comprehensive but somewhat out-of-date sources were suggested as a first source, with more up-to-date sources being consulted later for increased specificity. A general strategy of information retrieval was presented also. Innovations in computer-based educational information systems at a national level were described. Writing scientific reports in education was stressed and style, format, purpose, organization, and headings were covered. Special writing procedures for administrators and for proposals were offered. Special considerations of scientific writing were suggested, as were hints for novice writers and students on how to gain experience in this valuable professional capability.

STUDY AND DISCUSSION PROBLEMS

1. Read an educational research report. List the organization and the contents of each section.
2. List educational research literature review sources commonly used.
3. Pick an educational topic and indicate the procedures by which you would find recent material about it.
4. Follow the procedures you have suggested for learning about an educational topic and indicate the sources that were useful to you.
5. Describe the process of the writing of a research or evaluation report. What are the parts, and how is the content in each developed?
6. Assume you are starting on an educational research problem topic. Describe the procedure you would follow in a literature search, including specific sources and search words.
7. In a library available to you, locate and list five sources of information useful to you in designing and reporting a research or evaluation project.
8. What similarities and differences are there between research report writing and proposal writing?
9. List a number of general rules to be followed in writing a research report.
10. What are the most common abstracting and indexing sources for the educational literature.
11. What part of a report is not used in scientific style, but is of considerable value in reporting results of studies to administrators? How else do reports to administrators differ from strictly scientific reporting?
12. List some special aspects of style in scientific writing.
13. Use a correct publication style to cite a journal article and a book in which you are interested.

REFERENCES

American Psychological Association. *Psychological abstracts*. Washington, D. C.: 1927–.

American Psychological Association. *Publication manual*. Washington, D. C.: 1974.

Asher, J. W., and Kurfeerst, M. The computer and information retrieval: School law, a case study. *Harvard Educational Review*, 1965, *35*, 178–190.

Asher, J. W. Comment on "A comparison of i/t/a/ and T. O. reading achievement when methodology is controlled." *Elementary English*, 1968a, *XLV*(4), 452–457, 484.

Asher, W. Comment on "Spelling achievement i.t.a. instruction." *The Reading Teacher*, 1968b, *22*(2), 153–156, 169.

Buros, O. K., *The mental measurements yearbook*. Highland Park, N. J.: Gryphon Press, 1972.

Campbell, D. T., and Stanley, J. C. Experimental and quasi-experimental designs for research on teaching. In N. L. Gage (Ed), *Handbook of research on teaching*. Chicago, Ill.: Rand McNally, 1963, 171–246.

Child development abstracts and bibliography. National Research Council of the Society for Research in Child Development, 1927–.

Current index to journals in education. New York: Macmillan Information Service, Macmillan Publishing Co., 1969–.

Dissertation abstracts. Dissertation Abstracts, Ann Arbor, Michigan: University Microfilms, 1938–.

Ebel, Robert L. (Ed.). *Encyclopedia of educational research* (4th ed.). Toronto, Canada: Macmillan Co., 1969.

Educational administration abstracts. University Council for Educational Administration. Columbus, Ohio: E. A. Publishers, 1966–.

Education index: New York: H.W. Wilson, 1929–.

Exceptional child education abstracts. The Council for Exceptional Children, Arlington, Virginia, 1970–.

Gage, N. L. (Ed.) *Handbook of research on teaching*. Chicago, Ill.: Rand McNally, 1963.

Good, C. V. *Dictionary of education* (3rd ed.). New York: McGraw-Hill, 1973.

Goodman, F. *Thesaurus of ERIC descriptors*. New York: CCM Information Corporation, Crowell Collier Macmillan, 1972.

Kerlinger, F. N. (Ed.) *Review of research in education*. Itasca, Ill.: F. E. Peacock, 1973–.

The National Society for the Study of Education, 5835 Kimbark Avenue. Chicago, Ill.: University of Chicago Press, 1902–.

Reed, C. L., and Asher, W. Comment on "A multifactor admissions predictive system." *Psychological Reports*, 1971, *29*, 521–522.

Resources in education. Washington, D. C.: Superintendent of Documents, U. S. Government Printing Office, 1956–.

Review of educational research. Washington, D.C.: American Educational Research Association, 1931–.

Sociological abstracts. New York: Sociological Abstracts, Inc., 1954–.

Travers, R.M.W. (Ed.). *Handbook of research on teaching.* (2nd ed.). Chicago: Rand McNally, 1973.

Vockell, E., and Asher, W. Methodological inaccuracies in Croxen and Lytton's "Reading disability and difficulties in finger localization and right-left discrimination. *Developmental Psychology,* 1973, *8*(1), 112.

Vockell, E., and Asher, W. Perceptions of document quality and use by educational decision makers and researchers. *American Educational Research Journal,* 1974, *11*(3), 249–258.

Common
Errors in
Educational
Research

Chapter 11

Texts on scientific research methods are concerned primarily with procedures for conducting investigations in the field of study. A novice researcher in the sciences can follow the methodology of others. There might be a few precautions scattered here and there, alerting the careful investigator to problems of procedures, interpretation, or effort-saving methods. Unfortunately, in educational research, further precautions are necessary. The scientific and professional literature in education too often is inaccurate both in research methods and in the interpretation of data. Students or professionals doing research on a now-and-then basis—those who go to the literature to obtain a model for their research design—may be led astray. With good consultation and advice, the novice researcher's problems can be rectified, but what precautions can professionals take when they want to read the professional literature on a topic? It is almost impossible to have a research expert evaluate on a casual basis information quality for a broad range of articles.

Responsible professionals (and preprofessionals) will recognize the general problem and use the principles already presented in this book, especially those of internal validity of research, to judge information quality. They will seek consultation on important decision data, and, in addition, be alert to a number of specific problems and errors which will be presented in this chapter.

Topics covered will be: (a) the general problem of inadequate comparison groups, no real comparison groups, and groups that are explicitly in error because of the way in which they were developed; (b) interpretation of near-chance results as important; (c) cause-and-effect interpretations of correlated variables; and (d) a variety of problems involving poor use and interpretation of statistical analyses and measurement methods.

COMPARISON GROUP PROBLEMS

An initial theme of this book has been that comparisons are the essential concern in the interpretation of any data. It has been indicated that changes and developments in students cannot be ascribed automatically to an associated change in the educational system. Children and adolescents grow and develop all by themselves. It was suggested that sometimes students and children might develop more fully if some of the changes imposed in the name of education were not made! Politicians cannot take credit for rain; neither should educational administrators take full credit for many of the accomplishments of the students and alumni of their schools. The internal validity principle of maturation must be invoked and only tentative conclusions drawn about development, unless a carefully considered comparison group is available. Instances of omissions of comparison groups, or flawed comparison groups, were noted and explained in several of the previous chapters. A suggestion was even made that, on occasion, some recommended research methods actually led researchers into developing what now are recognized clearly as faulty comparison groups.

This faulty research method is termed "matching." The general procedure of matching can be done in several ways, and not all methods of matching, or use of the word, are faulty. In fact, some methods can be useful and valuable. The reader of research must note carefully what the writer means by the word "matching." Some researchers, recognizing the need for equivalent comparison groups, randomly assign individuals to groups and report that the groups were "matched." In this use of the word "matched," the groups indeed are comparable. However, the word "matching" has so many unfortunate connotations, it is recommended that the words "equivalent groups" be used to describe groups developed through the randomization of subjects.

A second worthwhile use of matching in the development of equivalent groups is the matching of individual subjects *followed* by the random allocation of one of the matched pair (triplet, etc.) to one group and the other to an alternative group. The end result of matching subjects followed by randomization is two (or more) equivalent groups which are particularly homogeneous with respect to one another.

However, there is a price paid for this homogeneity. The number of observations are not considered to be one for each person in both groups, but one for each *pair* of persons placed in the groups. The ability to detect differences in an experiment is based in part on the number of observations in the study. The pairing of subjects through matching reduces the number of observations by one-half. If the matching of the pairs is done on variables reasonably correlated with the criteria variables, however, the effectiveness of the experiment will be enhanced, despite the reduction in the number of observations.

Still, to obtain data for the matching process, it may be necessary to give several tests or collect observational data prior to the experiments. For example, intelligence tests must be given for people to be matched on these scores before they are randomly assigned to an experimental or control group. These data collection efforts and costs might well be used in other ways in the research effort to better advantage.

Another use of the term "matching" is in the phrase "matched groups." Here two (or more) existing groups are examined on several important characteristics. If the two groups are not different on these variables, the standard quasi-experimental model can be followed, using a treatment applied to one group and not to the other, and then the groups are compared on criteria. The use of the words "matched groups" in this sense is equivalent to the better types of quasi-experimental group research discussed in Chapter 5. To describe the design as "matched groups" in this case is not wrong, but the description may be confused with other research procedures which are in error.

Sometimes intact, existing groups have been studied in order to learn the effects of prior differing conditions or treatments on the matched groups. When the groups are not equivalent initially, selective matching of individuals from each of the groups sometimes is done in order to establish seemingly equivalent groups. The matching of these pairs of individuals has to be selective because the groups were not equivalent initially. There are some individuals (generally from both groups) that cannot be paired because their scores are either too high or too low to be coupled with another individual from the other group. (This situation is inherent in the matching process because the original intact groups were not equivalent. If the groups were equivalent, there is not too much point to matching.) Thus, the matching is selective. Individuals in the lower part of the distribution of the high-score group are matched with individuals from the higher part of the distribution in the low-score group. The subjects in the high end of high group and the bottom end of the low group cannot all be matched, and these subjects are no longer used in the research.

No randomization to groups after matching is possible, of course, because the groups are intact (already exist). This truncating selection (low scores from the high group, etc.) from the two original, intact groups produces an effect not recognized by some researchers in the behavioral and social sciences and some educational researchers. The matching of individuals from intact, unequal groups without subsequent randomization actually produces groups which are unequal! Thus, the whole logic of group comparison—equal groups, unequal results, and therefore the inference of unequal treatments—is thrown into turmoil. The reader will recall from Chapter 2 that attempting to make inferences about the equality or inequality of treatments is difficult, if not impossible, when the groups are initially unequal. This is because unequal groups acted on by either equal or unequal treatments generally produce unequal groups.

The reasons why matching of individuals from unequal, intact groups produces unequal groups is somewhat complex because it involves the theory of measurement in the behavioral and social sciences. However, unequal groups from this type of matching do occur. When selected individuals from high-score and low-score groups are matched on their test scores, a retesting of these individuals with the same test will show that the previously matched pairs now differ. The direction of the inequality can be predicted if the direction of the differences from the original intact groups is known. The movement of the average scores of the matched individuals will be toward the average (mean) score of the original groups. The resulting matched groups are primarily from the bottom of the higher group and the top of the lower group. Thus the shifting scores on retesting, termed *regression-toward-the mean*, will be up for the lower-scoring individuals matched from the high group and down for the higher-scoring individuals matched from the low group. With the opposite movements of the average scores in the two matched groups, it is inevitable that instead of the matched groups having been equated, they have been made unequal.

This opposite directionality of the shift in the matched groups' averages is important because it may confound the results of any treatment or condition effects. Sometimes educators and researchers take credit for the regression-toward-the mean effect, and at other times no formal reports of research are made because the regression-toward-the-mean effects are greater than the treatment effects and make the educational changes appear negative.

For instance, there are many reports in the educational literature of studies of the enhancing effect of various curricula for the mentally retarded. Upon examination, the careful reader may find that classes for retarded already existed in a school system and that a new curriculum was instituted in all classes. Not having a true experimental or control group available, some of the abler children in the retarded classes often were matched in regular classes with some of the children of less ability who were unable to be accommodated in the special classes. One of the major matching variables almost invariably is intelligence test scores. This means then that the higher-scoring children in the special classes would be matched with the children of lower ability in regular classes on the basis of existing or obtained intelligence test scores.

Should the investigators obtain intelligence test scores for the matched groups again after the end of the experimental curriculum period, they would find, even if the curriculum had no effect on intelligence test scores, that the obtained intelligence test scores seemingly had dropped in the special class groups. For the matched comparison group in the regular classes, the intelligence test scores would rise.

The explanation is that the matched sample from the retarded group has the top test scores of the low intelligence group. Their scores regress toward the mean of their own group, namely downward. The group from the regular classes has the bottom scores of the regular school group in terms of their intelligence. Their scores regress up to the mean of their original group. Further, the same phenomenon holds true for all scores positively correlated with intelligence test scores. Thus, the educational criteria that are related to intelligence test scores would also be influenced by the regression-toward-the-mean phenomenon. Unless the special curriculum is quite potent in its effect, the special class program would look as if it were harmful with respect to these criteria.

Tukey (1973) indicates that the problem of interpreting a descriptive study is not different when the matched variables are categorized, as with nominal variables, than when the variables are measured in interval form, as in the above discussion. He suggests that the difficulty of interpreting differences among categorical variables is the same as interpreting differences using intervally measured variables.

The phenomenon of regression-toward-the-mean has been known and well documented for many years (Thorndike, 1942). It also has been spelled out in detail in Campbell and Stanley (1963). Yet it continues to plague researchers and readers of research in education and related fields. Major, funded research, supposedly selected and monitored, is no guarantee that matching of individuals from intact groups will not be used as the design. (See Mazurkiewicz, 1966; Asher, 1968.) In fact, in one of the most important educational studies ever done, the federal government's Office of Economic Opportunity (OEO) evaluation of Head Start, used a matched individual design. The investigator in this case managed to match in such a way that it is likely some positive results of Head Start were obliterated by the regression-toward-the-mean phenomenon! Even more disheartening is the fact that the responsible federal officials in OEO's Evaluation Division, who prepared the general design for the Head Start evaluation, seem unaware of the real problem. (For an excellent discussion of these points, see Chapters 10, 10b, and 10c by Campbell and Erlebacher; Evans and Schiller; and Campbell and Erlebacher in *Disadvantaged Child*, Hellmuth, ed. 1970.) The behavioral sciences' literature in addition to education's also has this same error from time to time. (See Croxen and Lytton, 1971; Vockell and Asher, 1973.)

Another type of design problem, and related data interpretation, also involves regression. Occasionally investigators will test a group of students and select those who score lowest on the test for remedial treatment. After the treatment, they will then retest the students and report that there are gains on the test scores. They ascribe these gains to the quality of the treatment invoked. The treatment might indeed be good, but regression effects are also taking place and causing gains. The direction of the regression gain on the second testing for students selected from the bottom of the tested group will be upward toward the mean of the total group.

A typical example again is selecting children for special classes on the basis of low intelligence or school achievement score. If these children are given a remedial curriculum, or *even if they are not*, a second testing will show gains as the result of the regression effect. It is interesting to note that many reports of the effectiveness of remedial and special classes appear in the educational literature, but few present before-and-after test data on classes of gifted students, selected on the basis of their high-tested achievement. A second testing likely would show a *decrease* in scores because of a regression-toward-the-mean (unless maturation and learning effects were sufficient to overcome the regression effect). These results would suggest that when the outcome appears favorable and complimentary to the curriculum developer and administrator, the results are brought to the attention of their col-leagues; if not, they are not published. Perhaps readers of the educational literature should be wary of "favorable" results.

Another regression-like phenomenon is selecting an extreme (high or low) group on the basis of one measurement and then examining the group on other measurements. It is inevitable (except in highly unlikely circumstances) that any group will not be quite as extreme on any second measure as on the one on which they were selected. As an example, it is to be expected that the first string football team will not have a grade point average as high as the first eleven students in high school rank. Conversely, it is doubted that the academically top eleven students would perform too well as a football team. Similarly, it can be predicted that intellectually retarded children in school will be more like the rest of the children in the school in their athletic, social, and emotional capacities than in their academic capacities. The general rule is that groups of children and students selected because of their extreme placement on the basis of one measure will not be as extreme on other measures. The high groups regress downward and the low groups regress upward toward the general average or mean.

MEASUREMENT PROBLEMS

It is difficult to differentiate some comparison group problems from measurement problems since faulty comparisons sometimes arise because of faulty measurement procedures. The faulty comparisons caused by the regression of extreme or matched groups toward the mean are examples. There are other problems in interpretation of educational data, though, that are distinctly related to measurement. Measurement in the nonphysical sciences is inexact. Behavioral and social science measurement includes, almost by its nature, the presence of random errors. These random errors are not mistakes but simply the inability of man to make highly precise judgments about other men. As the result of this imprecision, behavioral, social, and educational measurement has some unusual properties often unanticipated by people using these measuring instruments.

First, a reduction in the range of individual differences in a sample makes relationships in those samples smaller than the corresponding relationships in unrestricted samples. Thus, a correlation of .60 of an intellectual variable with another variable in a general high school sample will drop precipitously in a sample of college seniors, and still further in a postgraduate sample. An example often recited is that success as a graduate engineer depends far more on personality variables than on academic ability. What the data interpreters fail to realize is that selection into engineering schools, and graduation from one, restricts the range of academic ability markedly while leaving an extensive range in the personality variables. The correlations between measures of success on the job and academic ability simply cannot be large in a sample of graduate engineers. However, given the relatively unrestricted range of personality variables, the correlations can be much larger. Likewise, intelligence test scores will correlate much higher with achievement test scores across all six grades of a grade school than these correlations in any one grade. A restriction of range of scores in a sample reduces correlations within the sample, compared to the correlations in an unrestricted range sample.

Another common misinterpretation of data in education because of measurement misconceptions is the size of predicted relationships. Prediction correlations (as all correlations) are restricted by the reliabilities of the predictor and criterion variables. Faculty of colleges and other critics often bemoan the fact that college-grade predictor correlations reached a peak of about .70 in the decade from about 1940 to 1950 and have not increased since then. These people are not familiar with measurement theory. The internal consistency reliability of college grades is about .60 to .70. The same reliability of the predictors is on the order of .90. However, over the period of time of a year the test-retest reliability of the standard tests probably would be reduced to the order of about .70. High school grades, by semester, are from zero to four years old when averaged and used for the prediction. Their reliability simply cannot be exceptionally high in these circumstances. Thus, all the variables in the prediction have restricted reliabilities.

Using a basic equation for measurement theory (Nunnally, 1967, p. 204), it can be determined that the maximum correlation among them can be only about .70. The equation is $r_{12} = r_{12} \sqrt{r_{11} \cdot r_{22}}$ where r_{12} is the highest value of the correlation that can be obtained between the two variables, 1 and 2 (a maximum of 1.00), r_{12} the observed correlation between the two variables, r_{11} is the reliability of variable one, and r_{22} the reliability of variable two. The equation is called the *correction for attenuation*, but it is also an estimate of what the correlation would be if the two variables were perfectly reliable. Note that if $r_{11} = .70$ and $r_{22} = .70$, the maximum value of r_{12}, the correlation between the high school record and tests and college grades, is also .70 (since r_{12} cannot be greater than 1.00). This is the ceiling on the relationship that has been found over the years. The true relationship between them (with error-free measurement) would be close to 1.00. However, it is not possible to predict perfectly an imperfect criterion.

This principle of interpretation of data leads to another principle of a similar nature. The square of a coefficient of correlation, r^2 (known as the coefficient of determination) multiplied by 100, yields the percent of the individual differences on a criterion explained by a predictor variable. As an example, if first-year college grades were correlated with high school records and tests with a correlation of .70, then the square of .70 is .49. Multiplying this latter value by 100, gives 49 percent, or about one-half of the criterion variable individual differences explained by the prediction. Unknowing critics will exclaim that, since only half of the college grades have been explained, half remain to be attributed to sources and variables other than the high school record and test data. This is not true. As was indicated in the example given just previously, only about half of the perfect explanation is possible because of imperfect measurement (often because of random error). Thus the thinking should be: How much of the criterion individual differences is being predicted compared to how much is predictable? If the correlation was .70 and the reliabilities of the variables in the prediction are about .70 (over the prediction time period), then not one-half, but perhaps 100 percent, or all, of the possible prediction is being made. Much of "unexplained" variance is due to random errors in measurement.

Another measurement-related problem of interpretation of data is that of ratios, difference scores, and gain scores. Because of the inability to measure with great precision in the sciences focused on humans, care must be taken in the arithmetic operations that are performed on data. Simply dividing one variable score by another variable score and obtaining a quotient, or subtracting one variable score from another to obtain a difference score (or a gain score) can lead to difficulties.

Earlier in the history of educational research it was popular to simplify data by developing a quotient from two variables. It was reasoned that intelligence and academic achievement are highly related; therefore, if standardized achievement scores were divided by a standardized intelligence test score, an accomplishment quotient (AQ) would be derived. If the quotient is multiplied by 100 (for ease in interpretation), an AQ of greater than 100 would indicate a student working above his native capacity. An AQ of less than 100 would indicate a student who is underachieving. To the extent that under and over achievement is a viable concept, the above is reasonably true.

Two additional problems arise, though. The first is that the unreliabilities of both the numerator variable and the denominator variable affect the derived quotient. Even with tests used in the quotient, in the higher ranges of reliability, the reliability of the quotient variable will not be much over .40. This is not good, but worse, the resulting quotient variable tends to be negatively correlated with the variable that is the denominator of the quotient (see Asher, 1962). As an example, the Intelligence Quotient for children and adolescents is a test of intellectual ability, scored in terms of a mental age, divided by a chronological age. If the sample of children differ from each other markedly in age, and the IQ score variable is correlated with a third variable, such as motor skills, height, weight (not too highly related to the ability being tested), the IQ may just turn out to be negatively related to the third variable. This would occur if the third variable is highly and positively correlated with the denominator. Thus, the interesting phenomenon occurs of three somewhat positively correlated variables having a seemingly negative relationship between two of them because of the way the scores were handled arithmetically, by division.

Subtracting one variable score from another tends to cause the same kind of problem. A variable B is subtracted from a variable A to obtain a difference score, D, in effect $A - B = D$. Then the variable D is likely to correlate negatively with variable B. In this case it is the subtraction that causes the problem.

The Accomplishment Quotient is seldom seen in recent literature in education, but difference scores frequently are found in the form of gain scores. Schools pretest students in a class to determine how much they know before an innovative educational method is presented. At the end of the program, six weeks, a semester, a year, or whatever, the same test (or another form of it) is given. The initial test scores are then subtracted from the final test scores for each person. These difference scores are used as indicators of gain or accomplishment in the course. As a general indicator of achievement, this procedure is acceptable for administrative decision-making. It is known that, in general, the true gain score ranks are the same as the rank order of these raw difference gain scores resulting from the simple subtraction of pretest scores from post-test scores.

However, if the raw gain scores are used for other analyses, particularly a correlational analysis, problems may arise. Outside variables that ordinarily would correlate positively with the pretest score may correlate negatively with the gain score. In fact, the gain score itself tends to correlate negatively with the pretest score! That simply means that students with high pretest scores tend not to have gain scores as large as students with low pretest scores. In addition to other possible factors, the simple process of subtracting one score from another contributes to the inaccurate results.

In order to avoid these problems, this rule must be followed: to relate a behavioral science, social science, or educational variable to any other such variable (especially by dividing and subtracting), use a regression equation or other statistical method of adjustment. Following this rule generally will eliminate many of the conceptual problems of negative correlations (where others find positive relationships), Accomplishment Quotients, difference scores, gain scores, underachievement, and regression-toward-the-mean. Again, the problems can be complex, and the now-and-then researcher and readers of the research and professional literature will want to consult a measurement theory expert about specific advice and interpretations.

PROBLEMS OF STATISTICAL INTERPRETATION

In addition to problems of good comparison groups and measurement errors, there are also some common errors made in the use and interpretation of statistical analyses of which readers of the literature should be aware. This topic may be somewhat less useful than the ones previously discussed because of the review of the problems of statistical analyses earlier in Chapter 3 and in Appendix A. Yet the topic is a necessary one because of the number of errors involving statistics that are found in the educational literature.

One of the first things a reader should do when studying an important article is to check the arithmetic. It is possible in the transfer of data and figures from analysis sheets, to draft copy, to final copy, and to the galley proof of the printer that a decimal point can be moved, figures transposed, and arithmetical errors made. (See Table 1 of Whitehill and Rubin, 1971, as an example. Here an error has been made which causes the F tests to be too large. Statistical significance probably is declared inaccurately.)

A way of understanding the procedures of a study is to make a chart and count out the number of subjects and the number of observations in each group and sample in the study. The next step is to review the tables and the text to determine where the observations and the subjects are that are being analyzed. In addition to organizing the study for the reader, occasionally a person with statistical training will find that inappropriate *degrees of freedom* have been calculated (see Asher, 1961). It is even a good idea to reevaluate the declared significance levels of the statistics. The presented statistical test values can be found in the tables with their degrees of freedom to see if the computed statistic is larger or smaller than the tabled values and to ascertain that the correct decision about significance has been made. Although this step seems simple, it is amazing how many errors will be found. After some practice, it will be found that an "eye" develops for the size of the outcome of statistical tests which are or are not significant. However, the precaution should be taken of consulting with an expert before any overt action is taken about seeming errors that are found.

In the area of statistics, the problem of chance findings again arises. In this era of computer analyses, hundreds, even thousands, of statistics may be computed for a single report. If the 5 percent level of significance is used, it follows from statistical theory that 5 percent of the statistical tests would be declared significant, even if the data were nothing more than randomly generated numbers. This does *not* mean that those 5 percent of the results are important and the others are not. It means that about 5 percent of statistical tests can be declared significant at the 5 percent level by chance alone. The rule to follow is to count the total number of statistical tests and the number that are significant at some given level. If the number of those significant is nearly at the significance level or less, consideration should be given to the belief that no important variables were operating in the study.

Another statistical problem is the use of a rather small number of subjects or observations. It is difficult to obtain statistical significance under these conditions. If, in addition, the reliability of the tests or observations used is not high, the problem is even greater. The researchers may find no (or few) statistics that are significant, and they then may conclude that there is no effect or no relationship. Perhaps a better conclusion would be not to draw a conclusion until further data could be gathered and analyzed. The absence of a conclusion in such a situation is a good signal for students to do further research using more subjects. The methods already are developed, and the area is of sufficient importance for the research to be published. If the new results confirm the older work, a contribution is made. If the students demonstrate that the relationships do indeed exist, they have made a contribution also and have an explanation for the differences in the findings.

One further problem in statistical interpretations is the use ·of multivariate analyses (such as multiple correlation) with groups that do not meet suggested ratios for the number of subjects to the number of variables in the study. Again, with the advent of computers, analyses of vast amounts of data became possible. Since it is easier to get a few subjects and give them a large number of tests than it is to get a large number of subjects and give them a few tests (or observe them, or interview them), researchers frequently do the former and then analyze at length. Such analyses tend to capitalize on random variations in the data and often important-looking "results" emerge.

In recent years, some guidelines have developed which are rules-of-thumb in such situations, and readers of the literature can use them to protect themselves. In relatively small studies of this type, with 200 to 300 subjects or less, the ratio of subjects to variables should be on the order of 10 to 1. In large studies in terms of the subjects involved (over 300), the ratio might approach 5 to 1.

Multiple correlation as a statistical technique poses special problems. This is a very common analytical method and a useful one in educational research. In addition to all of the usual problems of interpreting correlational data in terms of possible cause-and-effect relationships, multiple correlation has other interpretation problems as well. First, each time a new variable enters the multiple correlation prediction system (in addition to the variables already there), the multiple correlation will increase, whether added effectiveness of prediction is accomplished or not. Further, the interpretation of the results must be based on a study of the complete sets of interrelationships among the variables. Just because a variable has not entered into a multiple regression equation does *not* mean it is unimportant. It could be highly related to a variable already in the equation, and thus is excluded by the multiple correlation and regression process from further high priority consideration for entry into the equation. Multiple correlation, and multivariate analyses, in general, require considerable expertise to interpret accurately. Wherry (1975) has summarized and illustrated many of these problems in multivariate analysis interpretations. Again, the professional and the student without extensive knowledge in statistics and especially in multivariate analyses should seek consultation before using the methods and when attempting important interpretations of them.

Occasionally the reader of the literature in education will find writers who ignore, essentially, the analyses they have made. They evidently have made up their minds about the conclusions of a study after the data were collected (or perhaps even before) and ignore or slide over the data and the analyses lightly. Statements are made that the 5 percent level of significance will be used and then results are found at the 8 percent level. These are declared "near significance," but later the conclusions treat them as an established fact. At other times, the results of the analyses and the conclusions do not agree too well. The writer is unable to interpret the data accurately or does not wish to do so for some reason. A careful perusal of the methods, analyses, and results sections will bring these problems to light.

In addition to the problems of interpretation described here, a number of suggestions were presented in the prior chapters for the various kinds of research methods and approaches. Those chapters should be reread if the area of the literature being reviewed or the research being done involves a particular method. The number of errors that can be made is almost endless.

In attempting to determine just what the real world of education is like, care must be taken in reading research. In fact, one of the principal purposes of the scientific method is to learn what these errors are so that more accurate interpretations can be made and better methods used in the future. A key characteristic of science is that it has self-correcting mechanisms built into it. The users of research results are important to the continuing use of this mechanism.

SUMMARY

This chapter has presented a number of errors in research methods that often are found in the educational literature. In reading the scientific literature in most fields, the reviewer can ssume, in general, that the conclusions are accurate. In the field of education, this assumption is somewhat tenuous. Thus, it is necessary to indicate the nature of some of the more common problems in methodology and interpretation for its readers. Those planning educational research investigations also need to be wary if they pattern their research on examples found in the literature.

The first major area of problems in research methods is need for a comparison group which allows interpretations to be made. Throughout the early chapters of the book, methods of developing acceptable comparison groups were described. In this chapter matching was presented as a method *not* to be used generally. Matching of individuals from intact groups on variables of less than very high reliability is still found in the educational literature even though it frequently assures an uninterpretable research design. Again, some reminders of the principles of internal validity and invalidity were given. Regression-toward-the-mean errors within a variable as the result of truncated selection of groups, or the selection of high or low groups, was discussed. The effects of regression between and among variables as an error of interpretation was also presented. Students studied because they are high or low on one variable almost inevitably must be closer to the mean of the group on all other variables.

Examples of measurement problems in the interpretation of data were also given. Restriction of range, or the reduction of individual differences in a group, and the smaller indices of relationships among variables were illustrated. The influence of lack of perfect reliability of criterion and predictor variables and this influence on the upper limit of correlational prediction was presented. The equations for estimating the limiting influence of attenuation and determining the percentage of explainable predictive relationships were given also. Concerns and errors of interpretation of ratio, quotient, difference score, and gain score variable interpretations were described. Reversed correlation signs among variables sometimes are obtained inadvertently because one variable is divided or subtracted from another variable.

Statistical errors of commission and interpretation, while somewhat more technical than the other common errors, are important to readers of the educational literature. Some cues to quality and areas of concern are indicated. One of these is to count the subjects and the observations and to check these counts against the analyses. Checking the calculated statistics against the significance levels in the tables sometimes is revealing also. Determining the percent of chance findings of significance where large numbers of statistics have been calculated is often enlightening. The interpretation of no effect or no relationship in studies using small numbers of subjects and instruments of moderate reliability was discussed. The suggestion was made that no conclusion perhaps was appropriate unless further studies were done. Multivariate studies, now common in education, also received attention. The ratio of subjects to variables was the major concern. Ratios of less than five to one lead to problems. Multiple correlation is a multivariate method of particular value in education and is widely used. Suggestions for higher standards of use and interpretations were given.

The general problem of writers ignoring results or shifting conclusions for various reasons was indicated. Methods of reviewing the studies and the results in them such that the reader can draw his own conclusions were presented.

STUDY AND DISCUSSION PROBLEMS

1. List a number of the common errors to which you need to be alert in reading educational research and evaluation reports. Describe them briefly.
2. What problems are there in using difference scores, gain scores, accomplishment quotients, and ratios of scores?
3. List the ways in which the size of a correlation between two variables can be reduced, increased, limited, or distorted by the conditions under which the variable measurements are made.

4. Find a study in which groups were selected on the basis of a test score and then were retested on the same test. Determine whether regression-toward-the-mean might be a factor in the interpretation of the results.
5. Discuss the need for reasonable comparison groups in educational research and evaluation.
6. Find an educational study in which matching of individual subjects was used. Determine whether the matching was an acceptable research method or not. If not, determine the direction of the regression-toward-the-mean of the groups.
7. Write a brief critique of an educational article in which a common research error was found. (Consider publishing it!)
8. Read a journal article in a field of interest to you and make a chart counting the total number of subjects, the number of subjects in each group, and the number of observations made on each subject. Check the statistical analyses for their congruity with the number of subjects.
9. Check the accuracy of all the statistical significance levels in a journal article by looking up their reported values in the tables.
10. Count the number of significance tests in a journal article and determine how many are significant. How many would be significant by chance alone?
11. Look for a journal article in which there is either no comparison group or a flawed comparison group and report your conclusions about the data vs. those of the author.
12. What, in ordinary words, is a correction for attenuation of a correlation?
13. What is a coefficient of determination? How is it used with a correlation coefficient?
14. Can you find instances of writers ignoring their statistical test results in their written conclusions?
15. Can you find instances of writers converting statistical test results "that approach significance" into firm conclusions at the end of their reports?

REFERENCES

Asher, J. W. Comment on "A comparison of i/t/a and T. O. reading achievement when methodology is controlled." *Elementary English*, April, 1968, 452–457, 484.

Asher, W. Comment on the relationship between rigidity-flexibility in children and their parents. *Child Development*, 1961, *32*, 606–608.

Asher, W. Statistical problems of the accomplishment quotient. *Journal of Experimental Education*, 1962, *30*(3), 285–287.

Campbell, D. T., and Erlebacher, A. How regression artifacts in quasi-experimental evaluations can mistakenly make compensatory education look harmful. In J. Hellmuth (Ed.), *Disadvantaged child*. Vol. 3, New York: Brunner/Mazel, 1970, 185–210.

Campbell, D. T., and Erlebacher, A. Reply to the replies. In J. Hellmuth (Ed.), *Disadvantaged child*. Vol. 3, New York: Brunner/Mazel, 1970, 221–225.

Campbell,D.T., and Stanley, J.C. Experimental and quasi-experimental design for research on teaching. In N.L. Gage (Ed.), *Handbook of research on teaching*. Chicago, Ill.: Rand McNally, 1963, 171-246.

Croxen, M.H., and Lytton, H. Reading disability and difficulties in finger localization and right-left discrimination. *Developmental Psychology*, 1971, 5, 256–262.

Evans, J.W., and Schiller, J. How preoccupation with possible regression artifacts can lead to a faulty strategy for the evaluation of social action programs: A reply to Campbell. In J. Hellmuth (Ed.), *Disadvantaged child*. Vol. 3, New York: Brunner/Mazel, 1970, 216-220.

Hellmuth, Jerome (Ed.). *Disadvantaged child*, Volume 3. New York: Brunner/ Mazel, Inc., 1970.

Mazurkiewicz, A.J. A comparison of i/t/a and T.O. reading achieve nent when methodology is controlled. *Elementary English*, 1966, XLIII(ʋ), 601–606, 699.

Nunnally, J. *Psychometric theory*. New York: McGraw-Hill, 1967.

Thorndike, R.M. Regression fallacies in the matched groups experiment. *Psychometrika*, 1942, 7, 85–102.

Tukey, J.W. The zig-zagging climb from initial observation to successful improvement: Comments on the analysis of national data. In W.E. Coffman (Ed.), *Frontiers of educational measurement and systems*. Boston: Houghton Mifflin, 1973, 113–120.

Vockell, E.L., and Asher, W. Methodological inaccuracies in Croxen and Lytton's "Reading disability and difficulties in finger localization and right-left discrimination." *Developmental Psychology*, 1973, 8(1), 1, 2.

Wherry, R.J. Underprediction for overfitting: 45 years of shrinkage. *Personnel Psychology*, 1975, 28(1), 1–18.

Whitehill, R.P., and Rubin, S.J. Effectiveness of instrumental and traditional methods of college reading instruction. *Journal of Experimental Education*, 1971, 39(3), 85–87.

Chapter 12

Change, Research Support, and Ethics

Throughout this book research methods have been presented as aids in moving toward solutions for educational problems. Once these solutions have been found, efforts need to be made to incorporate them into the educational processes in order to change the educational system. Suggestions will be given in this chapter about how to effect these changes. Little research and evaluation can be done without support, and sources of support for these activities will also be presented in this chapter. Finally, a consideration of the ethics and law involved in doing research and evaluation in education will be considered.

CHANGE

In education the reason questions are asked, problems are stated, and research is done is to improve the education of children, adolescents, college students, and adults. However, improvement in the schools does not happen just because research is done or reported in the literature. Changes must be *made* to occur, especially in bureaucratic systems like education.

A book on educational research for professionals would not be complete unless suggestions were made on how to implement changes indicated by research. Fortunately, research has been done in this area so the ideas given do not have to be based entirely on a few personal experiences, folklore, old wives' tales, appeals to authority, or rank speculation. However, the answers are not complete—and may not always work.

Warren Bennis is a social psychologist with extensive experience in education. He is an expert on the topic of implementing changes in bureaucracies (Bennis and Slater, 1966), and has summarized his knowledge (Bennis, 1972) in the statement of several principles. First, he states that bureaucracies are an inevitable form of administration for large and complex organizations, which is what almost all educational systems are. Second, bureaucracies (that is, the people running them) resist change, if for no other reason than that change requires them to venture into the unknown. Personal security, value, esteem, and the worth of individuals in the organization may be at risk. Further, Bennis continues, nothing will make people resist change more than the feeling that change is being imposed on them.

Third, change is highly attractive to some unusual people. Some of these people are exceptionally able, others are covering a mediocrity with a superficial commitment to the new and different. Able educators in a bureaucracy will avoid, ignore, or reject mediocre persons and their ideas.

The fourth, and exceedingly important, principle stated by Bennis in the development, planning, and implementation of change is that the process must draw into it those who are going to be affected by it. One of the basic rules of successful change is to involve those whose jobs and lives will be altered. This was Corey's (1953) theme in action research. If those who saw problems in education did their own research on the problems, the results were more likely to be implemented. Involvement of those in education means teachers, administrators, staff, students, parents, and the community.

The implemented model for change can be revolutionary through a revolt, or by fiat from an administrative decree, or by successive, limited comparisons. Revolution changes the leadership, but the same old problems remain. They are not changed or resolved. Further, revolution inevitably produces reaction which may be worse than no change. Administrative decrees will bring about change and even solve some problems for a while. However, such tactics arouse resentment even when the administrator is right, and no administrator (or anyone else) can always be right. At the administrator's first major mistake, all affected by prior decrees will let the mistake be known and future effectiveness of the administrator will be limited.

The mode most often used for the implementation of change is successive, limited comparisons. In educational systems, the problems faced are so complex that some effects of a change are bound to be overlooked, alternative solutions neglected, and the impact of the ultimate outcome unpredictable. Incremental reform with successive, limited comparisons requires that research data be collected continuously on the educational system. These data should be interpreted in light of the rules for internal and external validity and prediction as suggested in this book. These data and interpretations should be given to those who are involved in the change process. They also should be encouraged to collect their own data and suggest additional data to be collected. This process should keep the changes away from procedures which are contrary to the achievement of the goals of the system.

The plans for change should have a sound, clear statement of what is to be achieved and how the changes will be implemented. The statement of goals alone, though, is not enough. The implementation plans should be coherent and have vitality. While the change itself may be incremental, the programs for change should not be a series of marginal events underfinanced and too small to make much impact on a major problem. Finally, time to consolidate gains must be allowed. Change takes time and requires continuous support by administrators and all involved.

Bennis (1972) makes an interesting analogy between the processes of change and research. He indicates that research involves a spirit of inquiry and experimentation, an examination of processes and criteria, risk-taking, and occasional defeats while not fearing the surprise of the future. The examination and change of an educational system also requires the pursuit of truth into the nature of the educational problems in a spirit of free inquiry. Bennis concludes (1972, p. 120), "The model for truly innovative and creative organizations in an era of enormous change becomes nothing less than the scientific spirit. The model for science becomes the model for all."

It is known that educators change behavior by first observing a successful innovative program in action under conditions not too different than those in their own school and then implementing the program in their own school. The most successful innovations involving teachers are accomplished through elaborate helping procedures as the teachers engage in the new behaviors. Multiple models of the innovation are helpful, and local fiscal support and leadership from the start of an innovation help maintain the local school's commitment to the change. There must be a plan for continuing the changes in the schools, however, or it will be difficult to institutionalize them.

The now-demised Eastern Regional Institute for Education (ERIE), a USOE supported regional laboratory, made a number of suggestions for curriculum changes in a report (1969), *Installing a New Curriculum: Observations and Recommendations.* The report suggested that the curriculum first be rigorously field-tested and reviewed before attempting other installations. It needs to be shown that it is indeed an improvement over existing programs. (This is certainly a theme of this book.) There must be administrative and teacher approval and support. The teachers should receive compensation and professional recognition for activities required beyond their regularly scheduled duties. Pre- and inservice training of teachers and administrators is necessary. Suitable equipment, materials, and supplies must be ready and available. Staff and administrative intercommunication is necessary, as is regularly scheduled consultant help. However, the consultants for the teachers must be perceived as being helping professionals rather than supervisors. The consultants also must be exceptionally knowledgeable about the innovative programs.

The ERIE report concluded that a number of factors were significant in a successful curriculum installation. The building principals are a most important figure in terms of their support of teachers and their resulting attitudes toward the innovation. They must be involved, not merely informed. Initial experiences with the new program are crucial. Teachers must be successful from the start, as the result of good planning, preparation, inservice training, advice on equipment, and so forth. Usually only one new curriculum should be introduced at a time in a district; more than one will cause some faltering. However, if the curriculum change emphasizes only one subject too long, an imbalance may occur and impede the installation efforts. Curriculum changes should start on a small scale and expand in subsequent years. Initial efforts should be made in just a few lower grades and later grades added each year.

Orlosky and Smith (1972) studied the origins, characteristics, and successes of major educational changes over a period of seventy-five years. They concluded that to solidify major change and make it permanent, the organization and administration of the educational system must be modified. For instance, a change in teaching practices must be accompanied by teacher retraining and strong incentives for teachers to change. Curriculum change by a considerable displacement of an existing pattern is not likely to be permanent. Curriculum changes that involve the addition of subjects or an updating of the content are more permanent than a reorganization or restructuring of the curriculum. Extensions and additions to the educational process, such as a community college, are more likely to be successful than an attempt to alter the total administrative structure.

A plan for diffusion is a must. Publicity alone will not cause change to become widespread. Changes that have the support of more than one major source of power, such as government, social groups, or educational professionals, are more likely to become permanent.

Educational personnel are important to change. If the new facts and procedures are few, and the educators do not have to relinquish power or have doubt cast on their roles, the changes are more likely to be lasting. Orlosky and Smith conclude that an educational system in a dynamic society cannot remain stagnant; therefore, these methods of implementing changes in education are important.

Change has become almost a fashion in education. Acclaim is given to proposals for change that deviate greatly from current practice. Certainly new ideas for change are needed in education, but if almost any idea is accepted and implemented, then educational change takes on the characteristics of a merry-go-round. The process of change becomes a game where winning comes from getting current procedures diverted so that one's own new activities can be substituted. Change that is circular or less effective than current procedures is worse than no change at all because of the eventual disillusionment that will set in.

The methods presented in this book can be used to test empirically innovative educational procedures for assurance that they indeed are superior to current methods. If this has not been done or has been done inadequately, the professional educator should be wary of claims of efficacy. The basic procedures for examining the data (if any) of others for reliability, validity, and prediction in connection with the suggested changes also have been given in this book. Most innovative programs in education have not been evaluated adequately on an empirical basis.

SOURCES OF SUPPORT

Research of any scope needs support, and research in a field as vast as education requires scope. Time, materials, workshops, observers, travel, and analyses are all facilitated if money and resources are available to be devoted to the investigation. Fortunately, support for educational research, evaluation, and program development is available primarily from the federal government and through the states, both to the professionals in the school systems and to researchers as such. There is some local money; also colleges and universities may be able to support educational research indirectly.

State and Local Sources.   The major state and local sources of educational research and evaluation support are through Titles I and III of the Elementary and Secondary Education Act of 1965. Though these titles are primarily for support of supplementary programs for low-income groups in one case (Title I) and for innovative educational activities for the other (Title III), both require "objective evaluation" of their results. These objective evaluations should be, of course, research in the broadly defined sense as used in this book. Further, there is no particular reason why the evaluation procedures could not be more rigorous than they often are and thus contribute much more to general knowledge about education. Title I funds are allocated to local school systems on a noncompetitive basis and often form an important part of these schools' yearly budgets. A part of these funds should be earmarked for evaluation research.

Title III funds for innovative programs are competitive within a state with some funds allocated directly from the U.S. Office of Education (USOE). Generally the competition is based on proposals which require considerable time to develop in order to assure feasibility, plan a program, meet deadlines, and await reviews. Other state sources of money, part of which may be used for research, can sometimes be found in the state education agency's divisions, such as vocational education, special education, and reading for programs in these areas. The State Office of Criminal Justice Planning may have some educational program support for activities designed to reduce juvenile delinquency and crime. Some of the more enlightened states have, from time to time, even had funds available for educational research as such—funds which were available on a competitive basis to schools within the state.

Local school systems sometimes have a research bureau, a testing or evaluation office, a school census department, a federal program office, or some combination of these functions. However, unless the system is of some size, these offices may be doing rather routine program activities. However, the personnel in these facilities may be aware of sources of support for various programs and people at the state and federal levels who should be contacted. It is always wise to obtain recent information directly from those in charge of programs in order not to waste time on last year's forms or an impossible budget or competitive situation.

National Sources. The National Institute of Education (NIE) is a major federal focus of support for formal educational research as such. Though NIE is a relatively new organization in the federal structure, it does have a considerable budget for educational research, and by law must expend the great majority of its funds outside of the Institute. The range of disciplines in which NIE is interested in attracting work on educational problems is great, extending throughout the behavioral and social sciences and into other areas as well. The NIE program areas of concern are somewhat set and are structured internally. Much of the research done is in response to Requests for Proposals (RFPs) which the staff of NIE and their consultants generate. The areas in which RFPs are issued are widely broadcast, and updated lists can be found in the bulletins of many professional organizations and from NIE itself.

Because of NIE, the U. S. Office of Education (USOE) has reduced its formal educational research support as such, but is continuing many of its innovative and developmental program activities. It also maintains its collection of statistical data about education. Some of these programs involve extramural (outside) contracts and grants to various educational systems. In addition, there has been for many years a strong national emphasis on Vocational Education, Adult Education, and Special Education in USOE. Educators and others interested in these several areas should determine what research, development, and evaluation programs are available in USOE.

Education interests in the federal government are not limited to NIE and USOE but are widespread. The National Science Foundation has been responsible for curriculum innovations in science and mathematics and continues with summer institutes and other programs relating directly to education. The Office of Child Development (OCD) has a number of programs relating to the pre-school child. The National Institutes for Health (NIH) are highly research oriented and have research and development support grants for education-related fields such as mental health, juvenile delinquency, and developmental psychology. The Department of Defense may be thought of as one of the major education and training enterprises of the federal government. In addition to its dependent children's schools, it has vast numbers of trade and vocational schools, specialized educational activities, and concerns about many matters closely related to education. In addition, those with particular educational interests may find programs at the federal level in substantive areas. The education of American Indians is handled by the Bureau of Indian Affairs, and education of prisoners is the concern of the Bureau of Prisons; many similar examples of the education foci in departments of federal agencies exist.

The most lasting statement that can be made about federal involvement in substantive education, educational research, and educational development is that it is constantly changing and shifting. No section, branch, division, bureau, office, or department's objectives, programs, or responsibilities remain the same for too many years. Keeping track of the federal government's educational activities has become an occupation in itself. The novice in the field should seek out those in their educational systems who are knowledgeable about such things. If all else fails, a letter to the district congressmen or a call to their local offices indicating rather clearly just what it is that you wish to do, in what area, and asking their assistance in finding an appropriate program will be a good start. Ultimately, phone calls to appropriate sections of federal agencies should be made in order to obtain up-to-date information, since bureaucracies are notably reluctant to commit themselves in writing. The changes in funding and redirection of programs are many.

Foundations.   Foundations also should be considered as sources of support for educational programs. The best single source of information in this area may be found in the publications of American Foundations Information Service (Lewis, 1971). Again, brief letters of inquiry followed by phone calls are appropriate to determine eligibility and current interests. While many of the foundations are national in their orientation, the listings within a state should not be ignored. Often foundations will have a local orientation and interest in some special area. Since eligibility may be limited, a given local program may have little competition for funds. On the other hand, a local program may be one of the few that will fit the guidelines of a local foundation.

COLLEGES AND UNIVERSITIES

Many of the sources of support previously indicated also are available to colleges and universities. Since research and development is a prime commitment of some of these institutions, they may have personnel who are quite knowledgeable about the sources of support and can be of considerable assistance in learning about the various programs. In addition, colleges and universities already may have ongoing grants which require staffing and from which dissertation material can be developed or in which local school cooperation is needed. Universities are also complex, and educational research activities may be found in them under a number of headings. Searching out research and testing bureaus, media research, institutional research, experiment station research, and faculty doing research in schools and departments of education, psychology, child development, and sociology may also yield support sources.

ETHICS AND EDUCATIONAL RESEARCH

There has been much public concern about the ethics of researchers in recent years, particularly in the field of medical research. This concern has become more widespread, and everyone considering doing research in education should stop to think about the ethical considerations of imposing various treatments, making certain observations, collecting some types of data, and making public the results of the research. Perhaps the issues can be summed by three primary elements: consent, confidentiality, and acceptable research procedures.

Informed consent is a first requisite of research. By this is meant that the procedures of the research are explained to those involved and written consent to those procedures obtained. It is impossible to obtain legal, informed consent from anyone less than eighteen years of age, and thus much care must be exercised in research in pre-school, elementary, and junior and senior high schools. Either parental consent must be obtained, or acceptance of the educational procedures by those responsible for implementing the school's curriculum and educational procedures must be obtained. This latter acceptance probably is sufficient where the research involves implementing educational programs and giving tests in the same general vein and type as those now being used. The community gives to its educational administrators and teachers power to implement educational programs with their students, subject only to general review, and the new educational programs would fall within that purview. Should educators be using the research data for their own purposes (such as a dissertation), it is recommended that, in addition to their own acceptance of the educational program, uninvolved administrators also review and accept the program and methods so that there is no conflict of interest.

Confidentiality is also of major importance. Particular care should be taken by the researcher that the individuals and the school systems are not embarrassed by their identification with the data that are collected. Since the higher level concerns of research are with theory and general variables rather than with specifics, the important aspects of a school's identification in a scientific report should be stated in general terms. Dimensions such as the general size, level, type of community and curriculum, and facilities can be given. No individual identification of subjects with their data ever should be made without the subject's consent. Even then, no data should be presented to anyone, including the subjects, unless it can be interpreted meaningfully to them, especially if there is a chance that anxiety or other problems might arise.

Particular care should be made not to collect data which might

involve evidence of violation of laws, unless there is provision for legal
protection against disclosure of the information. Self-report of the use
of alcohol by minors, use of some drugs, or participation in some sexual
activities are legal violations in many states. Testimony can be forced
under threat of contempt of court unless the data collector has the legal
immunity of privileged communications. This immunity is often
conferred upon physicians, lawyers, and ministers, priests, and rabbis.
In some states, licensed psychologists and some other professionals also
may be granted this immunity.

Even some rather innocuous questions may involve violations of
law and thus the confidentiality of communications with a subject. For
instance, questions about driving may yield data on underaged or
unlicensed driving. All data which can be identified with an individual
should be coded quickly and the subject number, subject name, and
raw data sheets kept in separate places to which access is restricted and
controlled.

Acceptable research procedures mean that the subjects should not
be inflicted with pain, injured, or given medication without their
informed consent, or, if underage, the consent of their parents or
guardians. The "intradermal barrier" (in or under the skin) of the
subjects should be protected at all costs. This means that professionals
licensed to practice medicine should be responsible for medical aspects
of a study. If the research is for the medical practitioners' benefit, their
judgment about procedures should be reviewed by a committee of other
licensed practitioners.

It probably is a wise procedure for every educational system to
have a research and evaluation committee to screen requests to collect
data and to do research in the system. This makes sense in at least two
ways. It involves the personnel of the system in the research, thus
helping with the research's acceptance and dissemination. Second, it
maintains established criteria for acceptance and reduces possible
conflicts of interest. In addition to a selective upgrading and vetoing of
research procedures, however, it is recommended that these commit-
tees perform an additional positive function as well. They should make
written recommendations to responsible administrators as to where
educational research is needed in the system, where evaluations should
be improved, and where subsequently unused data or data of question-
able validity are being collected as a part of standard educational
practice. They might even recommend who should do this suggested
research and evaluation, as well as submit an estimated cost projection.

It is elementary courtesy, when starting to do research in an educational system, to go through channels to the responsible administrator. In elementary and secondary schools, the building principals should be made aware of the researcher's purpose, clearance, and schedule of work in the building. If educational research is to be of value, the dissemination system should start immediately by the circulation of reports or summaries of reports to the involved professionals in the educational system where the work was done.

Research and evaluation should adhere to the highest standards. Literature read and reported should be the best available, and any shortcomings should be noted. Efforts should be made to upgrade the substantive professional literature in one's own area through professional organizations, personal contacts, letters to editors, and so forth. There is a specific set of ethical principles developed by Page (1966) for the educational researcher as such. He makes statements of ethical principles for six reference groups and areas: educational research as a science, as a profession, to clients, to students, to subjects, and to humans generally.

What was formerly a concern for ethics may now be a matter of federal law. The Family Educational Rights and Privacy Act of 1974 is of major importance to educators, researchers, and evaluators. (See the Federal Register January 6, 1975, Vol. 40, No. 3, pages 1208–1216 for a copy of the law and proposed rules by the Secretary of Health, Education, and Welfare.) Students and their parents may inspect all records, files, and data kept by a school which is related to them. Schools may not violate the privacy or allow others to violate the privacy of their students. Each school must obtain informed, written consent from the student or parents before a student's records are released to most other individuals, agencies, or organizations. Parents and older students must be informed at least annually of these rights as a matter of school policy. Generally, a system of monitoring and accounting for all personnel who have access to records is needed.

No federal funds will be made available to any school system or institution which violates this law. Thus this means that most educational organizations are included because few can afford not to use federal funds. Again the crucial age is eighteen. Those students under eighteen cannot give consent and must have the specific informed consent of their parents before they can participate in a study or before researchers can have access to the records of these students. A statement of legitimate interest must be placed in each record for each entry into the file which has been made by researchers and evaluators. These data then cannot be given to third parties.

EXCUSES

The human condition being what it is, everyone needs excuses for not doing what he or she knows ought to be done. Research is one of the better areas for excuse-making since it is put off so often. It always can be delayed until the "urgent" day-to-day operations are handled. That many of these day-to-day activities are educational pseudo-dynamics is irrelevant. To protect one's self-concept and the status of the organization, all professionals who know anything about research need a list of excuses to rationalize to themselves and explain to others why they are not doing research. (No citations can be given because the lists and ideas which follow are copies of copies, added to by graffiti, over a period of years.)

1. Say that the organization must not move too rapidly. This avoids moving at all.
2. Say that the problem cannot be separated from all the others. Therefore no problem can be resolved until all are resolved.
3. Show that the problem exists everywhere; therefore there is no need to be especially concerned about it locally.
4. Suggest that the problem needs considerable discussion by a large number of people before research can be done.
5. Suggest that if those who see problems are unhappy, they ought to go elsewhere to be unhappy.
6. Suggest that everyone wait until an expert is consulted.
7. Declare that no money is available for studying theoretical problems since there are so many practical problems to be handled.
8. Indicate that nobody in the university knows anything or will help anyway.
9. Indicate that nobody in the school systems will cooperate.
10. Declare that the really important aspects of education cannot be quantified anyway; therefore, what can statistics prove?
11. Make sure that you have enough routine work to do to keep you more than busy and therefore have no time for research.
12. If all else fails, appoint a large committee to look into it. This will keep research from being done for years. (Is it true that a camel was a horse put together by a committee?)

CONCLUSIONS

This book was written for professional and preprofessional educators to acquaint them with research methods that they would find useful in their everyday problems. Bachrack's (1965, p. 9) first law of research is, "People don't usually do research the way people who write books about research say that people do research." (His second law is that things take more time than they do.) This writer concurs and has tried to correct this impression by including several examples of practical research on educational problems by professional educators with whom he has been acquainted over the years. This has been possible because the methodology of educational research has matured rapidly over the past few decades. Computers have revolutionized the approach that is now taken to research analysis. Specific, local solutions to problems are now quite feasible and should be developed. Money is now available to work on important educational problems. Knowledge about research methods is now more widespread, and professional educators can do important research on their pressing problems. Today's educators can be better prepared now with less effort than the better researchers were in the not-too-distant past.

There are few major rewards in education other than the satisfaction of improving the general quality of the world by helping students learn. If the methods of learning can be improved, if more can be learned by students in the same time, if the costs can be reduced, more knowledge will be acquired by more people and perhaps a somewhat better world will result. The improvement and extension of learning is the ultimate goal of educational research.

The profession of education is an unusual mixture of emotional enthusiasm and cognitive rationality. A certain spirit is needed to inspire, or at least cajole, others into learning, but unexamined enthusiasm soon wears thin if, after the results become apparent, it becomes clear that the new ideas are no better (perhaps worse) than the old. Professionals with a knowledge of research methods can make quite good first approximations in examining new educational methods and techniques. They also can protect themselves and their clientele from those whose ideas are not backed by good evidence.

Louis Pasteur, the great French microbiologist of the nineteenth century, world renowned for his work is crystallography, spoilage of beer and wines, and his conquest of diseases of silkworms, as well as of chicken cholera, pig rouget, and rabies, derived great enthusiasm and motivation from his scientific discoveries which aided in the reduction of man's afflictions. Yet, as his life drew near its end, he said, on the occasion of the dedication of the Pasteur Institute:

> Worship the spirit of criticism. If reduced to itself, it is not an awakener of ideas or a stimulant to great things, but without it, everything is fallible; it always has the last word. What I am now asking you, and you will ask of your pupils later on, is what is most difficult to an inventor. It is indeed a hard task, when you believe you have found an important scientific fact and are feverishly anxious to publish it, to constrain yourself for days,

weeks, years sometimes, to fight with yourself, to try and ruin your own experiments and only to proclaim your discovery after having exhausted all contrary hypotheses. But when, after so many efforts, you have at least arrived at a certainty, your job is one of the greatest which can be felt by a human soul. (Vallery-Radot, 1919, pp. 443–444).

Turner (1973, p. 299) recently stated:

Educational researchers exist primarily, if not solely, to produce relevant and dependable information about education. Dependable information is relevant and significant when it aids in making intelligent decisions and accurate predictions. Information that is offered as dependable but is *not*, is not merely irrelevant: It is destructive to intelligent decision making and anathema to accurate prediction. It abets stupidities.

Education is still the way up the socioeconomic ladder and the way out of ghetto neighborhoods for millions of children and adolescents—as well as for many adults—in the United States. Throughout the world, in the areas where any education is a luxury to many, education is a means to sheer survival. If some of the fervor and commitment that brought the readers of this book to education, that keeps you in education, and that makes you a good teacher and educator, can be translated into improving the field of education through research, perhaps education will fulfill more of the promise that it holds for children and all the peoples of the world.

STUDY AND DISCUSSION PROBLEMS

1. Why is it important that the people to be affected be involved in the planning of change?
2. List and comment on each of Bennis' four statements for implementing change in a bureaucracy as each relates to educational systems.
3. Propose a change in an educational system with which you are familiar. Indicate how you would implement it.
4. What is the successive, limited comparison model of change?
5. What analogy is there between change procedures and research processes?
6. What procedures would you recommend for the implementation of a new curriculum?
7. What characteristics of change in an educational system aid in making it a continuing part of the system?
8. What concerns are there with the fads for change in education?
9. Seek out sources of support for educational projects in which you are interested. List them, amounts available, and limitations.
10. Of what ethical and legal problems must a researcher or evaluator in education be aware?
11. Why is confidentiality important in educational research and evaluation?
12. How is consent obtained for educational research and evaluation?

13. How important is the quality of the research and evaluation procedures in education?
14. Suppose you are a teacher who has consented to have research observers in your classroom. List what considerations you would expect from the observers.
15. What is the role of a research and evaluation committee in a school system? What screening criteria should they have? What ideas should be generated by the committee?
16. What professional courtesies should every researcher and evaluator extend to the personnel in a school system?
17. List several excuses you have heard for not doing research in your educational system.
18. What rewards ensue from doing educational research?
19. What is the role of criticism in research?
20. What is the ultimate purpose of educational research and evaluation?

REFERENCES

Bachrack, A. J. *Psychological research* (2nd ed.). New York: Random House, 1965.

Bennis, W. The sociology of institutions, or who sank the yellow submarine. *Psychology Today*, 1972, 6(6), 112-120.

Bennis, W., and Slater, P. *Changing organizations, American bureaucracy, and the temporary society*. New York: McGraw-Hill, 1966.

Corey, S. *Action research to improve school practices*. New York: Teachers College, Columbia University, 1953.

Eastern Regional Institute for Education. *Installing a new curriculum: Observations and recommendations*. Program Report R102, Syracuse, New York, 1969.

Ebel, R. L.(ed.). *Encyclopedia of educational research* (4th ed.). Toronto, Canada: Macmillan, 1969.

Federal Register. Privacy rights of parents and students. Vol. 40, No. 3, January 6, 1975, 1208–1216.

Lewis, M. O. (Ed.). *The foundation directory*. Addition 4, New York: Columbia University Press, 1971.

Orlosky, D., and Smith, B. O. Educational change: Its origins and characteristics. *Phi Delta Kappan*, 1972, LIII(7), 412–414.

Page, E. B. Some ethical principles for the educational researcher. *Educational Psychologist*, 1966, 3(3), 9.

Turner, R. L. Are educational researchers necessary? *Phi Delta Kappan*, 1973, LIV(5), 299.

Vallery-Radot, R. *The life of Pasteur*. London: Constable, 1919.

Glossary

ACCURACY. In sampling studies, a lack of bias in the sampling statistics. It is contrasted with "precision."

ACTION RESEARCH. In education, a type of applied scientific investigation or experimentation on curriculum and educational processes by practitioners. Its primary aim is to use research methods to change and improve educational practice in a class, school, or system.

ADOPTION. Part of the knowledge implementation and use processes in which changes are incorporated into educational operations. It includes installation, trial, and institutionalization.

ANALYSIS OF VARIANCE. A statistical analysis procedure used to determine possible differences among the means (averages) on a variable among two or more groups. It is generally used with interval data.

ANTHROPOLOGICAL RESEARCH. In education, the study of social and cultural patterns and their relationships to classrooms, schools, school systems, teachers, administrators, and educational phenomena. The variables tend to be values, attitudes, styles of behavior, role expectations, and modes of personal relationships.

BISERIAL CORRELATION. (See correlation.) A special type of correlation in which one of the two variables is measured in intervals and the other variable is artificially dichotomized.

CASE STUDIES. A method of research confined to one or a few persons or educational systems of particular interest. They are broadly descriptive and done in some depth. Many variables and relationships are studied.

CHI SQUARE. A statistical analysis procedure which generally uses counted (frequency) data. It is a general technique which takes two main forms: the first to show relationships between two variables in a sample; the second, to show possible differences among groups on a nominal (counted) variable.

CLASSIFICATION. The process of putting a person or object into a group or category.

CLUSTER SAMPLING. A method of determining representative persons or units from a part of a population under study. The units are drawn in groups of "clusters."

CONCURRENT VALIDITY. In measurement, a term indicating the relationship between a known, valid measure of a trait and a measurement procedure under study.

CONFIDENCE INTERVAL. A term used in statistics to denote the distance determined by the "confidence limits" within which a population value is likely to be found. The term is most often used in sampling studies.

CONFIDENCE LIMITS. A term to indicate the range within which a population value is likely to be found. They are set off by "confidence intervals" and are most often used in sampling studies.

CONSTRUCT VALIDITY. In measurement, the concern that the abstract, theoretical variables which a test is attempting to measure, are indeed being measured.

CONTENT VALIDITY. A measurement term indicating the representativeness of the behavior or topics being measured.

CONTROL GROUPS OR SUBJECTS. A group, persons, or units in an experimental research study to which either nothing is done or to which only prior standard or current educational activities are applied. They are used for comparison purposes with the various experimental groups or persons on which the research is focused.

CONTROL SERIES. A type of experimental design in which the research groups are not equivalent. Comparisons among the groups thus are in terms of greater or lesser differences than the original differences.

CORRELATION. A term used to indicate the degree of relationship between two or more variables for a group of subjects. It is represented in statistics by an index number which can range between -1.00 and $+1.00$.

COVARIANCE. A method of statistical analysis in which a criterion variable is adjusted mathematically to accommodate partially for initial differences in the groups to be compared.

CREDIBILITY. A term used in evaluation studies which is concerned with the belief in the capability and integrity of the persons doing the evaluation.

CRITERION (criteria). A variable measure used to assess the outcomes of a program or research activity.

CURRICULUM RESEARCH. Experimental methods used to appraise courses and patterns of instruction. It requires statements of theory, conditions, hypotheses, and data to be collected to test the hypotheses.

DEGREES OF FREEDOM. A phrase used in statistics indicating the absence of restraints in a set of scores. They are often used in entering statistical tables. They are closely related to the number of observations in a set of data. Often abbreviated "*df*."

DESCRIPTIVE RESEARCH. A method of determining interrelationships among variables in an education system. No systematic changes in treatments or conditions are made; only the relation of conditions and decisions on criteria variables and on each other is determined.

DEVELOPMENT. Part of the processes by which research knowledge is enhanced and extended for use in education. It also includes invention and design work.

DIFFUSION. Part of the knowledge implementation and use processes by which research knowledge is channeled to educators. It includes dissemination and demonstrations.

DISCREPANCY EVALUATION. A type of educational assessment and judgment concerned with differences between a standard of performance, intent, or proposed aspects of a program and actual performance. Resolving these differences is a major activity of discrepancy evaluation.

DISCRIMINANT ANALYSIS. A statistical procedure used in classifying persons or objects into group membership. The variables which determine the groups are usually purely descriptive, such as college major, religious affiliation, or profession.

ECOLOGICAL RESEARCH. The area of science concerned with the interrelationships or patterns of relations between organisms and their environment. In education this is often the relationship between the learning environment and the classroom milieu and the behavior of children and the teacher in the classroom or the school.

EDUCATIONAL RESEARCH. The systematic application of design, measurement methods, and analytical methods used to investigate and resolve problems of instructional design and related problems of schools. It attempts to develop, expand, and enhance conceptual and theoretical frameworks and includes application, development, dissemination, and adoption of knowledge in schools.

EFFICIENCY. A term used in educational evaluation which denotes being prudent with costs, personnel, and time.

ENGINEERING. The professional art of applying science and scientific methods to efficiently use people's and the world's resources for the benefit of individuals and groups.

EVALUATION. The process of determining, acquiring, and providing useful facts and information for the purpose of making decisions about educational processes and their alternatives. It is also used to determine the relationship between program objectives and accomplishments.

EX POST FACTO. The Latin words translated as "after the fact." When applied to research design, the term refers to the attempt to create a research or evaluation design after the fact of the grouping of subjects and application of conditions or treatments.

EXPERIMENTAL DESIGN. The plan for the allocation of subjects or units to groups, applying (or having applied) treatment (or conditions) or no treatments to groups or units, and the collection of data from the treatments and groups.

EXPERIMENTAL GROUPS OR SUBJECTS. The people or groups to which the innovative treatments or educational activities are applied.

EXPERIMENTAL INFERENCE. The judgment made in a controlled study about possible cause-and-effect relationships between treatment and outcome variables.

EXTERNAL CRITICISM. The process used in historical research which aids in the determination of the authenticity of the documents.

EXTERNAL VALIDITY. The sum of the characteristics of a research study which allows the research findings to be generalized to other populations, settings, treatments, and criteria similar to the ones in the study.

F TEST. A statistic generally derived from an analysis of variance. It estimates whether a set of means (averages) of groups are equal.

FORMATIVE EVALUATION. The processes of determining useful information about the educational programs, processes, staff, buildings, materials, and administrative actions. Answers the question: have they been procurred? Are they operating? Do they exist?

FREQUENCY DISTRIBUTION. The array of frequency of scores or sets of scores on a variable arranged into successive class intervals.

FREQUENCY POLYGON. When a frequency distribution is portrayed in graphic form, the result is a frequency polygon. The number of cases is one dimension of the graph and the scores on the variable is the other dimension.

HISTORICAL RESEARCH. A scholarly method of inquiry primarily descriptive, *ex post facto,* and longitudinal. It is an account of past events of societies of some magnitude, and is in part an art.

HISTORY. In research design, one of the threats to internal validity. It involves a change of external conditions of the experiment to the extent that they operate as another extra-experimental treatment or stimulus.

HYPOTHESIS. A proposed tentative statement, drawn from theory, which attempts to predict relationships, facts, or observations.

INSTABILITY. The threats to internal validity in research design represented by fluctuations in samplings and the inequality of equivalent measures. This is the only threat to internal validity in which statistical tests are relevant.

INSTRUMENTATION. The threat to internal validity of research design in which changes of calibration of the measuring devices are involved. It occurs because of use of nonequated test forms or changes in observers' standards.

INTERACTION. Unique interrelationships among treatment variables in which the effect of one treatment variable is influenced by the level of another treatment variable. The concept is important for considering inadvertent influences of extraneous conditions on subjects, treatments, and criteria of a study.

INTERACTION EFFECTS. The threats to internal validity in research design due to unique relationships of two or more of the primary threats to internal validity above and beyond the simple effects of these threats. Also the unique effects of the combination of the threats to internal validity and the treatments in the research design.

INTERNAL CRITICISM. In historical research the process concerned with the interpretation of data in authentic documents.

INTERNAL VALIDITY. The concerns and logical processes which allow a researcher or a reader of research to answer the question: Are the interpretations of the results of the research true for the situation in which the data were collected? It is the sum of the characteristics of research design which allow one to make statements about casual relationships among the variables in a research study.

INTERRUPTED TIME SERIES. A research design in which current classes' scores or a person's current behavior is compared to prior scores or behavior. The groups' prior scores or behavior act as the comparison base.

INTERVAL VARIABLES. The conceptual entities in research in which the values are on a single underlying dimension along which it is possible to determine equal units between successive values.

KURTOSIS. In an ordered distribution of data the tendency for the scores to be markedly peaked or markedly flat.

LEPTOKURTIC. A statistical term for describing an ordered distribution of an array of data in which the scores are closely clustered around the average and are markedly peaked.

LONGITUDINAL STUDIES. A research method in which data are collected on subjects as they develop and mature over an extended period of time. Prior data are related to later data.

MATCHING. A research design method in which subjects or groups are selected to be paired (or put in triplets, etc.) because they are like one another. One of the pair is given a treatment while the other is not.

MATURATION. A threat to the internal validity of research design involving systematic changes in the subjects that occur simply with the passage of time. Some of these changes are developing, aging, getting hungrier, and maturing.

MEAN. In statistics, a type of average in which a set of scores are added together and divided by the number of the scores. (An arithmetic mean.)

MEDIAN. In statistics, the middle score when a set of data are ordered from low to high.

MODE. In statistics, the most frequent score or the class interval with the most scores in it.

MORTALITY. A threat to the internal validity of research designs involving the reduction or loss of individuals in the groups being observed or tested that may or may not result from the treatment effects.

MULTIPLE CORRELATION. A statistical method for optimally weighting several available variables to predict a criterion variable.

NOMINAL VARIABLE. In measurement, a level of classification in which only descriptive labels and numerals (without a number meaning) are given to groups.

NONPARAMETRIC STATISTICS. Analytical methods which do not require assumptions of normality of distributions of scores or differences or samples of means.

NULL HYPOTHESIS. In statistics, the statement to be tested stating that there is no difference between the averages of two (or more) groups on a variable or no relationship between two (or more) variables in a group.

OBJECTIVE PROCEDURES. Observations or methods of unbiased persons in obtaining knowledge which are maximally in agreement with one another. Reliability is an equivalent of objectivity.

OPERATIONAL DEFINITIONS. A method in research of specifying a variable in terms of how it will be measured by tests or observational methods. Also procedures for eliciting behavior.

ORDER STATISTICS. Methods of analysis that use rank-ordered data.

PARAMETRIC STATISTICS. Analytical methods which assume normality of score distributions or of the distributions of samples of means or differences.

PERCENTILE RANK. The percentage of scores in a distribution equal to or lower than the score having the rank.

PERVASIVENESS. The concern in evaluation studies that the dissemination of evaluation reports is complete and usable by the varying audiences to which they are sent.

PHI COEFFICIENT. A statistical term for a type of correlation in which both the variables in the correlation are dichotomous.

PLATYKURTIC. The name in statistics for describing an ordered distribution of an array of data in which the scores are widely distributed and markedly flat.

POPULATION. All the subjects or objects which are of interest in research, in contrast to a sample which is the particular group studied.

PRECISION. A term used in sampling studies which indicates the relative size of the confidence limits around sample statistics. Smaller confidence limits are more precise than larger limits.

PREDICTION. In research, description of future status of a student, teacher, enrollment, group, and other individuals.

PREDICTIVE VALIDITY. In measurement, the ability of a measurement procedure to forecast the score of another measurement procedure in the future.

PREDICTORS. Those variables which are used to infer future status or conditions of subjects or groups.

PRE-EXPERIMENT. A faulty type of research design in which only one group is observed, treated, and again observed. Any changes are ascribed to the effects of the treatments. A case study can be a type of pre-experiment.

PROFESSIONAL. A person whose means of earning a living is based on unique theoretical knowledge and experience.

PSEUDO-EXPERIMENTS. A faulty type of research design in which a treated group is compared to a nontreated group with no attempt made to demonstrate that the groups were initially equated or that the criteria differences were greater or smaller than initial differences between the groups.

QUASI-EXPERIMENTS. A research method studying differences or changes of treatments on a group or groups, with subjects not randomly assigned to groups. There may be only one group observed over a series of time periods during which the group is treated differently. Pre- and post-measures for the groups are necessary.

QUOTA SAMPLING. A method of selecting units in descriptive studies in which variables of importance are established, such as age, race, residence, etc. Units under study are chosen on the basis of the incidence of their characteristics in the population.

RANDOMIZATION. A method of developing essentially equivalent groups of subjects in experimental research; in sampling or survey research, a method of selecting a group of subjects representative of the sampled population. The method uses a table of random numbers. These numbers are developed in such a way that there is no discernible pattern among numbers and all numbers have an equal chance of appearing.

RANGE. A statistical characteristic of an array of scores indicating the distance between the highest and lowest scores.

RAPPORT. In research studies, particularly in interviewing, the atmosphere of accord, harmony, and good feeling established between the researcher and the respondent.

REACTIVE ARRANGEMENTS. A threat to the external validity of research designs involving the effect of special testing, or observers, or conditions on groups being studied.

REACTIVITY. A threat to the internal validity of research designs caused simply by the process of doing the research and its accompanying observations and unusual circumstances.

REGRESSION-DISCONTINUITY. A type of quasi-experiment in which more subjects are available for a special program than accommodations are available for. Subjects are admitted on the basis of a regression equation and compared on criteria of success with those not admitted.

REGRESSION LINE. In statistics, the displayed path on a graph showing the relationship between two variables.

REGRESSION-TOWARD-THE-MEAN. A phenomenon of measurement in which extreme scores tend to become more centrally located, nearer the mean. High scores become lower and low scores become higher. This phenomenon is also a threat to internal validity in research studies.

RELEVANCE. The concern in evaluation studies that the data collected will serve the purposes of the evaluation.

RELIABILITY. A concept indicating replicability of studies, agreement among observers, or relationships among similar measures.

RESEARCH. A systematic and diligent investigative activity which attempts to find new general relationships or to apply knowledge in new useful ways.

RESEARCH DESIGN. The organization and logic of the subject, group, data sources, and treatment allocations from which the comparisons necessary to determine knowledge evolves.

RHO. A statistical term for a type of correlation in which both the variables are rank ordered.

SAMPLE. A portion of a whole group usually chosen in such a way as to be representative of the whole group; the particular group upon which observations are made.

SAMPLING UNIT. The individual elements, person, class, school, etc. under study, all of which comprise a population.

SCATTER DIAGRAM. In statistics, the display of the scores of a group of subjects on two variables to show the relationship between the two variables.

SCHOOL SURVEYS. A type of descriptive study of a school system by experts who make recommendations for educational practice based on their findings.

SCIENCE. A systematic body of knowledge about the natural world or the methods by which this knowledge is acquired or applied in new ways.

SELECTION. A threat to the internal validity of research design involving initial differences among groups at the start of a quasi-experiment. If these differences or related differences are taken to be the result of the treatment effects, the lack of validity of these conclusions is attributable to selection effects.

SELECTION RATIO. A statistical term used in choosing individuals to become members of a group. It is the number of persons to be chosen divided by the number of persons available to be chosen.

SKEWNESS. In an ordered distribution of data scores, the tendency for the most frequent scores to be at the left or the right of the distribution.

STANDARD DEVIATION. A statistical characteristic of an array of scores indicating the extent of differences or, range of the scores. Its square is the variance.

STATISTICAL REGRESSION. A threat to the internal validity of research designs involving the selection of high or low groups of subjects, on the basis of measurements, who have more average scores on retesting whether or not they have received intervening treatments.

STATISTICS. A primary method of analysis in educational research by which the rarity of a given result or the probably limits of a value in a population is determined.

STRATIFIED SAMPLING. A method of selecting units in a descriptive study in which the population is divided into groups (strata) and the units examined are selected from within these groups.

SUMMATIVE EVALUATION. The process of acquiring useful terminal information designed to yield judgments about the end results and effectiveness of an educational process or curriculum as a whole.

SYSTEMATIC SAMPLING. A method of selecting units in a descriptive study in which every Kth unit is selected from a sequence. K can be 2, 3, 4, 7, 5, 10, 20, 100, etc.

SYSTEMS ANALYSIS. Analysis of particular linkage of method, organization, institution; parts for determined, operation of whole. A method of making decisions based on incomplete data. It aids an administrator to choose a preferred alternative from among several choices or an optimal solution on a cost-benefit basis.

t TEST. A statistic generally used to estimate whether the means (averages) of two groups are either equal or unequal on a variable.

TESTING. A threat to the internal validity of research designs involving the effects on subjects of prior measurement or observation procedures which they have undergone.

TETRACHORIC CORRELATION. A statistical index for indicating the relationship between two variables which are artificially dichotomized.

THEORY. Generalization about the interrelationship of a number of variables and phenomena based on facts, definitions, and observations of the natural world. It attempts to explain *why* the phenomena occur or the facts are interrelated as they are.

THREATS TO VALIDITY. In research studies, the hindrances to the ability to state cause-and-effect relationships between the treatments and the criteria. They fall into two general classes: internal and external.

TIMELINESS. The concern in evaluation studies that the information developed arrives sufficiently in advance of decision dates so that the information can be used in making the decisions.

TREATMENT. In a research study the variable that is imposed on, withheld from, or presented in various degrees (levels) to the subjects.

TRUE EXPERIMENT. A research method in which subjects are allocated to various treatment groups at random and the groups are given the various treatments at random. The easiest research method in which to determine cause-and-effect relationships between treatments and criteria.

TYPE I ERRORS. The mistake in statistical logic in which a difference or relationship is stated to exist when, in truth, no difference or relationship exists.

TYPE II ERRORS. The mistake in statistical logic in which no difference or no relationship is stated to exist when, in truth, a difference or a relationship exists.

VALIDITY. In measurement, a concept indicating authenticity, truth, or genuineness of test results or observations which is useful for a purpose; also, the extent to which measurements can predict other measurements. In research, validity is the extent to which accurate conclusions about cause-and-effect relationships can be stated.

VARIABLE. The term used to define or identify concepts, properties, or dimensions of objects or functions studied, requiring a common element in the behavior or properties observed.

VARIANCE. A statistical characteristic of an array of scores indicating the extent of differences or range of scores. Its square root is the standard deviation.

Appendix A

More Statistics for Educational Research

In Chapter 3 several of the more common methods of statistical analyses were presented. In this Appendix an introduction to additional techniques will be given. Chi square techniques, the analysis of variance, an illustration of an interaction in analysis of variance, and some order statistics will be presented here.

CHI SQUARE ANALYSIS

When counted data, arising from enumeration of objects in categories of nominal variables, are analyzed statistically, X^2 (chi square) is often used. It is often called an enumeration statistic because of the counting, or enumerating, done in quantifying the variables. X^2 can be used for both purposes of statistics, showing differences among groups on one criterion variable at a time, for goodness of fit, or for showing relationships among nominal variables within one group at a time. Since this latter purpose is the same as that of correlation for interval data, which was presented in Chapter 3, the X^2 statistic for relationships within a group between two variables will be presented first.

Suppose that the learning of a mathematics concept is the object of concern in an educational system. There is a concern that, because of the content of the presentation, those students not interested in science may not learn the concept as quickly as those with this interest. An experiment is set up. Students are given an attitude scale of interest in science and divided at the middle of the distribution into high and low interest groups in science. The criterion measure is a quiz that tests the learning of the concept after one presentation and is split into those getting all items right and those who do not. Two hundred students are available for the study. Since both variables, "interest in science" and "concept learned or not," are dichotomized, a simple table can be set up with two dimensions, and each dimension divided into two parts. The students in each of the four categories can be counted. Suppose the results are as in Table A-1.

If indeed the students' interest in science made no difference in learning the concept, which is essentially the statement of a null hypothesis of no difference, then it would be expected that the number learning the concept would be about the same in both interest groups. Following the null hypothesis reasoning, then, 69 percent of both interest groups (138/200) would have been *expected* to learn the concept, and 31 percent in both interest groups (62/200) would *not be expected* to have learned the concept. With the *expected* numbers, calculated under the reasoning in the null hypothesis, a statistical test can be developed. Table A-2 is *observed* versus *expected* cases.

The expected values under the null hypothesis are calculated as follows: 31 percent of the 100 students who were the high-science interest group, if there were no differences between the old and new methods of teaching, would be expected not to have learned the concept. Similarly, 31 percent of the 100 students in the low-science interest group would also be expected not to have learned the concept. For the right-hand side of the table, similarly 69 percent of the 100 high-science interest students, under the null hypothesis of no difference, would be expected to learn the concept. The X^2 statistic is based on a comparison

TABLE A-1   Data for a Chi Square Test of Independence

	Did not learn the concept	Learned the concept	Total
High interest in science	2	98	100
Low interest in science	60	40	100
Total	62%	138	200
Percentage of Total	31%	69%	

TABLE A-2   Observed Versus Expected Cases in a Chi Square Test of Independence

	Did not learn		Learned		Total Observed
	Obs.	Exp.	Obs.	Exp.	
High interest in science	2	31	98	69	100
Low interest in science	60	31	40	69	100
Grand Total Observed					200

of the observed values in a cell versus the expected values derived from the statement of the null hypothesis.

These comparisons are, cell by cell, subtracted from one another, squared (cell by cell), and the squared values divided by the expected values in each cell (again cell by cell). All the individual cell values are then summed to produce the X^2 statistic. The X^2 test of independence has degrees of freedom equal to (Rows -1) times (Columns -1) or $(2 - 1) \times (2 - 1) = 1$. (When the degrees of freedom for a X^2 are equal to 1, a special rule applies. The absolute (unsigned) value of the observed values, minus the expected values in each cell are reduced by one-half. This is known as Yates' correction for continuity.) Thus the calculation of X^2 for this problem is as follows:

$$X^2_{1\,df} = \frac{(|2 - 31| - \frac{1}{2})^2}{31} + \frac{(|98 - 69| - \frac{1}{2})^2}{69} + \frac{(|60 - 31| - \frac{1}{2})^2}{31}$$

$$+ \frac{(|40 - 69| - \frac{1}{2})^2}{69}$$

$$X^2_{1\,df} = \frac{28.5^2}{31} + \frac{28.5^2}{69} \quad \frac{28.5^2}{31} + \frac{28.5^2}{69}$$

$$X^2_{1\,df} = 26.20 + 11.77 + 26.20 + 11.77$$

$$X^2_{1\,df} = 75.94$$

The degrees of freedom are used for entering the table of X^2. The tabled value of X^2 at the 1 percent level of probability with 1 df is 6.635. (See Table V of Appendix C.) The calculated value for this problem is 75.94, which exceeds the tabled value, thus the null hypothesis of no relationship between the row variable and the column variable is rejected.

TABLE A-3   A Chi Square Analysis of Goodness of Fit

	Heel Bar	Short Cleats	Regular Shoe	Total
Number of players' ankle and knee injuries	6	11	26	43
Total players	70	79	79	228

The two variables are related. Students with a high interest in science do learn the present mathematical concept more frequently than students with a low interest in science. By using this fact, further curricular decisions could be made by the curriculum supervisors and teachers.

Note that both the variables used were variables which were dichotomized from test score interval data. Interval data can be reduced to nominal data readily even after the data are collected, but remember this is not true in the opposite direction. To develop an interval variable from a nominal one requires a great deal of effort before the measurement instrument is used.

The second use of X^2 is to analyze enumeration data of the second major type of research study, that which attempts to show differences among two or more groups on one variable at a time. The football cleat study (Nedwidek, 1965) was research of this type and the criterion variable was counted data, the *number* of ankle and knee injuries. These data are presented in Table A-3.

The null hypothesis is that the number of ankle and knee injuries during the season is not related to the type of cleats being worn by the players. Under this hypothesis it is predicted that the rate of injury is the same among all players. This injury rate is 43/228 or 18.9 percent.

TABLE A-4   Observed and Expected Values for a Chi Square Goodness of Fit Test

	Heel Bar	Short Cleat	Regular Cleat	Total
Observed Injuries	6	11	26	43
Expected Injuries	12.93	14.63	14.63	43.09
Total	70	79	79	228

Thus 18.9 percent of the 70 heel bar players would be *expected* to be injured, or 12.93. For the 79 players using the short cleat shoes and the 79 players using the regular shoes, an 18.9 percent injury rate would be expected to yield 14.63 injuries in each of these groups. Thus the observed versus expected table would be as shown in Table A-4.

There are three groups; therefore the degrees of freedom equal $3 - 1 = 2$. (With more than one degree of freedom there is no need for a correction for the X^2.)

$$X_{2\,df}^2 = \frac{(6 - 12.93)^2}{12.93} + \frac{(11.00 - 14.63)^2}{14.63} + \frac{(26.00 - 14.63)^2}{14.63}$$

$$X_{2\,df}^2 = \frac{(-6.93)^2}{12.93} + \frac{(-3.63)^2}{14.63} + \frac{(11.37)^2}{14.63}$$

$$X_{2\,df}^2 = \frac{48.02}{12.93} + \frac{13.18}{14.63} + \frac{129.28}{14.63}$$

$$X_{2\,df}^2 = 3.71 + .90 + 8.84$$

$$X_{2\,df}^2 = 13.45$$

A calculated X^2 of 13.45 with 2 *df* exceeds the tabled value of X^2 with 2 *df* at the 1 percent level tabled value of probability. (See Table V of Appendix C.) Therefore if the X^2 is declared significant, the observed number of injuries per group are not likely to have arisen through chance alone. The research inference then, because of the way the experiment was set up and based on the statistical inference, is that the differing heel bars and cleats made a difference in the ankle and knee injury rate.

ANALYSIS OF VARIANCE AND THE F TEST

The next general statistic in common use is the F test. This statistic generally arises from the procedure Analysis of Variance (which has little to do with variances as such). The purpose of analysis of variance is understood more quickly if it is thought of as an extension of the t test. The t test is concerned with the equality of two means, that is, the possible difference between two groups (represented by their means) on one variable at a time. (It can also, as in the t test, test two groups, in which case the F test and the t test are functions of one another, $F = t^2$.) Since professional educators are generally interested in testing more than two kinds of treatments or conditions, the F test of the analysis of

TABLE A-5   Analysis of Variance Data and Summations

Method I		Method II		Method III	
X	X^2	X	X^2	X	X^2
7	49	4	16	3	9
8	64	6	36	2	4
4	16	3	9	4	16
7	49	5	25	5	25
		7	49	4	16
				6	36

$\sum X_1 = 26, \sum X^2 = 178$ $\sum X_2^2 = 25, \sum X^2 = 135$ $\sum X_3 = 24$ $\sum X^2 = 106$ $\sum \sum X = 75$
$\sum \sum X^2 = 419$

$n_1 = 4$ $\qquad\qquad$ $n_2 = 5$ $\qquad\qquad$ $n_3 = 6$ $\qquad\qquad$ $N = 15$

$\overline{X}_1 = 6.50$ $\qquad\qquad$ $\overline{X}_2 = 5.00$ $\qquad\qquad$ $\overline{X}_3 = 4.00$ $\qquad\qquad$ $\overline{\overline{X}} = 5.00$

variance is widely applicable to education problems. The analysis of variance generally uses interval data as the criterion variable being analyzed.

Again, an example will be helpful. Three methods of instruction are used to teach three randomized groups of children. A test is given after the instruction and is used as the criterion. The data are presented in Table A-5. The new symbols in Table A-5 are $\sum \sum X$ which stands for the sum of the sum of the X scores, and X which is the overall mean.

A correction term (CT) is calculated first:

$$CT = \frac{(\sum \sum X)^2}{n} = \frac{(75)^2}{15} = \frac{5625}{15} = 375.$$

Three components of an analysis of variance are calculated from the data: a Total sums of squares (SS_T), a Between Groups sums of squares (SS_B), and a Within Groups sums of squares (SS_W), and these values are then placed in an analysis of variance table before other values leading to the F statistic are calculated.

These analysis of variance sums of squares are:

The Total $SS = \sum \sum X^2 - CT = 419 - 375 = 44$

The Within Groups $SS = \sum X_1^2 - \frac{(\sum X_1)^2}{n_1} + \sum X_2^2 - \frac{(\sum X_2)^2}{n_2} +$

$X_3^2 - \frac{(\sum X_3)^2}{n_3} = 178 - \frac{26^2}{4} + 135 - \frac{25^2}{5} + 106 - \frac{24^2}{6}$

TABLE A-6   Analysis of Variance Summary

Source	Sums of Squares	df	Mean Square	F	Significance
Between Groups	15	2	7.50	3.10	N.S.
Within Groups	29	12	2.42		
Total	44	14			

$$= 178 - \frac{676}{4} + 135 - \frac{625}{5} + 106 - \frac{576}{6}$$

$$= 178 - 169 + 135 - 125 + 106 - 96 = 29$$

The Between Groups SS = Total SS − Within Groups SS = 44 − 29 = 15. Table A-6 shows the Analysis of Variance Summary.

The degrees of freedom (df) in Table A-6 are calculated as follows: for the Between Groups df, it is the number of groups minus one, or 3 − 1 = 2. For the Within Groups df, it is the number within each group minus one, and then all df within each group are summed, or $(4 - 1) + (5 - 1) + (6 - 1) = 12$.

The Total df is the total number of observations minus one, or 15 − 1 = 14. The various degrees of freedom add to the total degrees of freedom, as do the various Sums of Squares.

The Mean Square (average of the Sum of Squares) is equal to each Sum of Squares divided by its degrees of freedom. The F statistic is calculated in this type of Analysis of Variance by dividing the Between Groups Mean Square by the Within Groups Mean square, or $F = 7.50/2.42 = 3.10$.

The F value of 3.10 is evaluated in a table of F which is entered with two sources of degrees of freedom, one from the Between Groups, the numerator of the F ratio, and one from the Within Groups degrees of freedom, the denominator of the F ratio. In this case, the numerator is 2 and the denominator is 12. For 2 and 12 degrees of freedom, the tabled F values (See Table V of Appendix C) that could arise from chance processes alone are 3.88 at the 5 percent point and 5.94 at the 1 percent point.

In the usual fashion, the calculated F value, 3.10, is compared to the tabled values of F. If the calculated value is less than the tabled value, the F is not significant, and the null hypothesis that the differences among the means could have arisen by chance, mean one = mean two = mean three, is not rejected. The experimental inference is that the methods of instruction are not different in their effect on this criterion.

TWO-WAY ANALYSIS OF VARIANCE AND INTERACTIONS

The analysis of variance is quite versatile in its use and is the name given to a whole series of types of analyses. As was suggested in Chapter 2, manipulating one treatment variable at a time to determine its effect on a criterion variable is at best inefficient research. It is also rather unlike the real world of education where many variables impinge on students simultaneously, and the interaction among them can be quite important. The analysis of variance presented above is known as "one-way analysis of variance," since there is but one treatment variable. It is quite possible to have two or three or more treatment variables in the analysis of variance, and they are described as two-way, three-way, etc., analyses of variance. With the advent of computers, it has become possible also to analyze more than one criterion variable at the same time, using the analysis of variance format.

These analyses are called multivariate analyses of variance because not only do they have one or more treatment, or classification, variables, but two or more criteria variables that are analyzed simultaneously. These analyses allow for more complex research to be done and analyzed, research which in its form becomes much more like the day-to-day world of education. These analyses go well beyond what can be explained even briefly in this chapter, but may interest the reader sufficiently to study applied statistics as a topic in itself. One of the valuable aspects of multi-treatment analysis of variance is its ability to test specifically interaction terms—the unique interrelationship among the levels or two or more treatment variables.

For more understanding about interactions in analysis of variance, a last example will be presented. Suppose that three methods of instruction are to be tested on boys and girls, and it is of interest to determine whether the methods of instruction differ among themselves, whether the boys differ from the girls, and whether there is an interaction effect; that is, is there a unique interrelationship between the effect of sex of student and the method of instruction?

An achievement test would be the criterion variable. The data and calculations for a two-way analysis of variance are presented below.

	Instruction A	Instruction B	Instruction C	Total
Boys	2, 6, 4	5, 8, 5	2, 2, 2,	36
Girls	6, 4, 5	3, 1, 2	6, 7, 5	39
Total of Scores	27	24	24	75

Correction Term $= \dfrac{75^2}{18} = \dfrac{5625}{18} = 312.5$

Total Sums of Squares (SS) =

$2^2 + 6^2 + 4^2 + 5^2 + 8^2 + 5^2 + 2^2 + 2^2 + 2^2$

$6^2 + 4^2 + 5^2 + 3^2 + 1^2 + 2^2 + 6^2 + 7^2 + 5^2 - \text{CT}$

$$= 383 - 312.5$$

$$= 70.5$$

Boys vs. Girls SS $= \dfrac{36^2}{9} + \dfrac{39^2}{9} - \text{CT} = \dfrac{1296}{9} + \dfrac{1521}{9} - 312.5$

$$= 144 + 169 - 312.5$$

$$= .5$$

Instructional Methods SS $= \dfrac{27^2}{6} + \dfrac{24^2}{6} + \dfrac{24^2}{6} - \text{CT}$

$$= \dfrac{729}{6} + \dfrac{576}{6} + \dfrac{576}{6} - 312.5$$

$$= 121.5 + 96 + 96 - 312.5$$

$$= 1.00$$

Interaction SS: Boys vs. Girls $\times$ A vs. B vs. C

$= \dfrac{(2 + 6 + 4)^2}{3} + \dfrac{(5 + 8 + 5)^2}{3} + \dfrac{(2 + 2 + 2)^2}{3} + \dfrac{(6 + 4 + 5)^2}{3} +$

$\dfrac{(3 + 1 + 2)^2}{3} + \dfrac{(6 + 7 + 5)^2}{3} - \text{CT} - \text{Sex } SS - \text{Methods } SS$

$= \dfrac{12^2}{3} + \dfrac{18^2}{3} + \dfrac{6^2}{3} + \dfrac{15^2}{3} + \dfrac{6^2}{3} + \dfrac{18^2}{3} - 312.5 - .5 - 1.00$

$= 58 + 108 + 12 + 75 + 12 + 108 - 312.5 - .5 - 1.00$

$= 49$

Within Cells SS = Total SS $-$ Sex SS $-$ Methods SS

$$= 70.5 - .5 - 1.00$$

$$= 69$$

Table A-7 shows the summary of Two-Way Analysis of Variance.

TABLE A-7   Summary of Two-Way Analysis Variance

Source	Sums of Squares	df	Mean Square	F	Signi-ficance
Sex: Boys vs. Girls	.5	1	.50	less than 1.00	N.S.
Methods: A vs. B vs. C	1.00	2	.50	less than 1.00	N.S.
Interaction Sex × Methods	49.00	2	24.50	4.26	5%
Within Cells	69.00	12	5.75		
Total	70.50	17			

The interpretation is that the sex of the student makes no difference in the achievement on the criterion test, nor does the Method of Instruction: A, B, or C. Both of the F tests of the mean squares for these "main effects" (or dimensions) of the analysis of variance were not significant (N.S.) when tested against the term used for the denominator of the F ratio, Mean Square Within Cells.

The degrees of freedom for Sex: Boys vs. Girls, are $2 - 1$ or 1; for Methods of Instruction: A vs. B vs. C, $3 - 1$ or 2. For Within Cells the calculation of the degrees of freedom is a little more complex. There are three observations in each of the six cells produced by the product of the three Instructional Methods times the two sexes. Each cell's observational number is reduced by one to determine its degrees of freedom; thus $(3 - 1)$ times $6 = 12$ degrees of freedom for the Within Cells degrees of freedom.

The interaction of Sex × Methods is of particular interest. The method of calculating its sums of squares was shown. Its degrees of freedom are the product of the rows' degrees of freedom times the columns' degrees of freedom, or $2 \times 1 = 2$.

The mean square is, as always, the sums of squares divided by the degrees of freedom, or $49.00/2 = 24.50$.

The F ratio statistic is the interaction mean square, 24.50, divided by the Within Cells mean square, 5.75, or $24.50/5.75 = 4.26$.

The tabled F statistic values with 2 and 12 degrees of freedom are 3.89 at the 5 percent point and 6.93 at the 1 percent point. (See Table VI of Appendix C.) The calculated F ratio is greater than the 5 percent tabled value; therefore the null hypothesis of no unique interrelationship is rejected.

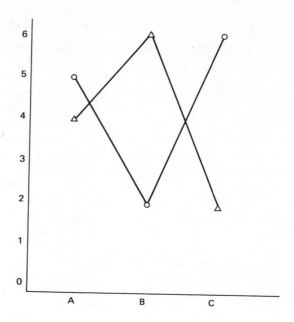

FIGURE A-1   Interaction of Sex × Instructional Method

To understand a significant interaction, a graph is desirable (see Figure A-1).

As can be seen from the graph, the boys do not differ significantly from the girls in amount learned, nor does the particular instructional method used seem to make any difference. However, there is a unique interrelationship, or interaction, which cannot be predicted from a general knowledge of the general level of the achievement of either boys or girls, or of the type of instruction used. Something about a particular instructional method when used with a particular sex produces a unique achievement effect. For Method A, there seems to be no difference at all between boys and girls. For Method B, boys do much better than girls, but the situation is reversed for Method C. It is this nonparallel quality, in this case a crossing of the lines connecting the means of the cells, that represents the interaction. Note that three hypotheses are tested in the analysis: one for Sex, one for Methods, and one for the Interaction effect of Sex × Methods. Further, the combined treatments in the experiment tell us more than would two separate experiments alone, one for Sex effects and one for Method effects.

PARAMETRIC AND NONPARAMETRIC DATA

Essentially the difference between ordered data and interval data represents a larger concern in statistical analyses in education and other social science fields, i.e., that of parametric versus nonparametric analyses. The parameter of major concern is the shape of the distribution of the data. In the abstract, the concern is an excellent one to consider each time a statistical analysis is done. In practice, however, some so-called nonparametric statistics use rank-ordered data that are treated as equal interval data. This latter assumption may be worse than the assumption that variables are normally distributed when developed through careful scaling and test construction procedures.

Data that involve counting of observations in nominal categories have the fewest assumptions involved in their analyses and are the most truly nonparametric. Note that data can be transformed readily from interval data to nominal data, but that nominal variables can only be transformed into interval variables with considerable prior work, if at all. For these reasons, variables were stated as generally being of two types, nominal or interval. Rank-order variables are sometimes classified as a third type of variable in the educational, psychological, and social science realms. (Note that percentile ranks are rank-order variables.)

ORDER STATISTICS

There are several statistical tests based on an ordered data measurement system which are seen in the research literature rather regularly. Their names and purposes will be indicated here so that the reader will have some knowledge of them. No attempt will be made in this brief chapter to show the analytical methods. These can be learned readily in Siegel's (1956) book *Nonparametric Statistics for the Behavioral Sciences*. For interpretation of ordered data statistical tests, however, Hays' (1973) Chapter 16, "Some Order Statistics," in his *Statistics for Psychologists*, is recommended.

The Mann-Whitney U test is the order data statistic approximation to the interval data, parametric *t* test. Both of these tests involve two groups of subjects and one criterion variable. For the *t* test the criterion is a normally distributed interval variable while for the Mann-Whitney U test the criterion is rank ordered. The Mann-Whitney U test is one of those unusual statistics in which the observed U must be *smaller* than the appropriate tabled value of the statistic for the null hypothesis to be rejected.

The Wilcoxon T (or T') test is much like the Mann-Whitney except that the subjects' observations are related, or paired, in some manner. Frequently these are two repeated observations on the same subject. There are two groups of scores for the subjects and the interest is to determine whether the two populations, represented by the sample of pairs, are identical.

The Kruskal-Wallis statistical H test is the ordered measurement data analogue of the one-way analysis of variance F test in interval measurement. If there are three or more groups and an ordered-data criterion, the null hypotheses to be tested could be that the samples have been drawn at random from a common population. As in the one-way analysis of variance, there is no need for the numbers of subjects in the samples to be equal in the Kruskal-Wallis H test.

The Median test is essentially the use of a type of X^2 to test much the same hypothesis that the *t* test is for means of groups. Do the two groups differ in their central tendencies, e.g., their medians, is the question of interest.

The Sign test uses exact probabilities for small samples and again a X^2 test for larger samples to determine whether two populations differ when the two samples from the populations consist of matched pairs of subjects. The criterion is again an ordered variable.

DETERMINING WHICH STATISTICAL METHOD TO USE

A number of statistical methods of analysis have been presented in this chapter and the previous one. Students generally can follow the purpose, types of data, and outcome of a given statistical procedure. The problem arises when the investigator is confronted with an array of different types of procedures, or worse yet, when confronted with data that need analysis. In a statistics course, a student can be fairly certain that the data problems at the end of a chapter can be analyzed by the methods presented in that chapter. In the real world, however, the data are not at the end of a chapter. Which analytical method should be used? For the statistical methods presented here, a brief table with type of variable, nominal or equal interval, on one dimension and purpose of the analysis, showing differences among groups on a variable or showing relationships among variables within a group, on the other dimension, is presented (see Table A-8). For statistical tests other than these that readers of the education literature may find, Table 1 (pages 154 and 155) of Tatsuoka and Tiedeman's Chapter 4 of *The Handbook of Research on Teaching* (1963) is recommended. That table is quite complete and the accompanying text describes each statistic briefly.

TABLE A-8   Statistical Procedure Classified According to Purpose

		Differences Among Groups (one criterion variable)	Relationships Among Variables (within one group)
Criterion Data Type	Nominal	X^2 (goodness of fit)	X^2 (test for independence) phi coefficient
	Rank	Mann-Whitney U (2 groups) H Kruskal-Wallis (3→K Groups) T Wilcoxon (2 Groups)	Spearman rho
	Interval	t test (two groups) Point Biserial (two groups) F test (analysis of Variance) (2→K groups)	correlation (r)

It is not suggested that statistical procedures be used without thorough, usually formal, systematic study. All statistical procedures have assumptions that are important in their use and interpretation. In addition, there are many limitations and specifics which must be considered as an understanding develops regarding the meaning of a statistical test. Two brief chapters cannot begin to present these assumptions, limitations, and considerations. Without further study of statistics, the reader of the professional literature must depend upon the quality of the journal, magazine, or book and its refereeing, and, as has been indicated, this is a somewhat hazardous position in which to be placed. A user of statistical methods without sufficient study is on even shakier grounds. It is imperative that consultation with an informed user of statistics in the behavioral, social science, or education fields be obtained *before* data are gathered and all during the collection, analysis, interpretation, and reporting phases of the research efforts.

SUMMARY

Two forms of X^2, goodness of fit, and tests of independence, were given along with data, examples, and interpretations of each. Finally two forms of analysis of variance, the associated F statistic, and interactions were described and calculated from examples. Implications for educational research of analysis of variance were discussed. Finally, some ordered data statistical analogues of the interval data statistics were named and their uses presented. These were the Mann-Whitney U, the Wilcoxon T, and the Kruskal-Wallis H test, the Median test, and the Sign test. Further use of statistics is not recommended without formal study and consultation with statisticians.

REFERENCES

Edwards, A. L. *Statistical analysis* (rev. ed.). New York: Rinehart, 1958.

Guilford, J. P., and Fruchter, Ben. *Fundamental statistics in psychology and education* (5th ed.). New York: McGraw-Hill, 1973.

Hayes, W. L. Some Order Statistics, Chapter 16 in *Statistics for the social sciences*, (2nd ed.). New York: Holt, Rinehart and Winston, 1973, pp. 760–808.

Nedwidek, R. A. *Football cleats and knee and ankle injuries.* Unpublished doctoral dissertation, University of Pittsburgh, 1965.

Tatsuoka, M. M., and Tiedeman, D. V. Statistics as an aspect of scientific method in research on teaching. In N. L. Gage (Ed.), *Handbook of research on teaching.* Chicago: Rand McNally, 1963, 142–170.

Appendix B Small-Grant Proposal

Title: Information Quality and Educational Decision
         Making

Applicant Organization: Purdue Research Foundation,
                          Purdue University, West
                          Lafayette, Indiana 47907

Principal Investigators:

William Asher, Project Director,
Purdue Educational Research Center,
West Lafayette, Indiana 47907
Area Code 317, Phone 749-2845

Edward Vockell, Principal Investigator
USOE Fellowship Holder, Bldg. G, SCC
Purdue University, West Lafayette,
Indiana 47907
Area Code 317, Phone 749-2845

Transmitted by:

Contracting Officer:

Duration of Activity: September 1, 1971 - August 30,
                        1972

Total Federal Funds Requested: $10,000

Date Transmitted:

Abstract

Title: Information Quality and Educational Decision
         Making
Project Director: William Asher, Purdue Educational
                    Research Center
Principal Investigator: Edward Vockell
Contracting Agency: Purdue Research Foundation,
                      Purdue University, West Lafayette,
                      Indiana 47907
Funds Requested: $10,000
Beginning and Ending Dates: September 1, 1971 –
                              August 30, 1972

The quality of the literature disseminated through
a major educational information channel, the acceptance
levels of this literature, and its effects upon decision
making and implementation in the educational systems
are the major considerations of this proposal.

In recent years, research and dissemination
specialists including Garvey and Griffith (1963, 1964a,
1964b, 1965, 1966, 1967, 1971), Glass (1968), Gideonse
(1968), Campbell (1969), Ziman (1969), Havelock (1969),
the National Academy of Sciences (1970), and Stufflebeam
(1971) have emphasized the need for high quality,
reliable research and evaluation literature as a basis
for decision-making processes in education. Many of
these same writers and others, including Michael (1963),
Campbell and Stanley (1963), Wandt (1965, 1967),
Scriven (1967), Asher (1969), Mann (1969), and Caro
(1971) have suggested that such quality and reliability
are often lacking.

It is proposed to randomly select a hundred reports from the <u>Research</u> <u>in</u> <u>Education</u> indexing and microfiche system of the Educational Resources Information Center, and to present these reports to educational practitioners and decision makers for evaluation of their quality and usefulness. The same reports will be submitted to specialists in educational research and evaluation to obtain an objective assessment of the quality of the content, methodology, and conclusions of the research. By analyzing and comparing these assessments, an attempt will be made to determine: (1) the quality of the information being disseminated; (2) the acceptance levels of the reports among educational decision-makers; (3) the plans educational decision-makers make as a result of the information being disseminated; and (4) how these implementation plans are related to the quality of the information being disseminated.

Information Quality and Educational Decision Making

In recent years, knowledge and information in education, as well as in science and technology in general, has proliferated rapidly. This proliferation has been accompanied in some quarters of the educational community by considerable concern about the adequate dissemination and implementation of reports, findings, collections, and summaries which have been gathered.

A National Academy of Sciences Committee (1970) listed five levels to which scientific information is disseminated: (1) the scholar, (2) the practitioner, (3) the elementary or secondary school teacher, (4) the policy-maker or administrator, and (5) the citizen. All persons in these various categories have a right and need for such information, but they do not all need it at the same level of specification, detail, special- ization, understanding, or speed. In view of such vary- ing levels of need and sophistication, it has become increasingly obvious that some outside organizational help, beyond the usual abstracts, yearly reviews, and summarizing books, is necessary for most users of scientific information to help them keep abreast of new developments in various fields of science and for their various purposes.

Dissemination of research findings can be either formal or informal. Informal dissemination includes such procedures as discussions with colleagues, cor- responding among interested parties, and conversations and exchanges at meetings. Garvey, et al. (1970)

present some interesting comparisons between such
informal presentations in the physical, social sciences,
and education, and their transition into more formal
dissemination through journals. They find that patterns
of information flowed somewhat differently in the
physical and in the social sciences and education. The
communications structures in education and the social
sciences are relatively incohesive as compared to the
physical sciences.

In formal dissemination of scientific information
through journals, there is a major role of review and
quality control which has traditionally been given to an
editor or board of editors or consultants. The National
Academy's Committee (1970) states: "The editor's task
is to decline work which is duplicative, incompetent,
incorrect, or totally pedestrian. This set of
editorial judgments is the backbone of the scientific
information system. It protects the inexpert reader and
those who provide research funds while assuring
scientists in the field that the published work has
been performed with competence and that the findings
are probably reliable." (p. 413)

Havelock (1969) presents a detailed study of the
processes of innovation, dissemination, and knowledge
utilization and of the characteristics of the individuals and organizations which facilitate or inhibit these
processes. Although this and similar studies reviewed
by Havelock provide useful and essential information
about the systems and linkages involved in the dis-

semination process, there is little explicit consideration of the quality of information being disseminated;
that it may be inaccurate or even have detrimental
effects in the dissemination processes as the result
of such inaccuracies.

There has long been criticism of the adequacy of
the literature on research and evaluation published in
the education journals. Speaking in general of the
era of pre-USOE research support and dissemination,
for example, Michael (1963), an editor of the Research
Methodology issue of the Review of Educational Research,
has suggested, somewhat harshly, that "Probably, on
the average, only 10 percent of published papers in
educational journals are worthy of being reported in the
Review." Similarly, Scriven (1967) has maintained
that, in education "by minimum acceptable research
standards, 95 percent of the work in the field....that
is concerned with causal analysis is, either by
theoretical or practical standards, invalid or trivial."

Wandt, as Chairman of an AERA Committee on
Evaluation of Research (1965 & 1967), published a
report on an empirical study on the quality of research
in education. He selected 125 articles which he
determined to be representative of the research articles
published in the broad field of education journals in
1962. These, also included associated fields of child
development, educational psychology, and sociology. He
submitted these articles to 125 judges who were deemed
experts in the field of educational research by an AERA

panel. The judges were asked to rate the articles "accept," "revise" or "reject" on the basis of their acceptability for publication in a journal of educational research. Of these published articles, the judges rated 19 percent "accept," 41 percent "revise," and 40 percent "reject." The judges also gave rather detailed lists of specific shortcomings which occurred in the articles which they felt should be rejected or returned for revision.

Campbell and Stanley (1963, p. 176) suggest, "Much research in education today conforms to a design in which a single group is studied only once, subsequent to some agent or treatment presumed to cause change...such studies have such a total absence of control as to be of almost no scientific value." Glass (1968) states that unless evidence of the worth of a new procedure, generated from a single case or group, is supported by public and replicable evidence, then the support for the ideas and procedures can only be appeals to authority. These authorities may be very able people, but it leaves the door open to self-interested persons, quacks, and frauds who to the public may seem to have equal, or even greater authority. Corey's book, Action Research to Improve School Practices (1953) points out, "The results of many educational experiments have been controversial because inadequate provision was made for obtaining data describing their success or failure. Those who substitute for the 'tried and true' newer and pre-

sumably more promising practices are under an especial
obligation to obtain objective evidence about
consequences (p. 100)."

More recently, Campbell (1969, p. 409) has
indicated possible political involvements accompanying many educational innovations which could make
accurate evaluations extremely difficult: "Most
administrators wisely prefer to limit the evaluations
to those the outcomes of which they can control,
particularly insofar as published outcomes or press
releases are concerned. Ambiguity, lack of truly
comparable comparison bases, and lack of concrete
evidence all work to increase the administrator's
control over what gets said, or at least to reduce
the bite of criticism in case of actual failure.
There is safety under the cloak of ignorance."
Further, as Caro (1971, p. 91) indicates, "Those who
actually carry out the programs to be evaluated are
subordinate to those to whom the evaluators report.
The issues addressed by the evaluation and the manner
in which results are reported are strongly related to
sponsorship. Consequently, the interests of the
general public, practitioners, and recipients of
services are not often fully served by evaluators."

Another difficulty arises out of the demand for
quick results. Man (1969, p. 13) states, "The better
the study, the longer it takes, and consequently the
less usefulness it may have. Conversely, the sloppier
the procedure, the more likely it is to provide

information on questions of interest even though this data will be of doubtful validity."

The implications of information quality for evaluation are proposed by Stufflebeam, _et al_. (1971) in his evaluational model. It distinguishes among four general types of decision settings: (1) decisions to effect large changes supported by a high level of relevant information grasp; (2) decisions involving small changes and high information grasp; (3) decisions involving small changes and low information grasp. (A change is "large" if society considers the variables to be altered important and if society considers the proposed change to be important rather than trivial.) The depth and quality of information demanded from the dissemination process will vary from setting to setting. Decisions which involve large changes will demand more detailed information than those involving smaller changes. Stufflebeam states that for educational practitioners "evaluation must be more extensive when there is only little information (or when the client cannot use available information in its present form)."

Asher (1969) points out that it is not possible for professional educators to read the literature in education and the related journals without a good knowledge of the theory of measurement, internal validity concepts of research design, and some statistics. This problem is more serious in education than in the physical and biological sciences. One

reason may be that engineers and physicians are
trained in measurement principles and research methods
of the physical or biological sciences, while most
professionals in education are not so well trained in
the behavioral sciences. Further comments, critiques,
and rejoinders are a standard part of the literature
in the physical sciences, whereas this is not the case
in the behavioral sciences. Asher and Vockell (1971b,
unpublished manuscript) determined the 17, most
frequently cited journals in the 1969 Encyclopedia of
Educational Research and sent questionnaires to the
editors of these journals to determine policy with
regard to critical comments. Thus far, 15 of the 17
have replied, and the results clearly indicate that
these journals do not as a general policy publish
critiques, comments, rejoinders, or critical letters to
the editor.

Kronick (1969) states that the scholarly journal
originally developed as an open record in which each
scholar submitted his findings to his fellow scientists
for their review and criticism. Such exchange of
critical comment is looked upon as an essential part
of the scientific dissemination process. Garvey and
Griffith (1971, p. 357) have reported on a study of
psychologists who have distributed preprints of their
scientific papers: "Over 60 percent of these authors
received feedback that prompted them to modify their
manuscripts. These modifications were not simply a
matter of improvement in grammar and style of the

manuscript but, instead, involved significant
modifications such as reanalysis of data, redefinition
of concepts, etc." The importance of good refereeing
and quality control at the editorial level is magnified
by the fact that teacher-oriented organizations seem to
be initiating publication policies which will put
"practical" information rather than research studies
into the hands of classroom teachers. For example,
Riedesel (1971) indicates that the future policy of
The Arithmetic Teacher, a journal of the National
Council of Teachers of Mathematics (NCTM), will be not
to publish research articles. Implicit in such a
policy change is the expectation that readers can
implement what they find useful without bothering with
the details of the research design.

Gideonse (1968) presented an output-oriented
model of research and development elaborating and
extending Guba and Clark's (1965) well known model.
Gideonse attempts to classify the processes related to
and necessary for change in education. The first stage
is Development, which includes both invention and
design of the innovation; the second stage, Diffusion,
includes dissemination and demonstration. (Gideonse's
definition of Demonstration includes such processes
as "to examine and assess" the qualities of the innovation.) The final stage is Adoption, which includes
trial, installation, and institutionalization. Here
part of the objective is "provide a basis for assessing
the quality, value, fit, and utility of the invention...

i.e., to test." Thus Gideonse considers systematic
evaluation of the material to be disseminated as an
integral part of Development, and Dissemination process.

Asher (1969) states, "Lack of systematic research
editing, critiques, and comments in the literature...
hurts in a non-negative way as well. It is often
stated that everybody knows the quality of the literature in education, and this is particularly true of
doctoral dissertations. But there are well done studies
in the literature of value to education that are
ignored....Again the total volume of the literature is
so large and generally of such poor quality in terms
of its objectivity that often the strategy in using
it is to implement those research ideas which occurred
most recently, that is, what is most popular at the
moment. This practice hardly builds enduring qualities
in an educational system. Meanwhile communications and
information of high quality tend to become obliterated
in the mass of documents." Asher recommends as a
partial solution an explicitly defined Elimination
process added to the Gideonse (1968) model.

Garvey and Griffith (1971) also view this problem
from a slightly different viewpoint. They maintain
that an _informal_ information system must exist along-
side the formal dimension, but they point out that
this informal domain is not meant to have the same
attributes as that published in the reputable journal
literature. These authors maintain that scientists

and authors need a forum where they can present half-
formed ideas for critical commentary from their peers
before reevaluating them and presenting them to the
public. Such information and ideas may turn out to be
completely false, but as long as they are contained
in the informal domain, they should be relatively
harmless. The potential difficulty is that such
informal information may be disseminated in such a way
that "regardless of efforts to keep these reports
from taking on the status of a formal communication,
the receiver gets the impression that the reported
findings are sound, and the discovery is original.
This conclusion may be reached simply because the
reports no longer have the characteristics of
informal communication and come to resemble the formal
journal article." (p. 361)

The computer has introduced new advantages and
opportunities for the storage and dissemination of
scientific information. Such advantages, however,
are accompanied by difficulties and responsibilities.
The work of Garvey and Griffith (1963, 1964a, 1964b,
1965, 1966, 1967, 1971) has shown the concentration on
retrieval techniques alone is not an adequate way to
improve a communication system if the desired outcome
is a net increase in the amount of relevant knowledge
available to the working scientist (Clark, 1971). An
excessive volume of information tends to swamp the
reader (Licklider, 1966). Holt (1971, p. 331) points

out that, "The undoubted merits of computers in this
kind of work seem to have made many of us overlook
the fact that the problems we face are not primarily
technological....It is becoming evident, however, that
the diagnosis of our communication problem is mainly
'information input overload' and the strategy of coping
with it that seems called for is reducing the amount
of input by better control of quality.

    With the increase in volume of information, there
is greater difficulty for the inexperienced reader in
determining what is good and what is bad in literature.
Ziman (1969, p. 319) points out that "We must be able
to rely on the basic accuracy and honesty of what we
read in other people's papers, for we are always using
their results in the construction of our own researches,
and simply cannot find the time to repeat all their
experiments, measurements, calculations, for ourselves
....I cannot see how this innocence could be preserved
against careerist pressures to publish, if there were
no scrutiny by expert referees." The National Academy
of Sciences Committee (1970) adds that even when a fully
computerized information retrieval system is eventually
developed"the role of the editors and reviewers will
remain unchanged: indiscriminate release of unedited
reports to a computer network could well be even more
disastrous than indiscriminate publishing would be
today."

    An example of the application of computerized
retrieval and dissemination systems to the field of

education is the Educational Resources Information
Center (ERIC), a program designed and supported by
the U. S. Office of Education for the purpose of
providing "a systematic and comprehensive link between
researchers and users." (ERIC, 1970b).

ERIC can be described as a national information
system designed and supported by the U. S. Office of
Education. Its purpose is to provide ready access to
results of "exemplary programs, research and development
efforts, and related information that can be used in
developing more effective educational programs"
(ERIC, 1970b). ERIC employs a system of specialized
clearinghouses, each of which is responsible for a
particular educational area. Current significant
information relevant to education is monitored,
acquired, evaluated, abstracted, indexed, and listed
in ERIC reference sources. Through these reference
sources, "any educator, anywhere in the country, has
easy access to reports of innovative programs,
conference proceedings, bibliographies, outstanding
professional papers, curriculum-related materials,
and reports of the most significant efforts in educational research and development, regardless of where
they were first reported" (ERIC, 1970b).

ERIC has two major publications; Current Index
to Journals in Education (CIJE) which indexes
published information in education; and Research in
Education (RIE), which indexes information which has

<u>not</u> been formally published in a scientific or
professional journal. A recent (1970a) ERIC newsletter states: "ERIC's two principal publications,
RIE and CIJE are remarkable efficient guides to what
is good in literature. Putting ourselves in the shoes
of potential users, we sagaciously clear only the
best for inclusion in RIE. Computerized indexing
of what is available in ERIC will facilitate your
'ferreting out' as no other information system has
ever done."

It would seem that the RIE aspects of ERIC may
present a contradiction. If the <u>published</u> literature
is of the quality Wandt, Campbell, Campbell and
Stanley, Glass, and Corey suggest that it is, what
value can there be in the massive dissemination of
unpublished literature, which has only minimal review
by scientists and professionals?

An investigation was initiated at Purdue University
(Asher and Vockell, 1971a, unpublished) to attempt
to evaluate the quality of ERIC's information
available through RIE. Twelve judges were selected
who had taken advanced courses in research design,
statistics, and measurement techniques. A total of
745 citations were randomly selected from RIE and
were assigned to the judges. The judges were
instructed to (a) determine the number of reports
cited involving any evidence of research or evaluation
to support the information included in the report,
and (b) evaluate the quality of the articles designated

as "research articles" according to predetermined
criteria.

Preliminary analysis indicates that of the 745
reports investigated, a total of only 155 were
classified as data oriented research. Of these, 22
were not available in either microfiche or hardback
from ERIC's reproducing service and therefore could
not be investigated further. Thus a total of 133
(17.3 percent) of the original 745 citations referred
to available research reports.

The judges then were asked to undertake three
forms of evaluation: (a) rank the reports on a
5-point scale according to the quality, (b) rank the
reports "accept," "reject" or "revise" according
to whether or not the articles should be accepted
for journal publication, and (c) list the possible
errors which appeared in reports listed either as
"reject" or "revise." A summary of the results is
given in Table I.

As the results indicate, a total of only 6.7
percent of the original 745 citations referred to
reports which were supported by research which is
either good or excellent. A total of only 2.60
percent of the original 745 citations referred to
reports which were considered worthy of publication
as they were written. These low ratings would seem
to be the result of the previously cited looseness
in the informal communication system and in evaluations
sponsored by the same organization which is being

evaluated. As suggested by Garvey and Griffith
(1971), a serious problem can arise when such information is transformed into a formal communication system.

Table I

Quality Ratings

	No.	%	Cum. %
Excellent--A model of good practice	13	1.69	1.69
Good--A few minor defects	39	5.07	6.76
Mediocre--Not good, not bad	33	4.29	11.05
Poor--Some serious defects	37	4.81	15.86
Completely incompetent--"horrible"	10	1.30	17.16
	132*		
Accept, Revise, Reject			
Accept	20	2.60	2.60
Revise	48	6.24	8.84
Reject	65	8.45	17.29
	133		

* = 1 report not rated

Dissemination is an integral and important aspect
of scientific and professional enterprises in general
and education and educational research specifically.
ERIC is a major effort in educational research dissemination process. Yet, the dissemination process is
based in great part on the assumption that what is
being disseminated is factual and worth disseminating.
In the light of the research reviewed and conducted it

seems that this might be a somewhat tenuous assumption.

Research Evaluation Instruments

Research has been reported on the development of
various objective instruments for judging the quality
of educational research and evaluation. Wandt (1967)
in his previously cited work with AERA developed a
list of 25 characteristics with a five-point quality-
rating scale for each characteristic. Wandt also
included an "accept-revise-reject" scale and a system
for classifying individual errors pointed out by the
judges. Persell (1966) uses a similar combination of
individual ratings of specific characteristics combined
with an overall rating of the quality of the work,
based on both the substance and the methodology of the
research. Suydam (1968) has developed an instrument
for evaluating experimental educational research
reports, based on an analysis of nine general areas
which results in a cumulative overall score for the
report. A similar instrument was developed by Kohr and
Suydam (1970) for evaluating survey research. Checklists and principles which can serve as guidelines for
evaluating education research and evaluation can be
found in Stufflebeam (1970), Scrivin (1967), Campbell
and Stanley (1963), Grobman (1968), Borg (1963),
Mouly (1963), Rummel (1964), Travers (1964), Van
Dalen (1966), and Farquahar and Drumboltz (1959).
McReynolds (1971) presents research on the reliability
of ratings of research papers.

Problem:

        The central problem of this proposal is to
determine the quality of the literature disseminated
through a major educational dissemination channel,
its acceptance, and the possible effects of its
implementation in educational systems. The following
questions will be investigated:

        1. What is the quality of the information in
            the material in this major dissemina-
            tion channel in education?

        2. What are the acceptance levels of these
            disseminated reports in the audience of
            educational practitioners, administrators,
            teachers, and developers?

        3. What implementation plans would these
            educational practitioners make as the
            result of the information disseminated
            in this channel?

        4. How are these implementation plans
            related to the previously determined
            quality of the information disseminated?

Method:

        First, five hundred ERIC citations will be
randomly selected from Research in Education, the
major dissemination channel of nonpublished educational
reports. These will be assigned to teams of judges
who will be asked to categorize the reports as either
research or nonresearch, depending on whether or not
the report shows evidence of replicable data collection

or methods and conclusions, and so forth, as opposed
to personal statements, bibliographies, curriculum
and administrative guides, and reviews of literature.
(Our previous research indicates that such classifications can be made reliably and that about 20 percent of the original five hundred reports will be
research oriented.)

Second, from the reports classified as research-
oriented, one hundred will be randomly selected and
sent to users of educational research. These will be
professional educators in elementary and secondary
school systems, in state educational agencies, and
in other education-related fields which are part of
ERIC's audience. Reports will be sent to appropriate
users, according to the level and content for which
the information would be used. Thus the reports will
be sent to administrative, supervisory, and curriculum personnel at appropriate levels, teachers,
teachers of teachers, guidance personnel, school
psychologists, and other decision makers in the field
of education. A broad range of personnel will be
tapped since ERIC itself includes such a broad scope.
The reports will be sent to persons who would find
the content area of the report of interest to them
in their professional decision making. These
educational practitioners will read the reports and
rate the informational quality and the value of the
report to them as a professional educator.

These users of educational information will be selected from Indiana and nearby states and major metropolitan areas for several reasons. First, this will be geographically convenient for researchers from Purdue University, who will be able to make the necessary personal follow-ups which the study will require if an exceptionally high rate of return is to be attained and individual interpretations and classifications are to be made. Second, a population of users of educational information will be available from up-to-date lists from state, city, and other education agencies. Third, it appears that Indiana and geographically close major metropolitan areas could not be considered atypical of school personnel, systems, and institutions. Indiana is known as the cross roads of the nation, and there is evidence available from Project TALENT that Indiana students are quite typical of U.S. students in aptitude and achievement (Asher and Dodson, 1969).

In the third step of this study, the ratings of these users of educational information on the quality of the information will then be compared to ratings of quality made of the same articles by expert judges who would be assigned the task of evaluating them according to their value as educational research. These judges will be members of the faculty in colleges and institutions in educational research and related areas, research oriented staff of state departments of education, researchers in public schools, and staff research personnel of regional laboratories, etc., who have done research on educational problems. These persons will be asked to rate the reports on the basis of their informational quality, as determined by their methodological soundness, conclusions, samples, statistical procedures and applications, summative and formative evaluation principles, and intrinsic and extrinsic validity, using as guidelines of rating procedures those developed by Wandt (1964), Persell (1966), USOE Small Grant Review Sheets parts 4a and 4c, educational and behavioral social science textbook writers (Kerlinger, 1964; Travers, 1964; Van Dalen, 1966; Mouly, 1963; Campbell and Stanley, 1963; Wandt, 1964; Fox, 1969, Suchman, 1967; Glass, 1968; Scrivin, 1967; Stufflebeam, 1971; Grobman, 1968; and Baxter, 1970), and checklists of areas of difficulty collected by the senior researcher in his teaching, research, and writing. This instrument will be pretested for ease and completeness of response.

Reliability of the instrument and judges for these situations will be determined by between judges' agreement using partial duplication of reviews; i.e., several of the studies will be rated by a second rater and the ratings will be correlated.

Both the users, who judge the value for possible implementation and the quality of the information, and the experts, who rate the methodology and soundness of the conclusions, will be paid for their services.

It is felt that by offering a small honorarium greater
cooperation, and a more complete response from the
selected samples, will be obtained.

If necessary, letter and telephone follow-ups
will be used to clarify information and to obtain
additional information in order to be thorough.

Probable Outcomes and Benefits to Education:

It is anticipated that the experts from the field
of educational research will tend to rate the reports
similar to the way they were rated in the pilot study
by Asher and Vockell (1971). It is expected that
several of the methodological problems in that study
can now be eliminated. Furthermore, a more specific
attempt will be made to ascertain objectively the
errors made in studies which are considered to be weak.
The reliability of the judges on the preliminary study
was good, and it is expected that even better reliability
will be obtained in the current study.

The ratings of the quality and value by the users,
e.g., administrators, supervisors, teachers, guidance
personnel, et al., generally will fall into the
following four quadrants:

(1) High ratings of information quality which are
     confirmed by educational research experts.

(2) High ratings of information quality which are
     not confirmed.

(3) Low ratings of information quality which are
     confirmed.

(4) Low ratings of information quality which
are not confirmed.

A preponderance of ratings in category one would
be taken as evidence that the research disseminated
through ERIC's RIE is indeed of good quality. Ratings
falling in category two would indicate that perhaps
the original selection of these articles in RIE is of
low quality and educational practitioners are not well
qualified to judge them accurately with respect to
methodological concerns. This would be taken as a
confirmation of the expectation from the review of
literature that such reports might do more harm than
good. Ratings falling in category three would be taken
as indications that the non-refereed, unpublished
literature under study is of highly dubious value.
Ratings in category four would be somewhat ambiguous,
but it is not anticipated that ratings in this
category will be frequent.

In addition, some general guidelines of the
normative standards of the ratings of the quality of
literature by research experts and professional
educators can be ascertained through this study.
Furthermore, insight into the way professional
educators consider using innovative educational
information made available through a major educational
literature dissemination channel can be obtained. The
interrelationship between educational literature
quality and the proposed implementation in educational
systems can be determined better. This aspect of the

study is of importance in the development of theoretical
aspects of the process of educational dissemination and
adoption.

Personnel:

Professor William Asher, Project Director

B.A.	DePauw	Psychology, 1950
M.S.	Purdue U.	Psychology, Measurement, 1951
Ph.D.	Purdue U.	Psychology, Statistics, 1955

Research Assistant, Speech Department, Purdue U.
1952-54.

Research Associate, Speech Department, Purdue U.
1954-55.

Research Analyst, Purdue-Calumet Development
Foundation 1955-56.

Research Coordinator, Cooperative Research
Program, USOE 1956-60.
Also Adjunct Professor American University
and U. of Maryland teaching Educational
Research Methods and Measurement.

Associate Professor and Professor of Educational
Research, U. of Pittsburgh 1960-66
Teaching statistics at all levels and research
methods.
Also taught principles of research and
statistics as a team teaching member in
Quantitative Methods in Medicine in School
of Medicine.
Also, on sabbatical for postdoctoral Harvard

University, 1964-65 as IBM Fellow in
Computing Center and School of Education.
Course work in multivariate analysis (Rulon),
computing, theory of measurement (Carroll),
Educational Sociology (Gross), etc.
Also, NSF Summer Institute, U. of Texas.
Applied Regression Analysis, 1964.

Professor of Education and Psychology, Purdue
U. 1966-date. Teaching Theory of Psychological
Measurement, Educational Research Seminars
and Methods, have taught a section of
Psychological Statistics with Winer.
Also Co-Director, Purdue Educational Research
Center, advising faculty on educational
research problems - design, measurement,
analysis, proposals, etc. 1967-date.
Also Co-Director USOE supported Graduate
Education Research Training 1967-date.
My load allocation is 25% teaching, 25%
administration, and 50% research.
Also spent one Winter at David Ryans'
Educational R. & D. Center at U. of
Hawaii 1968-69.

I have been a consultant and field reader for USOE
since 1960 and a Small Grant proposal reviewer since
Howard Hjelm started the program in 1963. I was also
one of the 100 "experts" chosen by Wandt in 1963 for
the AERA review of educational research article quality.
I have been a publishers' reviewer for the research

methods books by Kerlinger, VanDalen, Mouly, McGrath, and Tuckman (Harcourt Brace Jovanovich, 1972).

I have published some 60 papers in basic and applied research and evaluation. Selected citations to indicate the methodological and substantive scope are as follows:

Intelligibility Tests: A Review of Their Standardization, Some Experiments, and a New Test. Speech Mono., Vol. XXV, 1, 1958, 14-28.

Drop in Degrees. American Psychologist, Vol. 12, 12, December, 1957, 754-755.

Statistical Problems of Accomplishment Quotient, Journal of Experimental Education, Vol. 30, 3, March 1962.

Barnes, W. E., and Asher, J. W. Predicting a Student's Success or Non-Success in First-Year Algebra, The Mathematics Teacher, Vol. LV, 8, Washington, D. C., December 1962, 651-654.

Simun, P. B., and Asher, J. W. The Relationship in Undergraduate School to School Administrators' Ratings of First Year Teachers, The Journal of Teacher Education, Vol. 15, 3, 1964, 293-302.

Asher, W., and Kurfeerst, M. The Computer and Information Retrieval: School Law, A Case Study, Harvard Educational Review, Vol. 35, 2, Spring 1965, 175-190.

McCormack, J., and Asher, W. Aspects of the High School Record Related to the First Semester College Grade Point Average, Personnel and Guidance Journal, Vol. 42, 7, March 1964, 699-703.

Kurfeerst, M., and Asher, W. A Factor Analysis of the
Education Laws of Pennsylvania. Information Storage
and Retrieval, Vol. 4, 257-270.

Do Driver Training Courses Produce Better Drivers?
An Alternative Hypothesis, Traffic Safety Research
Review, Vol. 12, 1, March, 1968.

Asher, W., And Shively, J. E. The Technique of
Discriminant Analysis: A Reclassification of Harbison
and Myers' Seventy-five Countries, Comparative
Education Review, June, 1969.

Asher, W., and Dodson, B. The Prediction of Auto-
mobile Accidents Following the Senior Year in High
School, Behavioral Research in Highway Safety,
Vol. 1, 3, 1971.

I have as a teaching procedure for graduate
students and as a major research interest published
a number of "Comments" on articles appearing in the
educational research literature. These are as follows:

Comment on 'The Relationship Between Rigidity-
Flexibility in Children and Their Parents." Child
Development, Vol. 32, 1961, 607-608.

Comment on 'A Comparison of i/t/a and T.O. Reading
Achievement When Methodology Is Controlled,'
Elementary English, April, 1968.

Moller, N., and Asher, W. Comment on 'A Comparison
of Dropouts and Nondropouts on Participation in
School Activities.' Psychological Reports, 1968,
Vol. 22, 1243-1244.

Shively, J. E., and Asher, W. Comment on "The
Effects of Modified Programmed Lectures and Mathe-
matical Games Upon Achievement and Attitude of Ninth-
Grade Low Achievers in Mathematics,' Psychological
Reports, 1970, Vol. 26, 545-546.
Reed, C. L., and Asher, W. Comment on 'A Multifactor
Admissions Predictive System.' Psychological Reports,
1971, Vol. 29, 521-522.

It was through the lack of interest in, lack of
policy regarding, and refusal to publish many of
these comments and critiques by educational journal
editors that I became interested in the quality and
decision making uses of educational information in
the dissemination channels.
Membership and Associations:

Sigma Xi

Interamerican Psychological Association

Cited, American Men of Science 10th ed.

Fellow, American Psychological Association and
        Division 15 Educational Psychology
        Member Division 5 Measurement and Evaluation
        Member Division 16 School Psychology

Life Member, Phi Delta Kappa

Life Member, National Geographic Society

Fellow, American Association for the Advancement
        of Science

American Educational Research Association

American Driver and Traffic Safety Education Assn.

Certified for Private Practice of Psychology –
Indiana and Maryland.

National Council on Measurement in Education

National Society for the Study of Education

Edward L. Vockell

A. B.	Athanaeum of Ohio	Philosophy, 1967
M.S.	Xavier University	1969

Research trainee internship with the Southwestern Ohio
Educational Research Council (SWOERC), September
1967–August 1968.

Teacher of English and Latin, Ross H. S., Butler Co.,
Ohio, Feb.-June, 1968.

Teacher of English and Latin, Glen Este H. S., Clermont
Co., Ohio, Sept. 1968–June 1970.

Graduate Educational Research Trainee at Purdue
University, Sept. 1970–date.

Papers

Dating Behavior of High School Seniors (submitted for
publication to the Journal of Marriage and the Family).

Proposed Budget - William Asher and Edward Vockell
September 1, 1971 - August 30, 1972

		Purdue	U.S.O.E.	Total Budget
I. Direct Costs				
A. Personnel				
1. Wm. Asher Project Director. No payment allowed. See attached letter from John Hazard				
2. Ed. Vockell, Principal Investigator. No funds allowed since he is a USOE fellowship holder.				
3. Undergraduate Research Assistant 263 hr x $1.90/hr	$327	$ 173	$ 500
4. Secretarial Assistant $2.00/hr x 175 hrs.		350	350
TOTAL SALARIES	$327	$ 523	$ 850

Proposed Budget - William Asher and Edward Vockell

September 1, 1971 - August 30, 1972

			Purdue	U.S.O.E	Total Budget
B.	Fringe Benefits				
	1.	Major Medical and Life Insurance computed at .012 of total salaries	$ 4	$ 6	$ 10
	2	Workman's Compensation computed at .00113 of total salaries		1	1
		TOTAL FRINGE BENEFITS	$ 4	$ 7	$ 11
C.	Other Costs				
	1.	200 ERIC reports x $5.00/report		$ 1,000	$ 1,000
	2.	Postage		663	663
	3.	Computer Time		250	250
	4.	Communications (telephone calls) and Travel		745	745
	5.	Consultants (Reader/ Raters) 200 x $25.00/ rater = $5,000 40 (reliability raters) x $25.00/ rater = $1,000		6,000	6,000

Proposed Budget - William Asher and Edward Vockell
September 1, 1971 - August 30, 1972

		Purdue	U.S.O.E.	Total Budget
C.	Other Costs (contd)			
	6. Office Supplies		$ 300	$ 300
	7. Final Report		200	200
	TOTAL OTHER COSTS		$ 9,158	$ 9,158
	TOTAL DIRECT COSTS	$331	9,688	10,019
II.	Indirect Costs computed at 59.7% of total salaries	195	312	507
	TOTAL COST	$526	$10,000	$10,526

References

Asher, J. W. Development, dissemination, and adoption:
   The need for an elimination function. Paper
   presented at USOE Summer Institute, University
   of New Hampshire, Durham, N. H., 1969.

Asher, J. W., and Vockell, E. L. Dissemination
   processes in unrefereed channels. (Purdue
   University, unpublished manuscript, 1970a).

Asher, J. W., and Vockell, E. L. A study of critiques
   published in journals of educational research.
   (Purdue University, unpublished manuscript, 1970b)

Baxter, B. (Ed.). Evaluative research. Pittsburgh:
   American Institutes for Research, 1970.

Borg, W. R. Educational research: An introduction.
New York: David McKay Company, Inc., 1963.

Campbell, D. T. Reforms as experiments. American
Psychologist, 1969, 24, 409-429.

Campbell, D. T., and Stanley, J. C. Experimental and
quasi-experimental designs for research. In.
N. L. Gage (Ed.) Handbook of Research on Teaching.
Chicago: Rand McNally and Company, 1963.

Caro, F. G. Issues in the evaluation of social programs.
Review of Educational Research, 1971, 41, 87-114.

Clark, K. E. A critical examination of the National
Information System for Psychology. American
Psychologist, 1971, 26, 325-329.

Corey, S. M. Action research to improve school
practices. New York: Teachers College Columbia, 1953.

Educational Resources Information Center. How to use
ERIC. United States Government Printing Office,
1969 reprinted 1970.

Educational Resources Information Center. Keeping up.
ERIC Clearing House for Education and the Social
Sciences, Boulder, Colorado, 1970a.

Educational Resources Information Center. Your guide
to current educational information. ERIC
Clearinghouses, 1970b.

Farquhar, W., and Krumboltz, J. D. A checklist for
evaluating experimental research in psychology
and education. Journal of Educational Research,
1959, 52, 354.

Fox, D. J. The research process in education. Chicago:
    Holt, Rinehart and Winston, 1969.

Garvey, W. D., and Griffith, B. C. The American
    Psychological Association's Project on Scientific
    Information Exchange in Psychology. Journal of
    Counseling Psychology, 1963, 10, 297–302.

Garvey, W. D., and Griffith, B. C. Scientific
    information exchange in psychology. Science,
    1964, 146, 1655–1659.

Garvey, W. D., and Griffith, B. C. The structure,
    objectives, and findings of a study of scientific
    information exchange in psychology. American
    Documentation, 1964, 15, 258–267.

Garvey, W. D., and Griffith, B. C. Scientific
    communication: The dissemination system in
    psychology and a theoretical framework for planning
    innovations. American Psychologist, 1965, 20, 157–164.

Garvey, W. D., and Griffith, B. C. Studies in social
    innovations in scientific communication in
    psychology. American Psychologist, 1966, 21,
    1019–1036.

Garvey, W. D., and Griffith, B. C. Scientific
    communication as a social system. Science, 1967,
    157, 1011–1016.

Garvey, W. D., and Griffith, B. C. Scientific
    communication: Its role in the conduct of research
    and creation of knowledge. American Psychologist,
    1971, 26, 349–362.

Garvey, W. D., Lin, N., and Nelson, C. E. Communication in the physical and the social sciences.
   Science, 1970, 170, 1166-1173.

Gideonse, H. D. An output-oriented model of research
   and development and its relationship to educational
   improvement. Journal of Experimental Education,
   1968, 37, 157-163.

Glass, G. V. Educational piltdown men. Phi Delta
   Kappan, 1968, 50, 148-151.

Grobman, H. Evaluation of curriculum projects. AERA
   Monograph Series on Curriculum Evaluation.
   Chicago: Rand McNally and Company, 1968.

Guba, E. G., and Clark, D. L. An examination of
   potential change roles in education. Paper read at
   Symposium on Innovation in Planning School
   Curricula held by National Education Association
   Committee for Study of Instruction, Airielhouse,
   Virginia, October, 1965.

Havelock, R. G. Planning for innovation through
   dissemination and utilization of knowledge.
   Center for Research on Utilization of Scientific
   Knowledge, Institute for Social Research,
   University of Michigan, Ann Arbor, Michigan, 1969.

Holt, R. R. Some neglected assumptions and problems
   in psychology's information crisis. American
   Psychologist, 1971, 26, 331-334.

Kerlinger, F. N. Foundations of behavioral research.
   Chicago: Holt, Rinehart and Winston, 1964.

Kohr, R. L., and Suydam, M. N. An instrument for
    evaluating survey research. Journal of Educational
    Research, 1970, 61, 78-85.

Kronick, D. A. Information media. Encyclopedia
    Britannica. Vol. 12, 244D-244I, 1969.

Licklider, J. C. R. A crux in scientific and technical
    communication. American Psychologist, 1966,
    21, 1044-1051.

Mann, J. Evaluating educational programs: A symposium.
    The Urban Review, 1969, 3(4), 12-23.

McReynolds, P. Reliability ratings of research papers.
    American Psychologist, 1971, 26, 400-401.

Michael, W. B. (Ed.). Review of Educational Research,
    October, 1963, p. 443.

Mouly, G. J. The science of educational research. New
    York: American Book Company, 1963.

National Academy of Sciences Committee on research in
    the Life Sciences of The Committee on Science and
    Public Policy. Communication in the Life
    Sciences, The Life Sciences, Washington, D. C.
    National Academy of Sciences, 1970, 405-427.

Persell, C. H. Research evaluation instrument.
    Columbia University, Unpublished, 1966.

Riedesel, C. A. A change in "focus". The Arithmetic
    Teacher, 1971, 18, 113-114.

Rummel, J. F. An introduction to research procedures
    in education. (2nd ed.) New York: Harper and Row,
    Publishers, 1964.

Scriven, M. The philosophy of science in educational
    research. <u>Review</u> <u>of</u> <u>Educational</u> <u>Research</u>, 1960,
    <u>30</u>, 422-429.

Scriven, M. The methodology of evaluation. In B.
    Othanel Smith (Ed.) <u>Perspectives</u> <u>of</u> <u>Curriculum</u>
    <u>Evaluation</u>. Chicago: Rand McNally, 1967.

Stufflebeam, D. L., <u>et</u> <u>al</u>., Educational evaluation and
    decision-making (in press).

Suchman, E. A. Evaluative research: Principles and
    practice in public service and social action
    programs. New York: Russell Sage Foundation, 1967.

Suydam, Marilyn N. An instrument for evaluating
    experimental educational research reports. <u>Journal</u>
    <u>of</u> <u>Educational</u> <u>Research</u>, 1968, 61, 200-203.

Travers, R. M. W. An introduction to educational
    research. (3rd ed.) New York: Macmillan, 1969.

Van Dalen, D. B. <u>Understanding</u> <u>educational</u> <u>research</u>.
    New York: McGraw-Hill, 1966.

Wandt, E. <u>Cross-section</u> <u>of</u> <u>educational</u> <u>research</u>.
    New York: David McKay Company, Inc., 1965.

Wandt, E., <u>et</u> <u>al</u>. An evaluation of educational research
    in published journals. Report of the Committee on
    Evaluation of Research, American Educational
    Research Association, 1967.

Ziman, J. M. Information, communication, knowledge.
    <u>Nature</u>, 1969, <u>224</u>, 318-324.

Statistical Tables   Appendix C

TABLE I   Random Numbers (I)

```
03 47 43 73 86   36 96 47 36 61   46 98 63 71 62   33 26 16 80 45   60 11 14 10 95
97 74 24 67 62   42 81 14 57 20   42 53 32 37 32   27 07 36 07 51   24 51 79 89 73
16 76 62 27 66   56 50 26 71 07   32 90 79 78 53   13 55 38 58 59   88 97 54 14 10
12 56 85 99 26   96 96 68 27 31   05 03 72 93 15   57 12 10 14 21   88 26 49 81 76
55 59 56 35 64   38 54 82 46 22   31 62 43 09 90   06 18 44 32 53   23 83 01 30 30

16 22 77 94 39   49 54 43 54 82   17 37 93 23 78   87 35 20 96 43   84 26 34 91 64
84 42 17 53 31   57 24 55 06 88   77 04 74 47 67   21 76 33 50 25   83 92 12 06 76
63 01 63 78 59   16 95 55 67 19   98 10 50 71 75   12 86 73 58 07   44 39 52 38 79
33 21 12 34 29   78 64 56 07 82   52 42 07 44 38   15 51 00 13 42   99 66 02 79 54
57 60 86 32 44   09 47 27 96 54   49 17 46 09 62   90 52 84 77 27   08 02 73 43 28

18 18 07 92 46   44 17 16 58 09   79 83 86 19 62   06 76 50 03 10   55 23 64 05 05
26 62 38 97 75   84 16 07 44 99   83 11 46 32 24   20 14 85 88 45   10 93 72 88 71
23 42 40 64 74   82 97 77 77 81   07 45 32 14 08   32 98 94 07 72   93 85 79 10 75
 2 36 28 19 95   50 92 26 11 97   00 56 76 31 38   80 22 02 53 53   86 60 42 04 53
37 85 94 35 12   83 39 50 08 30   42 34 07 96 88   54 42 06 87 98   35 85 29 48 39
                              Start↓
70 29 17 12 13   40 33 20 38 26  (13)89 51 03 74   17 76 37 13 04   07 74 21 19 30
56 62 18 37 35   96 83 50 87 75   97 12 25 93 47   70 33 24 03 54   97 77 46 44 80
99 49 57 22 77   88 42 95 45 72  (16)64 36 16 00   04 43 18 66 79   94 77 24 21 90
16 08 15 04 72   33 27 14 34 09   45 59 34 68 49   12 72 07 34 45   99 27 72 95 14
31 16 93 32 43   50 27 89 87 19  (20)15 37 00 49   52 85 66 60 44   38 68 88 11 80

68 34 30 13 70   55 74 30 77 40   44 22 78 84 26   04 33 46 09 52   68 07 97 06 57
74 57 25 65 76   59 29 97 68 60   71 91 38 67 54   13 58 18 24 76   15 54 55 95 52
27 42 37 86 53   48 55 90 65 72   96 57 69 36 10   96 46 92 42 45   97 60 49 04 91
00 39 68 29 61   66 37 32 20 30   77 84 57 03 29   10 45 65 04 26   11 04 96 67 24
29 94 98 94 24   68 49 69 10 82   53 75 91 93 30   34 25 20 57 27   40 48 73 51 92

16 90 82 66 59   83 62 64 11 12   67 19 00 71 74   60 47 21 29 68   02 02 37 03 31
11 27 94 75 06   06 09 19 74 66  (02)94 37 34 02   76 70 90 30 86   38 45 94 30 38
35 24 10 16 20   33 32 51 26 38   79 78 45 04 91   16 92 53 56 16   02 75 50 95 98
38 23 16 86 38   42 38 97 01 50   87 75 66 81 41   40 01 74 91 62   48 51 84 08 32
31 96 25 91 47   96 44 33 49 13   34 86 82 53 91   00 52 43 48 85   27 55 26 89 62

66 67 40 67 14   64 05 71 95 86  (11)05 65 09 68   76 83 20 37 90   57 16 00 11 66
14 90 84 45 11   75 73 88 05 90   52 27 41 14 86   22 98 12 22 08   07 52 74 95 80
68 05 51 18 00   33 96 02 75 19  (67)60 62 93 55   59 33 82 43 90   97 37 38 44 59
20 46 78 73 90   97 51 40 14 02  (04)02 33 31 08   39 54 16 49 36   47 95 93 13 30
64 19 58 97 79   15 06 15 93 20  (01)90 10 75 06   40 78 78 89 62   02 67 74 17 33

05 26 93 70 60   22 35 85 15 13   92 03 51 59 77   59 56 78 06 83   52 91 05 70 74
07 97 10 88 23   09 98 42 99 64   61 71 62 99 15   06 51 29 16 93   58 05 77 09 51
68 71 86 85 85   54 87 66 47 54   73 32 08 11 12   44 95 92 63 16   29 56 24 29 48
26 99 61 65 53   58 37 78 80 70   42 10 50 67 42   32 17 55 85 74   94 44 67 16 94
14 65 52 68 75   87 59 36 22 41   26 78 63 06 55   13 08 27 01 50   15 29 39 39 43

17 53 77 58 71   71 41 61 50 72  (12)41 94 96 26   44 95 27 36 99   02 96 74 30 83
90 26 59 21 19   23 52 23 33 12   96 93 02 18 39   07 02 18 36 07   25 99 32 70 23
41 23 52 55 99   31 04 49 69 96  (10)47 48 45 88   13 41 43 89 20   97 17 14 49 17
60 20 50 81 69   31 99 73 68 68   35 81 33 03 76   24 30 12 48 60   18 99 10 72 34
91 25 38 05 90   94 58 28 41 36   45 37 59 03 09   90 35 57 29 12   82 62 54 65 60

34 50 57 74 37   98 80 33 00 91  (09)77 93 19 82   74 94 80 04 04   45 07 31 66 49
85 22 04 39 43   73 81 53 94 79   33 62 46 86 28   08 31 54 46 31   53 94 13 38 47
09 79 13 77 48   73 82 97 22 21  (05)03 27 24 83   72 89 44 05 60   35 80 39 94 88
88 75 80 18 14   22 95 75 42 49   39 32 82 22 49   02 48 07 70 37   16 04 61 67 87
90 96 23 70 00   39 00 03 06 90   55 85 78 38 36   94 37 30 69 32   90 89 00 76 33
```

Tables I–VI are taken from Tables XXXIII, I, III, VII, IV, and V of Fisher and Yates: *Statistical Tables for Biological, Agricultural and Medical Research*, published by Longman Group Ltd., London (previously published by Oliver and Boyd, Edinburgh), and by permission of the authors and publishers.

TABLE I   Random Numbers (II)

```
53 74 23 99 67    61 32 28 69 84    94 62 67 86 24    98 33 41 19 95    47 53 53 38 09
63 38 06 86 54    99 00 65 26 94    02 82 90 23 07    79 62 67 80 60    75 91 12 81 19
35 30 58 21 46    06 72 17 10 94    25 21 31 75 96    49 28 24 00 49    55 65 79 78 07
63 43 36 82 69    65 51 18 37 88    61 38 44 12 45    32 92 85 88 65    54 34 81 85 35
98 25 37 55 26    01 91 82 81 46    74 71 12 94 97    24 02 71 37 07    03 92 18 66 75

02 63 21 17 69    71 50 80 89 56    38 15 70 11 48    43 40 45 86 98    00 83 26 91 03
64 55 22 21 82    48 22 28 06 00    61 54 13 43 91    82 78 12 23 29    06 66 24 12 27
85 07 26 13 89    01 10 07 82 04    59 63 69 36 03    69 11 15 83 80    13 29 54 19 28
58 54 16 24 15    51 54 44 82 00    62 61 65 04 69    38 18 65 18 97    85 72 13 49 21
34 85 27 84 87    61 48 64 56 26    90 18 48 13 26    37 70 15 42 57    65 65 80 39 07

03 92 18 27 46    57 99 16 96 56    30 33 72 85 22    84 64 38 56 98    99 01 30 98 64
62 95 30 27 59    37 75 41 66 48    86 97 80 61 45    23 53 04 01 63    45 76 08 64 27
08 45 93 15 22    60 21 75 46 91    98 77 27 85 42    28 88 61 08 84    69 62 03 42 73
07 08 55 18 40    45 44 75 13 90    24 94 96 61 02    57 55 66 83 15    73 42 37 11 61
01 85 89 95 66    51 10 19 34 88    15 84 97 19 75    12 76 39 43 78    64 63 91 08 25

72 84 71 14 35    19 11 58 49 26    50 11 17 17 76    86 31 57 20 18    95 60 78 46 75
88 78 28 16 84    13 52 53 94 53    75 45 69 30 96    73 89 65 70 31    99 17 43 48 76
45 17 75 65 57    28 40 19 72 12    25 12 74 75 67    60 40 60 81 19    24 62 01 61 16
96 76 28 12 54    22 01 11 94 25    71 96 16 16 88    68 64 36 74 45    19 59 50 88 92
43 31 67 72 30    24 02 94 08 63    38 32 36 66 02    69 36 38 25 39    48 03 45 15 22

50 44 66 44 21    66 06 58 05 62    68 15 54 35 02    42 35 48 96 32    14 52 41 52 48
22 66 22 15 86    26 63 75 41 99    58 42 36 72 24    58 37 52 18 51    03 37 18 39 11
96 24 40 14 51    23 22 30 88 57    95 67 47 29 83    94 69 40 06 07    18 16 36 78 86
31 73 91 61 19    60 20 72 93 48    98 57 07 23 69    65 95 39 69 58    56 80 30 19 44
78 60 73 99 84    43 89 94 36 45    56 69 47 07 41    90 22 91 07 12    78 35 34 08 72

84 37 90 61 56    70 10 23 98 05    85 11 34 76 60    76 48 45 34 60    01 64 18 39 96
36 67 10 08 23    98 93 35 08 86    99 29 76 29 81    33 34 91 58 93    63 14 52 32 52
07 28 59 07 48    89 64 58 89 75    83 85 62 27 89    30 14 78 56 27    86 63 59 80 02
10 15 83 87 60    79 24 31 66 56    21 48 24 06 93    91 98 94 05 49    01 47 59 38 00
55 19 68 97 65    03 73 52 16 56    00 53 55 90 27    33 42 29 38 87    22 13 88 83 34

53 81 29 13 39    35 01 20 71 34    62 33 74 82 14    53 73 19 09 03    56 54 29 56 93
51 86 32 68 92    33 98 74 66 99    40 14 71 94 58    45 94 19 38 81    14 44 99 81 07
35 91 70 29 13    80 03 54 07 27    96 94 78 32 66    50 95 52 74 33    13 80 55 62 54
37 71 67 95 13    20 02 44 95 94    64 85 04 05 72    01 32 90 76 14    53 89 74 60 41
93 66 13 83 27    92 79 64 64 72    28 54 96 53 84    48 14 52 98 94    56 07 93 89 30

02 96 08 45 65    13 05 00 41 84    93 07 54 72 59    21 45 57 09 77    19 48 56 27 44
49 83 43 48 35    82 88 33 69 96    72 36 04 19 76    47 45 15 18 60    82 11 08 95 97
84 60 71 62 46    40 80 81 30 37    34 39 23 05 38    25 15 35 71 30    88 12 57 21 77
18 17 30 88 71    44 91 14 88 47    89 23 30 63 15    56 34 20 47 89    99 82 93 24 98
79 69 10 61 78    71 32 76 95 62    87 00 22 58 40    92 54 01 75 25    43 11 71 99 31

75 93 36 57 83    56 20 14 82 11    74 21 97 90 65    96 42 68 63 86    74 54 13 26 94
38 30 92 29 03    06 28 81 39 38    62 25 06 84 63    61 29 08 93 67    04 32 92 08 00
51 29 50 10 34    31 57 75 95 80    51 97 02 74 77    76 15 48 49 44    18 55 63 77 09
21 31 38 86 24    37 79 81 53 74    73 24 16 10 33    52 83 90 94 76    70 47 14 54 36
29 01 23 87 88    58 02 39 37 67    42 10 14 20 92    16 55 23 42 45    54 96 09 11 06

95 33 95 22 00    18 74 72 00 18    38 79 58 69 32    81 76 80 26 92    82 80 84 25 39
90 84 60 79 80    24 36 59 87 38    82 07 53 89 35    96 35 23 79 18    05 98 90 07 35
46 40 62 98 82    54 97 20 56 95    15 74 80 08 32    16 46 70 50 80    67 72 16 42 79
20 31 89 03 43    38 46 82 68 72    32 14 82 99 70    80 60 47 18 97    63 49 30 21 30
71 59 73 05 50    08 22 23 71 77    91 01 93 20 49    82 96 59 26 94    66 39 67 98 60
```

TABLE I   Random Numbers (III)

22 17 68 65 84	68 95 23 92 35	87 02 22 57 51	61 09 43 95 06	58 24 82 03 47
19 36 27 59 46	13 79 93 37 55	39 77 32 77 09	85 52 05 30 62	47 83 51 62 74
16 77 23 02 77	09 61 87 25 21	28 06 24 25 93	16 71 13 59 78	23 05 47 47 25
78 43 76 71 61	20 44 90 32 64	97 67 63 99 61	46 38 03 93 22	69 81 21 99 21
03 28 28 26 08	73 37 32 04 05	69 30 16 09 05	88 69 58 28 99	35 07 44 75 47
93 22 53 64 39	07 10 63 76 35	87 03 04 79 88	08 13 13 85 51	55 34 57 72 69
78 76 58 54 74	92 38 70 96 92	52 06 79 79 45	82 63 18 27 44	69 66 92 19 09
23 68 35 26 00	99 53 93 61 28	52 70 05 48 34	56 65 05 61 86	90 92 10 70 80
15 39 25 70 99	93 86 52 77 65	15 33 59 05 28	22 87 26 07 47	86 96 98 29 06
58 71 96 30 24	18 46 23 34 27	85 13 99 24 44	49 18 09 79 49	74 16 32 23 02
57 35 27 33 72	24 53 63 94 09	41 10 76 47 91	44 04 95 49 66	39 60 04 59 81
48 50 86 54 48	22 06 34 72 52	82 21 15 65 20	33 29 94 71 11	15 91 29 12 03
61 96 48 95 03	07 16 39 33 66	98 56 10 56 79	77 21 30 27 12	90 49 22 23 62
36 93 89 41 26	29 70 83 63 51	99 74 20 52 36	87 09 41 15 09	98 60 16 03 03
18 87 00 42 31	57 90 12 02 07	23 47 37 17 31	54 08 01 88 63	39 41 88 92 10
88 56 53 27 59	33 35 72 67 47	77 34 55 45 70	08 18 27 38 90	16 95 86 70 75
09 72 95 84 29	49 41 31 06 70	42 38 06 45 18	64 84 73 31 65	52 53 37 97 15
12 96 88 17 31	65 19 69 02 83	60 75 86 90 68	24 64 19 35 51	56 61 87 39 12
85 94 57 24 16	92 09 84 38 76	22 00 27 69 85	29 81 94 78 70	21 94 47 90 12
38 64 43 59 98	98 77 87 68 07	91 51 67 62 44	40 98 05 93 78	23 32 65 41 18
53 44 09 42 72	00 41 86 79 79	68 47 22 00 20	35 55 31 51 51	00 83 63 22 55
40 76 66 26 84	57 99 99 90 37	36 63 32 08 58	37 40 13 68 97	87 64 81 07 83
02 17 79 18 05	12 59 52 57 02	22 07 90 47 03	28 14 11 30 79	20 69 22 40 98
95 17 82 06 53	31 51 10 96 46	92 06 88 07 77	56 11 50 81 69	40 23 72 51 39
35 76 22 42 92	96 11 83 44 80	34 68 35 48 77	33 42 40 90 60	73 96 53 97 86
26 29 13 56 41	85 47 04 66 08	34 72 57 59 13	82 43 80 46 15	38 26 61 70 04
77 80 20 75 82	72 82 32 99 90	63 95 73 76 63	89 73 44 99 05	48 67 26 43 18
46 40 66 44 52	91 36 74 43 53	30 82 13 54 00	78 45 63 98 35	55 03 36 67 68
37 56 08 18 09	77 53 84 46 47	31 91 18 95 58	24 16 74 11 53	44 10 13 85 57
61 65 61 68 66	37 27 47 39 19	84 83 70 07 48	53 21 40 06 71	95 06 79 88 54
93 43 69 64 07	34 18 04 52 35	56 27 09 24 86	61 85 53 83 45	19 90 70 99 00
21 96 60 12 99	11 20 99 45 18	48 13 93 55 34	18 37 79 49 90	65 97 38 20 46
95 20 47 97 97	27 37 83 28 71	00 06 41 41 74	45 89 09 39 84	51 67 11 52 49
97 86 21 78 73	10 65 81 92 59	58 76 17 14 97	04 76 62 16 17	17 95 70 45 80
69 92 06 34 13	59 71 74 17 32	27 55 10 24 19	23 71 82 13 74	63 52 52 01 41
04 31 17 21 56	33 73 99 19 87	26 72 39 27 67	53 77 57 68 93	60 61 97 22 61
61 06 98 03 91	87 14 77 43 96	43 00 65 98 50	45 60 33 01 07	98 99 46 50 47
85 93 85 86 88	72 87 08 62 40	16 06 10 89 20	23 21 34 74 97	76 38 03 29 63
21 74 32 47 45	73 96 07 94 52	09 65 90 77 47	25 76 16 19 33	53 05 70 53 30
15 69 53 82 80	79 96 23 53 10	65 39 07 16 29	45 33 02 43 70	02 87 40 41 45
02 89 08 04 49	20 21 14 68 86	87 63 93 95 17	11 29 01 95 80	15 14 97 35 33
87 18 15 89 79	85 43 01 72 73	08 61 74 51 69	89 74 39 82 15	94 51 33 41 67
98 83 71 94 22	59 97 50 99 52	08 52 85 08 40	87 80 61 65 31	91 51 80 32 44
10 08 58 21 66	72 68 49 29 31	89 85 84 46 06	59 73 19 85 23	65 09 29 75 63
47 90 56 10 08	88 02 84 27 83	42 29 72 23 19	66 56 45 65 79	20 71 53 20 25
22 85 61 68 90	49 64 92 85 44	16 40 12 89 88	50 14 49 81 06	01 82 77 45 12
67 80 43 79 33	12 83 11 41 16	25 58 19 68 70	77 02 54 00 52	53 43 37 15 26
27 62 50 96 72	79 44 61 40 15	14 53 40 65 39	27 31 58 50 28	11 39 03 34 25
33 78 80 87 15	38 30 06 38 21	14 47 47 07 26	54 96 87 53 32	40 36 40 96 76
13 13 92 66 99	47 24 49 57 74	32 25 43 62 17	10 97 11 69 84	99 63 22 32 98

TABLE I   Random Numbers (IV)

```
10 27 53 96 23   71 50 54 36 23   54 31 04 82 98   04 14 12 15 09   26 78 25 47 47
28 41 50 61 88   64 85 27 20 18   83 36 36 05 56   39 71 65 09 62   94 76 62 11 89
34 21 42 57 02   59 19 18 97 48   80 30 03 30 98   05 24 67 70 07   84 97 50 87 46
61 81 77 23 23   82 82 11 54 08   53 28 70 58 96   44 07 39 55 43   42 34 43 39 28
61 15 18 13 54   16 86 20 26 88   90 74 80 55 09   14 53 90 51 17   52 01 63 01 59

91 76 21 64 64   44 91 13 32 97   75 31 62 66 54   84 80 32 75 77   56 08 25 70 29
00 97 79 08 06   37 30 28 59 85   53 56 68 53 40   01 74 39 59 73   30 19 99 85 48
36 46 18 34 94   75 20 80 27 77   78 91 69 16 00   08 43 18 73 68   67 69 61 34 25
88 98 99 60 50   65 95 79 42 94   93 62 40 89 96   43 56 47 71 66   46 76 29 67 02
04 37 59 87 21   05 02 03 24 17   47 97 81 56 51   92 34 86 01 82   55 51 33 12 91

63 62 06 34 41   94 21 78 55 09   72 76 45 16 94   29 95 81 83 83   79 88 01 97 30
78 47 23 53 90   34 41 92 45 71   09 23 70 70 07   12 38 92 79 43   14 85 11 47 23
87 68 62 15 43   53 14 36 59 25   54 47 33 70 15   59 24 48 40 35   50 03 42 99 36
47 60 92 10 77   88 59 53 11 52   66 25 69 07 04   48 68 64 71 06   61 65 70 22 12
56 88 87 59 41   65 28 04 67 53   95 79 88 37 31   50 41 06 94 76   81 83 17 16 33

02 57 45 86 67   73 43 07 34 48   44 26 87 93 29   77 09 61 67 84   06 69 44 77 75
31 54 14 13 17   48 62 11 90 60   68 12 93 64 28   46 24 79 16 76   14 60 25 51 01
28 50 16 43 36   28 97 85 58 99   67 22 52 76 23   24 70 36 54 54   59 28 61 71 96
63 29 62 66 50   02 63 45 52 38   67 63 47 54 75   83 24 78 43 20   92 63 13 47 48
45 65 58 26 51   76 96 59 38 72   86 57 45 71 46   44 67 76 14 55   44 88 01 62 12

39 65 36 63 70   77 45 85 50 51   74 13 39 35 22   30 53 36 02 95   49 34 88 73 61
73 71 98 16 04   29 18 94 51 23   76 51 94 84 86   79 93 96 38 63   08 58 25 58 94
72 20 56 20 11   72 65 71 08 86   79 57 95 13 91   97 48 72 66 48   09 71 17 24 89
75 17 26 99 76   89 37 20 70 01   77 31 61 95 46   26 97 05 73 51   53 33 18 72 87
37 48 60 82 29   81 30 15 39 14   48 38 75 93 29   06 87 37 78 48   45 56 00 84 47

68 08 02 80 72   83 71 46 30 49   89 17 95 88 29   02 39 56 03 46   97 74 06 56 17
14 23 98 61 67   70 52 85 01 50   01 84 02 78 43   10 62 98 19 41   18 83 99 47 99
49 08 96 21 44   25 27 99 41 28   07 41 08 34 66   19 42 74 39 91   41 96 53 78 72
78 37 06 08 43   63 61 62 42 29   39 68 95 10 96   09 24 23 00 62   56 12 80 73 16
37 21 34 17 68   68 96 83 23 56   32 84 60 15 31   44 73 67 34 77   91 15 79 74 58

14 29 09 34 04   87 83 07 55 07   76 58 30 83 64   87 29 25 58 84   86 50 60 00 25
58 43 28 06 36   49 52 83 51 14   47 56 91 29 34   05 87 31 06 95   12 45 57 09 09
10 43 67 29 70   80 62 80 03 42   10 80 21 38 84   90 56 35 03 09   43 12 74 49 14
44 38 88 39 54   86 97 37 44 22   00 95 01 31 76   17 16 29 56 63   38 78 94 49 81
90 69 59 19 51   85 39 52 85 13   07 28 37 07 61   11 16 36 27 03   78 86 72 04 95

41 47 10 25 62   97 05 31 03 61   20 26 36 31 62   68 69 86 95 44   84 95 48 46 45
91 94 14 63 19   75 89 11 47 11   31 56 34 19 09   79 57 92 36 59   14 93 87 81 40
80 06 54 18 66   09 18 94 06 19   98 40 07 17 81   22 45 44 84 11   24 62 20 42 31
67 72 77 63 48   84 08 31 55 58   24 33 45 77 58   80 45 67 93 82   75 70 16 08 24
59 40 24 13 27   79 26 88 86 30   01 31 60 10 39   53 58 47 70 93   85 81 56 39 38

05 90 35 89 95   01 61 16 96 94   50 78 13 69 36   37 68 53 37 31   71 26 35 03 71
44 43 80 69 98   46 68 05 14 82   90 78 50 05 62   77 79 13 57 44   59 60 10 39 66
61 81 31 96 82   00 57 25 60 59   46 72 60 18 77   55 66 12 62 11   08 99 55 64 57
42 88 07 10 05   24 98 65 63 21   47 21 61 88 32   27 80 30 21 60   10 92 35 36 12
77 94 30 05 39   28 10 99 00 27   12 73 73 99 12   49 99 57 94 82   96 88 57 17 91

78 83 19 76 16   94 11 68 84 26   23 54 20 86 85   23 86 66 99 07   36 37 34 92 09
87 76 59 61 81   43 63 64 61 61   65 76 36 95 90   18 48 27 45 68   27 23 65 30 72
91 43 05 96 47   55 78 99 95 24   37 55 85 78 78   01 48 41 19 10   35 19 54 07 73
84 97 77 72 73   09 62 06 65 72   87 12 49 03 60   41 15 20 76 27   50 47 02 29 16
87 41 60 76 83   44 88 96 07 80   83 05 83 38 96   73 70 66 81 90   30 56 10 48 59
```

TABLE II   The Normal Distribution

P	·00	·01	·02	·03	·04	·05	·06	·07	·08	·09
·0	∞	2·575829	2·326348	2·170090	2·053749	1·959964	1·880794	1·811911	1·750686	1·695398
·1	1·644854	1·598193	1·554774	1·514102	1·475791	1·439531	1·405072	1·372204	1·340755	1·310579
·2	1·281552	1·253565	1·226528	1·200359	1·174987	1·150349	1·126391	1·103063	1·080319	1·058122
·3	1·036433	1·015222	·994458	·974114	·954165	·934589	·915365	·896473	·877896	·859617
·4	·841621	·823894	·806421	·789192	·772193	·755415	·738847	·722479	·706303	·690309
·5	·674490	·658838	·643345	·628006	·612813	·597760	·582842	·568051	·553385	·538836
·6	·524401	·510073	·495850	·481727	·467699	·453762	·439913	·426148	·412463	·398855
·7	·385320	·371856	·358459	·345126	·331853	·318639	·305481	·292375	·279319	·266311
·8	·253347	·240426	·227545	·214702	·201893	·189118	·176374	·163658	·150969	·138304
·9	·125661	·113039	·100434	·087845	·075270	·062707	·050154	·037608	·025069	·012533

The value of P for each entry is found by adding the column heading to the value in the left-hand margin. The corresponding value of x is the deviation such that the probability of an observation falling outside the range from $-x$ to $+x$ is P. For example, P = ·03 for x = 2·17009o; so that 3 per cent. of normally distributed values will have positive or negative deviations exceeding the standard deviation in the ratio 2·170090 at least.

TABLE III   Distribution of t

Probability

df	·05	·01	df	·05	·01
1	12·706	63·657	18	2·101	2·878
2	4·303	9·925	19	2·093	2·861
3	3·182	5·841	20	2·086	2·845
4	2·776	4·604			
5	2·571	4·032	21	2·080	2·831
			22	2·074	2·819
6	2·447	3·707	23	2·069	2·807
7	2·365	3·499	24	2·064	2·797
8	2·306	3·355	25	2·060	2·787
9	2·262	3·250			
10	2·228	3·169	26	2·056	2·779
			27	2·052	2·771
11	2·201	3·106	28	2·048	2·763
12	2·179	3·055	29	2·045	2·756
13	2·160	3·012	30	2·042	2·750
14	2·145	2·977			
15	2·131	2·947	40	2·021	2·704
			60	2·000	2·660
16	2·120	2·921	120	1·980	2·617
17	2·110	2·898	∞	1·960	2·576

THE CORRELATION COEFFICIENT

TABLE IV Values of the Correlation Coefficient for Different Levels of Significance

df	·05	·01	df	·05	·01
1	·99692	·999877	16	·4683	·5897
2	·95000	·990000	17	·4555	·5751
3	·8783	·95873	18	·4438	·5614
4	·8114	·91720	19	·4329	·5487
5	·7545	·8745	20	·4227	·5368
6	·7067	·8343	25	·3809	·4869
7	·6664	·7977	30	·3494	·4487
8	·6319	·7646	35	·3246	·4182
9	·6021	·7348	40	·3044	·3932
10	·5760	·7079	45	·2875	·3721
11	·5529	·6835	50	·2732	·3541
12	·5324	·6614	60	·2500	·3248
13	·5139	·6411	70	·2319	·3017
14	·4973	·6226	80	·2172	·2830
15	·4821	·6055	90	·2050	·2673
			100	·1946	·2540

TABLE V   Distribution of x^2

Probability

df	·05	·01
1	3·841	6·635
2	5·991	9·210
3	7·815	11·345
4	9·488	13·277
5	11·070	15·086
6	12·592	16·812
7	14·067	18·475
8	15·507	20·090
9	16·919	21·666
10	18·307	23·209
11	19·675	24·725
12	21·026	26·217
13	22·362	27·688
14	23·685	29·141
15	24·996	30·578
16	26·296	32·000
17	27·587	33·409
18	28·869	34·805
19	30·144	36·191
20	31·410	37·566
21	32·671	38·932
22	33·924	40·289
23	35·172	41·638
24	36·415	42·980
25	37·652	44·314
26	38·885	45·642
27	40·113	46·963
28	41·337	48·278
29	42·557	49·588
30	43·773	50·892

TABLE VI   5 Percent Points of the F Distribution

df_2 \ df_1	1	2	3	4	5	6	8	12	24	∞
1	161·4	199·5	215·7	224·6	230·2	234·0	238·9	243·9	249·0	254·3
2	18·51	19·00	19·16	19·25	19·30	19·33	19·37	19·41	19·45	19·50
3	10·13	9·55	9·28	9·12	9·01	8·94	8·84	8·74	8·64	8·53
4	7·71	6·94	6·59	6·39	6·26	6·16	6·04	5·91	5·77	5·63
5	6·61	5·79	5·41	5·19	5·05	4·95	4·82	4·68	4·53	4·36
6	5·99	5·14	4·76	4·53	4·39	4·28	4·15	4·00	3·84	3·67
7	5·59	4·74	4·35	4·12	3·97	3·87	3·73	3·57	3·41	3·23
8	5·32	4·46	4·07	3·84	3·69	3·58	3·44	3·28	3·12	2·93
9	5·12	4·26	3·86	3·63	3·48	3·37	3·23	3·07	2·90	2·71
10	4·96	4·10	3·71	3·48	3·33	3·22	3·07	2·91	2·74	2·54
11	4·84	3·98	3·59	3·36	3·20	3·09	2·95	2·79	2·61	2·40
12	4·75	3·88	3·49	3·26	3·11	3·00	2·85	2·69	2·50	2·30
13	4·67	3·80	3·41	3·18	3·02	2·92	2·77	2·60	2·42	2·21
14	4·60	3·74	3·34	3·11	2·96	2·85	2·70	2·53	2·35	2·13
15	4·54	3·68	3·29	3·06	2·90	2·79	2·64	2·48	2·29	2·07
16	4·49	3·63	3·24	3·01	2·85	2·74	2·59	2·42	2·24	2·01
17	4·45	3·59	3·20	2·96	2·81	2·70	2·55	2·38	2·19	1·96
18	4·41	3·55	3·16	2·93	2·77	2·66	2·51	2·34	2·15	1·92
19	4·38	3·52	3·13	2·90	2·74	2·63	2·48	2·31	2·11	1·88
20	4·35	3·49	3·10	2·87	2·71	2·60	2·45	2·28	2·08	1·84
21	4·32	3·47	3·07	2·84	2·68	2·57	2·42	2·25	2·05	1·81
22	4·30	3·44	3·05	2·82	2·66	2·55	2·40	2·23	2·03	1·78
23	4·28	3·42	3·03	2·80	2·64	2·53	2·38	2·20	2·00	1·76
24	4·26	3·40	3·01	2·78	2·62	2·51	2·36	2·18	1·98	1·73
25	4·24	3·38	2·99	2·76	2·60	2·49	2·34	2·16	1·96	1·71
26	4·22	3·37	2·98	2·74	2·59	2·47	2·32	2·15	1·95	1·69
27	4·21	3·35	2·96	2·73	2·57	2·46	2·30	2·13	1·93	1·67
28	4·20	3·34	2·95	2·71	2·56	2·44	2·29	2·12	1·91	1·65
29	4·18	3·33	2·93	2·70	2·54	2·43	2·28	2·10	1·90	1·64
30	4·17	3·32	2·92	2·69	2·53	2·42	2·27	2·09	1·89	1·62
40	4·08	3·23	2·84	2·61	2·45	2·34	2·18	2·00	1·79	1·51
60	4·00	3·15	2·76	2·52	2·37	2·25	2·10	1·92	1·70	1·39
120	3·92	3·07	2·68	2·45	2·29	2·17	2·02	1·83	1·61	1·25
∞	3·84	2·99	2·60	2·37	2·21	2·10	1·94	1·75	1·52	1·00

TABLE VII 1 Percent Points of the F Distribution

df_2 \ df_1	1	2	3	4	5	6	8	12	24	∞
1	4052	4999	5403	5625	5764	5859	5982	6106	6234	6366
2	98·50	99·00	99·17	99·25	99·30	99·33	99·37	99·42	99·46	99·50
3	34·12	30·82	29·46	28·71	28·24	27·91	27·49	27·05	26·60	26·12
4	21·20	18·00	16·69	15·98	15·52	15·21	14·80	14·37	13·93	13·46
5	16·26	13·27	12·06	11·39	10·97	10·67	10·29	9·89	9·47	9·02
6	13·74	10·92	9·78	9·15	8·75	8·47	8·10	7·72	7·31	6·88
7	12·25	9·55	8·45	7·85	7·46	7·19	6·84	6·47	6·07	5·65
8	11·26	8·65	7·59	7·01	6·63	6·37	6·03	5·67	5·28	4·86
9	10·56	8·02	6·99	6·42	6·06	5·80	5·47	5·11	4·73	4·31
10	10·04	7·56	6·55	5·99	5·64	5·39	5·06	4·71	4·33	3·91
11	9·65	7·20	6·22	5·67	5·32	5·07	4·74	4·40	4·02	3·60
12	9·33	6·93	5·95	5·41	5·06	4·82	4·50	4·16	3·78	3·36
13	9·07	6·70	5·74	5·20	4·86	4·62	4·30	3·96	3·59	3·16
14	8·86	6·51	5·56	5·03	4·69	4·46	4·14	3·80	3·43	3·00
15	8·68	6·36	5·42	4·89	4·56	4·32	4·00	3·67	3·29	2·87
16	8·53	6·23	5·29	4·77	4·44	4·20	3·89	3·55	3·18	2·75
17	8·40	6·11	5·18	4·67	4·34	4·10	3·79	3·45	3·08	2·65
18	8·28	6·01	5·09	4·58	4·25	4·01	3·71	3·37	3·00	2·57
19	8·18	5·93	5·01	4·50	4·17	3·94	3·63	3·30	2·92	2·49
20	8·10	5·85	4·94	4·43	4·10	3·87	3·56	3·23	2·86	2·42
21	8·02	5·78	4·87	4·37	4·04	3·81	3·51	3·17	2·80	2·36
22	7·94	5·72	4·82	4·31	3·99	3·76	3·45	3·12	2·75	2·31
23	7·88	5·66	4·76	4·26	3·94	3·71	3·41	3·07	2·70	2·26
24	7·82	5·61	4·72	4·22	3·90	3·67	3·36	3·03	2·66	2·21
25	7·77	5·57	4·68	4·18	3·86	3·63	3·32	2·99	2·62	2·17
26	7·72	5·53	4·64	4·14	3·82	3·59	3·29	2·96	2·58	2·13
27	7·68	5·49	4·60	4·11	3·78	3·56	3·26	2·93	2·55	2·10
28	7·64	5·45	4·57	4·07	3·75	3·53	3·23	2·90	2·52	2·06
29	7·60	5·42	4·54	4·04	3·73	3·50	3·20	2·87	2·49	2·03
30	7·56	5·39	4·51	4·02	3·70	3·47	3·17	2·84	2·47	2·01
40	7·31	5·18	4·31	3·83	3·51	3·29	2·99	2·66	2·29	1·80
60	7·08	4·98	4·13	3·65	3·34	3·12	2·82	2·50	2·12	1·60
120	6·85	4·79	3·95	3·48	3·17	2·96	2·66	2·34	1·95	1·38
∞	6·64	4·60	3·78	3·32	3·02	2·80	2·51	2·18	1·79	1·00

Lower 1 percent points are found by interchange of df_1 and df_2, i.e. df_1 must always correspond with the greater mean square.

Index